College Financial Aid For Dummies®

W9-BHK-767

Express Financial Aid To-Do List

✔ **Collect cost data on colleges you like.**

Use college guidebooks, software, and college Web sites to gather information on financial aid and other key factors — curriculum, population, faculty, location, and reputation.

✔ **Request admission and financial aid applications.**

Ask each college on your list for entry and finaid apps in the fall of your senior high school year; fill out and send in. Answer "yes" to *all* college acceptances and *all* financial aid. Sort it out later.

✔ **Send finaid applications before you're accepted.**

Most important forms: Free Application for Federal Student Aid (FAFSA) for all colleges and also Profile for expensive colleges. Mail FAFSA right after January 1 of senior year. Forms are vital — don't mess up.

✔ **Provide additional information hyperfast.**

Respond immediately to requests for additional information and documentation from FAFSA or Profile processors or colleges. Ask colleges if you're short any forms. **Important:** annually resubmit finaid requests.

✔ **Carefully review finaid reports and award letters.**

Double-check confirmations from colleges; return all corrections instantly. Review your federal Student Aid Report (SAR) for errors. Examine your award letters, comparing loans and jobs to gift money.

✔ **Negotiate for more free money.**

Don't hesitate to ask your finaid counselor to substitute gift aid for loans when possible. If you win an outside scholarship that subtracts from your total aid package, ask that the amount subtract from your loans, not from gift money.

✔ **Look everywhere for aid.**

Check admissions recruiter, faculty in your major, dean's office, on-campus organizations, and alumni office for aid sources. Ask your guidance counselor and libraries to steer you to private programs.

✔ **Consider alternatives.**

Some colleges offer tuition and/or fee waivers to certain categories of students, returning students, children of alumni, employees, or family members enrolled simultaneously. Colleges may offer special payment plans or other discounts.

✔ **Investigate loans.**

Research all loans before you borrow — interest rates and repayment conditions. Expect your loan application to take at least six weeks to be processed. Borrow only what you need to scrunch through school.

IDG BOOKS WORLDWIDE

...For Dummies®: Bestselling Book Series for Beginners

College Financial Aid For Dummies®

Quick Reference Card

Finaid Pocket Calendar

High School

FIRST YEAR

Begin drafting a four-or-more year college financing plan.

SOPHOMORE YEAR

Start a college scholarship resource file. Collect information.

JUNIOR YEAR

October: Research finaid opportunities and lenders. Take the PSAT.

November: Attend finaid workshops and college fairs. Collect information on colleges and finaid resources.

December: Complete asset structuring and position student for maximum finaid eligibility. See PSAT results.

February: Register for May or June SAT. Plan to visit college campuses.

March: Discuss colleges with counselors.

April: Research scholarships for free in the career center and online.

May: Write to college admission offices requesting entrance and scholarship info. See college Web sites.

Summer: Visit college campuses. Request applications for private finaid.

SENIOR YEAR

September – October: Update college list based on research. Complete and send admission applications.

October – December: Request scholarship applications. Prepare Profile. Attend college fairs for costs and forms.

November: Take SAT. Get a Free Application for Federal Student Aid. Attend finaid workshops. Mail Profile. Complete school aid applications.

January: Complete and send early income taxes, FAFSA, and other finaid applications.

February: Review and save Student Aid Report. Add any updates and return. Send tax information to school finaid offices.

March: Complete scholarship applications. Apply for Federal Stafford and Federal Parent loans.

April: Compare each college's award package. Send admission acceptance and award letters to schools.

May: Send appeal letters and negotiate with colleges. Choose a college; notify those you're not interested in.

June: Send deposit and apply for loans. Work to save money. Begin scholarship research for next year.

College

FIRST-THROUGH-SENIOR YEAR

September: Interview for on-campus jobs.

October – December: Apply for private scholarships.

January: Renew FAFSA.

February: Complete and send taxes. Resubmit SAR with updated data. Send tax info to school finaid office.

March: Send returned, updated SAR to college finaid office.

May: Sign and accept renewal award letters.

Praise, Praise, Praise

For Dr. Herm Davis

"Thanks to Dr. Davis's wonderful advice, I have just received another $2,500 grant! This is in addition to my child's previous award based on an appeal letter that reflected changes in our income and resources. I couldn't have done it without him!"

> — *A. Chapeton,* Mother, Bethesda, Maryland

"High school counselors, career specialists, parents and school administrators look to Dr. Herm Davis for quality financial aid guidance. Without question, Dr. Davis is one of the leading financial aid information experts in the United States."

> — *Joseph A. Monte,* Past President of the National
> Association of College Admission Counselors.

"Dr. Davis has combined heavy-duty research and resources with clear, sound advice to save college students thousands of dollars."

> — *Jacqueline Daughtry,* Vice President of Student
> Loans, Independence Federal Savings Bank

"Dr. Davis gives street-smart advice and on-the-money research that gives you an edge in the college money market."

> — *Dr. Ulysses Glee,* Chief of the Office of Postsecondary
> Education for the District of Columbia

"Dr. Davis's insights to the financial aid world have given thousands of students and their families flotation devices when they were sure to sink under mammoth tuition bills. His exhaustive knowledge and practical advice help students make the most of some of the best days of their lives."

> — *K. Michael Ayers,* Department Adjutant,
> Indiana American Legion

"Our institution used college financial aid software and scholarship database information that Dr. Herm Davis was instrumental in developing for use by colleges and students. Dr. Davis was found to be extraordinarily aware of financial aid resources that are available throughout the United States."

> — *William Cordero,* Dean of Student Services,
> Santa Barbara City College, California

Praise, Praise, Praise

For Joyce Lain Kennedy

"Joyce Kennedy is at the top of her field."
> — *John D. Erdlen,* CEO, Strategic Outsourcing, Inc.

"Books by Ms. Kennedy are what got me started along the path of careers in education. Another individual has been converted by your books."
> — *Patty McLarty,* Gary, Indiana

"I have read many books and articles about 'how to, what to, and why not to,' but none seem to be as insightful and logical as yours."
> — *Peter Lamberton,* E. Providence, Rhode Island

"Joyce Lain Kennedy's career kowledge is the answer to any job-seeker's prayers."
> — *J. Herbert Wise,* Executive Recruiter, Dallas

"Your trio of books really energized me to get back in the job hunt and rethink my approach to prospective employers. Thanks to you, I'm working at a job I enjoy."
> — *Mark Luboski,* Cleveland, Ohio

"...Kennedy (no relation) ... having spent more than a few years observing and writing about career planning and job hunting, covers the subject thoroughly in *Resumes For Dummies* and *Job Interviews For Dummies*, practically, and with high good humor....Kennedy is a seasoned professional who knows what works."
> — *Marilyn Moats Kennedy,* Kennedy's Career Strategist, Chicago

Job Interviews For Dummies by Joyce Lain Kennedy is the winner of the Ben Franklin Award for Best Career Book of 1996.

TM

References for the Rest of Us!™

BESTSELLING BOOK SERIES

Do you find that traditional reference books are overloaded with technical details and advice you'll never use? Do you postpone important life decisions because you just don't want to deal with them? Then our *...For Dummies*® business and general reference book series is for you.

...For Dummies business and general reference books are written for those frustrated and hard-working souls who know they aren't dumb, but find that the myriad of personal and business issues and the accompanying horror stories make them feel helpless. *...For Dummies* books use a lighthearted approach, a down-to-earth style, and even cartoons and humorous icons to dispel fears and build confidence. Lighthearted but not lightweight, these books are perfect survival guides to solve your everyday personal and business problems.

> "More than a publishing phenomenon, 'Dummies' is a sign of the times."
>
> — The New York Times

> "...you won't go wrong buying them."
>
> — Walter Mossberg, Wall Street Journal, on IDG Books' ...For Dummies books

> "A world of detailed and authoritative information is packed into them..."
>
> — U.S. News and World Report

Already, millions of satisfied readers agree. They have made *...For Dummies* the #1 introductory level computer book series and a best-selling business book series. They have written asking for more. So, if you're looking for the best and easiest way to learn about business and other general reference topics, look to *...For Dummies* to give you a helping hand.

IDG BOOKS WORLDWIDE®

1/99

COLLEGE FINANCIAL AID FOR DUMMIES®

by Dr. Herm Davis and Joyce Lain Kennedy

IDG Books Worldwide, Inc.
An International Data Group Company

Foster City, CA ♦ Chicago, IL ♦ Indianapolis, IN ♦ New York, NY

College Financial Aid For Dummies®

Published by
IDG Books Worldwide, Inc.
An International Data Group Company
919 E. Hillsdale Blvd.
Suite 400
Foster City, CA 94404
www.idgbooks.com (IDG Books Worldwide Web site)
www.dummies.com (Dummies Press Web site)

Library of Congress Catalog Card No.: 97-72418

ISBN: 0-7645-5049-7

Printed in the United States of America

10 9 8 7 6 5 4

1B/RQ/QT/ZZ/IN

Distributed in the United States by IDG Books Worldwide, Inc.

Distributed by CDG Books Canada Inc. for Canada; by Transworld Publishers Limited in the United Kingdom; by IDG Norge Books for Norway; by IDG Sweden Books for Sweden; by Woodslane Pty. Ltd. for Australia; by Woodslane (NZ) Ltd. for New Zealand; by TransQuest Publishers Pte Ltd. for Singapore, Malaysia, Thailand, Indonesia, and Hong Kong; by ICG Muse, Inc. for Japan; by Norma Comunicaciones S.A. for Colombia; by Intersoft for South Africa; by Le Monde en Tique for France; by International Thomson Publishing for Germany, Austria and Switzerland; by Distribuidora Cuspide for Argentina; by Livraria Cultura for Brazil; by Ediciones ZETA S.C.R. Ltda. for Peru; by WS Computer Publishing Corporation, Inc., for the Philippines; by Contemporanea de Ediciones for Venezuela; by Express Computer Distributors for the Caribbean and West Indies; by Micronesia Media Distributor, Inc. for Micronesia; by Grupo Editorial Norma S.A. for Guatemala; by Chips Computadoras S.A. de C.V. for Mexico; by Editorial Norma de Panama S.A. for Panama; by American Bookshops for Finland. Authorized Sales Agent: Anthony Rudkin Associates for the Middle East and North Africa.

For general information on IDG Books Worldwide's books in the U.S., please call our Consumer Customer Service department at 800-762-2974. For reseller information, including discounts and premium sales, please call our Reseller Customer Service department at 800-434-3422.

For information on where to purchase IDG Books Worldwide's books outside the U.S., please contact our International Sales department at 317-596-5530 or fax 317-596-5692.

For consumer information on foreign language translations, please contact our Customer Service department at 1-800-434-3422, fax 317-596-5692, or e-mail rights@idgbooks.com.

For information on licensing foreign or domestic rights, please phone +1-650-655-3109.

For sales inquiries and special prices for bulk quantities, please contact our Sales department at 650-655-3200 or write to the address above.

For information on using IDG Books Worldwide's books in the classroom or for ordering examination copies, please contact our Educational Sales department at 800-434-2086 or fax 317-596-5499.

For press review copies, author interviews, or other publicity information, please contact our Public Relations department at 650-655-3000 or fax 650-655-3299.

For authorization to photocopy items for corporate, personal, or educational use, please contact Copyright Clearance Center, 222 Rosewood Drive, Danvers, MA 01923, or fax 978-750-4470.

About the Authors

Dr. Herm Davis spends the majority of his time consulting with students and parents on paying for college. One of the nation's top student aid authorities, Dr. Davis heads the National College Scholarship Foundation, a nonprofit organization providing information to students. Additionally, he directs College Financial Aid Counseling and Education Services Inc. (CFACES).

A resident of Rockville, Maryland (a Washington, D.C. suburb), Dr. Davis is a 25-year veteran in financial aid and scholarship information for higher education. He was, for 15 years, Director of Financial Aid at Montgomery College in Rockville, Maryland, before leaving to devote all of his time to financial aid counseling and scholarship information management. He writes a weekly column on student financial aid for a Maryland newspaper and has published numerous reports on paying for college.

Dr. Davis has served on several government and professional boards concerned with financial aid. He is the financial aid advisor to the nonprofit Special Operations' Warriors Foundation, an organization that provides college planning for children of men and women who died or became disabled while serving the nation in special military operations.

Dr. Davis presents financial aid programs to such high profile groups as the Department of Justice, Department of Defense, Department of State, The Washington Post Scholarship Incentive Program, The American Legion's Boys Nation, and the Fannie Mae Foundation — Futures 500C Club.

Each year Dr. Davis presents college financial aid programs in more than 70 high schools as a community service, including ten schools that feature English as a Second Language programs. In addition to his work with middle-income students, he has helped more than 3,000 low-income and minority students receive financial aid totaling more than $4,000,000.

His doctorate in higher education administration in 1978 from George Washington University in Washington, D.C. featured a dissertation on *Financial Aid and Academic Progress*. Dr. Davis was born in Indiana, is a U.S. Navy veteran, and was graduated from Indiana State University in Terre Haute with a bachelor's and a master's degree in education.

Joyce Lain Kennedy is the author or senior author of seven books. Her most recent are *Resumes For Dummies, Cover Letters For Dummies,* and *Job Interviews For Dummies* (IDG Books Worldwide), which recently received a Ben Franklin award as the best careers book of 1996. She also writes a Los Angeles Times Syndicate column, CAREERS. Kennedy's column, now in its 29th year, appears in more than 100 newspapers. Kennedy was for 20 years the executive editor of *Career World*, a national magazine for secondary and college students, where she became interested in student financial aid. Writing from Carlsbad, California (a San Diego suburb), Kennedy is a baccalaureate business graduate of Washington University in St. Louis.

ABOUT IDG BOOKS WORLDWIDE

Welcome to the world of IDG Books Worldwide.

IDG Books Worldwide, Inc., is a subsidiary of International Data Group, the world's largest publisher of computer-related information and the leading global provider of information services on information technology. IDG was founded more than 30 years ago by Patrick J. McGovern and now employs more than 9,000 people worldwide. IDG publishes more than 290 computer publications in over 75 countries. More than 90 million people read one or more IDG publications each month.

Launched in 1990, IDG Books Worldwide is today the #1 publisher of best-selling computer books in the United States. We are proud to have received eight awards from the Computer Press Association in recognition of editorial excellence and three from Computer Currents' First Annual Readers' Choice Awards. Our best-selling ...*For Dummies*® series has more than 50 million copies in print with translations in 31 languages. IDG Books Worldwide, through a joint venture with IDG's Hi-Tech Beijing, became the first U.S. publisher to publish a computer book in the People's Republic of China. In record time, IDG Books Worldwide has become the first choice for millions of readers around the world who want to learn how to better manage their businesses.

Our mission is simple: Every one of our books is designed to bring extra value and skill-building instructions to the reader. Our books are written by experts who understand and care about our readers. The knowledge base of our editorial staff comes from years of experience in publishing, education, and journalism — experience we use to produce books to carry us into the new millennium. In short, we care about books, so we attract the best people. We devote special attention to details such as audience, interior design, use of icons, and illustrations. And because we use an efficient process of authoring, editing, and desktop publishing our books electronically, we can spend more time ensuring superior content and less time on the technicalities of making books.

You can count on our commitment to deliver high-quality books at competitive prices on topics you want to read about. At IDG Books Worldwide, we continue in the IDG tradition of delivering quality for more than 30 years. You'll find no better book on a subject than one from IDG Books Worldwide.

John Kilcullen
Chairman and CEO
IDG Books Worldwide, Inc.

Steven Berkowitz
President and Publisher
IDG Books Worldwide, Inc.

Eighth Annual
Computer Press
Awards ≥1992

Ninth Annual
Computer Press
Awards ≥1993

Tenth Annual
Computer Press
Awards ≥1994

Eleventh Annual
Computer Press
Awards ≥1995

IDG is the world's leading IT media, research and exposition company. Founded in 1964, IDG had 1997 revenues of $2.05 billion and has more than 9,000 employees worldwide. IDG offers the widest range of media options that reach IT buyers in 75 countries representing 95% of worldwide IT spending. IDG's diverse product and services portfolio spans six key areas including print publishing, online publishing, expositions and conferences, market research, education and training, and global marketing services. More than 90 million people read one or more of IDG's 290 magazines and newspapers, including IDG's leading global brands — Computerworld, PC World, Network World, Macworld and the Channel World family of publications. IDG Books Worldwide is one of the fastest-growing computer book publishers in the world, with more than 700 titles in 36 languages. The "...For Dummies®" series alone has more than 50 million copies in print. IDG offers online users the largest network of technology-specific Web sites around the world through IDG.net (http://www.idg.net), which comprises more than 225 targeted Web sites in 55 countries worldwide. International Data Corporation (IDC) is the world's largest provider of information technology data, analysis and consulting, with research centers in over 41 countries and more than 400 research analysts worldwide. IDG World Expo is a leading producer of more than 168 globally branded conferences and expositions in 35 countries including E3 (Electronic Entertainment Expo), Macworld Expo, ComNet, Windows World Expo, ICE (Internet Commerce Expo), Agenda, DEMO, and Spotlight. IDG's training subsidiary, ExecuTrain, is the world's largest computer training company, with more than 230 locations worldwide and 785 training courses. IDG Marketing Services helps industry-leading IT companies build international brand recognition by developing global integrated marketing programs via IDG's print, online and exposition products worldwide. Further information about the company can be found at www.idg.com.   1/24/99

Authors' Acknowledgments

Thanks "Big Time" to the good men and women in the **U.S. Department of Education, The College Board, American Legion, National Association of Student Financial Aid Administrators, National Association of College and University Business Officers, American Association of State Colleges and Universities,** and **scholarship sponsoring organizations** who have gone out of their way to assist the authors in preparing this book.

Josey Vierra and **Carol Daigle** in Maryland worked hard on resource data. They've been in the trenches of student financial aid and know where the resources are buried.

Charity De Oca in California wove magic in the words of several chapters.

Zoiner Sonny Tejada served as the California computer communications chief.

Financial authority and author of *Personal Finance For Dummies* **Eric Tyson** graciously reviewed a key chapter.

Johns Hopkins University Director of Student Financial Services **Ellen Frishberg** meticulously and carefully reviewed the entire book and made numerous contributions that improved its quality.

More Thanks to **Dummies Trade Press Stars** for making this book a top-of-the-charts event: **Kathleen M. Cox,** Project Editor, and **Tamara S. Castleman,** Copy Editor; and for liking this book and putting it in print: **Kathleen A. Welton,** Vice President and Publisher, and **Mark Butler,** Acquisitions Editor

Publisher's Acknowledgments

We're proud of this book; please register your comments through our IDG Books Worldwide Online Registration Form located at http://my2cents.dummies.com.

Some of the people who helped bring this book to market include the following:

Acquisitions, Development, and Editorial

Project Editor: Kathleen M. Cox

Acquisitions Editor: Mark Butler

Associate Permissions Editor:
Heather H. Dismore

Copy Editor: Tamara S. Castleman

Technical Editor: Ellen Frishberg, Director of Student Financial Services, Johns Hopkins University

Editorial Manager: Mary C. Corder

Editorial Assistants: Donna Love, Chris H. Collins

Production

Project Coordinator: Debbie Stailey

Layout and Graphics: Cameron Booker, Pamela Emanoil, Angela F. Hunckler, Todd Klemme, Jane E. Martin, Anna Rohrer, Deirdre Smith, Ian Smith, Kate Snell

Proofreaders: Christine Berman, Kelli Botta, Michelle Croninger, Joel K. Draper, Robert Springer Carrie Voorhis, Jon C. Weidlich,

Indexer: David Heiret

Special Help: Jamie Klobuchar

General and Administrative

IDG Books Worldwide, Inc.: John Kilcullen, CEO; Steven Berkowitz, President and Publisher

IDG Books Technology Publishing: Brenda McLaughlin, Senior Vice President and Group Publisher

Dummies Technology Press and Dummies Editorial: Diane Graves Steele, Vice President and Associate Publisher; Mary Bednarek, Director of Acquisitions and Product Development; Kristin A. Cocks, Editorial Director

Dummies Trade Press: Kathleen A. Welton, Vice President and Publisher; Kevin Thornton, Acquisitions Manager

IDG Books Production for Dummies Press: Michael R. Britton, Vice President of Production and Creative Services; Cindy L. Phipps, Manager of Project Coordination, Production Proofreading, and Indexing; Kathie S. Schutte, Supervisor of Page Layout; Shelley Lea, Supervisor of Graphics and Design; Debbie J. Gates, Production Systems Specialist; Robert Springer, Supervisor of Proofreading; Debbie Stailey, Special Projects Coordinator; Tony Augsburger, Supervisor of Reprints and Bluelines

Dummies Packaging and Book Design: Patty Page, Manager, Promotions Marketing

♦

The publisher would like to give special thanks to Patrick J. McGovern, without whom this book would not have been possible.

♦

Dedication

This book is dedicated to the countless members of the **professional financial aid community** who have spent their lives serving students and parents.

It is dedicated to those from whom I have been privileged to learn, especially the late **Dr. Doug McDonald,** who served as the director of financial aid at the Community College of Baltimore, the University of Delaware, and was the executive director of the Maryland State Scholarship Board. Dr. McDonald provided leadership as president of the Eastern Association of Financial Aid Administrators, and as a board member of the National Association of Financial Aid Executives.

It is dedicated to my family for the enduring support they've given in allowing me to take time away from family happenings to grow into a committed financial aid professional as I attended endless financial aid meetings and family workshops, took college courses on higher education issues, and worked on this book. To my daughter, **Shauna Davis,** to my son **Craig Davis,** and to my friend and wife **Sara Jo Davis,** I thank you.

And it is dedicated to **each of you readers** whose need for funding to pay for the next leg of your life's journey inspired me to focus my attention on cutting-edge financial aid practices.

— Dr. Herm Davis

Contents at a Glance

Cartoons at a Glance

By Rich Tennant

"Someone put a financial aid form in our tip cup."

page 73

"My daughter's college education is costing me an arm and a leg and over 60 noses a year."

page 5

"...and here's our returning champion, spinning for her 3rd & 4th year college tuition..."

page 299

"It's part of my employer tuition assistance agreement with the 'Pizza Bob' corporation."

page 275

"Our plan is to buy the rest of it when we pay off our college loan."

page 237

"I really can't have a relationship now - I'm afraid it might impact my 'needs analysis form'."

page 167

Fax: 978-546-7747 • E-mail: the5wave@tiac.net

Table of Contents

Our book has a dual focus:

1. **What you must know to navigate the financial aid system to your advantage.** Using information rooted in Dr. Davis's extensive experience, we share with you the kinds of insider knowledge that most guidebooks just can't deliver.

2. **What you must know to create a financial plan for four or more years of college.** You should not merely scrabble together a quick fix to pay for the next semester (although we do tell you what to do if school's about to start and you're cashless and clueless).

We identify some of the best private scholarships available, and coach you on how to work the system to shake loose gift money. We tell you what to watch out for when taking out loans. We reveal how much you can really count on work aid. We tell you how a tiny blunder on your forms can mean a giant loss of money.

We tell you how to negotiate with school financial aid counselors without ticking them off. We dissect little-known options such as using the state National Guard to collect on the GI Bill.

We focus on the undergraduate financial aid challenge but look too at the graduate finaid scene.

A glance through the table of contents tells you that this is a mother lode of a guidebook to find college gold.

Icons Used in This Book

A helpful feature of the ...*For Dummies* series is the liberal use of cute pictures called icons that draw your attention to information too useful to ignore. These are the icons used in this book and what they signify:

The bare essentials of student financial aid you absolutely, positively, for sure must understand. Or else the universe blows apart.

Look for this icon to identify the authors' expert tips on getting the most money without selling a sibling.

This icon points to bargains or rewards that you'd camp out in line overnight to get.

This icon identifies niches of riches — outstanding sources of college money.

Despite what you may have heard, this icon directs your attention to myths and realities about college aid.

An icon reminding finaid seekers to keep precious copies in case your school or financial aid processor loses your paperwork, a not infrequent occurrence.

An alarm-bell icon that says wake up, it's time to act!

This icon shows it's important for you to record a fact for future reference in your indelible memory.

When you think you make too much money (but not enough to pay school bills), read what this icon highlights and be reinspired to get that money you need.

This icon highlights information useful to international students seeking a college education in the United States.

If you're not fresh out of high school but want a chance at a college education, these tips will help you achieve your goals.

These tips help maximize your chances of getting the most college aid.

Making these mistakes can torpedo your chances for financial aid, so watch out!

In this part . . .

Few students understand the financial aid system well enough to navigate its complex ins-and-outs, let alone plan paying for four years in advance. Because the earnings premium attached to a college degree may be as high as 80 percent, more people are enrolling than ever. To beat the rising competition for finaid, you need to combine an in-depth understanding of the college money system and good old-fashioned resourcefulness.

This part helps you steer through the finaid-finding maze. You find stockpiles of information on qualifying for college money, the intricate workings of college funding, and the cost of higher learning. You also learn how to get financial aid when your circumstances are unique. And you get tips on highlighting your most finaid-worthy attributes. Read on to find out how to help the financial aid system help you.

Chapter 1

College Money: Who Gets It

In This Chapter

▶ Bringing middle-income families in from the cold

▶ Previewing central concepts of aid

▶ Shifting assets to qualify for more aid

*A*s a student or parent paying college bills, do you agree or disagree with the following statements?

✔ Middle-income students are shortchanged when financial aid is passed around. (In financial aid circles, middle-income families are defined as those with annual incomes of $45,000 to $95,000; upper-middle incomes continue to about $150,000. We don't have enough fingers and toes to count higher than that.)

✔ If you had lots more money, or lots less, paying for college wouldn't be a problem.

✔ The American financial aid system punishes families who work hard and save their money.

If you agree with these contentions, join the crowd. Middle-class families across the nation are howling in unison about feeling like afterthoughts when student aid is passed around.

A recent national survey reported in *Student Poll* (a product of Baltimore's Art & Science Group, Inc., institutional marketing consultants to higher education and the nonprofit sector) confirms that a whopping majority of people who pay tuition bills say the financial aid system doesn't meet the requirements of the beleaguered middle class.

"On paper it looks as though we have a big income," says Greta, a Virginia mother whose family is experiencing the sticker shock of college costs. "We're not going hungry, but we have old cars, and my husband's job may set sail at any time. We don't eat meals out, buy more than the bare minimum of clothing, or take vacations. Every dime we can hang onto goes toward tuition."

The amount that your family is expected to pay remains about the same no matter where you enroll. The more expensive the college, the more aid for which you are eligible. All you need is to apply and qualify academically. At least, that's the way the system is supposed to work — and, very often, it does. Academically speaking, however, schools have fallen on difficult economic times.

Although most schools still insist that they hew to a *need-blind admissions policy,* which means that the decision to accept or turn down an applicant is made without regard to that student's financial need, many educators admit privately that students who can pay have the edge over equally qualified students who are less able to pay.

In practical terms, all but the most selective and well-endowed schools tilt toward students who can pay their way without dipping into the institutions' coffers. (For a list of colleges and universities with deep endowment pockets, see Chapter 6.)

Keeping your nose in the books is the key to snagging merit scholarships. The people handing them out are GPA groupies. They love applicants who emerge from high school in the upper regions of their class and demolish SAT and ACT tests as if they were child's play.

Some colleges, for example, knock 40 percent off tuition to students who graduate in the top 5 percent of their high school class and are selected for a grant; others give the best students whatever money they need to attend — the best students being those graduating in the top 2 percent of their class, with a GPA of 3.9 out of 4.00 and SAT scores higher than 1450.

The bar is high, too, for those who leap over it to win sports, music, drama, or art scholarships: Both talent plus academic achievement often must be stellar.

But what if talented applicants have only so-so grades? They may still make the scholarship cut. Sometimes talent outweighs academic records by a country mile — just ask any football coach.

Colleges frequently aim their merit scholarships toward students they want but who may not show up without the inducement of serious aid. Aid offers are designed with an eye toward the school's diversity mix of brains, talent, and cultural composition.

If you're lucky enough to be in the most-wanted category — with some combination of great grades, leadership activities, fine arts ability, desirable major, geography, or minority status — don't let the school know that your enrollment is a done deal or its limited aid budget may go to those who need persuasion.

Popular essay topics for finaid applications

Pick five topics below most likely to apply to your situation. Write a 500-word essay on each and file for your core essay database. If you don't know how a good academic essay should read, get a copy of *100 Successful College Application Essays* by Christopher J. and Gigi E. Georges for samples of some great ones.

While essay topics are never entirely predictable, here are some scholarship favorites:

- Describe yourself as a person living in the 21st Century.

- Explain how your background, experience, personality, values, interests and goals qualify you for this award. Include the influence of other people in your life.

- Recount an accomplishment that you had to struggle to achieve. Include what it is, how you tackled it, and how it changed you.

- What personality traits do you value most in yourself? Choose a few and jot down the examples of how each has helped you.

- Discuss an activity (extracurricular, community, family, or work) that has had the most meaning for you and tell why.

- Discuss your educational and/or your career objectives.

- If you could spend an evening with any person — living or dead — who would it be, why would you choose that person, and what would you talk about?

- Our school seeks a diverse and unique population. How will your distinctiveness enrich our learning environment and enhance your prospects for success as a — ?

- Submit an essay on "The Value of Teachers" (or other career field).

- Why are you the most qualified person to receive this award?

- Evaluate yourself as a student. What are your areas of academic strength and weakness? Do you think your transcript (and counselor/teacher reports) is a fair evaluation of your academic abilities?

- Show us the imaginative side of your personality.

- Describe an ethical dilemma you have personally encountered. What alternative actions did you consider and why? Do not tell what you decided to do.

For more examples of good essays, you might try calling or e-mailing scholarship providers. Ask if sample winning essays from previous years are available if you send them a stamped, self-addressed envelope. A number of scholarship providers do have sample essays on hand.

Suppose your talent is nonexistent. Your grades are in the "not bad" category, and the processional line between you and the valedictorian is 200-people deep. You may get admission but probably no federal grant aid whatsoever from elite schools, regardless of how strapped you are. If your middle-class family's income tops the federal and state aid caps (adjusted to about $40,000), you need to shop for low-interest loans. However, these same colleges may offer you funds from their own resources.

Qualifying for Finaid (Financial Aid)

Question: Who qualifies for college financial aid?

Answer: Surprise! You and most of the people you know!

If you and your family do each financial aid task (1) correctly and (2) in a timely manner, you will receive student financial aid of some kind.

Although each aid program defines its own special criteria, certain eligibility requirements are common to virtually all programs:

- ✔ You must be enrolled in an eligible program at an eligible institution. The finaid program defines what is eligible.

- ✔ You generally must show satisfactory academic progress toward a degree or certificate to keep finaid.

- ✔ Typically, you must be "in good standing" with the institution you attend.

- ✔ For federal student aid programs, you must be a United States citizen, or a noncitizen who is a permanent resident. Refugees or those granted political asylum may be eligible.

- ✔ Aid programs sponsored by colleges and private organizations may require that you be a U.S. citizen or permanent resident.

- ✔ As a rule, you must be a legal resident of the state from which you seek finaid to receive it. Out-of-state residents may be able to participate in state-backed loan programs.

- ✔ Many finaid programs require that you be at least a half-time student (six semester hours of courses per semester, or the equivalent).

- ✔ Some programs sponsored by schools and private organizations require that you attend college on a full-time basis (12 semester hours minimum).

- ✔ International students qualify for special programs sponsored by colleges and private organizations. (See Chapter 2 for more information.)

Federal aid programs usually apply to more than 9,000 eligible colleges, universities, and vocational-technical schools (which means everything from computer repair to cosmetology). You can also use federal aid money at hospital schools of nursing and two-year colleges.

Rarely are less-than-half-time students eligible for federal funds. The exception is Pell grants, which can be used for less-than-half-time students; you just won't receive as much as if you were enrolled full-time.

Unlike federal programs, state aid programs may not consider vocational-technical school students eligible for some aid programs. Other types of study that may not qualify for aid from various programs include religious studies and voc-tech programs of less than six months' duration.

Perceived versus demonstrated need

Need means the amount of money your family can't afford to pay for your education — it's the difference between the cost of your college education and the dollars your family is expected to ante up for college expenses. Need does not mean poverty status.

The concept of need has a particular meaning in finaid offices, however. You may tell your college financial aid counselor you have need just because you're on thin shoe leather, and bill collectors are hot on your trail. While that's not a good position to be in, aid givers consider that type of informal reporting as *perceived need*. It doesn't mean a thing to them.

What you have to do is show *demonstrated need*, as explained in Chapter 3. You do so by filling out a mass of paperwork supported with financial documents. The complex paperwork evaluates families' income and assets to determine how much of the overall college tab individual students and their parents can afford.

Financial aid personnel at various schools put approximately the same ceiling on how much they expect a family to pay, regardless of costs at their college. Once you're accepted for admission, they try to offer an aid package that makes up the difference.

Expect aid packages to be a mixed bag

The aid package, described in greater detail in Chapter 3, is comprised of self-help money and gift money. *Self-help money* includes work-study jobs and loans that must be paid back. *Gift money* includes grants (based on demonstrated need) and scholarships (based on merit), which aren't paid back. Gift money is also called *free money*. Once you grasp the concept of demonstrated need, you can act to increase your eligibility for aid by following the advice given throughout this book.

Financial aid for students with disabilities

Students with disabilities may face such additional expenses as special equipment related to the disability and its maintenance, expenses of services such as readers, interpreters, note takers or personal care attendants, special transportation requirements, and medical expenses relating to the disability but not covered by insurance.

Scholarships specifically designated for students with disabilities are very limited (see the Resource Guide at the end of this book). If you have a disability, be sure to pursue scholarships available for qualities other than disability.

In addition, the state vocational rehabilitation agency, as well as organizations of and for people with disabilities, may be able to help you realize your college goal.

Moreover, at each college, students with disabilities should ask about financial support not only at the financial aid office, but at the Office of Student Services, 504 coordinator, or Office of Disability Support Services.

For a fuller discussion of available resources for college students with disabilities, obtain an annually revised information paper, *Financial Aid for Students with Disabilities.* The paper is free. Order from:

HEATH Resource Center
American Council on Education
One Dupont Circle NW, Suite 800
Washington, DC 20036
V 202-939-9320
F 202-833-4760
E heath@ace.nche.edu

A Plan for the Long Haul! Way to Go!

When you get into the college financial aid game, approach it with a four-year plan that allows you to shift assets and avoid eating beans when tuition deadlines strike, as the following story illustrates.

Both of Hilton's parents worked and were proud that they could send their son to an Illinois name-brand university. But last year, when Hilton, a sophomore, returned home to Maryland for the December break, they broke staggering news:

> *Mom lost her job. We can't afford to send you back to your school for the spring semester. Sorry, we'll try again in the fall.*

Hilton's family had not sought college financial aid when he graduated from high school, assuming that their family income — $78,000 — was too high to qualify for more than good wishes. And Hilton was neither scholar, jock, nor talented musician, so the idea that a "good" school would offer Hilton a bundle of money to grace its campus was unlikely. What's more, the family found the complex financial aid process to be just too much trouble.

Hilton's parents had saved a few dollars and assumed that with their jobs and careful money management, they could handle Hilton's college. They would deal with the tuition year by year.

All went as anticipated until Mom lost her job and Hilton's college costs threatened to sink the family. Good news: Mom landed another job within a few months, and Hilton returned to his college in the fall. Bad news: Hilton unnecessarily lost a semester of school because he failed to file an emergency appeals letter with his school. He didn't know he could.

The moral to Hilton's story is apparent:

- ✔ Learn as much as you can about the college financial aid system.
- ✔ Use that knowledge to plan how to pay for all your college years.
- ✔ Ask questions; don't assume.

Beyond an unexpected financial crunch and lost time, you need a four-year family college financial plan for other reasons, too — not the least of which is to allow yourself adequate time to plan how you will shift assets and increase your family's share of the aid money.

Playing the Aid Game: Asset Control

The key to getting aid based on your financial status is clear: *The more impoverished you look, the more aid you get.*

For example, aid-analysis programs require you to count your savings in regular taxable accounts as wealth, not the savings you have in your home equity, retirement accounts, and cash-value life insurance policies. (Some schools, however, do throw all of a family's wealth into one big pot to measure how much aid the student's entitled to receive.)

Even Washington politicos are concerned that, with the exception of unsubsidized loans, the middle-income student gets the short end of the financial aid stick. The president and the Congress have responded with varying proposals to create a huge new (mostly middle-class) entitlement in the form of tax breaks. At press time, they had not yet come to a meeting of the minds. The end result is likely to be a compromise of some sort, giving middle-class students more than they have but less than they want.

Play or pay?

Autumn was just beginning and Shawn, an outstanding California high school senior with a GPA of 4.9 (out of 4.0 — extra points for advance placement college courses), was trying hard to get into Stanford on an early-decision basis. As the son of a single mother, inexpensive macaroni-and-cheese casseroles were a popular supper in Shawn's home.

To increase your aid eligibility, you can make these other short-term strategic moves. All of them should be accomplished *prior to December 31 of your junior year in high school.* (Or, if a nontraditional student, the year before you intend to apply for aid. See Chapter 2 for more about nontraditional students.)

Because need-analysis standards vary from school to school, make anonymous calls to target schools asking what specific assets are included in their calculations.

A key point to remember: Your ability to pay *this* year's tuition is based on your income and assets of *last* year. That's because colleges can't see into the future and verify your family's financial status this year.

Federal need analyzers don't count assets like the value of your car or home when they figure how fat a cat your family is. Nor do they subtract debts from your assets. But they seem to smell money in the bank, and they count every cent as an asset after the asset protection allowance. (Remember, the more assets, the less aid.)

Most of the following tips suggest that you shift cash into assets that aren't counted or pay off debts that don't help you look poor on paper. For instance, suppose you have $50,000 in a savings account but owe $20,000 on a consumer debt. The federal formula recognizes the $50,000 in your bank account loud and clear. Frustratingly, they ignore the $20,000 you owe. By withdrawing the money from savings and using it to pay your debt, and because you have a $30,000 asset protection allowance, your assets drop from $50,000 to zero. Presto! You qualify for more financial aid.

Here are pointers for parents to help reframe your aid eligibility. All of them are legal and legitimate. As an East Coast financial planner says: "There is no reward in heaven for paying extra money for college."

- **Spend down and pass over.** Any asset keeps you from receiving maximum aid dollars. Getting rid of the money by paying tuition and other legitimate college-related expenses is to your advantage as it can increase the amount of financial aid you'll receive every year after that.

- **Reduce a child's kitty.** Finaid administrators expect parents to spend 5.65 percent of their assets (and that's *after* subtracting an asset protection allowance), but they expect students to spend 35 percent of their savings each year for school with no asset protection allowance. If you're thinking of a tax savings, forget it — the tax benefits of putting money in a child's name are small compared to the big cut in family finaid.

- **Pay off consumer loans and home mortgages.** Home equity loans generally reduce assets; so consider taking out a home equity loan to pay off automobile loans, credit card debt, or other consumer loans. Watch out: Although most schools don't count home equity as an asset, some do to determine eligibility for institutional aid only.

✔ **Time your purchases.** If you have assets of $50,000 or more, make major purchases before December 31 of a child's junior year in high school. If you are 45 years or older, for every $1,000 you withdraw from savings, the amount you're expected to fork over for college decreases by about $120.

✔ **Time your income.** If you plan to cash in high-performing stocks or other investments to pay for college, do so before December 31 of the year before you are evaluated for your aid award. That is, if you want aid in the 2000-2001 school year, try to report the big money before December 31 of 1998; remember that 1999 is the base year on which your income and assets will be evaluated. The same timing applies to extravagant bonuses or commissions — although this timing is harder to arrange. Capital gains can inflate your income dramatically, and if you sell after December 31, that boost in income will slash your aid eligibility the next year.

✔ **Put assets off-limits.** Rules are far from universal, but schools do not include retirement funds, such as 401(k)s and individual retirement accounts, when totaling a family's assets for federal need analysis, but some higher cost colleges use these assets to measure a family's ability to pay.

✔ **Start your own home business.** Some parents, who have always wanted to operate a little business from home, reduce assets by making capital investments in their enterprise. The business, which is unlikely to make money in the initial years, probably will result in a tax deduction as well as more aid for their child. (Warning: Some colleges discount paper losses.)

Caveats when shifting assets

Keep the following caveats in mind when applying for financial aid:

✔ **Some of the preceding strategies carry risk.**

You could lose your investment in your home business, for instance.

✔ **Tax accountants and financial planners can slash your aid eligibility.**

Accountants and planners who lack in-depth knowledge of college financing can torpedo your chances to receive aid. Certain income strategies, such as shifting money to a child's account, may work well for long-term tax reduction planning but are ill-advised for the college years unless your income precludes grant aid eligibility.

✔ **Before moving money out of a kid's name and stashing it in the parent's name, double check that the transfer passes two acid tests:**

• Is the move legal with the IRS? Ask your accountant or the bank involved to be sure that no rules are broken.

• Do not transfer any asset until you determine that the action will give you the increased-aid-eligibility results you seek.

Chapter 2

What if You're Adult, Part-Time, International, or Other?

*M*oving forward on a financial aid journey when you're a part of the traditional crowd — attending full-time college on campus in your home country in your teens or early 20s — is difficult enough even though your pathway is well marked and you know what to expect.

Seeking out aid funds when you're a nontraditional learner set apart from the crowd is altogether a more challenging task, because you may not know where your pathway *begins*, much less how it twists and turns.

This chapter is designed for learners who don't fit the traditional mold — learners like these:

✔ **Adult at Risk:** At 47, Dan is a successful and talented craftsworker in the construction trades. But Dan frets about the future, worrying that he's getting too old to continue the heavy lifting that his work requires. Is construction management the answer? Can Dan afford to go after the construction-focused college degree many companies now demand?

✔ **Part-time wake-up call:** Twenty-seven-year-old Kelly's two children are now in school. Kelly dropped out of a community college after high school because she said, "I wasn't sure what I wanted to do." She traveled around the country working as a waitress, fell in love, and married a co-worker. Kelly plans to stay home for another few years but worries that her beginner's skimpy accounting skills, acquired at the community college, are inadequate for today's tough job market. She'd like to study part-time, but her family's budget is stretched as thin as the rubber band that keeps her bills together. The cost of baby-sitters, as well as tuition, is more than Kelly can handle. Can Kelly receive finaid to study part-time?

✔ **College without a campus:** David's on an unsuccessful archaeology dig in a remote mountainous area. He knows he needs graduate credentials to advance in his field and so he's been looking into using his computer as a distance-learning campus. David's earnings are as sparse as the expedition's findings. Paying for college online has him stumped. Can David reap aid for virtual study?

✔ **World-class student:** Chang's family has decided he would benefit by an obtaining a graduate engineering education in the United States. Chang's Korean family can get most of the money together for his studies but they are short about $10,000. Is all financial aid for U.S. colleges saved for U.S. citizens? Or is there a glimmer of hope that help is available for this international student who wants an American graduate college education?

✔ **American in Paris:** Ever since she was a young girl of eight, Rosemary had her heart set on studying art in Paris. But her father, a high school teacher, and mother, a paralegal, were responsible for the nursing-home bills of Rosemary's grandmother, as well as bringing up Rosemary and her brother. For Americans, studying overseas is an unrealistic goal unless you're well-heeled. Or is it? Can student aid save Rosemary's dream?

Dan, Kelly, David, Chang, and Rosemary represent the new faces in higher education today.

Exploding numbers of nontraditional students are changing the profile of the prototypical American student.

Collectively, the majority of all American undergraduates now fit nontraditional descriptions — they're not in the bloom of youth, not full-time, not campus-bound, not hailing from within the borders of the United States, and not staying on their side of an ocean to study.

These older, nontraditional faces are standing shoulder-to-shoulder with the learners we think of as traditional: young, full-time, campus-based, home-grown, and home-loving students. From the perspective of a U.S. citizen, the nontraditionals fall in five broad groups:

✔ Adults who have been buffeted by the winds of work and are highly focused on tuning up their workplace skills or on making themselves over with fresh skill sets to fit into new fields.

- Part-time students who must hold onto their day jobs or family duties as they slog it out in the halls of academe.

- Far-away students who crack the books in distance education programs, sit in front of a computer maintaining serious e-mail discussions with their professors, and download lecture notes. Sometimes the distance learners get back to basics by watching a course on television, picking up the telephone, or even sending correspondence by postal mail.

- International students who recognize the borderless economies of the world translate to borderless education; often their learning destination of choice is the United States.

- Students who travel outside the United States to study find that an educational exchange of ideas flows two ways. Privileged families of old sent their offspring to spend a "junior year abroad." Now society's rank-and-file think an international experience may be just what the competitive workplace ordered.

Nontraditional students have a catalog of special problems, from getting off work in time to study, to child care, to getting a visa, to getting health insurance. But for all five groups, no problem looms larger than paying for college. We discuss the money angle one group at a time.

Adult Students: Paying the Back-to-College Tab

Jerry Fushianes, PA-C, is a certified physician assistant who recently graduated from the University of Detroit Mercy, a private Catholic institution. Jerry entered graduate school to build on his old career of paramedic. After being in the workplace for several years, Jerry said he became "very excited" about going back to school. "Until I learned what it cost!" he says.

"The University of Detroit Mercy is one of the most expensive PA (physician assistant) schools out there. The cost is $470 per credit hour, making my tuition bill over $6,500 per semester, including books and fees," Jerry explains.

The hard realities of coming up with that kind of money sent Jerry scurrying to the university's financial aid office: "No two ways about it, I just couldn't afford retraining."

Jerry's first clue that his dream was reachable was when he received a $2,000 grant from the state of Michigan, a benefit available to all the state's students who attend a private university. The eligibility requirements for the state grant were, according to Jerry, "a pulse and an acceptance letter from a college."

Next, Jerry began to look at other opportunities. He found Harper Hospital in Detroit, which would trade $6,000 per year for two years' service after graduation. Jerry took that as well and revved up his financial aid hunting:

"I looked at civic and religious organizations for sponsorship. I came up dry. So I took out both subsidized and unsubsidized loans."

Then he received a scholarship from the Physician Assistant Foundation for $2,000. Jerry's aid hunt was a hit! He totaled up his costs and income.

How does Jerry feel about his experience? "Student aid for adults is real and very attainable. And I had a job waiting for me when I graduated," he says.

The newly minted physician assistant doesn't seem worried about paying back the $50,000 in student loans. He jumped right in and took two jobs to pay his loans off quickly, working nights at Harper Hospital and days at The Family Doctor, a family medical practice. Good thinking!

Jerry is one of the nearly half of today's college students who are over the age of 25, a figure up from one third in 1974. Jerry already had a bachelor's degree when he began his return trip for a master's degree to become a physician assistant. Some students need only a stray course or two to flesh out workplace skills but most are angling for the bachelor's degree they didn't take seriously when they dropped out years ago.

Whatever the motivation or career field, here's the key fact to remember if you are an older student headed back: The mechanics of obtaining student financial aid are exactly the same for adults 25 years or older as for younger students in the traditional age group of 18 to 22.

Jerry's total two-year PA education costs:

Tuition	$33,480
School Expenses	$2,500
Living expenses	$33,000
Total costs	$68,980

Jerry's financial aid figures:

State tuition grant ($2,000 x 2 yrs.)	$ 4,000
Harper Hospital ($6,000 x 2 yrs.)	$12,000
PA Foundation	$2,000
Student loans	$50,000
Total financial aid	$68,000

How to receive more than the standard Stafford loan in a calendar year

Jerry's loan amounts are more than the norm. Briefly, here's what happened: The U.S. Department of Education requires postsecondary educational institutions to establish a *standard academic year (AY)* for awarding federal aid.

Colleges have two choices. They may choose to standardize with a calendar year, in which all students begin and end at the same time; this type of AY is called a *scheduled academic year (SAY)*.

Or they may choose another type of AY that permits students to start when they wish and progress at their own speed, which is called a *borrower-based academic year (BBAY)*. After the student completes the required number of credit or clock hours, the student can be considered for the next grade level of loan eligibility, which permits a second loan to be awarded within a shorter time period than is true for a student in a SAY program.

Thus, when a college uses the BBAY, a graduate student can indeed receive an additional $9,250 within a 12-month period of time.

In neither SAY nor BBAY programs can a student receive more than the total allowed under the federal student loan program — for undergraduate studies, the total is $23,000, and for graduate studies, $65,500.

Beware of phony college degrees

People who are stalled in their careers because they lack a needed educational credential and can't find the money to pay for it may be tempted to take the easy way out — buying a degree facsimile from a degree mill.

Degree mills usually claim to have libraries, classrooms, and other essential facilities, but the truth is they have a couple of desks and telephones. Their professors are untrained or nonexistent. Admission requirements are such that anyone who breathes can earn a doctorate (highest academic degree).

Fake colleges often advertise in small ads that look legitimate in magazines and newspapers. Some mills advertise on the Internet. Sometimes they claim to be "accredited." The so-called accrediting agency is a work of fiction concocted by mill operators.

Employers are smarter about degree mills than you might suspect. At the hiring stage, if you try to float a worthless degree, you'll be passed over; later discovery of your questionable credentials may result in job termination.

College and university degrees aren't the only counterfeit credential. Business thrives in the private trade-school industry where mill operators, anxious for federal student loan money, may provide classrooms but the classes themselves are virtually worthless.

Degree or diploma mill fakery appears in many variations. The blatant exchange of money for an instant credential is obvious but the novice eye may have trouble distinguishing between a borderline degree mill and a legitimate, accredited distance learning program.

Here are two ways to separate the bogus from the beautiful:

- If you're studying to get or upgrade a job or obtain a license to work, call a few employers' human resource departments and ask if the company ever hires graduates of the school in question.

- Be sure the school is accredited by a recognized accrediting body. The U.S. Department of Education maintains a list of these bodies and you can verify your school's accreditation by calling 1-800-4FEDAID.

Part-Time Students: Bummer! You're Tossed a Bone

The student aid system does very little to assist part-time students, who often have low-paying jobs and kids to support.

The lack of resources to help part-timers climb out of a career hole has not gone unnoticed by professionals who monitor student aid trends:

"Despite their growing presence on the nation's campuses, part-time students are much less likely than their full-time counterparts to receive financial assistance from federal, state, or institutional sources, even though their needs may be greater," says a 1993 report from the well-known American Council on Education.

The report, *Part-Time Enrollment: Trends and Issues,* found that between 1970 and 1990, the number of part-time undergraduates more than doubled from 2.1 million to nearly 5 million (out of a total of about 15 million college students); by 2002, the ranks of part-time students are expected to swell to 5.7 million.

What's new since 1993 for part-time students? Nothing much. Part-timers are more likely to be women and minorities and to attend public community colleges. Despite dramatic changes in the world's economies that are forcing people to look for jobs far more frequently than in the recent past, critics of present financial aid policies for part-timers make the argument that to the neediest goes the least.

Part-timers are technically eligible for most financial aid programs if they attend college at least half time (even less for Pell grants). In real life, financial aid officers first award full-time students; then, if any dollars remain, they disburse the leftovers to part-time students.

Employers and private organizations may prove to be a more fruitful source of finaid for part-time students.

Uncovering the Money for Distance Learning

New and old communication technologies permit learning to take place beyond the classroom — in the home, workplace, commuter train, car, and even under the spreading chestnut tree.

You can earn an undergraduate or advanced degree at honest-to-goodness accredited colleges and university programs available through computer, television, telephone, videocassette, audiocassette, and that familiar standby, postal mail.

Off-campus programs vary in cost but usually compare favorably to on-campus study. Still, they're not cheap. At one well-known online private university, a typical undergraduate course costs about $1,000 and a graduate course $1,250; a bachelor's degree at the same virtual university costs $30,000 to $40,000; a master's as much as $15,000. State schools are much less expensive — about half as much or less than private institutions.

In addition, some distance colleges charge small-change fees for such sundry things as study guides, telecommunications, and tapes. Once in awhile, you'll be hit with a substantial "nonresident charge." Always ask about additional charges before figuring your total distance learning cost.

The happy news is that financial aid is available to distance learners; less cheerful is the revelation that aid is not as generous to distance learners as to resident students. Here's a quick look at the requirements:

- ✔ The number one requirement for receiving federal student aid is that you be a candidate for a degree.

  Skipping around with a course here and there won't make you eligible for federal funding.

- ✔ The number two requirement is that you are signed up for at least half-time study (a minimum of six credit hours).

  As noted in Chapter 1, however, you may receive aid through Pell grants, which require less than half-time enrollment.

- ✔ The number three requirement is that you choose a course or program that is accredited by the U.S. Department of Education through an accrediting body the DOE recognizes.

  The institution you choose for distance learning may not pass accreditation muster for several reasons, ranging from quality of its offerings to the unfortunate rule that an institution doesn't qualify for federal aid if more than half of its courses are offered by telecommunications.

If you and your program meet these requirements, you are eligible for the same federal student aid programs available to resident students, except for a few fine-print qualifiers that your potential school's financial aid chief should know.

You begin your quest for finaid by applying at the school's financial aid office, just as you would if you were physically on campus.

Other than federal funds, most of the other student aid resources, from scholarships to loans, are technically available to the distance learner. The problem is the same as with the part-time learner — your aid comes at the bottom of the barrel, after full-time, on-campus students have been awarded.

Can Your Boss Send You to College?

Maybe you need a year or two more of college to finish your bachelor's degree or you want to earn a graduate or professional degree. In these uncertain times you can never have too many marketable skills polished by solid education and training.

If you are getting your education bit by bit over a period of years, rather than in one straight line through college, maybe you should try to find a boss who is willing to foot the bill.

BASICS

Do you have to pay taxes when your company pays tuition?

Companies offer two kinds of EAP funding: those that are specifically job-related, and those that are for general employee self-improvement (such as getting your college degree).

The first category, funds for job-related training assignments, are tax free to employees and a business expense to employers. When your company says "Go get training to do your job," you go get training, end of discussion.

But the second category, degree or certificate completion for self-improvement with some relationship to your job, or what is termed Section 127 in the U.S. Tax Code, is the more ambiguous form of EAPS. For 20 years companies have been able to deduct employee tuition reimbursement as a business expense, and employees have been able to escape paying taxes on it as long as the annual per-student expense was no higher than a given cap. The current cap is $5,250 per year. The law authorizing this tax break is not permanent, but reauthorized every three years or so. The 1997 tax law once again provides tax-free employer-provided educational assistance for undergraduate courses that begin before June 1, 2000. Remember, the tax-free benefits don't apply to graduate courses.

Educational Assistance Programs (EAPs) are more commonly found among sizable companies than small firms. Such industries as insurance, hospitals, and public utilities are among those that offer the most generous EAPs, according to an annual survey by the Chamber of Commerce of the United States. Fewer than half of retailers offer EAPs and manufacturing plants aren't high on education benefits either.

Who pursues degrees?

Studies by the National Association of Independent Colleges and Universities show that of employees who go to college on the employer's nickel: 33 percent pursue associate (two-year) degrees, 23 percent pursue bachelor's degrees, 22 percent pursue master's degrees, and 13 percent pursue certificates (any postsecondary level study).

Must you repay tuition with service?

Twenty years ago, employers weren't fussy if you didn't stick around after you completed your schooling. That's changed, says Cynthia Pantazis, senior government relations associate for the American Society of Training and Development: "Increasingly employers want to be sure they get a return on their educational investments." Don't be surprised if you're asked to sign an agreement stating that you'll repay the company if you depart the premises before a specific period of time.

How many employers offer tuition assistance?

Surveys vary, but it appears that the majority of employers provide some form of tuition assistance to their employees. Two studies say as many as 90 percent of employers pay for all types of education assistance programs.

Two other recent studies say that seven out of ten employers reimburse employees for courses that are part of a degree program, with slightly more covering bachelor's degree programs than graduate programs.

What percentage of tuition costs are reimbursed?

Most employers reimburse employees for the tuition bill, rather than pay it outright. About half of employers return 100 percent of tuition costs, 18 percent reimburse between 50 percent and 90 percent, while the remaining 30 percent refund less than 50 percent Almost all employers insist you get at least a "C" in a course before you see a dime.

Do only full-time employees get EAP help?

Only one quarter of employers pay tuition benefits to part-timers.

How can you prospect for EPA-friendly employers?

Check company Web sites for employee benefit statements. Anonymously call human resource offices and ask about education benefits for employees.

International Students: Destination USA

In this age of globalization, are you a citizen of a country outside the United States who is thinking, "Hmmmn…maybe I'd love to study at a U.S. college or university if only I had the funds to do so?" With perseverance, you may be able to gather the funds you need.

Starting on the homefront

Start your mission in your home country. Begin with the premise that you will gather your own money in your country before shipping out. Of the half-million students who come to the United States from abroad each year to attend college, some 80 percent of undergraduate students and nearly 50 percent of graduate students accumulate the funds from their own re-sources and those of their families, according to NAFSA: Association of International Educators.

Some international students receive funding from their governments, which usually expect them back home when school's over.

The very few scholarships awarded from within U.S. borders to internationals may only be granted while you are in your home country; you often become ineligible once you reach U.S. shores.

Whatever methods you use to collect educational funds, have a plan to pay for the entire four years or you may have to pack up and ship out after a year or so. A few institutions of higher education require that international students provide proof of funding for the entire planned period of study.

Targeting stateside student aid

The deepest pockets of funding for students from abroad are the colleges and universities themselves. In a recent year, the schools gave international students nearly $147 million, according to reports filed with The College Board. Table 2-1 identifies the top 15 U.S. *undergraduate* student international aid givers; collectively, they awarded more than $50 million to students from afar in the 1995-1996 school year.

Table 2-1 Top Aid-Giving Schools for International Undergraduates

College	Number Students	Number Int'natl	Dollars Awarded to Int'natl	Number Given Aid
1. Harvard & Radcliff	6,691	458	6,681,455	299
2. Massachusetts Institute of Technology	4,495	340	5,463,510	234
3. Mount Holyoke	1,884	242	4,497,579	198
4. Univ. of Miami	8,289	859	4,497,357	474
5. Univ. of Pennsylvania	10,186	907	3,986,883	181
6. Princeton	4,609	276	3,500,000	159
7. Middlebury	2,087	141	3,445,950	137
8. Dartmouth	3,861	217	3,022,980	131
9. Macalester	1,768	238	2,390,000	157
10. Brown	5,942	432	2,340,475	100
11. Brandeis	2,998	166	1,942,049	89
12. Stanford	6,577	314	1,930,000	120
13. Clark	1,884	323	1,728,000	171
14. College of Wooster	1,669	117	1,700,000	110
15. Franklin and Marshall	1,866	103	1,669,900	71

(Source: Calculations by Dr. Herm Davis based on data in The College Board's College Handbook: Foreign Student Supplement, 1997. Data reflects schools with large international student funding programs or a significant ratio of international students who received financial assistance during the 1995-1996 academic school year.)

Financial aid information of all types is time-sensitive. The data in Table 2-1, the latest available, is significantly useful in targeting schools where you will have a better-than-average chance of receiving institutional aid.

Table 2-2 provides a more comprehensive listing of more than 100 U.S. schools that provide financial aid to non-U.S. students.

Table 2-2	Undergraduates: Colleges that Award Significant Aid to International Students			
State/ College	**No. Students Enrolled**		**International Students**	
	College-Wide	**Int'natl**	**Total Dollars**	**Students Awarded**
ALABAMA				
Univ. of Alabama (Huntsville)	14,796	429	$396,091	66
Univ. of Mobile	1,937	59	334,161	51
ALASKA				
Univ. of Alaska (Anchorage)	15,613	500	591,201	
ARIZONA				
Arizona State University	31,212	1,171	441,270	90
ARKANSAS				
Harding University	1,513	140	1,111,353	131
Ouachita Baptist University	1,463	70	252,265	41
CALIFORNIA				
California Inst. of Technology	923	88	1,175,000	53
Menlo College	458	75	153,506	31
Stanford University	6,577	314	1,930,000	120
Thomas Aquinas College	540	34	297,800	29
University of Redlands	1,318	103	230,282	28
Whittier College	1,330	39	181,150	19
COLORADO				
Colorado College	2,008	47	250,000	10
DELAWARE				
Wesley College	1,316	20	172,000	15

State/College	No. Students Enrolled		International Students	
	College-Wide	Int'natl	Total Dollars	Students Awarded
DISTRICT OF COLUMBIA				
George Washington University	6,378	641	$533,700	59
Georgetown University	6,374	618	326,138	19
FLORIDA				
Bethune-Cookman College	2,402	106	264,314	58
Eckerd College	1,366	152	350,000	70
Florida Atlantic University	12,900	474	841,039	287
Florida Institute of Technology	1,780	400	694,785	108
Florida Southern College	1,610	77	387,011	63
Lynn University	1,449	252	371,225	63
University of Miami	8,289	859	4,497,357	474
University of South Florida	23,994	397	274,396	120
University of Tampa	2,049	244	353,366	83
GEORGIA				
Mercer University	4,045	133	234,187	75
HAWAII				
University of Hawaii (Manoa)	13,357	404	201,936	315
ILLINOIS				
Illinois Institute of Technology	2,262	272	554,604	134
Illinois Wesleyan University	1,875	47	382,240	30
Know College	1,127	85	704,111	67
Monmouth College	923	41	488,000	41
North Park College	1,324	109	408,654	68
Principia College	565	65	694,168	46
University of Chicago	3,453	147	397,460	29
INDIANA				
Earlham College	1,017	47	365,000	34
Goshen College	1,000	93	433,000	80
Purdue University	27,982	721	483,551	65
Tri-State University	1,172	245	537,389	140
Wabash College	790	27	417,310	27
IOWA				
Coe College	1,312	66	269,442	37
Dordt College	1,209	187	600,000	175
Drake University	3,802	130	258,449	69

(continued)

Table 2-2 *(continued)*

State/ College	No. Students Enrolled		International Students	
	College-Wide	Int'natl	Total Dollars	Students Awarded
LOUISIANA				
Louisiana State Univ. A & M	20,363	619	$1,468,421	390
Tulane University	6,327	271	1,088,000	65
MAINE				
Bates College	1,636	52	531,090	24
Bowdoin College	1,595	36	281,000	22
Colby College	1,785	99	539,945	25
MARYLAND				
Hood College	1,099	31	296,181	19
St. John's College	419	20	324,700	17
Univ. of Maryland	22,922	761	242,761	41
MASSACHUSETTS				
Amherst College	1,600	49	687,709	33
Boston Conservatory	342	75	324,940	55
Brandeis University	2,998	166	1,942,049	89
Clark University	1,884	323	1,728,000	171
Eastern Nazarene College	670	29	228,000	29
Gordon College	1,229	31	294,833	31
Harvard & Radcliff College	6,691	458	6,681,455	299
Massachusetts Inst. of Technology	4,495	340	5,463,510	234
Mount Holyoke Collge	1,884	242	4,497,579	198
Smith College	2,668	212	1,970,883	90
Suffolk University	2,762	350	279,000	55
Wellesley College	2,257	121	816,955	35
Williams College	1,982	55	526,401	24
MICHIGAN				
Eastern Michigan University	18,176	535	794,616	267
Kalamazoo College	1,272	44	516,184	31
Michigan Tech. University	5,699	225	362,141	47
MINNESOTA				
Concordia College (Moorhead)	2,958	89	364,872	78
Gustavus Adolphus College	2,398	51	240,000	33
Macalester College	1,768	238	2,390,000	157
St. Olaf College	2,936	79	365,000	53
University of St. Thomas	4,908	61	314,098	39

State/College	No. Students Enrolled		International Students	
	College-Wide	Int'natl	Total Dollars	Students Awarded
MISSISSIPPI				
University of Southern Mississippi	7,946	189	$334,867	34
MISSOURI				
College of the Ozarks	1,509	22	$200,200	22
St. Louis University	6,123	467	1,030,029	130
Truman State University	6,073	170	200,598	66
University of Missouri (Kansas City)	5,447	318	55,000	100
Washington University	4,993	313	463,535	55
NEW HAMPSHIRE				
Dartmouth College	3,861	217	3,022,980	131
NEW JERSEY				
Princeton University	4,609	276	3,500,000	159
NEW YORK				
Colgate University	2,921	60	500,000	21
Columbia Univ.-Columbia Col.	3,573	103	750,000	30
D'Youbille College	1,433	344	262,025	284
Hamilton College	1,670	88	1,193,260	
Hartwick College	1,522	60	366,440	23
Hobart & William Smith College	1,770	42	365,440	23
Hofstra University	7,846	268	317,712	46
Ithaca College	5,559	96	617,900	53
Manhattan School of Music	439	141	314,420	42
Parsons School of Design	1,810	531	562,000	157
Rochester Institute of Technology	10,552	382	273,000	68
St. John's University	12,395	364	922,830	115
St. Lawrence University	2,006	74	1,326,797	63
University of Rochester	5,182	386	1,500,000	200
Vassar College	2,334	60	560,042	35
NORTH DAKOTA				
Jamestown College	1,064	59	242,478	52
OHIO				
Cleveland Institute of Music	214	43	249,658	34
College of Wooster	1,669	117	1,700,000	110

(continued)

Table 2-2 *(continued)*

State/ College	No. Students Enrolled		International Students	
	College-Wide	**Int'natl**	**Total Dollars**	**Students Awarded**
OHIO *(continued)*				
Denison University	1,882	69	$725,431	57
Franciscan Univ.of Steubenville	1,554	88	366,947	80
Kenyon College	1,522	35	364,500	25
Miami University (Oxford)	14,119	156	527,538	54
Mount Union College	1,583	85	232,390	46
Ohio Wesleyan University	1,712	128	1,483,000	114
OREGON				
Lewis & Clark College	1,837	153	393,521	53
Linfield College	1,588	81	238,090	23
Reed College	1,276	96	345,070	21
PENNSYLVANIA				
Allegheny College	1,838	41	271,570	21
Bryn Mawr College	1,122	102	829,000	48
Dickinson College	1,840	60	200,360	9
Elizabethtown College	1,753	34	295,800	28
Franklin and Marshall College	1,866	103	1,669,900	71
Gettysburg College	2,017	38	381,520	21
Lafayette College	2,190	100	1,145,060	58
Shippensburg Univ. of PN	5,576	59	209,186	30
Slippery Rock Univ. of PN	6,757	211	500,686	182
Swarthmore College	1,353	71	1,054,554	45
Univ. of Pennsylvania	10,186	907	3,986,883	181
RHODE ISLAND				
Brown University	5,942	432	2,340,475	100
Columbia Bible College	476	17	296,416	17
TENNESSEE				
University of the South	1,242	25	262,048	15
TEXAS				
Abilene Christian University	3,680	270	660,639	195
Ambassador University	860	177	716,396	170
Southern Methodist University	5,297	128	498,438	86
Texas Christian University	5,886	205	495,699	84
University of Houston	21,426	979	1,073,797	248
University of Texas (Arlington)	17,897	431	240,344	355

State/College	No. Students Enrolled		International Students	
	College-Wide	Int'natl	Total Dollars	Students Awarded
VERMONT				
Bennington College	285	38	$373,770	34
Middlebury College	2,087	141	3,445,950	137
WASHINGTON				
Whitman College	1,354	15	264,860	15
WEST VIRGINIA				
West Virginia Wesleyan College	1,620	57	372,884	26
WISCONSIN				
Beloit College	1,249	133	844,752	86
Lawrence University	1,219	108	1,226,212	108

(Source: The College Board, The College Handbook Foreign Student Supplement, 1997)

Most of the available U.S.-sponsored financial aid that does not require you to be a U.S. citizen or permanent resident comes from the colleges themselves.

Graduates pull in more aid than undergraduates

Graduate students outrank undergrads when U.S. student money is handed out. Table 2-3 lists the top 15 graduate schools that give aid to international students.

Table 2-3 Graduate Aid: The 15 Schools that Award the Most Aid to International Graduate Students

State/College	No. Students Enrolled		International Students	
	College-Wide	Int'natl	Total Dollars	Students Awarded
1. Vanderbilt University	1,732	446	$8,660,000	365
2. University of Notre Dame	1,334	422	7,149,048	422
3. Louisiana State A & M	5,231	1,064	7,142,000	903

(continued)

Table 2-3 *(continued)*

State/ College	No. Students Enrolled		International Students	
	College-Wide	Int'natl	Total Dollars	Students Awarded
4. University of Miami	3,134	618	$5,777,584	575
5. New York University	15,281	2,135	5,398,266	478
6. University of Virginia	4,085	433	3,647,037	327
7. Dartmouth College	541	122	3,200,000	122
8. University of Delaware	3,103	597	2,876,476	345
9. North Carolina State University	5,192	798	2,676,784	561
10. Georgetown University	2,616	517	2,640,650	177
11. Lehigh University	1,999	359	2,100,628	369
12. SUNY at Binghamton	2,296	436	1,704,081	240
13. Oklahoma State University	3,150	755	1,361,350	396
14. St. John's University	3,300	305	1,290,130	187
15. Medical College of Ohio	406	124	1,176,000	98

(Source: The College Board, The College Handbook Foreign Student Supplement, 1997)

"By far, the most scholarship dollars go to Ph.D. students at USC," says Mary E. Randall, associate dean and director of graduate education and admissions: "We award virtually no funds to undergraduates; a small amount goes to master's candidates; the lion's share goes to doctoral candidates in the form of teaching and research assistantships. These are awarded only to the cream of the crop, the very best students. We present aid to internationals because we attract the finest minds in the world and create a stimulating environment for all our students. Our international learners add cultural richness to our student body and help prepare our graduates to work in a world-wide economy."

Graduate aid tends to be academic-based, not need-based. Table 2-4 lists U.S. schools that award significant amounts to international graduate students.

Table 2-4 Graduate Aid: Universities Awarding Significant Aid to International Graduate Students

State/College	No. Students Enrolled		International Students	
	College-Wide	Int'natl	Total Dollars	Students Awarded
ALABAMA				
Tuskegee	173	11	$112,280	14
CALIFORNIA				
Monterey Inst. of International Studies	638	207	211,000	51
San Francisco Conservatory of Music	107	31	122,500	15
University of San Francisco	2,252	294	197,017	35
COLORADO				
University of Northern Colorado	1,283	67	$268,859	73
CONNECTICUT				
University of Bridgeport	814	176	101,265	29
DELAWARE				
University of Delaware	3,103	597	2,876,476	345
DISTRICT OF COLUMBIA				
Catholic Univ. of America	2,773	290	1,153,482	126
Georgetown University	2,616	517	2,640,650	177
FLORIDA				
Florida Atlantic University	2,352	293	756,404	181
Florida Institute of Technology	2,452	293	538,703	92
Florida State University	5,686	548	114,695	48
University of Miami	3,134	618	5,777,584	575
University of South Florida	6,202		751,875	266
GEORGIA				
Medical College of Georgia	211	44	374,000	44
HAWAII				
Univ. of Hawaii (Manoa)	4,501		112,661	67
ILLINOIS				
Bradley University	1,847	216	212,000	71
Eastern Illinois University	1,600	67	131,976	42

(continued)

Table 2-4 *(continued)*

State/College	No. Students Enrolled		International Students	
	College-Wide	Int'natl	Total Dollars	Students Awarded
INDIANA				
Rose-Hulman Institute of Tech.	175	56	$470,000	46
University of Notre Dame	1,334	422	7,149,048	422
IOWA				
Maharishi Univ. of Management	212	66	468,00	61
Univ. of Northern Iowa	1,390	119	223,896	76
KANSAS				
Wichita State University	3,024	444	456,816	256
LOUISIANA				
Louisiana State Univ. A & M	5,231	1,064	$7,142,000	903
MASSACHUSETTS				
Boston Conservatory	121	50	164,250	34
Boston University	8,055	1,593	258,390	802
Suffolk University	1,419	114	245,000	27
MICHIGAN				
Central Michigan University	1,853	133	296,474	92
MINNESOTA				
Univ. of Minnesota (Duluth)	346	105	1,000,000	80
MISSISSIPPI				
U. of Southern Mississippi	2,538	152	551,274	116
MISSOURI				
St. Louis University	1,889	140	1,019,036	94
NEW HAMPSIRE				
Dartmouth College	541	122	3,200,000	130
NEW MEXICO				
NM Institute of Mining and Tech.	243	87	580,592	88
NEW YORK				
Hofstra University	2,547	71	476,966	71
Manhattan School of Music	435	195	411,000	641
New York University	15,281	2,135	5,398,266	478
St. John's University	3,300	305	1,290,130	187
SUNY at Binghamton	2,296	436	1,704,081	240

State/College	No. Students Enrolled		International Students	
	College-Wide	Int'natl	Total Dollars	Students Awarded
NORTH CAROLINA				
North Carolina State University	5,192	798	$2,676,784	561
Univ. of NC (Charlotte)	2,890	202	688,956	106
Univ. of NC (Greensboro)	2,241	55	194,920	59
OHIO				
Medical College of Ohio	406	124	1,176,000	98
Miami University	1,482	143	650,522	118
OKLAHOMA				
Oklahoma State University	3,150	755	1,361,350	396
OREGON				
Oregon Graduate Institute	474	120	825,000	75
PENNSYLVANIA				
Lehigh University	1,999	359	2,100,628	359
Thomas Jefferson Univ. College of Allied Health	512	27	551,517	47
TENNESSEE				
Vanderbilt University	1,732	446	8,660,000	365
TEXAS				
Southern Methodist University	3,579		751,706	159
Texas A & M University	8,852	2,112	1,011,920	1,679
University of Houston (Houston)	6,457	1,019	618,557	142
VIRGINIA				
University of Virginia	4,085	433	3,647,037	327
Virginia Commonwealth Univ.	4,119	164	765,496	82
WEST VIRGINIA				
West Virginia Wesleyan College	63		372,884	26

(Source: The College Board, The College Handbook Foreign Student Supplement, 1997)

Few major universities across the nation reported their financial aid for graduate international schools in this College Board survey, including three major California institutions with large international student populations: UC Berkeley, University of Southern California, and UCLA. Even so, the

We have discussed only the highlights of aid for international students in this chapter. Other topics — exchange rates, visas, taxes, health insurance, filling out forms — are mentioned in various books (noted at the end of this chapter) and on Web sites. The best Web site we've found is *FinAid: The Financial Aid Information Page* at www.finaid.com. See Chapter 12 for more on this and other Web sites.

Obtaining aid is challenging for U.S. citizens; obviously doing so is much harder for students from other lands. If you think the task is overwhelming, remember the words of a great American poet, Henry Wadsworth Longfellow:

> *Perseverance is a great element of success. If you only knock long enough and loud enough at the gate, you are sure to wake up somebody.*

U.S. Students Going Abroad Can Get Traveling Money

Eleven American college students recently were awarded scholarships by the Winston Churchill Foundation for graduate study in mathematics, engineering, and the sciences. These students, who attend one of the 50 accredited institutions participating in the program, study for one year at Churchill College, Cambridge University, in Great Britain. They receive $23,000 toward tuition, travel, and living expenses.

Before you get too excited at the thought of grantors in other nations footing the education bill for you as a U.S. student, you should know that the Churchill awards come from the Winston Churchill Foundation of the U.S., which is located in New York City.

With a few exceptions — such as Japan, Germany, and Canada — don't count on other nations' governments or private resources being too generous with their study money for non-citizens. Get your cash at home before hopping on a plane to schools abroad.

The basic guidelines for Americans who wish to be eligible for financial aid as they study abroad are the following:

- ✔ As a U.S. student who attends an accredited U.S. institution overseas as an extension of your stateside institution, you are eligible for the full range of federal financial aid programs.

  You may also be eligible from your home school for study abroad. The home school sets its own policies for institutional aid.

- ✔ As a U.S. student who attends an international institution overseas, you are eligible for federal and private loan programs only, not for any gift aid.

The idea of an international experience thrills many American students until they find out the old spoilsports who give out aid insist that you shoulder at least a half-time load at the foreign institution and receive credit toward your degree. You can't just be coasting along for enrichment.

Although only about 100,000 Americans study off U.S. shores each year, many helpful programs are available. To find out about aid that may be accessible to you, the American student who wants to study abroad, contact

✔ **American Institute for Foreign Study**
102 Greenwich Ave.
Greenwich, CT 06830
Telephone 800-727-2437
Internet: www.aifs.org/

The organization arranges cultural exchange and study abroad programs throughout the world for more than 40,000 students each year.

✔ **Council on International Educational Exchange**
205 E. 42nd St.
New York, NY 10017
Telephone: 212-822-2600
Internet: @www.ciie.org

✔ **Institute for International Education (IIE)**
809 United Nations Plaza
New York, NY 10017
Telephone: 212-883-8200
E-mail: webmaster@www.iie.org

✔ **NAFSA: Association of International Educators**
1875 Connecticut Ave. NW, Suite 100
Washington, DC 20009, USA
Internet: www.nafsa.org

Work Hard at Looking Hard for Money

Yes, even when you don't fit the mold of the traditional college student, you can pay for the education and training to end up where you want to be. Be prepared to work hard at looking hard.

Jerry Fushianes, PA-C, mentioned earlier in this chapter, recounts his first days at seeking aid, when a financial aid officer gave him superb advice:

> *Jerry, it's obvious you're going to need $20,000 a year in financial aid. If you want $20,000 in aid, you need to put $20,000 worth of effort into finding it.*

That financial aid counselor was so right.

The finaid process is made even more difficult because of occurrences beyond your control. Your college's financial aid staff may give conflicting directives or penalize you by failing to update your account on their computers. Congress may not pass financial aid legislation quickly enough for the process to work smoothly. Your aid application may be lost.

Nothing about applying for college money is simple.

- ✔ When students are turned down for aid, it's often because they have failed to file an application on time — *they haven't learned the process.*

- ✔ Or they miss turning in a required document — *they haven't learned the process.*

- ✔ Or they don't know how to compete for resources — *they haven't learned the process.*

Learning the process is the real key to your college financial aid. If you arm yourself with knowledge and make a four-year financing plan, you'll get the education you want at a price that you can handle.

This chapter rolls out the big pieces of the U.S. financial aid system in which the process takes place. After clearing the cobwebs from the basic structure of finaid, the chapters that follow fine-tune the particulars of what you should know to cut the best deals you can in paying for college.

Don't take "no" for an answer

Financial aid assistants are such big time "no" people there's even a joke about it in financial aid circles. The old-timer instructs the new finaid assistant: *"Start with 'no.' You can always move to 'yes.'"*

Here are three familiar phrases to expect:

- ✔ No, you can't have an appointment.

- ✔ No, you haven't submitted the right information and documents to support your aid request.

- ✔ No, you can't appeal your case to anyone else.

Of course, you do your utmost to avoid hearing all those infuriating "no"s from finaid assistants by submitting all aid application documents on time and correctly filled out.

When your applications are blemish free and submitted before deadline, you need not put up with this string of "no"s from assistants who are paid to screen you out. You can fight it.

The vast majority of students do not appeal a turndown. They assume the aid spout was turned off by a higher power who must know best. Another reason students shut up and smile no matter what is the fear that making waves in the financial aid office will brand them as troublemakers throughout the campus. The reality is: The finaid office is isolated from academic departments, and very little chitchat flows between them.

If "no" is your answer, find out why. If a mistake has been made, don't be silent.

Demonstrated Need: The Key to Aid

Question: What is financial need?

A short answer: *Need* is the difference between what a student's family is expected to contribute and the total cost for one year of the college or university where a student hopes to enroll. Amazingly enough, the term for what a family is expected to contribute is called the *Expected Family Contribution (EFC)*. Both the family contribution and the student contribution are included in the EFC.

A longer answer: Qualifying for financial aid depends on family income and assets, family size, how many parents work, age of the oldest parent, number of family members in college at the same time, and the cost of attendance.

To treat everyone as fairly as possible, everyone fills out the same instrument of torture, which is something like a tax form. The system used to determine the EFC is called the *Federal Methodology,* a need-analysis formula approved by the U.S. Congress. You arrive at your Expected Family Contribution by filling in the blanks of a form called the *Free Application for Federal Student Aid (FAFSA),* which is described later in this chapter.

Under the Financial Aid Umbrella

In case you don't get enough freebie dollars — and face it, you probably won't — find out all you can about the disorganized, freewheeling financial aid system. Learn how the system works so that you can make the system work for you. Figure 3-1 shows a simple diagram of how the financial aid system is organized.

Self-help money

On the left side of the financial aid umbrella you find self-help financial aid, which includes loans and work.

Loans: Money you pay back

A loan for education is student financial aid that must be repaid. Loans differ in their availability and repayment terms. Loans come in three basic types: federally subsidized, state-subsidized, and private loans or lines of credit.

Availability may or may not be based on your demonstrated need, as described earlier:

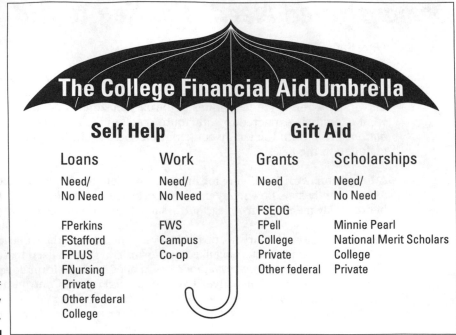

Figure 3-1:
The
financial aid
umbrella
covers a
variety of
money
sources.

The College Financial Aid Umbrella

Self Help		Gift Aid	
Loans	**Work**	**Grants**	**Scholarships**
Need/ No Need	Need/ No Need	Need	Need/ No Need
		FSEOG	
FPerkins	FWS	FPell	Minnie Pearl
FStafford	Campus	College	National Merit Scholars
FPLUS	Co-op	Private	College
FNursing		Other federal	Private
Private			
Other federal			
College			

✔ Need-based loans, chiefly those in which the federal or state government subsidizes the interest payments, require that you show financial need in order to obtain them.

✔ Loans that are not need-based (you pay the full interest with no subsidies are available to you or your family even if your folks are rolling in money).

Loans come from a rich variety of sources: government, colleges and universities, banks, foundations, organizations, employers, and individuals.

A sampling of loans are identified under the umbrella in Figure 3-1: the Federal Perkins, Federal Stafford, and Federal PLUS loan programs, nursing, and private loan resources. We talk more about federal loan programs in Chapter 7.

Availability of a loan may or may not be related to your or your family's credit record and ability to repay. Commercial lenders usually take credit ratings and repayment potential into account before making an education loan, while government and nonprofit sources do not.

You or your family may be forced to start repayment of some loans while you are still in school, but you can delay repayment of others until you graduate and are out in the job market making an income. For more about becoming an educated borrower, see Chapter 16.

Work: Earn as you learn

Well over half of those attending college have jobs to keep the money flowing in and to gain marketable work experience.

The federal and state work-study programs are prime examples of work as student aid. The part-time (often 10 hours or less), campus-based jobs are usually for undergraduates, but graduates can sometimes arrange to join the work crowd. What kinds of jobs are on the work-study menu? Government program designers ambitiously aim to make the jobs appetizingly career oriented, but you may have to settle for a plain-fare grunt job. Students work during the academic year, and pay is usually the minimum wage.

Other employment-based aid includes regular part-time jobs on or off campus, co-operative education that alternates classroom study with jobs, and paid internships. See Chapter 11 for more about working as your way to pay.

Gift money

Gifts are everyone's favorite because repayment is not required and the money is usually not taxable. Whee — free money! Chapter 10 has more information about qualifying for gift aid.

Grants: No payback

A grant is based on need and is not repaid. Pell grants are the federal government's most ambitious gift program. Annual awards range from about $400 to $3,000 yearly, depending on the funds that Congress provides and the number of applicants. Chapter 7 has more information about federal grant programs.

Scholarships: Your money to keep

Scholarships may or may not be awarded on the basis of need. *Merit* — how well you do during high school and college years in both grades and activities — is the basis for most undergraduate non-need awards.

Scholarships that are not based on merit or need rely on uncommon criteria. For instance, people who have a severe-to-profound bilateral hearing loss can apply for a $2,000 scholarship from the Minnie Pearl Scholarship Program administered by the EAR Foundation.

The Resource Guide at the back of this book lists a sampling of scholarship resources. Available state aid is listed in Chapter 8.

Finaid: It's bundled in packages

When you get the good news — that, yes, you're on the aid list! — expect the college's wherewithal to be offered in a combination package: loans, work, grants, and scholarships. Everyone hopes for the gift side of the aid umbrella: The more free money, the better.

Your aid package isn't a do-it-yourself project; your college's financial aid department puts the aid mix together.

Meet the Forms that Drive Financial Aid

Where college financial aid is involved, the dead-tree industry lives! You'll be filling out enough forms to start your own paper farm. Here's a list of forms you can't escape.

Free Application for Federal Student Aid (FAFSA)

The FAFSA is unavoidable to apply for all federal need-based aid. When you and your family have finished writing yards of answers to everything about your clan's financial status, you send your FAFSA off to an official processor for the U.S. Department of Education (a government subcontractor in real life). A few weeks later, you'll receive a Student Aid Report that reveals the Expected Family Contribution figure (EFC). Each college to which you have applied uses this information to determine your family's contribution.

To receive maximum aid, send your FAFSA form by March. (Each college determines its own deadline you have to meet to receive maximum funding.) Don't forget to fill out a renewal FAFSA for every year that you want federal aid.

The FAFSA is the only need application form required for federal student financial aid programs and the majority of state scholarship programs. The majority of all state institutions as well as all two-year colleges and proprietary vocational-technical schools use only the FAFSA for a need-analysis form.

Get a copy of FAFSA at your college's financial aid office, public library, or from your high school guidance office.

Figuring out your family's portion

Turn to the Resource Guide at the back of this book to see a real FAFSA. In the meantime, Table 3-1 is a generalized guide to what a family of four at various levels of income is expected to pay to send one child to college for one year, in this case the 1998-1999 school year.

Table 3-1 Expected Family Contributions	
Income (before taxes)	Expected Family Contribution
$30,000	$668
$35,000	$1,431
$40,000	$2,194
$45,000	$2,319
$50,000	$4,148
$55,000	$5,464
$60,000	$6,799
$65,000	$7,817
$70,000	$9,287
$75,000	$10,757
$80,000	$12,227
$85,000	$13,697
$90,000	$15,166
$95,000	$16,636
$100,000	$18,106

Source: The College Board

The figures in Table 3-1 are calculated on the assumption that one parent works and that the older parent is age 45. If both parents work, or if one parent is older than 45, the expected contribution is lower. Net assets are presumed to be less than $40,300. If the family's assets are greater, the expected contribution will be higher. Use this table as a warm-up to gain a quick idea of the amount of cash your family will have to dig up for your schooling.

✔ Colleges may have exotic scholarships for students who

- are left handed (Fred and Mary Beckley Scholarship — Fred and Mary were left-handed tennis players who met on the court. They married and established an endowment for left-handed students with need).

- have a last name of Murphy, Baxendale, Borden, or Smith (Harvard College).

- have calf-roping skills (University of Arizona).

- plan to quit smoking, drinking, or using drugs (Bucknell University).

- are female, majoring in athletics, and graduated from Seneca Valley High School (University of North Carolina-Greensboro).

Some colleges use their own financial aid application form *instead* of the Profile. Their customized application forms can become grisly in the depth of detail requested; in addition to all the other data, the college may ask about funds in siblings' accounts.

Examples of rationales for using a customized application form:

✔ For placement purposes in the work-study program, the college aid office may need to know about your work experience, driver's license, life guard experience, or other facts to make a job placement.

✔ If you've indicated an interest in a study-abroad program, the college aid office adjusts your budget depending on costs for transportation and overseas housing.

✔ When you have a special medical consideration, you may require a boost in aid for medication.

✔ If you're a graduate student, the finaid office will look for loans that directly relate to your discipline: MedLoans (medical students), EdLoans (education students), LawLoans (law students), and MBA loans (business school students).

✔ A married graduate student who brings the spouse to campus has extra expenses.

Why can't colleges get together and devise one comprehensive form used by all? Why do you need several different application documents to request aid? Good questions, but you won't find a succinct answer. What you have to know is: The colleges call the tune and you dance the jig.

Financial Aid Transcript (FAT)

If you're planning to jump ship from one college or university to another and want finaid, you'll need a *financial aid transcript.* **Note:** You need the FAT whether or not you received aid at the old school. In fact, you must have the FAT submitted by each college or university previously attended whether you received aid from it or not.

The skinny on the FAT is that it is free, but it's your responsibility to tell your old college to send your FAT to your new college.

Timing Finaid: Go with the Flow

The U.S. Department of Education distributes money to each college to disburse to students who meet eligibility requirements. The college financial aid offices also fatten their aid kitties with endowment-generated funds and awards they administer from other sources, such as general revenues.

No matter where the aid money comes from, most of your greenbacks will be awarded by your school.

You begin by completing and submitting your FAFSA to the specified DOE processing center. Personnel at the center process your paperwork and return the results to you within four to six weeks.

✔ Each college you specify receives the results of your FAFSA on a document called the *Institutional Student Information Report (ISIR)*. The college will receive your results electronically.

✔ You receive your FAFSA results on a document called the *Student Aid Report (SAR)*. The color of the paper used for SARs changes from year to year, and so you may hear others refer to them as "blue forms" or "pink forms" or "yellow forms." You receive your SAR in two parts.

   • SAR Part I is a summary of the FAFSA information you submitted. SAR Part II is a form to use if you need to correct or update Part I data. Review your SAR Part I for accuracy; if you fail to spot and correct errors, you can lose thousands of dollars. Return only Part II to the specified Department of Education processor in the provided return envelope if you need to make corrections.

   Note: Make copies of the corrections on Part II and send them to the financial aid office of each college you've targeted and to your state's scholarship agency. If your SAR was completely accurate and you made no corrections, send nothing to the schools and state agency; they are supposed to receive the information on the Institutional Student Information Report (ISIR) mentioned earlier.

• Occasionally a college will ask that you send the original Part I and Part II of your SAR. Go ahead and send it. Immediately order a duplicate SAR from the Department of Education by calling 319-337-5665. Duplicate SARS are free.

Although you get feedback from FAFSA, don't expect to be told your expected family contribution by the central processor of the CSS Profile. You'll get an acknowledgment, but that's all it is. However, each college that required you to provide a CSS Profile receives the results, which are then reviewed by your financial aid counselor who decides the amount of your demonstrated need.

Suppose you filled out your FAFSA, CSS Profile, and a college's own financial aid application form. Here's how one young man fared who did that very thing, according to his award notification letter from a major university.

Federal Pell Grant	$2,550
Federal Supplemental Grant	$2,000
University Grant	$15,000
Federal Work-Study Program	$2,000
Federal Subsidized Stafford Loan Referral	$2,625
Federal Perkins Loan	$2,000
Total	$26,175
Cost of Attendance (COA)	$28,607
Expected Family Contribution (EFC)	$2,432
Demonstrated Need	$26,175

When to Apply for Aid

The $64,000 question for many students is the following: Do I apply for financial aid before or after I have been admitted to a college?

The answer is: **"Apply for admission and financial aid at the same time."** You should not wait for one procedure to be completed before starting on the other.

When students apply for regular admissions, the college normally notifies them of acceptance in April, May, and June. But most financial aid priority deadlines are in February. If you wait until admission to apply, you will miss the deadlines for the awarding of financial aid.

The student financial aid process is tiresome, sometimes agonizing. But if spending a few hours with some forms means the difference between an education and no education, the choice is obvious.

Chapter 4

Dr. Davis's Comprehensive Finaid Calendar

- -

In This Chapter

▶ A timeline for finaid success

▶ What to do when

- -

*H*ere's a handy calendar you can use to keep your finaid search on track. Consider writing action items on actual calendar pages.

Sophomore year of high school

☐ **Continuing:** Start a college scholarship resource file. Save private scholarship sources sponsored by organizations, service groups, corporations, government agencies, and individuals.

☐ Explore career options through high school career studies and self-discovery. (Many scholarships are available from career-related professional organizations.)

☐ Join appropriate clubs or participate in activities associated with scholarships such as Scouts, service clubs, and jobs.

Junior year of high school

☐ Register with your school counselor to take the PSAT, National Merit Scholarship Qualifying Test, and the ACT.

☐ Apply for advanced placment to be eligible to take college courses in high school.

☐ Investigate banks, credit unions, and other institutions that make educational loans; open an account if that's a requirement for being able to borrow.

☐ **October:** Take the Preliminary Scholastic Assessment Test (PSAT).

❑ **November:** Attend financial aid workshops to get a head start on early financial aid planning and to understand the finaid process.

❑ Attend college fairs. Gather information about colleges and financial aid resources.

❑ **December:** Complete steps to avoid being penalized for unwise asset structuring. Complete positioning of student assets for maximum financial aid eligibility. (See Chapter 1.)

❑ Review PSAT result.

❑ **February:** Register for May or June SAT II for schools that require it.

❑ Make plans to visit colleges to see the campus "in action."

❑ **March:** Visit the high school guidance and career center to discuss colleges.

❑ **April:** Do a free computer scholarship search using Internet services (see Chapter 12):

❑ **May:** Write to the college admission offices where you want to enroll, asking for information on entrance and scholarships. Ask for college's admission video if one is available.

❑ Check Internet for college Web sites to see if your target schools offer an electronic admission option.

❑ Contact your state's scholarship administration (see Chapter 8) to determine state financial aid opportunities and application procedures.

❑ **Summer:** If you haven't already done so, visit colleges of interest.

❑ Request applications from private scholarship sponsors.

❑ Prepare for early decision applications.

Senior year of high school

❑ **October:** Continue to pursue scholarship resources.

❑ Send letters to scholarship providers requesting scholarship applications.

❑ Send college applications.

❑ Prepare College Scholarship Service's Profile for those colleges that require this document to award institutional funding.

Attend college fairs to collect admission and financial aid information.

❑ **November:** Secure a Free Application For Federal Student Aid (FAFSA) from your high school counseling/career center.

❑ Attend free college financial aid workshops (minimum of two) offered by your high school or organizational sponsors to review the correct method of completing the FAFSA and the Profile.

❑ Mail the Profile to the CSS processing center.

❑ Complete institutional aid applications if required by the college.

❑ **December:** Fill out the FAFSA form but do not mail.

❑ **January:** Mail an original FAFSA or a renewal FAFSA form after January 1 and not before, using the self-addressed envelope that came with the form. Even if you're using estimated income, mail your FAFSA before February 1. You may also be required to complete an institution's supplemental form(s).

❑ **February:** Receive the results of the FAFSA, called a Student Aid Report (SAR). Keep these forms in a safe place until your and your family's federal taxes are completed.

❑ You and your family each complete U.S. Federal Taxes Form 1040.

❑ Update the SAR from the information on the Form 1040. Make additional corrections such as new colleges of interest that should receive the SAR.

❑ Sign, date, and return the SAR to the designated address on the SAR.

❑ Send copies of your and your family's 1040 with W-2(s) attached to each targeted college's financial aid office.

❑ **March:** Receive corrected SAR, which reflects the actual tax data.

❑ Send a copy of the corrected SAR results to each college financial aid office. *Note:* Colleges should already have received the corrected results through the relatively new and sometimes imperfect electronic data exchange (EDE), but play it safe and send the colleges a copy until the EDE is working well at all schools.

❑ **April:** Continue to receive admission acceptance letters. Accept all admission offers until the corresponding financial aid award letters are finalized to weigh offers.

Note: You may have to pay a deposit at several schools to hold your admission status until you have your financial aid plan intact.

❑ Receive college financial aid notification (award letters). Accept all awards from all schools; return award letters promptly. Prepare financial aid appeal letters as required (see Chapter 9). Remember, you are still negotiating and deciding, although you accept everything at this point.

❑ **May:** Receive outside scholarship notification.

❑ Compare all award letters and institute final negotiations with the college(s) of choice.

❑ Finalize college selection.

❑ Notify each nonselected college admission office that you have made another choice and will not be enrolling in the fall. Report to each nonselected college financial aid office that you are relinquishing your earlier aid acceptance because you will not be enrolling in the fall.

❑ Receive your award letter from your number-one-choice school. Obtain and complete your family's section of the Federal Stafford and FPLUS loan forms. Submit these by certified mail to your prime-choice school.

❑ Complete paperwork for on-campus housing at the selected college.

❑ **June-August:** Work during the summer and save at least $1,000 for college expenses. (Your financial aid award is already completed so this money will not count against your funding for the year.)

Complete a computerized scholarship search for the next academic year. New scholarship sponsors are available for each year that you advance in college.

College freshman through senior year

❑ **September:** Meet with financial aid office's college placement coordinator to interview for a campus job as authorized in the award letter.

❑ **October-December:** Apply for private scholarships.

❑ **January:** Complete and submit new or renewal FAFSA for the next school year.

❑ Complete new or renewal CSS Profile.

❑ Complete Institutional Aid Application if required by the college.

❑ **February:** Prepare federal income tax forms.

❑ Receive Student Aid Report (SAR) and update with tax information. Resubmit SAR. Send copies of your and your family's income tax forms to the college's financial aid office, if required. (Be sure that tax forms are signed or they won't be accepted.)

❑ Interview for a dorm assistant position for the next school year.

❑ **March:** Receive corrected SAR. Send copy of corrected SAR to the college's financial aid office to assure they have your new information.

❑ **May:** Receive renewal award letter. Renewal letters usually are distributed after the spring grades are posted. Sign and return award letters promptly.

Chapter 5

College Costs: Upward and Onward

- -

In This Chapter

▶ The number one area of spending in higher education

▶ At private colleges, almost no one pays full price

▶ Cost increases may be slowing down

▶ Getting real about student expenses

- -

*T*owering tuition increases over the past 20 years — often double the rate of increase in the overall cost of living — have made the college tab so high that almost no one can pay the full freight at private colleges these days, and many families are unable to handle ramped-up bills at public institutions.

Aid Is Fastest Growing College Expense

Not only families are taking hits. The tuition runup has placed dramatic pressure on budgets of colleges and universities too, resulting in a stunning new statistic:

Financial aid is the fastest growing institutional expense in American higher education today.*

Not faculty salaries, not academic support services, not maintenance of campus facilities, but the disbursement of funds to help students attend school is the number one growth item for budgets at colleges and universities across the land, according to the National Center for Education Statistics, *Digest of Education Statistics 1996*. In computing financial aid expenditures, only scholarships and fellowships are included; the figures do not include Pell grants or college work-study programs.

* Expense refers to those costs directly associated with educating students, not including capital construction.

Fewer than 10 percent pay list price at private colleges

Providing discounts on tuition and living costs is another way of saying "institutionally funded financial aid offered to students to help defer the cost of an education." It means gift money (scholarships and grants), not self-help aid (loans and jobs).

A nationwide study among 232 members of the National Association of College and University Business Officers (NACUBO), a nonprofit professional organization, reveals that *fewer than 10 percent of students in those schools actually pay the published tuition price.* This statistic may surprise you — it did us.

The practice of discounting rates is growing faster at small colleges with tuitions below $15,700 than at small colleges with higher tuition and at large colleges and universities.

Remember that these are only typical figures. For cost details about specific institutions, the College Board reports tuition and fees and other expenses for more than 3,000 colleges in its annual *College Costs and Financial Aid Handbook.* This information is also posted on The College Board's Web site (www.collegeboard.org).

Good News! Cost Cutting Coming On

Here's a news flash in a *Forbes* magazine issue late last year.

> *Because what they sell is such a good investment, colleges have gotten away with obscene price increases. Not much longer.*

The magazine then cites a countertrend in which "dozens and dozens" of colleges are cutting tuitions, maintaining prices, or not increasing them as fast as usual.

A recent *USA Today* survey concurs, reporting that a number of colleges have listened to consumers and are planning lower tuition raises. And the *Chronicle of Higher Education* a few months ago proclaimed that many private colleges are reporting small tuition increases, the smallest in years (but most still outpace inflation).

Once You're Hooked, You're History

The NACUBO study confirms what many students and parents have long suspected: *Gift money is far more generous coming in than going out.* After generous financial aid lures you inside the college's door, don't expect the same juicy awards the following years.

Colleges and universities today are run as businesses, not as what one writer describes as "bastions of high-minded collegiality." The higher education marketing strategy at many schools presumes that once you're established on a campus, you'll hang around without being fed the substantial discount that induced you to enroll.(Alert: Ask your college if the awards are renewed at substantially the same rate, assuming family resources remain static!)

That's why all types of private colleges and universities discount the rate for first-year students substantially more than for all undergraduates. The shift as you move through the education pipeline may be from gifts to self-help, or from gifts to nothing.

To avoid the ghastly surprise of having your aid award sink under your feet, make a four-year financial aid plan (see Chapter 1) and religiously revisit your plan every semester. Check in with the finaidmeisters at your school well in advance of each new school year.

If you prove to be the exception and the money keeps on coming year after year, thank your lucky stars. Your vigilance paid off!

Colleges everywhere are paring down operating costs, from hiring fewer faculty to slotting in more teaching graduate assistants.

Student daily cash needs are higher than you think

Don't forget to add $2,000 or more for a computer, a requirement at many schools. (Before you buy a computer, find out if your school's computer system is running on Mac OS or Windows.)

And how much walking-around money will you need? That depends on too many things to dip the answer in bronze and display it, not the least of which is whether your campus is rural or urban. Bear in mind that estimates by colleges tend to be conservative. If you're a party animal, increase your school's estimate of spending for food and drink, dorm room necessities, clothing, and recreation by 50 percent. If you're prone to ski weekends or hosting keg parties and haven't budgeted adequately, you may have to take in laundry.

Private colleges aren't alone in trying to make do with less reliance on runaway tuitions. State educators are planning a variety of actions to chop costs. Among the most discussed are

✔ **Prepaid tuition plans**

These plans, usually operated statewide, permit families to lock into a tuition rate years in advance and set aside money in a state account. Texas recently began its Tomorrow Fund. More than 350,000 Florida families have joined a similar tuition savings program in recent years. Virginia launched a state plan in 1996.

✔ **Lowering costs by speeding academic progress**

Students are taking longer to graduate than did earlier generations. A University of Illinois study discovered half the degree recipients didn't finish in four years. A State University of New York report found that 60 percent of the university's students — and 45 percent of students nationally — receive their bachelor's degrees within six years.

Ideas of how to move things along range all over the map: Take more college-level courses while in high school; improve academic counseling to help students more effectively choose a major and sequence their courses; advise high school juniors of courses they need during their senior year to better prepare for college-level work.

More proposals: States make policy decisions to freeze tuition, shifting funds from other programs (like prisons and Medicaid) to pay the difference. Some tie tuition increases to the cost-of-living index. Students get guaranteed four-year graduation by making four-year plans, meeting with advisers every semester to accommodate changes and review progress.

Still more proposals: Beef up high school education in math and other courses often requiring remedial courses in college; provide a computer-generated list of unmet degree requirements to each college student as well as student's adviser.

The list of proposed fixes for atrocious college costs is lengthy. Some may take root soon enough to benefit you. At least the unremitting upward spiral of tuition increases seems to have found brakes.

Additional reading

Both references list tuition costs for individual colleges and universities:

✔ *Peterson's Two Year Colleges* (annual) P.O. Box 2123 Princeton, NJ 08548

✔ *The Princeton Review Complete Book of Colleges,* Random House, Inc. 2315 Broadway, 3rd Floor New York, NY 10024

Part II

How to Find the Aid You Need

The 5th Wave   **By Rich Tennant**

"Someone put a financial aid form in our tip cup."

In this part ...

Some people have such talent that they can replay a Mozart composition after hearing it once. The exceptionally bright bulbs don't even need sheet music. Most of us, though, need months of practice and reams of sheet music to manage the same feat.

Finding financial aid isn't that much different. Whether you've got the endless talent that wins merit-only scholarships, or you need a diagram to clap, you need top tips to earn the aid you need. This book gives you the direction for winning college money. But what about detailed techniques for increasing your payload chances?

These chapters show several success stories, with behind-the-paperwork interviews with big finaid winners on how they struck finaid gold. You also learn how to access federal, institutional, and private aid, whatever your merits.

But you won't necessarily have to settle for what you're awarded — you also pick up little-known facts about negotiating finaid packages, even when you're broke and school starts in 30 days. And don't skip the chapters on the hidden finaid market and other frequently asked questions.

Chapter 6
Tapping the School's Own Aid

*B*ank robber Willie Sutton knocked off banks in the 1930s because, he said, "That's where the money is."

In the 1990s, you should knock *on* campus doors because that's also where the money is.

Find Vaults of Money All Over Campus

When you activate the student financial aid process, the staff at a school's financial aid office processes your application for the normal federal, state, and institutional awards. Institutional aid, as you may recall, is the school's own money that it can do with as it pleases.

This hide-and-seek chapter takes you behind the scenes. We go beyond the normal, routine aid resources to find money, money everywhere on a big campus treasure hunt. We start where you start: the admissions office.

Calling All Allies: Find Me Funds

You have secret allies on campus: the people in the admissions office, in general, and the college recruiter who is responsible for your file in particular.

The expense of recruiting you and others like you costs out at more than $2,400 a head. Once you're recruited and admitted, admissions personnel want to hang on to you, especially at institutions that are in danger of opening a semester with empty seats. The recruiter in charge of your file can do two kinds of things to help fatten your wallet:

- ✔ Double-check that all the required documentation you need in order to receive finaid is on file in the financial aid office.

- ✔ Recommend you for any special scholarships that are used to entice students and lock up their enrollments. In the workplace, a comparable practice is called a sign-on bonus — you are rewarded for committing to join the company or enroll at a specific college. Be sure your name is in the hat for these scholarships that are budgeted by the admissions staff.

Your advocate in the admissions office has a stake in your staying committed to the school and may also convey helpful information about new scholarships from the campus grapevine. A graceful way to establish your relationship is to ask the admissions recruiter to describe how other students have financed their way through your school-to-be.

If you find that your admissions recruiter at College A is more dedicated to your success than your admissions recruiter at College B, you may want to weigh this disparity of service as yet another factor in your final choice of schools.

The college's athletic office is a sure stop if you have athletic ability; ask your high school coach to assist. A good resource if you're athletically inclined is *How to Win a Sports Scholarship* by Penny Hastings and Todd D.Caven (published by Hastings Communications, P.O. Box 14927, Santa Rosa CA 95402; 707-579-3479). Cost is $17.95 by mail.

Still another place to prospect for finaid is the department where you'll major or at least spend a lot of time.

Don't overlook matching grants

More than 250 four-year colleges have a policy that matches outside grants with institutional awards. Lafayette College in Pennsylvania gives matching grants up to $5,000 if you can drag in a comparable outside scholarship. The University of Kentucky will match up to $3,400. Hood College in Maryland and Marymount College in New York will match up to $3,000. Nationwide, the average matching grant is $1,000 per student, with a range from $100 to full tuition. Your college's financial aid or business office keeps the matching-grant books; ask for chapter and verse.

Try for Departmental Scholarships

Some scholarships are controlled by specific college departments. Contact heads of those departments directly; you can get their names and contact information from your admissions office ally.

Look over Table 6-1, which lists a sampling of merit-based scholarship opportunities offered by college departments of art, drama, music, and various other academic disciplines. Demonstrated need is not required to qualify for these awards.

Table 6-1   Dr. Davis's Sampling of Departmental Scholarships

Institution	Art	Drama	Music	Merit/ Academic
ALABAMA				
Alabama State University	X	X	X	X
Tuskegee University		X	X	X
ALASKA				
University of Alaska	X	X	X	X
ARIZONA				
Arizona State University	X	X	X	X
Arizona Western College	X	X	X	X
CALIFORNIA				
Pepperdine University	X	X	X	X
San Diego State University	X	X	X	X
University of California, Berkeley	X	X	X	X
University of California, Santa Barbara	X	X	X	X
University of Southern California	X	X	X	X
COLORADO				
University of Colorado, Boulder	X	X	X	X

(continued)

Table 6-1 *(continued)*

Institution	Art	Drama	Music	Merit/ Academic
CONNECTICUT				
University of Connecticut	X	X	X	
DELAWARE				
University of Delaware	X	X	X	X
DISTRICT OF COLUMBIA				
Catholic University		X		X
George Washington University	X	X	X	X
FLORIDA				
Jacksonville University	X	X	X	X
University of Miami			X	X
GEORGIA				
Mercer University	X	X	X	X
Morehouse College		X		X
HAWAII				
Brigham Young University-Hawaii	X	X	X	X
ILLINOIS				
Bradley University	X	X	X	X
DePaul University	X	X	X	X
Knox College	X	X	X	X
Northwestern University		X	X	
INDIANA				
Earlham College				X
Indiana State University	X	X	X	X
Indiana University	X	X	X	X
KENTUCKY				
Kentucky Wesleyan College	X	X	X	X
University of Louisville	X	X	X	X

Institution	Art	Drama	Music	Merit/ Academic
LOUISIANA				
Tulane University				X
Xavier University of Louisiana	X	X	X	X
MARYLAND				
Johns Hopkins University			X	X
University of Maryland	X	X	X	X
MASSACHUSETTS				
Boston University	X	X	X	X
University of Massachusetts	X	X	X	X
MICHIGAN				
University of Michigan	X	X	X	X
MINNESOTA				
Mankato State University	X	X	X	X
University of Minnesota	X	X	X	X
MISSISSIPPI				
Mississippi State University		X	X	X
MISSOURI				
University of Missouri	X	X	X	X
Washington University	X			X
NEW HAMPSHIRE				
Colby-Sawyer College	X	X	X	X
NEW YORK				
Fordham University	X	X	X	X
Ithaca College		X	X	X
New York University		X	X	X
Parsons School of Design	X			
St. John's University	X	X	X	X
Syracuse University	X	X	X	X

(continued)

Table 6-1 *(continued)*

Institution	Art	Drama	Music	Merit/Academic
NORTH CAROLINA				
Duke University	X	X	X	X
East Carolina University	X	X	X	X
Elon College		X	X	X
North Carolina A & T State University	X	X	X	X
University of North Carolina		X	X	X
Wake Forest University	X	X	X	X
OHIO				
Denison University	X	X	X	X
Miami University	X	X	X	X
Oberlin College			X	X
OKLAHOMA				
University of Tulsa	X	X	X	X
OREGON				
Lewis and Clark College		X	X	X
Pacific University	X	X	X	X
PENNSYLVANIA				
Drexel University	X	X	X	X
Duquesne University		X	X	X
Gettysburg College				X
Wilkes University	X	X	X	X
RHODE ISLAND				
Rhode Island School of Design	X			X
SOUTH CAROLINA				
Clemson University		X	X	X
Furman University	X	X	X	X
TENNESSEE				
Fisk University				X
Vanderbilt University				X

Institution	Art	Drama	Music	Merit/ Academic
TEXAS				
Rice University		X	X	X
Southern Methodist University	X	X	X	X
UTAH				
Brigham Young University	X	X	X	X
VERMONT				
Bennington College	X	X	X	X
VIRGINIA				
James Madison University	X	X	X	X
University of Richmond		X	X	X
WASHINGTON				
Gonzaga University		X	X	X
Seattle University	X	X	X	X
Whitman College	X	X	X	X
WEST VIRGINIA				
University of Charleston	X	X	X	X
West Virginia Wesleyan College	X	X	X	X
WISCONSIN				
Beloit College		X	X	X
Marquette University	X	X		X

Discover Colleges with Deep Pockets

Harvard, the University of Texas, and a few others among America's wealthiest colleges can admit any student they want without worrying about how much finaid that student needs. They can welcome anyone they wish because these institutions have a big enough private endowment to make up the difference between tuition cost and ability to pay.

The schools that are rolling in endowment money spend it to lure students who really soar, such as the top 1 percent or 2 percent of high school classes. They may base full-rides totally on merit, not demonstrated need. Table 6-2 lists American colleges and universities with the best endowments.

Table 6-2	America's Best-Endowed Colleges	
Rank	**Institution**	**Dollars (thousands)**
1	Harvard University	$8,811,785
2	Texas System, University of	5,697,150
3	Yale University	4,853,010
4	Princeton University	4,467,000
5	Stanford University	3,779,420
6	Emory University	3,013,112
7	California, University of	2,572,492
8	Columbia University	2,558,090
9	Massachusetts Institute of Technology	2,476,630
10	Texas A & M U. System	2,458,043
11	Washington University	2,305,686
12	Pennsylvania, University of	2,108,961
13	Rice University	1,850,312
14	Cornell University	1,829,185
15	Northwestern University	1,763,000
16	Chicago, University of	1,675,559
17	Michigan, University of	1,624,349
18	Notre Dame, University of	1,227,256
19	Dartmouth College	1,082,934
20	Southern California, University of	1,022,339
21	Case Western Reserve University	995,700
22	Johns Hopkins University	982,618
23	Duke University	966,669
24	Virginia, University of	937,206
25	Minnesota and Foundation, University of	856,227
26	California Institute of Technology	823,225
27	Rochester, University of	808,381
28	New York University	793,085

Rank	Institution	Dollars (thousands)
29	Brown University	$789,254
30	Purdue University	752,334
31	Rockefeller University	708,353
32	Ohio State University & Found.	649,585
33	Swarthmore College	623,981
34	Wellesley College	605,509
35	UNC at Chapel Hill & Foundation	596,841
36	Boston College	587,000
37	Smith College	578,039
38	Delaware, University of	574,250
39	Grinnell College	571,512
40	Cincinnati, University of	563,432
41	Southern Methodist University	562,838
42	Richmond, University of	551,542
43	Pittsburgh, University of	542,756
44	Texas Christian University	534,448
45	Indiana University & Foundation	529,378
46	Carnegie Mellon University	524,305
47	Williams College	510,006
48	Macalester College	509,496
49	Washington & Lee University	501,295
50	Wake Forest University	499,798

(Source: National Association of College and University Business Officers)

The size of an institution's endowment is certainly not the most important consideration in your planning, but it can be one of your considerations. Think about including rich colleges on your enrollment wish-list, as the following guidance tips explain.

Old conventional wisdom: A free education is not worthwhile if it is not the education you want. Identify schools you want to go to, then look for finaid.

New conventional wisdom: Factor in a school's endowment-driven generosity in selecting a college. Or, don't choose your school for money, but go where money is and fall madly in love.

Early Decision May Shrink Aid

Colleges in droves are rushing to offer *early decision enrollments,* meaning that you apply in the fall (usually by mid November) and, if the school accepts you (usually by mid December), you immediately agree to enroll.

Most of the issues involved in this controversial topic are beyond the purpose of this book, but the problem with early decision enrollment from the financial aid viewpoint is that you may be offered a downsized finaid package because you are already hooked.

You might think that the early bird would get more financial-aid worm, but what more likely happens is that you're considered a "sure thing," so why not save money for others who need enticement to enroll?

"I am going to be pretty tempted to give you a larger loan [rather than gift money] or gap you [award an aid package that falls short of meeting documented need] if I've already got you under contract," is what an admissions director of a liberal arts college in the Midwest told a major newsmagazine.

If merit based financial aid is a determining factor, don't apply under early-decision timelines. For those schools that offer need-based (like the Ivies), early decision is not a disadvantage.

What bad thing happens to you if you do enroll under early-decision time lines and you later find out that you've been stiffed on financial aid? Can you change your mind and go to another school where they're less sure of signing you up and treat you better? Maybe nothing happens. The early-decision you make is supposedly binding — the schools consider the contractual agreement an ethical issue. Even so, we found no evidence that you will be sued or banished from higher education if you change schools.

Jobs on campus

Your college's financial aid office coordinates the need-based Federal Work-Study Program (FWSP), but most college employment offices handle all part-time jobs on campus: cafeteria, janitorial, groundskeeping, library, parking attendant, and security guard, to name a few. These jobs often pay more than the FWSP jobs, and you can work more hours because they are not restricted by FWSP regulations.

You may be in great demand if you have a skill certification or experience, such as computer skills, campus day care, lifeguarding, and tutoring for individuals with disabilities. Campus offices that are responsible for supportive services offer financial assistance to students who have experience or certificates (lifesaving certificate, driver's license, special instructor license, sign language, or any other documentation of your special skill or experience) qualifying them to handle specialized jobs.

Chapter 7

What Uncle Sam and Aunt Feddie Are Willing to Fork Over

• •

In This Chapter

▶ Federal grant programs

▶ Federal loan programs

▶ Federal work-study programs

• •

*T*he capital city on the Potomac (Washington, D.C., for those of you geographically disinclined) is home base to the world's largest single source of financial aid: the federal government.

The U.S. government furnishes about 75 percent of all available financial aid — a commitment far outstripping that of any other major country.

Despite the largesse that's been rolling on since the 1950s, federal funding of student aid programs has slipped behind the cost of education. (Don't bother wondering why — knowing the answers won't put a dime in your pocket.) Opposing forces continue to knock heads over revving up or slowing down the federal education money machine, depending on their philosophy and politics, and it looks as though some changes are in the wings.

If you want to stay current on what the pols are up to, punch up the Web site of the U.S. Department of Education (www.ed.gov/money.html) to monitor new program additions and changes in existing programs.

Another way to stay on top of federal finaid things is to obtain a copy of the free pamphlet *The Student Aid Guide,* published by the federal government and cited at the end of this chapter.

As matters stand as we write this, the following key programs can affect the funding of your college education.

Federal Grant Programs

The federal government offers the following grant programs to assist in funding your higher education.

Federal Pell Grant Program

The 800-pound gorilla in the need-based programs, the Federal Pell Grant Program awards gift money to nearly 4 million students in amounts ranging from $4 to $3,000 yearly (1997-1998 school year).

The grants are off-limits to graduate students, as well as students who have already received a bachelor's degree.

The amount you get depends on your demonstrated need, the costs of education at the particular college you want to attend, the length of the program in which you are enrolled, whether your enrollment is full- or part-time, and the amount of money the Congress approves divided by the number of qualifying students.

You apply by filling out the FAFSA (see Chapter 3).

Federal Supplemental Educational Opportunity Grant Program

Do you have exceptional demonstrated need? Like you can't make the oatmeal or corndogs stretch to the end of the month? The Federal Supplemental Educational Opportunity Grant Program, fondly known as SEOG (pronounced SEE-og) is for you. To qualify, you must be enrolled at least half time in an undergraduate program at an accredited institution. Grants in the neighborhood of $4,000 are possible on the basis of pure, unadulterated need (poverty). However, most colleges don't receive enough SEOG funds to pay out maximum eligibility, and $1,000 to $1,500 is considered a good award. Roughly 1 million students are tapped for this desperately needed funding designed to equalize college opportunity.

This program is *campus-based,* which means that although the money comes from the federal government, the colleges hand it out to students who show exceptional need. (Typically you are eligible if you were eligible for a Pell grant award.) If you think you qualify for the SEOG, ask your school financial aid counselor to put you down for one.

Federal Loan Programs

We report the information you positively, absolutely must know about private loans in Chapter 16. The loans here are awarded directly or guaranteed by Uncle Sam and Aunt Feddie.

Federal Direct Student Loan Program and Federal Stafford Loan Program

These two programs are for student borrowers. The difference is where the money comes from. Funds from the Federal Direct Student Loan Program are federal money disbursed through your college. Funds from the Federal Stafford Loan Program come from private sources such as banks, credit unions, savings and loan associations, and educational organizations.

Either program — Direct or Stafford — can be subsidized or unsubsidized.

- ✔ If you have demonstrated need, the loan is *subsidized,* meaning the government pays the interest while you're in school.

- ✔ If you don't have demonstrated need, you pay interest from the time you get the loan until it is paid in full (although you may elect to defer interest payments until after you graduate). This loan is *unsubsidized.*

You can't borrow more money than the amount needed to study for a year. First-year students can borrow up to $2,625; sophomores can borrow some $3,500. Limits during the third and fourth and fifth years rise to $5,500. Graduate students can borrow $18,500 per year ($8,500 subsidized and $10,000 unsubsidized).

The cost of the Federal Direct or Federal Stafford student loans can't rise above 8.25 percent interest rate, plus an origination fee of 3 percent and sometimes an insurance premium of 1 percent. These fees are deducted from the amount of your loan before you receive payment.

FAFSA starts the sequence of action that permits you to borrow a Federal Direct or Federal Stafford loan, subsidized or unsubsidized. Lots of niggling details attend these two loans. Ask your high school guidance counselor or college financial aid counselor to help you understand these loan packages if you're having trouble.

Federal Parent Loans for Undergraduate Students (FPLUS)

FPLUS loans and Direct FPLUS loans are for parent borrowers. The difference is where the money comes from. Direct FPLUS loans are federal funds disbursed by your college's financial aid office. FPLUS loans come from private sources such as banks, credit unions, savings and loan associations, and educational organizations.

The maximum that can be borrowed under either of these loan programs depends upon the cost of the college and the amount of financial aid that the student receives.

The formula for maximum eligibility for an FPLUS loan follows:

Cost of education	(for example) $28,000
(Minus) Student aid awarded	(for example) $14,000
(Equals) Amount of FPLUS eligibility	$14,000

The interest rates for the FPLUS loans are figured annually by adding 3.1 percent to the rate of the 52-week U.S. Treasury bill. The rate is capped at 9 percent for the life of the loan. A one-time origination fee of 3 percent is paid to the federal government to help offset program costs. A one-time 1 percent insurance fee is paid to the state guarantee agency (Note: PHEAA, the Pennsylvania Higher Education Assistance Authority waives the 1 percent insurance fee).

Credit checks

FPLUS loans require a credit check, but student loans do not. The credit check doesn't use the formula applied to commercial credit. A commercial credit check formula consists of an income-to-debt ratio. The FPLUS credit check is less rigid, requiring only that the lender investigate to see if the parents pay their credit accounts within a reasonable period of time.

Will a bankruptcy experience by itself prevent a parent from receiving an eligibility rating for an FPLUS loan? No, but you do need a healthy credit history.

Several services complete an early credit check for pre-approval for an FPLUS loan. The Independence Federal Savings Bank offers a free pre-approval credit check. Ask someone at your finaid office to call toll-free at 800-733-0473, look at the bank's Web site (www.ifsb.com), or send e-mail to IFSB@aol.com.

If you are turned down for an FPLUS loan, call the lender and ask why. Often the reason is that the credit bureau provider has not updated its files on your family. Call a loan officer at the lending institution to help you resolve any error. If nothing works, call the American Express (1-800-814-4595). They have a 70 percent success rate in getting a rejected FPLUS reversed and approved.

Silver linings

When parents are rejected for an FPLUS loan, it may actually be good news for the student who wants to enroll in a lower-cost college. Students get loans at a lower interest rate than do parents, and repayment doesn't begin as quickly even though the interest is being capitalized.

When the family credit is poor and you anticipate an FPLUS or Direct FPLUS loan rejection, go ahead, Mom and/or Dad, and apply for an FPLUS or Direct FPLUS loan. Make a copy of the rejection letter and you, the student, send it with a new Federal Stafford or Federal Direct loan application to your college's financial aid counselor.

To make up for the turndown for an FPLUS or Direct FPLUS loan, you as a college student are allowed to borrow an additional unsubsidized Federal Stafford or Direct loan as long as you submit the parents' rejection letter along with your application. Through this process, you can borrow $4,000 for each of the first two years and $5,000 for each of the last two years. Although a parent's interest rate can rise to 9 percent, yours is capped at 8.25 percent. Further, your repayment on principal begins after graduation or when you're no longer attending college at least half time. By contrast, your parents' repayment on principal begins 60 days after they receive their final payment. In short, this type of borrowing is great for your cash flow.

Federal Work-Study Programs (FWS)

A campus-based program in which federal dollars are distributed by colleges, you must have demonstrated need and be enrolled for at least half-time study at either the undergraduate or graduate level to qualify for these jobs. Employment is almost always on campus, although jobs are also arranged off campus in community service programs.

The pay is at least the current federal minimum wage and may be higher. Compensation for off-campus jobs is left to the discretion of the employer and may be greater than campus jobs.

More Federal Educational Support

The military offers a cornucopia of financial aid opportunities. These are described in Chapter 17. Additionally, an assortment of other resources offered by Uncle Sam and Auntie Fed range from medical and nursing scholarships to those from the Bureau of Indian Affairs.

The federal government tries hard to help you make sure that your education money numbers add up to an affordable year of college.

Additional reading

For additional information, request a free copy of *The Student Guide* (annual) by the U.S. Department of Education Office of Student Financial Assistance. You can order it from Federal Student Aid Programs, P.O. Box 84, Washington, D.C. 20044 or call 800-433-3243.

Chapter 8

The Shape of State Aid

*Y*our state helps you go to college in two ways:

✔ It provides an affordable college education in state schools. Sometimes the quality of the education is as good as that offered by the best private colleges. The terms used to describe top public colleges and universities include *Public Ivys* and *Flagship Universities*.

✔ It provides grants and loans to qualifying students who enroll at either public or private colleges and universities within their own state. All states offer need-based awards; about half the states deliver merit-based aid. A handful of states don't cut off the money at the state line: They maintain reciprocal arrangements with other states that allow you to spend your education state dollars in reciprocating states. You stand to gain thousands of dollars, particularly in the big states such as California, Florida, Wisconsin, Minnesota, Maine, Ohio, and Pennsylvania.

When Feds Say No, States May Say Yes

Hailing Middle- and Upper Middle-Income Families: Don't forget to apply to your state for a hand even if your federal government finaid foray was a dismal flop.

Some states are more generous than the federal government in figuring whether you qualify for financial aid. Federal awards are based on your adjusted gross income, which includes some notice of your assets. By contrast, in some states, aid is based solely on taxable income without notice of your assets.

In some states you can own a posh estate, a stable of race horses, and several fast sports cars and theoretically still qualify for thousands of dollars of aid so long as your taxable income falls within state limits.

States like to do their own things. A number of states award a full ride including room and board to in-state students who participate in the federal free lunch program. In others, programs such as the Hope Scholarships in Georgia require students to maintain a 3.0 academic grade point average.

The rules are all over the map. Don't overlook inquiring about possible aid awards at your state's student financial aid agency.

Applying for State Aid

If the forms you need to apply for student aid aren't available at your high school or college financial aid office, contact your state financial aid agency at the address listed in the directory in the following section. States vary in the information they need to decide if you're award-eligible; some use the data from the FAFSA, while others require a supplemental aid form that is processed by the state's agency for higher education financial aid.

If you snag aid from one state but attend school in another, you'll have to contact your state financial aid agency to learn the ropes.

Look to your home state to play a substantial role in supporting your education. Tuition at state schools is always much less costly when you are a resident of a state than when you live outside of that state (because your taxes haven't been filling the state's coffers). The difference between being an in-state student and an out-of-state student can be as much as $10,000 per year.

Although establishing residency in a state used to be fairly simple, rules are tightening. Many states now insist that parents pay taxes within their borders and live in the state as a primary residence.

Even so, if you have your eye on another state's public university, it may be worthwhile to morph your way in from outsider to resident. You may have to drop out of college for at least a year, work in that state, and pay taxes to establish residency and meet all the rules.

Residency requirements not only vary from state to state, but sometimes *from school to school within a state*.

Don't count on backing into education during that year that you're establishing your residency. Community colleges, usually operated by a county, add another tier of residency. You not only have to live in the state, you have to live in the school's county — or pay higher tuition rates.

A Directory of State Requirements and Finaid Agencies

To review what your state and others offer, here is a directory of state residency requirements you must meet to qualify for in-state student status and state scholarships. The state's financial aid agency contact information follows each residency statement.

When you contact a state's college financial aid agency, don't expect the agency to know details about state residency requirements, which may change from year to year. What the financial aid agencies know about are the financial aid programs sponsored within the state.

But these agencies may know whom to contact to verify residency requirements. When you call a state financial aid agency's telephone number in the following directory and wish to verify residency requirements, ask two questions:

- ✔ Whom should I call to verify eligibility for state residency?
- ✔ Whom should I call at (name of college) to verify residency eligibility?

The most common answer will be the institution's financial aid office, but it never hurts to ask. Without fail, verify residency requirements with the college you hope to attend.

Key to listing:

Following is a key to the terms that appear in the following state listings:

Requirement: Residency requirement, how long you must live in the state to attend state colleges and universities and pay in-state tuition (always much less than out-of-state tuition)

Exception: Certain institutions in a state require more or fewer years to establish residency

Student aid eligibility: How long you must reside in the state to be eligible for college financial aid

Military waiver: Some states grant instant resident status to members of the military and their families

Documents required to prove residency: States vary in number and type of documents required

Reciprocity: Some states have reciprocity agreements with other states to give each other's citizens the lower in-resident rate for tuition

V: Voice telephone number
F: Fax telephone number
I: Internet URL (Web address)
E: E-mail address

Alabama

Student aid eligibility requirements: 2 yrs. residency, driver's license or voting card, bank account, state tax return
Reciprocity: Yes, for certain majors, members of the Southern Regional Education Compact
Military waiver: Yes
Agency: Alabama Commission on Higher Education
100 N. Union St. P.O. Box 30200
Montgomery, AL 36130-2000
V: (334) 242-1998
F: (334) 242-0268
E: acbbxholi@asnmail.asc.edu
I: www.webserver.dsmd.state.al.US/ACHE.htm

Alaska

Student aid eligibility requirements: 1 yr. residency, driver's license or voting card, postal service verification
Reciprocity: No
Military waiver: No
Agency: AK Commission on Post-secondary Education and Alaska Student Loan Corp.
3030 Vintage Blvd.
Juneau, AK 99801-7109
V: (907) 465-2962
(800) 441-2962 (Alaska only)
F: (907) 465-5316
I: www.educ.state.ak.us/acpe/acpehome.html
E: execdir@educ.state.ak.us

Arizona

Student aid eligibility requirements: 1 yr. residency, driver's license, vehicle registration, voting card, state tax return
Reciprocity: Yes, WICHE-certain western states
Military waiver: Yes
Agency: AZ Commission for Post-secondary Education
2020 North Central Avenue, Suite 275
Phoenix, AZ 85004-4503
V: (602) 229-2591
F: (602) 229-2599
E: www.acpe.asu.edu

Arkansas

Student aid eligibility requirements: Driver's license, vehicle registration, state tax return, residency requirement varies
Reciprocity: Yes, varies by institution
Military waiver: Yes
Agency: AR Department of Higher Education
114 East Capitol
Little Rock, AR 72201-3818
V: (501) 371-2000; (800) 54-STUDY
F: (501) 371-2001
E: luh@adhe.arknet.edu
I: http://www.adhe.arknet.edu

California

Student aid eligibility requirements: 1 yr. residency for state grant; Each state institution determines residency; University of California: 3 yrs.; driver's license, voting card, vehicle registration, state tax return; considers all documents
Reciprocity: no
Military waiver: Yes
Agency: CA Student Aid Commission
P.O.Box 510845
Sacramento, CA 94245-0845
V: (916) 445-0880
F: (916) 327-6599
I: www.csac.ca.gov
E: custsvcs@csac.ca.gov

Colorado

Student aid eligibility requirements: 1 yr. residency immediately preceding the first day of classes; driver's license, vehicle registration, voting card, state tax return
Reciprocity: Yes, New Mexico
Military waiver: Yes
Agency: CO Commission on Higher Education
Colorado Heritage Center
1300 Broadway, Second Floor
Denver, CO 80203
V: (303) 866-2723
F: (303) 860-9750
I: www.state.co.us/cchedir/hecche.html

Connecticut

Student aid eligibility requirements: 1 yr. residency; driver's license, vehicle registration
Reciprocity: No
Military waiver: Yes
Agency: CT Department of Higher
Attn: Financial Aid
61 Woodland St.
Hartford, CT 06105-2391
V: (860) 566-5766
(860) 566-3910
(800) 842-0229
(800) 4-FED-AID
F: (806) 566-7865
I: ctdhe.commnet.edu

Delaware

Student aid eligibility requirements: 1 yr. residency; driver's license, voting card, state tax return
Reciprocity: Yes, PA
Military waiver: No
Agency:
DE Higher Education Commission
Carvel State Office Building
820 North French Street, 4th Floor
Wilmington, DE 19801
V: (302) 577-3240
F: (302) 577-6765
I: www.state.de.us/high-ed/commiss/
webpage.htm

District of Columbia

Student aid eligibility requirements: 15 consecutive months residency; voting card, state tax return, lease, deed, or real estate tax bill
Reciprocity: No
Military waiver: Must pay D.C. taxes
Agency: Office of Postsecondary Education, Research and Assistance
2100 Martin Luther King Jr. Avenue,
Suite 401, SE
Washington DC 20020
V: (202) 727-3685
F: (202) 727-2739
I: www.ciwashington.dc

Florida

Student aid eligibility requirements: 1 yr. residency before the first day of classes; proofs of residency determined by institution
Reciprocity: No
Military waiver: Yes
Agency: FL Department of Education
Office of Student Financial Assistance
325 W. Gaines St.
Tallahassee, FL 32399-0400
V: (850) 487-0649
F: (850) 921-4378
I: www.bor.state.fl.us

Georgia

Student aid eligibility requirements: 1 yr. residency immediately preceding; driver's license, vehicle registration, voting card, state tax return
Reciprocity: No
Military waiver: Yes
Agency: Georgia Student Finance
Commission
State Loans and Grants Division
2082 East Exchange Place, Suite 200
Tucker, GA 30084
(800) 546-HOPE (4673)
GA only: (800) 776-6878
F: (770) 414-3162
I: www.gsfc.org

Hawaii

Student aid eligibility requirements: 1 yr. residency; voting card, state tax return
Reciprocity: Yes, Pacific Islands
Military waiver: Yes
Agency: Hawaii State Postsecondary
Education Commission
University of Hawaii
2444 Dole St., Room 202
Honolulu, HI 96822-2394
V: (808) 956-6624
F: (808) 956-5156
I: www.hern.hawaii.edu/hern
E: ishii@hawaii.edu

Idaho

Student aid eligibility requirements: 1 yr. residency; determined by institution
Reciprocity: WA, UT
Military waiver: Yes
Agency: Idaho State Board of Education
650 West State St.
P.O. Box 83720
Boise, ID 83720-0037
V: (208) 334-2270
F: (208) 334-2632
I: www.sde.state.id.us
E: board@osbe.state.id.us

Illinois

Student aid eligibility requirements: 1 yr. residency; driver's license, vehicle registration, voting card, state tax return
Reciprocity: No
Military waiver: Yes
Agency: Illinois Student Assistance Commission
1755 Lake Cook Road
Deerfield, IL 60015-5209
V: (847) 948-8550 or (847) 948-8500
(800) 899-4722 (IL, IA, IN, MO, WI only)
F: (847) 831-8549
I: www.isac1.org

Indiana

Student aid eligibility requirements: On or before Dec. 31 of the year preceding application for award; driver's license, vehicle registration, voting card, state tax return
Reciprocity: No
Military waiver: No
Agency: State Student Assistance Commission of Indiana
150 West Market Street, Suite 500
Indianapolis, IN 46204-2811
V: (317) 232-2350
F: (317) 232-3260
I: www.che.state.in.us
E: sjones@che.state.in.us

Iowa

Student aid eligibility requirements: 1 yr. residency; state tax return
Reciprocity: No
Military waiver: Yes
Agency: IA College Student Aid Commission
200 Tenth Street, 4th Floor
Des Moines, IA 50309- 3609
V: (515) 281-3501 or (515) 281-4890 or (800) 383-4222
F: (515) 242-5996
I: www.state.ia.us/government/icsac/index.Htm
E: icsac@max.state.ia.us

Kansas

Student aid eligibility requirements: 1 yr. residency prior to first time college attendance; driver's license, vehicle registration, voting card, state tax return
Reciprocity: MO, with limitations
Military waiver: Yes
Agency: Kansas Board of Regents
700 SW Harrison, Suite 1410
Topeka, KS 66603-3760
V: (913) 296-3517
F: (913) 296-0983
I: www.ukans.edu/kbor
E: christy@kbor.state.ks.us

Kentucky

Student aid eligibility requirements: 1 yr. residency; state tax return, property ownership, driver's license, vehicle registration, voting card
Reciprocity: Contact agency
Military waiver: Yes
Agency: KY Higher Education Assistance Authority
1050 U.S. 127 South, Suite 102
Frankfort, KY 40601-4323
V: (502) 564-7990
(800) 928-8926
F: (502) 564-4190
I: kheaa.state.ky.us
E: jernst@mail.state.ky.us

Louisiana

Student aid eligibility requirements: 1 yr. residency; driver's license, vehicle registration, voter registration, document of employment in-state for 1-year
Reciprocity: No
Military waiver: Yes
Agency: LA Student Financial Assistance Commission
LA Office of Student Financial Assistance
P.O. Box 91202
Baton Rouge, LA 70821-9202
V: (800) 259-5626; (504) 922-1012
F: (504) 922-1089
E: dpfeifer@osfa.state.la.us

Maine

Student aid eligibility requirements: 1 yr. residency; state tax return; the burden shall be on the student to prove that he/she has established a Maine domicile for other than educational purposes
Reciprocity: CT, MA, NH, RI, VT, MD, DE, DC, AK, PA
Military waiver: Yes
Agency: Finance Authority of Maine (FAME)
119 State House Station
Augusta, ME 04333-0949
V: (207) 626-8200
(in state only) (800) 228-3734
F: (207) 626-8208
I: www.fame.maine. com
E: rochelle@famemaine.com

Maryland

Student aid eligibility requirements: 3 months to 1 yr. residency; driver's license, vehicle registration, voter card, state tax
Reciprocity: Yes, contact state agency
Military waiver: Yes
Agency: MD Higher Education Commission
Jeffrey Building
16 Frances Street
Annapolis, MD 21401-1781
V: (410) 974-5370
(410) 974-2971
F: (410) 974-5994
I: www.ubalt.edu/www/mhec
E: staylor@mhec.state.md.us

Massachusetts

Student aid eligibility requirements: 1 yr. residency; driver's license, vehicle registration, voter card, state tax return
Reciprocity: Yes, New England states, PA, DC
Military waiver: No
Agency: MA Higher Education Coordination Council
330 Stuart Street
Boston, MA 02116
V: (617) 727-9420
F: (617) 727-0667
I: www.mde.state.mi.us

Michigan

Student aid eligibility requirement: residency determined by each institution; driver's license, vehicle registration and insurance in-state, voter card, state tax return, other documents as required
Reciprocity: Determined by institution
Military waiver: Yes
Agency: MI Higher Education Assistance Authority
Office of Scholarships and Grants
P.O. Box 30462
Lansing, MI 48909-7962
V: (517) 373-3394
F: (517) 335-5984
I: www.mde.state.mi.us

Minnesota

Student aid eligibility requirements: residency determined by institution; state tax returns, auto insurance in-state, other documents as needed
Reciprocity: Yes, ND, SD, WI, IA, Manitoba Midwest Student Exchange Program
Military waiver: No
Agency: MN Higher Education Services Office
400 Capitol Square Building
550 Cedar Street
St. Paul, MN 55101-2292
V: (612) 296-3974
(800) 657-3866
F: (612) 297-8880
I: www.heso.state.mn.us
E: info@heso.state.mn.us

Mississippi

Student aid eligibility requirements: 1 yr. residency; state tax returns, driver's license
Reciprocity: Yes, AL, AR, FL, GA, KY, MD, SC, TN, TX, VA, WV
Military waiver: Yes
Agency: MS State Institutions of Higher Learning
Financial Assistance Board
Office of Student Financial Aid
3825 Ridgewood Rd.
Jackson, MS 39211-6453
V: (601) 982-6623
In state only: (800) 327-2980
F: (601) 987-4172
I: www.ihl.state.ms.us
E: sledge@ihl.state.us

Missouri

Student aid eligibility requirements: 1 yr. residency; driver's license, vehicle registration, voting card, state tax return, personal and property taxes
Reciprocity: Yes, some state schools have agreements with selected members of the Midwestern Higher Education Commission
Military waiver: Yes, military personnel assigned to MO institutions pay non-resident fees; if stationed for other purposes, personnel and their dependents pay resident fees
Agency: MO Coordinating Board for Higher Education
3515 Amazonas Drive
Jefferson City, MO 65109-5717
V: (573) 751-2361
F: (573) 751-6635
I: www.mocbhe.gov

Montana

Student aid eligibility requirements: 1 yr. residency; driver's license, vehicle registration, voting card, state tax return
Reciprocity: No
Military waiver: Yes
Agency: MT University System
2500 Broadway
Helena, MT 59620-3103
V: (406) 444-6570
F: (406) 444-1469
I: www.montana.edu
E: rcrofts@oche.montana.edu

Nebraska

Student aid eligibility requirements: 1 yr. residency; driver's license, vehicle registration, voting card, state tax return
Reciprocity: Yes, at certain institutions in specific areas of study
Military waiver: Yes
Agency: NE Coordinating Commission for Postsecondary Education
140 N. Eighth Street, Suite 300
P.O. Box 95005
Lincoln, NE 68509-5005
V: (402) 471-2847
F: (402) 471-2886
I: nol.org/nepost secondaryed
E: dpowers@ccpe.state.ne.us

Nevada

Student aid eligibility requirements: 6 months residency prior to application, 1 year residency after; driver's license, voting card, state tax return
Reciprocity: Yes, WICHE, WWE, Good Neighbor
Military waiver: Yes
Agency: University of Nevada-Reno
Office of Financial Aid, Rm. 076
Reno, NV 89557
V: (702) 784-6181 or (702) 784-4666
F: (702) 784-4283
I: www.unr.edu
E: records@admon.unr.edu

New Hampshire

Student aid eligibility requirements: 1 yr. residency; driver's license, vehicle registration, voting card, state tax return
Reciprocity: New England states
Military waiver: Yes
Agency: New Hampshire Postsecondary Education Commission
2 Industrial Park Drive
Concord, NH 03301-8512
V: (603) 271-2555
F: (603) 271-2696
E: j_knapp@tec.nh.us

New Jersey

Student aid eligibility requirements: 1 yr. residency; driver's license, vehicle registration, voting card, state tax
Reciprocity: No
Military waiver: No
Agency: NJ Office of Student Financial Assistance
4 Quakerbridge Plaza, CN540
Trenton, NJ 08625
V: (609) 588-3268
(609) 292-4310
(800) 792-8670
F: (609) 292-7225
I: www.state.nj.us.highereducation

New Mexico

Student aid eligibility requirements: 1 yr. immediately preceding the term for which the resident classification is requested; driver's license, vehicle registration, voting card, state tax return, evidence of employment. Exceptions exist: marriage, Navajo Nation, etc. (contact state agency)
Reciprocity: Yes, TX, CO, AZ
Military waiver: Yes
Agency: New Mexico Commission on Higher Education
1068 Cerrillos Rd.
Santa Fe, NM 87501-4925
V: (505) 827-7383
(800) 279-9777
F: (505) 827-7392
I: nmche.org
E: bhamlett@che.state.nm.us

New York

Student aid eligibility requirements: 1 yr. residency prior to attending a postsecondary institution, regardless of receipt of financial aid; driver's license, vehicle registration, voting card, state tax return
Reciprocity: No
Military waiver: Yes
Agency: New York State Higher Education Services Corporation
One Commerce Plaza
Albany, NY 12255
V: (518) 473-7087
TAP Inquiry Unity: (518) 474-5642
F: (518) 473-3749
I: www.hesc.state.ny.us

North Carolina

Student aid eligibility requirements: 1 yr. residency; driver's license, vehicle registration, voting card, state tax return
Reciprocity: No
Military waiver: Yes
Agency: NC State Education Assistance Authority
P.O. Box 2688
Chapel Hill, NC 27515-2688
V: (919) 549-8614
(800) 700-1775
F: (919) 549-8481
I: ias.ga.unc.edu/ncseaa

North Dakota

Student aid eligibility requirements: 1 yr. residency; driver's license, voting card, vehicle registration, state tax return
Reciprocity: Information not provided
Military waiver: Yes
Agency: ND University System
ND Student Financial Assistance Program
600 East Boulevard Ave.
Bismarck, ND 58505-0230
V: (701) 328-2960
F: (701) 328-2961
I: www.nodak.edu
E: wipf@prairie.nodak.edu

Ohio

Student aid eligibility requirements: 1 yr. residency immediately preceding enrollment; driver's license, vehicle registration, voting card, state tax return, parent or employer statement evidencing residency
Reciprocity: Yes, MN, KY, WV, VA, limited to specific institutions and programs
Military waiver: Yes
Agency: Ohio Student Aid Commission
P.O. Box 182452, 309 South Fourth St.
Columbus, OH 43218-2452
V: (614) 644-5230

(888) 833-1133
F: (614) 752-5903
I: www.bor.ohio.gov

Oklahoma

Student aid eligibility requirements: 1 yr.
residency; Each case judged on its own
merit by the appropriate institutional
official consistent with State Regents' Policy
Reciprocity: Academic Common Market, Call
(405) 524-9144
Military waiver: Yes
Agency: Oklahoma Tuition Aid Grant
Program
500 Education Building State Capitol
Complex
Oklahoma City, OK 73105-4503
V: (405) 524-9120
F: (405) 524-9235
I: www.osrhe.edu
E: hbrisch@osrhe.edu

Oregon

Student aid eligibility requirements: 1 yr.
residency; driver's license, vehicle registra-
tion, voting card, state tax return
Reciprocity: Yes, WA, Northern CA
Military waiver: Yes
Agency: Oregon State Scholarship
Commission
1500 Valley River Drive, Suite 100
Eugene, OR 97401
V: (541) 687-7400
F: (541) 687-7426
I: www.osshe.edu

Pennsylvania

Student aid eligibility requirements: 1 yr.
residency; driver's license, vehicle registra-
tion, voting card, state tax return, lease,
deed or real estate tax bill, employer letter
stating Full Time employment
Reciprocity: Yes, except NY, NJ, MD
Military waiver: No
Agency: Pennsylvania Higher Education
Assistance Agency (PHEAA)
1200 N. Seventh St.
Harrisburg, PA 17102-1444
V: (800) 692-7435 (in state)
(717) 720-2800
F: (717) 720-3904
I: www.pheaa.org

Rhode Island

Student aid eligibility requirements: 1 yr.
residency immediately preceding first day
of semester; driver's license, state tax
return, rent receipts
Reciprocity: New England Board of Higher
Education Regional Student Program
Military waiver: Yes, spouse or child of
Armed Forces member stationed in state
pursuant to military orders
Agency: Rhode Island Higher Education
Assistance Authority
560 Jefferson Blvd.
Warwick, RI 02886
V: (401) 736-1100; (800) 922-9855
F: (401) 732-3541
I: www.uri.edu/ribog/
E: ribog@uriacc.uri.edu

South Carolina

Student aid eligibility requirements: 1 yr.
residency; driver's license, vehicle registra-
tion, voting card
Reciprocity: No
Military waiver: Yes, stationed in SC no later
than September 1st of preceding year
Agency: SC Higher Education Tuition Grants
Commission
1310 Lady St., Suite 811
Columbia, SC 29201
V: (803) 734-1200
F: (803) 734-1426
I: www.state.sc.us/tuitiongrants

South Dakota

Student aid eligibility requirements: 1 yr.
residency immediately preceding the first
scheduled day of classes; driver's license,
vehicle registration, voting card, state tax
return, income of student, residence of
student's parents, marriage to SD resident,
ownership of property, institution's required documents
Reciprocity: MN Western Interstate Commission on Higher Education, Western Undergraduate Exchange (WICHE)
Military waiver: Yes
Agency: SD Department of Education and
Cultural Affairs
700 Governors Dr.
Pierre, SD 57501-2291

V: (605) 773-3134
F: (605) 773-6139
E: roxit@bor.state.sd.us
I: http://www.ris.sdbor.edu

Tennessee

Student aid eligibility requirements: residency determined by institution; driver's license, vehicle registration, voting card, state tax return
Reciprocity: Within 30 miles of Austin Peay State University
Military waiver: Yes
Agency: TN Higher Education Commission
404 James Robertson Pkwy, Suite 1950
Nashville, TN 37243-0820
V: (615) 741-1346
In-state (800) 447-1523
Out-of-state (800) 257-6526

Texas

Student aid eligibility requirements: 1 yr. residency; driver's license, vehicle registration, voting card, employment records
Reciprocity: States adjacent to TX
Military waiver: Yes
Agency: TX Higher Education Coordinating Board
P.O. Box 12788, Capitol Station
Austin, TX 78711-2788
V: (512) 427-6340
(800) 242-3062
F: (512) 427-6420
I: www.cb.state.tx.us

Utah

Student aid eligibility requirements: 1 yr. residency; driver's license, vehicle registration, voting card, state tax return, institution may require additional documents
Reciprocity: Some graduate programs, (WICHE) states (certain western states) WVE with ID, WY, NV
Military waiver: Yes
Agency: Utah Education Assistance Authority
355 W. North Temple, #3 Triad, Ste. 550
Salt Lake City, UT 84180-1205
V: (801) 321-7200; (800) 418-8757
F: (801) 321-7198

I: www.utahsbr.edu
E: CFOXLEY@utahsbr.edu

Vermont

Student aid eligibility requirements: 2 yrs. residency prior to enrollment in postsecondary institution; driver's license, vehicle registration, voting card, state tax return, ownership of residential property
Reciprocity: Certain majors, New England Regional Student Program
Military waiver: No
Agency: VT Student Assistance Corporation
Champlain Mill
P.O. Box 2000
Winooski, VT 05404-2601
V: (802) 655-9602
F: (802) 654-3765
I: www.vsac.org
E: info@vsac.org

Virginia

Student aid eligibility requirements: 1 yr. residency; application for in-state tuition plus any documents required by the institution
Reciprocity: AL, AR, FL, GA, KY, LA, MD, MS, SC, TN, TX, WV, (Academic Common Market)
Military waiver: Yes
Agency: State Council of Higher Education for Virginia
James Monroe Building,
Ninth & Tenth Floors
101 N. Fourteenth St.
Richmond, VA 23219
V: (804) 225-2137
F: (804) 225-2604
I: www.schev.edu
E: mcdowell@schev.edu

Washington

Student aid eligibility requirements: 1 yr. residency; driver's license, vehicle registration, voting card, state tax return
Reciprocity: OR, ID, British Columbia
Military waiver: Yes
Agency: WA State Higher Education Coordinating Board
P.O. Box 43430, 917 Lakeridge Way, SW
Olympia, WA 98504-3430

V: (360) 753-7850
F: (360) 757-7808
I: marcg@hecb.wa.com

West Virginia

Student aid eligibility requirements: 1 yr. residency, and not primarily for the purpose of attendance at a WV institution; driver's license, vehicle registration, voting card, state tax return
Reciprocity: PA
Military waiver: No
Agency: WV College and University System
1018 Kanawha Blvd. East
Charleston, WV 25301
V: (304) 599-2691
(304) 558-4614
F: (304) 558-0048

Wisconsin

Student aid eligibility requirements: 1 yr. residency, not primarily than to obtain an education; driver's license, vehicle registration, voting card, state tax return
Reciprocity: MN
Military wavier: Yes
Agency: Higher Educational Aids Board
P.O. Box 7885
Madison, WI 53707-7885
V: (608) 267-2208
F: (608) 267-2808
I: www.uwsa.edu/bor/index.htm
E: heab@macc.wisc.edu

Wyoming

Student aid eligibility requirements: 1 yr. residency; driver's license, vehicle registration, other documents required are determined by the institution
Reciprocity: CA, OR, WA, AZ, NV, ID, MT, CO, AK, NM, NE, HI, UT, ND, SD
Military waiver: Yes
Agency: Wyoming Community College Commission
2020 Carey Avenue, Eighth Floor
Cheyenne, WY 82002-0110
V: (307) 777-7763
F: (307) 777-6567
E: hkitchen@antelope.wcc.edu

American Samoa

Board of Higher Education
American Samoa Community College
P.O. Box 2609
Pago Pago, AS 96799-2609
V: (684) 699-9155

Guam

University of Guam Education Council
303 University Dr.
Mangilao, Guam 96923
V: (671) 734-4469

Trust Territory of the Pacific Islands

College of Micronesia-FSM Drawer 159
Ponape, FM 96941

Puerto Rico

Council on Higher Education of Puerto Rico
P.O. Box 23305-UPR Station
Rio Piedras, PR 00931
V: (809)758-3350

Virgin Islands

VI Joint Boards of Education
Charlotte Amalie, P.O. Box 11900
St. Thomas, VI 00801
V: (809) 774-4546

Federated States of Micronesia

1725 N. St., NW
Washington D.C. 20036
V: (202) 223-4383

Republic of the Marshall Islands

RMI Scholarship Grant and Loan Board
P.O. Box 1436
3 Lagoon Road
Majuro, MI 96960
V: (692) 625-3108

Republic of Palau

Ministry of Education Bureau
P.O. Box 9
Koror, Republic of Palau, TT96940
V: (686) 488-1003

Florida is first state to approve lottery scholarships

Thanks to the players of the Florida Lottery, the *Bright Futures Scholarship* program has been funded. We're talking big money — the initial year's pot of money for college students, $78 million, is expected to grow to between $150 million and $180 million annually after four years. As many as 42,000 Florida high school graduates stand to benefit each year.

If you're a high school graduate in that state with at least a B average, such as a 3.2 GPA, you can collect $1,500 a year for college, plus some money for books. This is 75% of tuition and fees at a state university, community college, or vocational school.

If you boast a GPA of 3.5 or higher, Florida's new program will pay about $2,000 annually — 100% of tuition and fees — plus $600 a year for books at state schools.

The money began flowing for the 1997-1998 school year. "The kids hit the jackpot this year," said Gov. Lawton Chiles, as he signed the lottery scholarship bill into law.

To other states with lotteries: Take notice!

Chapter 9
Negotiating: Get Ready to Bargain

· ·

In This Chapter

▶ Gaining a clear understanding of your negotiating room

▶ Using research to equalize the gap between need and aid

▶ Profiting from 23 insider tips to negotiate more aid

▶ Writing appeals: Three sample letters show you how

· ·

*I*t's the last spring before you enter college. You know you're embarking on some of the best years of your life, but the next couple of months are pure torture, waiting for answers from the half dozen colleges you applied to, requesting aid from each. You live from one mailbox visit to the next, ready for good news or — perish the thought — bad news.

Finally the envelopes come straggling in. At first glance, you're happy to see that they're all thick acceptances, not thin little notes of rejection. But wait a minute . . . what's this on the bottom line of your number one college choice? Good grief, your financial aid award is $4,000 short of the amount you need to make it through the year. Bummer!

Isn't it strange how the college you love above all others is the one that either turns you down or doesn't give you enough money? "It's frustrating," says Gina, a high school senior in St. Louis, "when you get enough aid everywhere else but the place where you really want to go."

Don't give up. The unfortunate shortfall — in this example, $4,000 — doesn't spell doom for your chances of attending your first choice. If you strategize correctly, you may be able to negotiate your way through that $4,000 gap. This chapter shows you how to do it.

A Backgrounder on Bargaining

Parents of young students, more often than students themselves, conduct finaid negotiations because they usually are the ones who pay the bills. Nevertheless, on the theory that life is one big negotiation, we address most of our suggestions to students — of any age — who probably need practice in the dynamics of bargaining. *Remember:* Thousands of dollars are at stake.

Before earnestly considering ways to upgrade your financial aid award, don't bother looking for negotiating partners in all the wrong places: Certain schools do not negotiate. You don't have to guess which schools will bargain and which ones won't. Colleges usually state their appeal policies early on in an acceptance or award letter. When you're in doubt about the negotiation policy, anonymously call the financial aid office and ask if award appeals are accepted.

The colleges that say *take our offer or leave it* tend to be elite institutions in the top tier of schools. (The number of top-tier colleges ranges between 30 and 65, depending upon who's counting.) These selective and elite schools take a rigid stance because they can. The esteemed institutions like Harvard enjoy a surplus of academically qualified applicants whose parents are able to pay cash without a quibble.

Fortunately for you and most people, colleges that refuse to reconsider award offers are relatively few. The great majority of colleges in the United States are so pressured to enroll students that they discount tuitions by accommodating financial needs whenever possible.

Most colleges will negotiate their financial aid award offers if you provide a good enough reason to do so or make a sincere plea for guidance. Basing your negotiation on facts — presenting new information or calling attention to factors the finaid counselor may have overlooked — is the surest way to win an appeal.

But when a "new fact" can't be found for miles around, make an emotional appeal to the college's financial aid counselor. Admit that you have a power failure in your financial circuits and ask the counselor's help in finding more aid rocks to turn over.

Try to make your appeal face-to-face. If that's not possible, write your appeal in a letter and follow up with a telephone call.

Now that's negotiating!

The Baroness von Trapp (the real life heroine in *The Sound of Music*) was a charming negotiator. When producer Leland Hayward offered her 5 percent of the stage musical, the Baroness said she'd have to think about it a bit.

Returning a few hours later, the Baroness said: "Whenever I have a puzzle in my head, or a decision to make, I always pray to the Holy Ghost. And I prayed to the Holy Ghost, and the Holy Ghost says 10 percent."

Why threats and ultimatums won't work

Some parents make a big mistake by irately threatening to educate their child elsewhere if a college doesn't cough up more funding. The selection of another college indeed may be the logical answer and you may have to say so — but *say it nicely*. The point here is not what is said but the way in which it is said.

As an East Coast finaid counselor in a public school candidly admits:

"When a parent tries to push me around with demands for more money or baldly threatens to send his or her child to another school if I don't offer more aid, I do the best I can to raise the offer if the amount isn't over $3,000 or $4,000 — but only if I have the grounds to justify the increase.

"When a parent wants more than this modest amount, I reply that i'll have to call a school committee meeting, which is true for authorization of a larger amount of expenditures, and admit that I'm not sure when the committee can get together. Maybe the committee won't meet in time for the student to enroll.

"You [the authors] asked how I feel about parents who demand more funding — or else! Well, I don't react well to huffy ultimatums from people in ski masks. What a contentious parent doesn't realize is that whether a particular student enrolls or goes elsewhere may affect admission office personnel, but it doesn't affect my job. When a parent threatens to pull a potential student away from here, I pleasantly agree that decision is the parent's right and give the appeal no more thought.

"My reaction is different when the parent or student has exhausted all their known possibilities and there doesn't seem to be any recourse except to study at a less expensive college. That's when I try very hard to help.

"I can't speak for my colleagues in the field, particularly in student-starved, non-elite, regional private schools, but that's my reaction to families that demand more just because they think they're entitled to more."

Hold back one fact for the appeal

As we said earlier in this chapter, initiating an award appeal that pays off is easier when you can bring up new or overlooked information.

Consider omitting a minor (never a major) special circumstance as a negotiating strategy to keep the door open for an appeal.

What could be considered a minor special circumstance? Child care expenses or health insurance for students no longer covered by parental health plans, to name two. (We describe other special circumstances in the family-based tips given later in this chapter.)

The special circumstance you forget to mention in your original aid request need not be earth-shattering in importance, just true and logical enough to give you a graceful entry to an appeal process.

The Dynamics of Issue-Based Appeals

Everyone who has tried to get more of anything knows that background information is needed to unravel the basic dynamics of friendly persuasion.

The following analysis looks at the underlying factors, marketing issues, and family complexities that impact the aid process.

Fat cat schools: Follow the money

Colleges with large endowments have greater flexibility than do their poorer cousins in awarding their own funds. They can afford to recruit students who best meet their institutional objectives rather than concentrating on meeting students' financial needs. This largesse can work to your advantage with a well-crafted negotiation. Chapter 6 contains a list of endowment-driven colleges and universities.

The discussion spells out reasons why the college may be predisposed to honor your request for more aid in general or more aid in gift money. It offers an arsenal of strategies to use in negotiating your award. To make the issues easier to use, we split the negotiating tips into two camps — issues that are *college-based* and issues that are *family-based*.

- ✔ **College-based issues:** We give you the issue's framework, noting why the factor may sway the aid decision makers to act in your favor. We follow that with a strategy to try and cinch the increased funding you need. You usually need not document with paperwork college-based issues in your aid appeal.

- ✔ **Family-based issues:** These are special circumstances. We give you only a reminder list of conditions that you can use to expand your aid, assuming any of them fit your family circumstance. We omit the depth of detail found in the college-based issues because you already know how the circumstance impacts your family, and the strategy does not vary from issue to issue. You simply relate the issue and prove it with paper documents. The documentation is essential to back your claims of family-based issues that qualify you for an increase in finaid.

Your family-based special circumstance will not be taken into consideration in your aid appeal if you fail to include documentation.

Negotiating tips for college-based issues

The information you need to effectively implement the negotiating strategies presented in the following sections is available from four sources:

- ✔ **Printed information:** The college's catalog or letters to you are the first stops on your research trail.

- ✔ **Personal inquiries:** Ask an admissions counselor at the college's admissions office; for example, if you can't find out what percentage of demonstrated need the college has historically granted, call an admissions counselor and ask. (Admissions office personnel tend to be very cooperative because this staff must "meet its numbers" of expected enrollments or jobs will roll.)

  Query the college's representatives who attend college fairs.

  Check, too, with other fountains of information, such as your high school guidance counselors and the college's alumni.

- ✔ **Software and college Web sites:** The College Board's software *ExPAN* (see Chapter 12) contains specific information about institutions' diversity, financial aid history, and typical aid package mix. Each college's Web site may also contain the information you need.

✔ **Networks of friends:** Reaching out for information from your friends and their friends who attend or have graduated from the college may provide the data you need to pull the finaid system's levers.

First, the issue that may be particularly effective with a specific college (because the college is vulnerable), followed by comments and a suggested strategy. You may be able to combine several of these tips in your appeal.

Issue 1 — How badly does the college need students?

Discover trends in the college's enrollment figures. Is the enrollment down?

When a college is experiencing a smaller-than-usual application pool, its management team may be frantic to add students, advertising such enticements as sushi and waffle bars in the student unions and prime cable service in the dorms. You can bet its institutional ears are open to student pleas for more aid.

Strategy: After making your appeal, ask if it isn't better to have a student paying at a reduced level than having an empty seat in the classroom or an empty bed in the dorm? You need not mention an anemic enrollment — school managers are well aware of the problem. This strategy is useless, of course, at MIT and other high flyers, and at state schools that are swamped with applicants.

Issue 2 — How do costs compare with those of other institutions?

With the exception of the top-tier schools that would sooner allow their students to saunter naked across campus than negotiate price, colleges that punch a high tuition ticket have room to discount tuition rates.

Strategy: Incorporate research into your appeal, noting that the college is whatever percent more expensive than the average annual tuition cost of four-year private schools, which is approximately $11,500. Ask if the tuition structure possibly has enough margin to offer you more consideration? By researching tuition at somewhat similar colleges, you can refine the over-and-above comparison even more by citing "comparable private schools."

Issue 3 — Geographic diversity: Does the college value it?

Most Ivy and near-Ivy League schools believe all types of diversity enhance the education of all students because diversity provides a window on the real world.

One example is geographic diversity. Consider these:

- ✔ Indiana University, located in southern Indiana, intentionally recruits students from outside the Hoosier state to enrich its population with students from other parts of the nation and the world. Even though this school is located outside of major metro areas, it has reached out to recruit a large Jewish population of more than 2,500 students, has developed a major Jewish studies option, and maintains an active Hillel program.

- ✔ Some Eastern colleges cast nets for students hailing from Wyoming, Idaho, and the Dakotas.

- ✔ Some Southern schools recruit students from Northern states.

Your first step is to identify the region that provides most of the school's student body — if you're not living in that region, you have ammo to use in your appeal.

Strategy: Whether you offer new facts or make a personal plea, when your research shows that your intended alma mater is blessed with endowment money, emphasize your geographical desirability as an enrichment of perspectives on campus.

Liberally use the word *diversity* in your appeal. Say you can contribute to the cultural richness of the student body but that you need help with the level of your financial aid. Ask how you can help the finaid counselor help you to cover the last $4,000 you need to enroll.

Issue 4 — Cultural diversity: Does the school need more minorities?

Colleges are pressured by the Feds, states, their alumni, their faculties, and even their student bodies to increase minority student representation on campus. Student protesters at the University of Massachusetts ended a six-day takeover of an administration building early in 1997 after winning many of their demands, which included increasing the enrollment of minority students. Overall in the United States, one-fourth of college students come from minority groups.

If you're a minority student, you're a hot commodity at top schools seeking diversity if your grade point average is high — above 3.5 out of 4.0.

Many minority students grow up in big cities and select urban campuses over those in less populated areas, providing another clue about where to use this negotiation — at colleges located in small towns with a relatively uniform population. For this diversity tip, minority includes religion and heritage, as well as race and color.

At colleges where 90 percent of applicants from all racial and ethic groups are admitted, minority group status has little or no negotiating muscle. Florida International University, for instance, has stopped awarding Hispanic students minority-based scholarships because half of its students are Hispanic.

Strategy: If you are a member of a minority group and are negotiating with a school where your group is in short supply, remind them of your status. You can say something like the following:

> *According to your catalog you appear to be underrepresented in Hispanic students, of which I am one, although I may have overlooked indicating that fact on my admissions application. In fact, I may have overlooked several things that would count in my favor — I'm the first one in my family to go to college and my high school counselor has been pretty busy so I haven't had much expert advice. My goal is to attend (name of college), but the numbers in my award letter are going to keep me out of this wonderful school. What additional information would you need to increase my award (or scholarship aid), making it possible for me to enroll?*

The bottom line: At institutions that value and recruit for cultural diversity, the odds weigh heavily in the direction of the minority student who has a well-prepared appeal for any credible reason.

Issue 5 — *What is the college's track record on financial aid?*

This tip calls for super sleuthing on your part. You must discover the college's *going rate* for aid awards by ferreting out two pieces of information:

- ✔ What is the typical mix (self-help and gift) of aid the college has historically awarded?
- ✔ What percentage of demonstrated need has the college traditionally met?

Without comparative reports, you lack a basis for comparison with how the school has dealt with other students. You can't be certain you haven't already received the school's best offer.

A well-kept secret within the collegiate financial aid industry is one you should know:

The college financial aid process doesn't always result in the best deal for every student. Often what the industry terms the *initial offer* comes first, which means the opening bid is less than you need and less than the college can deliver. The rationale is that the offer can always be raised if that's what it takes to get you enrolled. When you bite and accept the initial offer without trying for more, the college is richer and you are poorer.

Strategy: Even when a college's aid policy is straightforward — their first offer is their last offer — it pays to determine the school's norms in aid awards before you launch an appeal. A computer probably ground out your award letter with programming based on specific parameters. Financial aid counselors routinely modify your award if the parameters are unreasonable after you submit new information.

You can frame your comments with these thoughts in mind:

> *As I understand it, the normal gift aid mix for a student with my EFC is (20 percent to 50 percent). I didn't understand why my letter specified so little gift aid until I realized you may not have figured in (bit of new information, such as parent lost a job or the high cost of medical care for a family member). Does this fact mean I'm eligible for more gift funding? How much more? How soon can you make it happen?*

Or

> *My research indicates the university usually meets 100 percent of demonstrated need. My award seems to be only 75 percent of my demonstrated need. I think I'm dead here. That missing $4,000 may make it impossible for me to enroll. Did I get something wrong somewhere? I am not sure that I let you know that (bit of new information). What else must I do to help you close the gap to 100 percent so I can become one of your students?*

Issue 6 — Why has the college decreased your Year 2 award?

In this situation, you are no longer a freshman. The college has given you enough money for your first year. But now for the next year, you are advised that (1) your actual dollars have been cut, or (2) that your aid package has been reworked — you are now expected to come up with more funding in self-help aid (loans and jobs) as you receive less in gift aid (scholarships and grants).

When the shock wears off, you wonder what happened. Chances are high that you've received an initial award to test the water. The college's slash-and-churn tactics are designed to find out if you'll hang in as an educational customer if they cut off big chunks of your aid. Race to the financial aid office and find out exactly why your aid went down, not up.

Strategy: No single strategy is inclusive but, in general, anticipate your talking points:

- ✔ Did your grades slip? Note that you had to study twice as hard for a difficult semester.

- ✔ Are you a low-income student? Remind them that you depend almost entirely on finaid for the basic necessities, including the food on your table.

✔ Are you a middle-income student? Point out that your family already faces sacrifice, debt, and hard choices. You aren't even sure that you can stay in school if more, not less, help isn't forthcoming. Everyone knows that for the past two decades college costs have risen much faster than inflation.

Issue 7— Does the college seek National Merit finalists?

Academic excellence casts a come-hither glow over future student recruitment as well as fundraising efforts. A great way for colleges to give their academic standards a shot in the arm is to populate their campuses with National Merit finalists. Some colleges, such as Macallister College in Minnesota, even set aside financial aid funds for students who are National Merit finalists.

Approximately 7,300 National Merit Scholars attend nearly 400 different colleges and universities. Despite the fact that far more students generally attend public rather than private colleges, among National Merit scholars more than half (about 4,000) choose to attend private colleges and are funded by institutional merit-based aid. The highest numbers choose Harvard (about 400), Texas at Austin (300), and Rice (200).

Strategy: Lace your language with comments about excellence and achievement. You are establishing an environment to deliver your true agenda:

> *As I am a National Merit finalist, I believe I can meet your academic standards and bring value to the student body at (name of college). What's stopping me is the high ratio of debt in the financial aid package you offer. It's towering. I'll be paying it off until the 22nd century. Or at least until my own future children are old enough for college. Can you possibly restructure the offer with more scholarship or grant funding? Is there something else I can do? I really need your help.*

Issue 8 — Is the college seeking special talent?

Students who can tutor in computer labs, handle art materials, catalog library books, work the cafeteria cash register, stock supplies in a bookstore, handle school intramural programs, or fill any school need are in demand.

Your appeal should embrace all of your accomplishments and skills — in high school you were a newspaper editor, musician, theater performer, or whatever.

Strategy: Frankly admit that your family is stumbling over the very high level of loans in an era of downsizing and employment instability. Career experts agree that if a job is lost over the age of 45, one or two years may pass before the individual finds a comparable job making parental loans very difficult to repay on schedule. Put your request in human terms, like the following:

> *I am experienced at sports equipment management — I did it for the high school football team and the softball team. I'm glad to work as much as I can and still keep my grades up, but are any scholarships or grants available that we missed out on? What can you advise at this point other than sinking into a mountain of debt? Should we conclude that the cost of college has risen above the average person's ability to pay?*

Issue 9 — What's the ratio of finaid recipients to total enrollment?

Does your research reveal that a large proportion of the college's student population is receiving financial aid, chiefly gift aid? If so, the college's financial aid professionals are sensitive to the college's high costs and the students' needs. This college is student-oriented, rather than research-oriented, and is investing in its potential alumni. This college is receptive to aid appeals.

Strategy: Pull out all the stops with a factual or emotional appeal. Here's an example.

> *Your offer, while greatly appreciated, leaves a void of $4,000, which I can't handle. Is it true that 67 percent of your student population receives aid and that much of it doesn't have to be repaid? There must be some factor in my background that can help you find another $4,000 in scholarships. Did I tell you that my mother just changed jobs and she earns less than she did at her old job? Did I mention that my computer was stolen and I didn't have replacement insurance? Isn't there something you can do to help me work this out?*

Issue 10 — Does the college respond to competing offers?

Colleges may respond to being played off against each other, but their managers don't like to admit that they're as affected by market forces as anyone else. When dealing with financial aid counselors, who are professionals and proud of it, be sensitive in how you leverage one finaid offer to increase another. Always use tact and polite language. Finaid professionals wince and tell you to take the other offer and run when your appeal style is too slick.

Strategy: Share the competitive letter with the counselor you hope will raise the amount or quality of your award. State that you had your sights set on attending your first-choice college but without more aid, you'll be forced to attend the college with the better offer because (give a reason — no money, your family can't or won't support the higher price, or any true justification). Ask the counselor to match the award. You may not get an equivalent offer, but you'll get something more.

Negotiating points for family-based issues

Although the amount of financial aid awarded is based on standard formulas, your family may be far from standard issue. Each factor increases your award and reduces the amount of expected family contribution.

We said it before but because so many people forget, we say it again:

Prove every claim for nonroutine, diminished family income with such documents as expense charts, canceled checks, medical bills, divorce papers, employment termination notices, and Social Security notifications.

The following points provide legitimate reasons for the college's financial aid counselor to enlarge your award.

Your budget is not standard-issue

Financial aid is based on a standard student budget. You must prove that your expenses will be greater than the standard. The areas of health, diet, disability, transportation, and even special tutorial expense if you need remedial work justify an appeal.

Education costs escalate for other family members

Do other members of your family have uncommon costs that take away from your family's ability to pay the assessed expected family contribution? Perhaps a brother or sister is required to attend a private school because of learning disabilities or other disabilities, for example. The FAFSA or CSS Profile has no place to put this information. You have to focus on it in your appeal.

Family obligations drain money from your family's income

Many parents are caught in the "sandwich" generation. They provide for children and for their own aged parents. Costs of providing care in a home, a nursing facility, or a residence on another continent can be overwhelming. Use such expenses in an appeal because the higher the expense total, the greater your demonstrated need.

Income cuts mean more aid

Social Security benefits for children are reduced at age 18 or on the last day of high school attendance, whichever date comes last. Usually this occurs after the FAFSA documents are filed, which means the college's financial aid counselor has no way of knowing that your SS benefits are lower and your family will have fewer dollars for college.

Another income cut that your finaid officer won't know about unless you announce it in an appeal occurs in families where parents are split apart. Most noncustodial divorced or separated parents are not obligated to contribute child support after your 18th birthday.

In a related issue, when a divorce or separation of parents occurs after the financial aid forms have been submitted, all income and asset information must be corrected. Inform your financial aid counselor how much child support and/or home maintenance support your custodial parent expects to receive from the other. In any event, your expected family contribution is likely to be lower under the new arrangement. The divorce or separation must have actually taken place; it can't be an action that may happen in the future.

Illness or death in the family is reason to appeal

Similar to divorce, if the parent who was a wage earner during the base year of income is no longer able to contribute, your income drops and aid rises.

Educational transportation may qualify for funds

When you are required to complete an internship, co-op education assignment, or another program that requires an automobile for transportation, ask for additional aid funding to cover the related expenses.

Required study abroad requires another look at aid

If you are enrolled in college for credit and must complete a study-abroad program to fulfill curriculum requirements, you may be able to get more money for transportation and living expenses.

A parent is out of work

Because your demonstrated need is assessed on income earned by your parent(s) in the previous calendar year (base year), if a parent's job is lost, you have a ready-made aid appeal. Use it.

Bad credit ratings make good aid awards

When you and your parents are borrowed out, have a bad credit history, owe the IRS, are overextended on credit cards, or for any other reason can't borrow more college money, share that fact with your financial aid counselor. The counselor may be sympathetic and award you more gift funds.

Family size increases

Is a new sibling on the scene? A central element in calculating your eligibility for aid is the number of household members. Count all your family's *children who will receive more than half their support from your parents* between July 1, 1998, and June 30, 1999. Your appeal is based on your mother being pregnant and expecting birth in the spring of 1998, which adds another mouth to feed during your school year.

Parents retire

The college financial aid counselor has no way of knowing your mater or pater is planning to retire during your school year. Explain the retirement benefits, presumably lower than employment earnings, and ask the counselor to calculate a new base year.

New academic statistics may increase dollars for scholars

Many colleges give discounts related to class rank or SAT/ACT scores, sometimes as much as 50 percent for high achievers. If your SAT/ACT scores have increased or your high school rank has risen, you may qualify for favored status.

Scholars, don't let this one fall between the cracks.

Family obligations force finaid layaway

When you've already received your award letter and suddenly find that family responsibilities will keep you out of school until the second semester, negotiate with the finaid counselor to hold your second semester funding for you and not give the money away to someone else.

Writing a Winning Aid Appeal

Many avenues for appeal are open once you begin to think through the college's issues and your family's fiscal fitness. Learn to write a good appeal letter. Even when you plan a face-to-face encounter in the financial aid office, bring a letter stating the facts with you.

The following three letters show you how to construct an effective appeal. Two are written by parents, which is what's normally done, and the third is written by a student.

March 26, 1998

Mr. Reynold Ellman
Office of Student Financial Aid
Adelphi Universtiy
Garden City, New York 11530

Subject: Letter of Appeal, Loss of Income

Re: John Scholar, SSN 000-000-000

Dear Mr. Ellman:

I write to you to inform you of my loss of income for the current year, 1998. I understand that students' financial aid is based on their demonstrated need, which involves the parents' and student's income and assets for the 1997 calendar base year.

My income has reduced significantly. I have enclosed a copy of a letter from the International Medical Group that confirms that my service agreement with them will not be renewed. On my 1997 income tax, I listed the income from this contract, $21,300. My income for 1998, however, will only consist of my full-time job, which pays me a salary of $58,358. This is a tremendous decrease from the original $79,658.

I hope you can consider this new and disheartening information in a reevaluation of my son's financial need. John and I would greatly appreciate it.

Thank you for what you have already done for John; our family would treasure any additional assistance towards John's education as he pays his own way at Adelphi University.

Most sincerely yours,

Jane Scholar
Mother

enc: (1)

July 10, 1998

Jeremy Ivers, Director of Financial Aid
Bluffton College
280 West College Avenue, Box 788
Bluffton, OH 45817-1196

Subject: (1) Self-Employment Business Statement and (2) Special Circumstances

Reference: Rebecca Heart, SSN#000-000-000

Dear Mr. Ivers:

As per your office's request, we have enclosed information and documents regarding our self-employment and special circumstances. My husband and I write you to summarize our current situation. We are self-employed and have no tangible assets except for the file cabinets and computer we use to provide our services. My husband is a private counselor and I am a writer.

1) Because of these circumstances, we have not completed the business form; we have relevant information for this section. We declared the business income as $98,010 on our Federal income tax form 1040, and have enclosed copies of related documents.

2) We understand that our application and request for aid missed the established deadline. When our daughter, Rebecca, applied for early decision acceptance, we assumed that because we have only one child and, in light of our combined income, we could not qualify for financial assistance.

However, we recently consulted a general financial advisor regarding our need for self-employed retirement coverage, and a college financial aid advisor regarding our financial planning. Both advisors agreed that without better planning, we will face tremendous difficulties funding both our retirement and Rebecca's education. These advisors gave us the following reasons to apply for college financial aid:
* our relatively low net worth
* our highly variable income
* our current medical expense burden: in addition to paying $1,700 per month to Blue Cross Blue Shield, we must pay significant medical fees for a serious, chronic mental health condition, which is only partly covered by our medical insurance. This treatment will not decrease in the next five years. We have also learned that we will require $10,000 in dental, nonelective, noncosmetic work over the next six months. We have no dental insurance and our dentist can only allow three monthly payments. We can provide documentation to verify such facts.

In conclusion, we expect a shortfall of at least $6,000 after considering Rebecca's unsubsidized Stafford and the PLUS program. We would greatly appreciate any advice from your offices as we struggle to meet our financial obligations and keep Rebecca in college.

Sincerely yours,

Maria Heart
(Mother)

enc.(s): 10 documents related to above areas of concern

April 10, 1998

Mr. John Moneypenny   Subject: Financial Aid Appeal Letter
Director of Financial Aid   Ref: William Wilneed (SSN: 000-000-000)
Carnegie Mellon University   Telephone # 555-555-1342
Pittsburgh, PA 15213

Dear Mr. Moneypenny:

I have signed and enclosed the award notification from your institution, but I write to ask for
your guidance.

My parents and I have reviewed our family's plan for paying for college. As you are aware, I
have two brothers who will apply for college in the next three years. You may recall my that
brother Thomas is a junior with a 3.9 GPA and SAT scores of 1380. My sophomore brother,
Timothy, has similar academic achievements.

I am the brother with a less awesome academic record -- 3.6 GPA and SAT 1250. Even so, I
am troubled because I was not found eligible for more than a $2,625 Stafford loan.

My parents are concerned that they will not have the funds to support me for the next four
years without some help from CMU. I have taken the liberty of describing our budget plan,
which shows a gap of $4,375. Can you assist me in identifying resources to fill the gap in our
unmet need?

C.O.A. at Carnegie Mellon including living on campus.................$28,000

Student's contribution from savings........... $ 2,000
Student's contribution from summer work..... 1,000
Student's contribution from Stafford Loan..... 2,625
Parent's contribution from savings............... 10,000
Parent's contribution from PLUS................... 8,000
TOTAL.. $23,625
Balance...$4,375

As you can see, we are only short about $4,000 in our budget. Your assistance in identifying
additional financial aid will be appreciated.

Sincerely yours,

William Wilneed
Class of 2002

Fine-Tuning Your Bargaining Skills

Negotiating is a skill you should learn. Because a college financial aid counselor has the authority to use "professional judgment" on a case-by-case basis, fine-tuning your bargaining skills really pays.

Third-party (outside) scholarships prove the point. The average award package is made up of 60 percent self-help funds (loans and/or jobs) and 40 percent gift funds. When you receive an outside scholarship, some colleges want to take back their gift aid in like proportion, leaving you with the same amount of debt. Ugh. Good negotiation may modify that disappointment by persuading the college to reduce each type of assistance in the award letter by 50 percent of the outside award.

Example: Suppose you win an outside scholarship of $2,000, and your award letter specifies a $3,500 loan and a $2,000 grant. You want your loan reduced by $1,000 and your grant reduced by $1,000. You don't want your grant reduced by $2,000 leaving you with $3,500 to pay off.

If you don't really understand the financial aid formulas and don't really know what's going on, you're going to pay thousands of dollars more than you really must. In any industry — and education is an industry — business managers try to get you to pay as much as possible, while you try to pay as little as possible.

Chapter 10
Merit Scholarships for the Talented

● ●

In This Chapter
▶ Inspiring student wins $542,681
▶ Secrets of winning scholarships
▶ Personal finaid inventory checksheet

● ●

amon Darnell Williams of Washington, D.C. is on the A-Team of scholarship winners.

Damon made it his business to know so much about the financial aid system that he racked up an astonishing $542,681 in college scholarship offers, including full-ride prizes from seven highly regarded colleges and universities. He won so many awards that the excess pays for books and other school expenses. Damon knows that having too much money is better than having too little and so he went all out in his search.

Ultimately, Damon chose George Washington University because he wanted to complete his education, at least through his undergraduate college years, within Washington, D.C., boundaries.

So awesome is Damon's high scoring that he recently shared the awards spotlight in the Second Annual NAACP Pathway to Excellence Awards Gala with such celebrities as Dr. Maya Angelou, Whoopi Goldberg, Phil Donohue, and Marlo Thomas.

Now a hospitality (hotel and restaurant management) major, Damon began learning the finaid system during the summer after his sophomore year at H.D. Woodson High School. He read books and watched videos, but placed heavy emphasis on the personal touch. Damon spent time with his high school guidance counselor and called financial aid counselors at colleges. He asked for advice. "I wanted people who could affect my future to perceive me as a person, not just as a name on a piece of paper," Damon says.

We asked Damon for suggestions on becoming a big scholarship winner.

"First, learn how the financial aid system works. Learn to work within the system and how to work around it," Damon advises.

Work around the system?

"Find a connection! Getting student aid is a form of networking. When you can't find a person who knows a student aid director or counselor at a college, call the director cold. In my experience, some directors mentioned new scholarships that might fit me. I always tried to tailor my approach to scholarships that I really wanted by showing I'm a serious-minded individual who goes after what he wants."

Other tips from Damon:

- ✔ Start early and be persistent. Don't wait until you're a high school senior to suddenly realize college is just around the corner. And no matter how tired you are, make time to complete your applications and turn them in by the deadlines.

- ✔ Write sincere letters to presidents of colleges and universities. (Usually they're passed to the financial aid office.) Use the name and precise title of the president and spell everything correctly. You want to project the image of a student with great promise of being a mature person who will contribute to society. Your letters show purpose and that you care enough to make an all-out effort worthy of reward. The letters also show you're worth helping and that a helping hand extended to you now will be returned to society many times over.

- ✔ Prepare an essay pool of perhaps four or five core essays, on topics such as what you hope to be doing in 20 years, why you want to go to a specific college, an so forth. Adapt your core essays quickly to scholarship programs or to college finaid offices. Having a starting point on essays keeps your momentum going — you then have no excuse to delay sending in the application because you don't know what to say in a required essay.

- ✔ Go in person to local colleges and universities, or call the institution if it is out of town. If you, for example, live in Washington, D.C., you may be able to travel to a college in Philadelphia but you would telephone a college in Chicago. Give financial aid counselors the details of your financial history so they can understand your circumstances. Try to establish a relationship with finaid counselors.

Don't think that Damon spent all his time grinding out finaid applications — his academic record was superb. Valedictorian of his class, Damon graduated from high school with a 4.29 in his school's 4.0 system. (He received extra points for college-level and honors courses.)

Damon's leadership record was also impressive. Among a raft of activities, he served in two citywide positions: as president of Future Business Leaders of America and as a member of the student government executive committee.

Damon's scholarship resume, which is a compilation of all his financial aid awards, stretches over four pages and misses nothing. It cites distinctions in education, honors and awards, vocational leadership, other leadership, community service, work experience, affiliations, public speaking experience, television and radio appearances, and newspaper clips about him.

His scholarship resume also includes Damon's career objective to be an entrepreneur specializing in hotel and restaurant management, and his hobbies of chess, miniature golf, reading and watching films and sports.

Few students can hope to match Dynamo Damon's record-breaking performance, but it's a goal worth eyeing.

Good Prospects Even if You're Not a Budding Einstein

You may not be a world-class competitor like Damon, but are you an above-average student in academics, sports, music, art or another ability? Colleges and universities pant for your presence. They, being competitive creatures, have school reputations to keep up and need to brag that they're the place to be.

That's why virtually all colleges and universities put their money where their mouths are by awarding a combination of merit and need-based scholarships.

That's why nine out of 10 four-year colleges give no-need scholarships. That's why all schools want the best talent they can attract.

The very students the schools are trying to attract may not be fully cooperating. The biggest problem in lining up free money for college is understanding how the system works, from the point of discovery to the point of receiving the awards.

Much like you have to buy a ticket to win the lottery, you have to heavily invest yourself in the system if you hope to reap substantial scholarship rewards. Many students and their parents don't get the message. They have a feeling that what they're doing is so monumentally valuable that scholarships will seek them out.

Need is in eye of the beholder

You may have little idea whether or not you are a financially needy student when you apply for a scholarship. Most students don't.

Many private scholarship organizations have their own definition of demonstrated need, and they don't adhere — and may not even be close — to the Federal Methodology (based on the FAFSA) that colleges use to determine a student's eligibility.

✔ Always assume that you have demonstrated need and allow the scholarship sponsor to determine its level.

✔ Never disqualify yourself based on the level of need specified by the government or your college.

That's not how the big-scholarship-money printing presses roll. To receive major private scholarships, you have to do more than distinguish yourself academically, athletically, in arts, or in community service. Throwing in your status as an all-around great kid isn't enough either. *You have to work the system before all of these virtues pay off.*

Nine Rules of the Scholarship Hunt

When it comes to scholarship money, you can't afford to let opportunity go knocking. But as someone once observed, the trouble with opportunity is that it always comes disguised as hard work. That's certainly the case with the scholarship hunt. We wish we could say the hunt is like a walk on the Baywatch beach, but really there are no shortcuts if you want to end your treasure hunt with at least two fists full of college money — enough to pay for four years of college.

With that goal in mind, here are nine rules for a winning scholarship hunt.

Shed the lead, think ahead

When should you start smartening up about scholarships? Sit down for startling news: Don't wait until your junior year — start in your first year of high school.

Even though you may already be pushing yourself so hard to get into a "good" college that there's little time to sleep or have fun, the burdens of debt for years after college are so debilitating that the sooner you plan, the easier you land.

In your first year, you can begin participating in high school governance, newspaper journalism, Girl Scouting or Boy Scouting, community service, school club activities and any other activity that shows you are developing skills and making labor contributions to worthy causes. This early start can develop into a strong visible credential to use in your scholarship search by the time you graduate.

During your first year, begin collecting information on scholarships. Get everyone in the family to help you clip news of scholarships to add to your collection. At this stage, don't limit the type of scholarship information you collect because you're unsure of your college major or career pathway. Save information on any type of scholarship.

Reviewing your scholarship collection at this early stage can save you time in the long run. You quickly see what is important and what is not important to win a particular scholarship.

You must learn the answer to this question: *How is a student evaluated for a specific scholarship?*

If you have no demonstrated need, you'd be wasting your time to apply for the $2 million Elks National Foundation's "Most Valuable Student" scholarship award, for example. For this award, the selection committee assesses applicants on leadership and activities, but the final decision tilts toward demonstrated need.

True scholarships do not have a financial need criteria. Many students who spend time looking for private scholarships do not have need. Students who have need try for aid from the college.

Become an awards detective

Arguably the most important part of the scholarship hunt is research. Most parents and students don't know where to begin. A good place to start is the career center at your high school. Most centers have software you can use to make a computerized search.

Find sponsors and causes dear to your future

Many service organizations — Kiwanis Clubs, Lions, Eagles, Elks, and Moose — raise scholarship funds to sponsor college students. These same organizations usually have a national project, such as eye banks, food and shelter for the homeless, and children's hospitals. If, by chance, you plan to major in a career field related to the areas of interest to an organization's national project, track down the local scholarship chairman of the organization, share your goals and ask for sponsorship.

If you attend a high school that refuses to let you get your hands on the scholarship computers until you're a senior, turn to the Internet and do a free scholarship search online. See Chapter 12 for the best sources of online help.

Does searching free online databases have drawbacks?

✔ The free search is advertising-driven, designed to collect your name and address for marketing efforts.

✔ The database may not be frequently updated or validated. Value in a database is based on accuracy and currency. Who wants to spend hours and wasted postage applying for scholarships you'll never receive?

Nevertheless, the free online searches can help you discover where scholarships are located.

Alternative computerized searches are available:

✔ The National College Scholarship Foundation provides a computer scholarship search and literature, *College Aid Resources for Education,* for $24.

✔ The American Legion offers a booklet, *Need a Lift,* and a computerized search for $20.

Both organizations are cited at the end of this chapter.

Scholarship research is not a one-time exercise. It starts in the early years of high school and continues through graduate school. Your motto should be "Start early, stay late." Make collecting snippets and chunks about scholarships a family affair as brothers, sisters, aunts, uncles, grandparents and friends join your parents and you in forming a *scholarship research team.* Devote a file drawer or a bedroom corner for your scholarship library.

Despite the part you, the student, should play in financing your own education, the reality is that mom and dad become the true scholarship team leaders. The sad fact is that most students see a college education as an entitlement and are not concerned about who pays the bill. Isn't it true that you value more highly the things in which you personally invest? You'll never be tempted to ditch classes if you're busting your chops to pay by winning scholarships or by working.

Research includes not only finding hidden scholarship funds but being able to get the applications to apply for the money. One of the reasons so many students fail to receive scholarships is they don't get the application in time to compete for the award, a topic we discuss later in this chapter.

Stockpile marketing ammo

Give your research team ammunition to win your battle for money. Prepare a Personal Financial Aid Inventory by photocopying and filling out the form shown as Figure 10-1.

Using your Personal Financial Aid Inventory, look for connections with all organizations, agencies, clubs, and the like that may have scholarships available. Don't overlook such local groups as parent-teacher associations, professional organizations, and veterans groups. Include corporations. Parents should check with employers and unions to see if aid for offspring is offered. Ethnic heritage groups like the Alliance of Poles or the German-American Club may also provide financial aid.

Your scholarship team will benefit from your personal aid inventory. They need to know about all of your characteristics, skills, and experiences. Consider these awards:

- ✔ **St. John Fisher College** in New York awards more than $150,000, without regard to demonstrated need or GPA requirement, to students who've contributed to community service activities.

- ✔ **Juniata College** in Pennsylvania gives scholarships to people who are left-handed.

- ✔ **Lyon College** in Batesville, Arkansas, pays students who play the bagpipes between $1,000 and $6,000 without regard to need or merit.

- ✔ At **North Carolina State University,** students who are named Gatlin or Gatling can receive up to $6,000 with no requirements for academic excellence or need.

- ✔ The **University of Rochester in New York** passes out $5,000 to any student who is a New York resident when enrolling.

Personal Financial Aid Inventory

ACADEMIC INFORMATION

High School grades _____ Rank in Class _____

Special aptitudes,
abilities, and hobbies _____

Special awards and
recognition _____

School and community
activities _____

College major(s) _____

Career plans _____

STUDENT INFORMATION

Citizenship _____

Ethnic heritage _____

Age _____ Gender _____

Clubs _____

Physical traits _____

Religious affiliations _____

PARENT INFORMATION

Occupations   Mother _____ Father _____

Veteran status   Mother _____ Father _____

Professional
organizations/unions   Mother _____ Father _____

Figure 10-1: Review your financial aid inventory.

Save every scrap of accomplishment

The scholarship hunt is the perfect reason for comprehensive, systematic record keeping.

You and your parents should retain copies of any significant happening during your high school years — special award for scouting, 4-H, music, community service, or any kudos.

Keep your records by activity, separating your high school activities from your community activities.

Although your high school transcript will be sent to scholarship sponsors to verify grades and how they've improved or worsened from year to year, the transcript doesn't tell your entire story.

The transcript doesn't describe your award for the honor roll or an award for most-improved student. The transcript says nothing about how your research paper in a particular class received special recognition.

Special notes and special awards catch the eye of the scholarship readers who review and evaluate your application.

Keep careful records, too, each time you put your name in the ring for a specific scholarship. Save a list of the forms required by the scholarship sponsor, and keep dates when the documents were mailed to the sponsor. Note for each sponsor that although you have sent an unofficial (high school or transfer) transcript, your school must mail an official copy of your transcript before the scholarship committee can act on your file.

Record keeping focuses your attention on each potential scholarship application and whether you need to follow up your initial effort.

Follow, follow the finaid road

Imagine this scene: A room filled with civic-minded, good-hearted, unpaid women and men sitting at tables sorting through gazillions of scholarship applications, getting a little punchy in the process because scholarship selection is just one more assignment they've unselfishly taken on to help others. We call these people *volunteers*, bless 'em all.

Many volunteers today have full-time jobs or kids to look after, and the time they spend wading through pounds of the aspirations and dreams of college hopefuls isn't their number one priority in life.

The reading and clerical load of processing scholarship applications can become overwhelming, causing some volunteers to put aside work for the "next time" or to take student mail home to finish their assignments. Let's face it: Day-in-day-out continuity of tasking can be missing in many volunteer organizations.

If you've been a member of a volunteer organization, you know first-hand how easily inefficiencies occur — inefficiencies that can leave you the scholarship-seeker out in the cold in one or both of the two stages of scholarship solicitation, as the following disqualifying scenarios illustrate:

✔ **Stage 1: You ask for an application.**

But you don't receive the application and you're automatically disqualified.

So what happened to your request for an application, assuming it wasn't lost in the mail? In a volunteer environment, your request may be stuck in someone's desk drawer or hiding in a stack of unopened mail or locked in a car trunk beside the reader's bowling shoes that won't be worn for the next ten days.

✔ **Stage 2: You complete and mail an application and enclose documents.**

But you forget to enclose one or more required documents. No one gets back to you with that oversight. You are automatically disqualified because of lack of information.

So why didn't someone notify you that your scholarship application is incomplete? Maybe a reader thought that if you are unable to follow directions, you're not college material. Who knows? Who cares? The answer could be any number of reasons, none of them important in the sense that you're out of the running if you don't fix the problem.

The willingness to follow-up on every single application request is vital. If you don't receive a requested application form after two or three weeks, pick up the telephone and call the scholarship sponsor. (Yes, we agree that long-distance telephoning is expensive, but ask yourself which is more expensive — telephone calls or paying for college?)

Never assume that one request should suffice and drop the scholarship when you don't get the application.

✔ After you get the form and return your comprehensive scholarship application package, telephone to ask if the sponsor received it, and confirm that all your supporting documents are present and accounted for.

✔ When you speak to a sponsor's employee or volunteer, be certain to get the person's name and job title.

✔ Record pertinent facts of your conversations in your records. If, at a later time, a sponsor says your application was not received on time, you can nail that misstatement on the spot by tactfully quoting dates, chapter and verse.

When you receive an award, you've got one more follow-up job to handle: Write to the sponsor with your acceptance and thanks for the award.

Keep a close watch on each scholarship application as it moves through the system and follow up relentlessly.

Get thee to finaid on time

Pay attention to your scholarship calendar (see Chapter 4). in general and to an October deadline in particular in making sure you have received virtually all scholarship application forms. This gives you time to prepare a powerful application package complete with endorsements, letters of recommendation, notices of honors, 500-word essays when required, and other self-marketing materials.

Throughout the scholarship application process, don't fail to meet all deadlines. As Duke University financial aid director Jim Belvin says, "It wouldn't matter if the student were the son of the president of the university, if he did not meet the deadline he would not be considered for financial aid."

Are there no extenuating circumstances that would justify an extension if you miss a deadline? We can think of one — being shipwrecked at sea.

There are usually more applicants for aid than there is aid to distribute. Most finaid staff are looking for ways to rule you out. Don't give them the opportunity by neglecting to completely fill out your application and mail it in on time.

Tailor your application to win the prize

When you whip out a generic (one-size-fits-all) application for every scholarship you come across, what you prove is that you have access to a working photocopy machine.

But when you design your scholarship application package to maximize your appeal in a specific scholarship award environment, you prove you have access to a working mind.

Cut to the chase: Get the rules

Find out what really matters in each scholarship award. Request a copy of the scholarship's rules. You want to know how many points are given for need, for the essay, for leadership, for scholarship, for part-time work while in college, for participation in extra-curricular activities, for volunteer work, and the like. Aim your application where the points are.

Develop a core application and then tailor it to fit specific scholarships. You are trying to get the scholarship selection readers to see that your qualifications match the award's criteria.

In addition to your core scholarship application, select appropriate items from the following list that show how well you match the kind of student the scholarship sponsor says it seeks:

- ✔ Unofficial high school transcript (college transcript for returning adults)

  Official transcripts must be mailed by originating schools so there's no chance that you could alter them. But scholarship sponsors will accept even photocopies as unofficial transcripts until they receive official versions.

- ✔ Recommendation letters from teachers, community leaders, business and professional people, members of the clergy

- ✔ A 500-word essay on national theme

- ✔ A list of all awards such as those bestowed for scouting, debating, poster design, and so forth (scholarship watchers say half of all students who apply for scholarships will not complete an application if the scholarship requires an essay)

- ✔ A list of references who can comment on your skills and work experience

- ✔ A list of volunteer or community service activities in which you have participated

- ✔ A list of positions held in school that show leadership and responsibility

- ✔ A list of work experiences that show you can manage your time between school, work, and extracurricular activities

- ✔ Copies of documents and newspaper clippings verifying your awards, honors, commendations

Go all out to gain an edge against your competitors. Present scholarship decision-makers with a superb, self-marketing application package that shows that you, a strong match for the award's requirements, are among the top tier of candidates. Show them why they should give you the money.

An outstanding and targeted presentation package is the secret weapon that wins you the big prizes. But even if you don't have the greatest qualifications, gift money may be available.

Find your strong suits: Money's out there for average people, too

Maybe you're no great shakes as a scholar, your SAT or ACT wasn't cheering material, and your athletic abilities don't rival Michael Jordan's. If you've got a talent, it's wrapped away in tissue paper and hasn't been seen for 17 years. Even so, you'd be surprised at how much money is available that has little to do with academics, but relies on

- ✔ Ethnic or racial heritage
- ✔ Membership in clubs
- ✔ Community activities
- ✔ Career plans or field of study
- ✔ Hobbies and special interests
- ✔ Physical traits (very tall, short) or disabilities (asthmatic)
- ✔ Religious affiliation
- ✔ Parents' employers or their unions

Scholarships based on some of these aspects are profiled in the Resource Guide at the back of the book.

Set your hounds on finaid

Maintain a resolute determination to win and don't take "no" for an answer. After following up on the receipt of your application package and confirming that it's in order with no pieces missing, you may not hear a word back for months and months.

- ✔ If you have not heard from a sponsor in three months, call and find out the status of your application.

- ✔ If you have received notice that you're not in the final cut for a scholarship award, call and find out why. Maybe the scholarship committee didn't receive all of your material although it all arrived at the sponsoring organization. Student records are frequently misfiled, and applicant documents disappear from the scholarship folders. If you detect an irregularity, ask that your application be reinstated with all the required documents present.

✔ If you have been awarded a scholarship but haven't received the funds by July 15, ask the person who signed your award letter when you can expect to receive your scholarship money.

Once in a while an unusual situation develops: You are notified that you were a finalist but, unfortunately, the money ran out. If this happens to you, wait until college starts in the fall and, about mid-term, call the person who signed the bad-news letter to find out if any of the finalists failed to attend college or have dropped out; if so, ask if you can have funds returned by the college where the no-show or drop-out enrolled. Scholarship committees generally don't want to have to report to their organizations that funds raised for scholarships are sitting idle.

Lock that scholarship dream in steel jaws and hang on. Cease only if you are told by someone important to "Stop calling us, you bowser." Until that happens, continue with the determination of Hannibal the elephant-riding conqueror, who, as he sought a way to cross the forbidding Alps, clenched his teeth and announced: "We will either find a way, or make one."

Mother is right: Say thanks

Although you aggressively pursue the scholarship prize, once you've made yourself known, stand down and allow the system to work and stop kissing up.

In addition to the acceptance and thank-you letters you write when you do win, make yourself available for the scholarship luncheon or similar event. Not only is it gracious behavior, but you want to make sure that when your name comes up for renewal awards for the next three years, they know who you are.

Fighting over Scholars

Schools give the largest number of no-need awards for academic achievement. Why? Colleges need bright students who in turn attract good faculty who in turn generate research funds. And bright students who graduate remember their colleges fondly and make alumni gifts.

Now you know why colleges treat finalists in the annual National Merit Scholars, the nation's most prestigious high school academic-talent competition, like uncrowned royalty.

In Louisville, Kentucky, Garet Thomas — who scored 33 out of a possible 36 on the American College Test and 1,510 out of a possible 1,600 on the Scholastic Assessment Test — was wooed by three or four colleges a day, finally including at least one from every state.

Thomas, according to news reports, chose the University of Kentucky. His prize was spectacular — a full ride with money left over. Because that school and others, such as the University of Oklahoma, have determined to upgrade their academic standing, they are aggressive about recruiting National Merit Scholars and give excellent awards.

To National Merit finalists who list the University of Kentucky as their first choice, the school offers free tuition, free room and board, and $450 per year for books.

Finalists who name the University of Oklahoma as their first choice get free or heavily discounted tuition, an additional $2,875 a semester, and the right to register for classes before other students. In 1984, academic scholarships cost the school $100,000; this year, awards by the merit-aid office topped $3.2 million, and academic scholarships university-wide totaled nearly $6 million.

But the National Merit finalists don't find similar blandishments of automatic financial aid at highly selective schools like Princeton and Duke Universities. These schools choose instead to emphasize need-based aid.

The trick is to apply to schools that especially want what you have to offer (athletics, drama, art, for instance) or to schools where your grades and test scores place you in the upper 25 percent of the applicant pool. Your upper-level status will influence the attractiveness of your aid package.

How can you tell if you're in the top 25 percent? Look at the college's *selectivity score range*. Nearly half of four-year colleges report selectivity by average or median selectivity figures in terms of the middle 50 percent of entering students, such as 60 to 75. If your selectivity rating is above 75, you're in the top 25 percent. Your high school guidance counselor can expand on this concept, or you can look in the College Board's reference, *The College Handbook*, or study its software, *ExPAN*, both of which are cited at the end of this chapter.

Edison in the making

At 17, Adam Ezra Cohen has "Inventor" stamped across his future. As a high school senior at New York's Hunter College High School, Cohen was already the creator of 152 inventions, including one that allows computer users to guide a cursor with their gaze. In 1997, he took top honors in the annual Westinghouse Science Talent Search with an "electrochemical paintbrush" that prints characters so infinitesimal that 50 words would fit within the width of a human hair. Cohen's prize? A $40,000 scholarship he'll use to study physics at Harvard.

Alternatives to Scholarships

Suppose the unthinkable happens and you receive no scholarship money to speak of. Apart from loans, you can consider other ways to pay for college, such as work-study and co-op programs, participation in the ROTC and working for an employer with a tuition assistance plan — all of which are discussed in this book.

Remember, too, that some career-oriented programs only kick in with finaid after you become a sophomore, so be alert to reapplying for your second year.

Additional resources

The following resources can help you in your search for merit aid:

✔ *College Costs and Financial Aid Handbook*; The College Entrance Examination Board; annual; available from booksellers or for $16.95 from College Board Publications, Box 886, New York, New York 10101.

✔ *ExPAN software*; from The College Entrance Examination Board; priced for institutional use — check your school or library.

✔ *College Aid Resources for Education*, available for $24 from the National College Scholarship Foundation; Box 8207, Gaithersburg, MD 20898 .

✔ *Need a Lift?*; revised annually by the American Legion, Indianapolis, Indiana; Available for $3 from The American Legion, National Emblem Sales, PO Box 1050, Indianapolis, IN 46204; 317-630-1251.

✔ *The Scholarship Book* by Daniel J. Cassidy, revised frequently; $24.95; Prentice-Hall, 800-432-3782.

Chapter 11

Keep Up the Good Work

● ●

In This Chapter

▶ The truth about getting finaid when you work

▶ Student jobs as a transition to adult careers

▶ What every dollar earned costs in finaid eligibility

● ●

*M*ia Mendez (not her real name) attends a prestigious and pricey college. She pays for classes in political theory and international policy by serving drinks at a popular lunchtime bar. To cover the costs of practical needs like rent, food, and clothing, Mia scrubs hospital rooms at a local hospital. To make time for studies, she works weekends, nights, and holidays.

What does Mia do for fun? She laughs and rolls her eyes, admitting, "Fun is a theoretical concept to me. Everybody keeps asking me how I do it — I just tell them I give up having a life."

Mia and nearly half of U.S. college students work while in college. About 25 percent work 20 or more hours a week; 6 percent work 35 or more hours.

"Last year I worked an average of 56 hours a week, and the people in financial aid basically told me I'd have to work less to prove I need money to qualify for financial aid. They won't give me all I need to survive; it's like they're saying I should plunge into debt rather than try to work my way through," says Mia.

Like this hard-working young woman, many dedicated college students must put their shoulders to the work-wheel long before they enter the field they're studying.

What the cost of today's college comes down to for most people is this: You can work, you can borrow, or you can try to do a bit of both.

The high educational price of working for tuition

In response to students' growing work habit, college administrators have begun to worry about student burnout and *attrition* (dropout rates). In the last 20 years, the number of students who complete their degrees has dropped from 47 percent to about 40 percent. The numbers sink another 10 percent for those who work more than 20 hours per week, according to a study by University of California at Los Angeles.

Job Experience Is Essential for New Grads

Need a job? Get experience. Need experience? Get a job. The old beginner's dilemma is getting harder to solve, not easier. Today's competitive job market demands that new graduates have some sort of workplace experience, whether it's gained in jobs or internships, paid or unpaid.

The days are gone when you could graduate, go into the job market experience-naked and expect to be hired on the basis of your fine education. Few organizations are looking for blank canvases to paint on. Employers want skills validated by work experience.

Summer jobs are one means to more than extra money. Whether you spend your summer developing software or selling shoes, you can make your experience pay off on your resume. To find out what transferable skills you can polish on any of the above jobs, crank up your computer and read the online article *Make your Summer Work Experience Pay* (www.jobweb.org/jconline/features/summer/default.shtml)

Get the experience that employers want and avoid becoming one of those graduates who, according to the Education Resources Institute, owes an average of $16,000 in loans. If you're not a beginner but an adult going back to school, you already know how important work experience defined by skills has become.

Won't I Lose Finaid by Working?

Perhaps you've heard that the greedy financial aid monster gobbles 50 cents in aid eligibility for every $1 earned above $2,000 and, if you the student save the money you earn, you lose an additional 35 cents. So when you try to avoid overdosing on debt as well as putting muscle in your resume, you come out ahead by only 15 cents on the dollar. Have you heard that? Don't believe it hook, line, and sinker.

The work-and-lose-money story does contain a kernel of fact. But the truth is that the financial aid consequences of your student job depend on how much you earn, your tax bracket, your assets, and your family status. Moreover, the financial aid counselor has the power to make a *professional judgment*, which can modify the consequences if it looks as though the system is unfairly knocking you down for having the ambition to go out and earn money to pay a few bills.

Suppose, for instance, that you take a year off school to work, making an income of $15,000. When you go back to school, your FAFSA results shown on your SAR will say you are obligated to pay an ESC (expected student contribution) of $7,700. Your financial aid counselor knows that's a crazy tab to expect you to pay — you won't be working and making that much money while attending college. The counselor has the authority to reduce that $7,700 to much less. How much less depends on a number of considerations, but your ESC could even go down to zero.

When you hear that working during college is a dumb idea because you lose money in financial aid, remember the divisions of financial aid — gift (free money which means scholarships and grants) and self-help (jobs and loans). The aid you're losing by virtue of a larger expected student contribution could well fall into the loan column. The less money you can borrow while in school, the less encumbered your future as a new worker will be.

As for giving up 35 cents for each dollar you save, why would you put any excess funds in a savings account? Go back and read Chapter 1 on asset shifting.

How Your Paycheck Shapes Your Share of Tuition

Table 11-1 shows how much financial aid eligibility you give up in return for a paycheck. Subtract your taxes, and you'll have an idea how many cents on the dollar you may forfeit for each dollar you earn.

Table 11-1 — Expected Student Contribution (ESC) from Student's Annual Earnings

Earnings	Single (Dependent)	Single (Independent)	Single (One Child)	Married
$1,650	$0	$0	$0	$0
$2,000	$0	$0	$0	$0
$2,500	$205	$0	$0	$0
$3,000	$420	$0	$0	$0
$3,500	$636	$0	$0	$0
$4,000	$852	$0	$0	$0
$4,500	$1,068	$0	$0	$0
$5,000	$1,284	$0	$0	$0
$5,500	$1,500	$0	$0	$0
$6,000	$1,716	$41	$0	$0
$7,500	$2,363	$426	$0	$0
$10,000	$3,443	$1,468	$0	$0
$15,000	$5,601	$3,626	$0	$2,126
$17,500	$6,681	$4,706	$311	$3,286
$20,000	$7,760	$5,785	$532	$4,285
$22,500	$8,840	$6,865	$996	$5,365
$25,000	$9,919	$7,944	$1,460	$6,444

Note: This table shows pretax income and does not reflect assets. Pretax income and assets vary by student. Dr. Davis created this table using calculations based on data from the College Scholarship Service Fund Finder (Federal Expected Student Contribution).

From Table 11-1, you get a general idea of how much financial aid you can expect to lose based on your earnings:

- ✔ For example: You can earn $2,000 and lose nothing. But if you earn $5,000 and are a single dependent student, you'll be expected to kick in $1,284.

- ✔ Another example: If you earn $15,000 as a single dependent student, you will lose $5,601; if you are a single independent student, you will lose $3,626; if you are a single parent with one child, you'll lose nothing; if you are married, you'll lose $2,126.

Chapter 12

Use This Hotlist and Get Wired for Finaid

- -

In This Chapter

▶ Forty awesome Internet places to ferret out finaid

▶ More than 100 dynamite telephone contacts for quick answers

▶ Five great software programs to ease your efforts

- -

*H*ere comes a practical listing of electronic tools to ease your financial aid search. Whether you're a techno-buff or you've just unpacked your first computer, these lists have something for everyone. Internet Web sites, telephone resources, and computer software — we've got them all. We've checked and rechecked these resources and at press time, they're right on the money!

Internet Resources

Check out the following sites for great finaid information.

Adventures in Education, Financial Aid Office
www.tgslc.org/adventur/fao.htm

The Texas Guaranteed Student Loan Corporation's Financial Aid Office has a large collection of scholarships, grants, and fellowships. The site also includes a reference that gives you facts and a beginner's guide to finaid.

Alliance to Save Student Aid
www.student-aid.nche.edu

This site provides updated information on congressional cuts on student aid and new, related legislation.

The Ambitious Student's Guide to Financial Aid
www.signet.com/collegemoney/toc1.html

This online book includes tables, worksheets, and advice on how to get the funds you need to attend college.

Chinook College Funding Service
www.chinook.com/

This site contains a broad spectrum of information about the finaid process, meeting deadlines, and sample finaid sources. Chinook is an award-winning, high-scoring search service, so we figured you should check it out, even if its service isn't free.

Chronicle of Higher Education
www.chronicle.merit.edu

This is a good place to find information on changes in the finaid process.

Citibank Student Loan Corporation
www.citibank.com/student/CSLC.html

Citibank provides practical advice for planning and financing college along with a smorgasbord of finaid loans and financing plans.

College Board Online
www.collegeboard.org

This site offers information about colleges, financial aid, admission, entrance exams, and FAQs.

CollegeEdge
www.CollegeEdge.com

CollegeEdge offers a scholarship search of finaid at 3,443 educational institutions and 3,973 scholarship sponsors. Involving a short questionnaire, CollegeEdge enables you to explore specific schools, ferreting out info on tuition and fees, finaid application procedures, payment plans, and statistics. The site also contains relevant articles and an "Ask CollegeEdge" question and answer forum.

College Fund Finder
www.apollo.co.uk/a/cff

This site is a financial search service.

College Xpress
www.collegexpress.com/index.html

Providing information on college, admission, and finaid for every level of student, this site includes financial aid databases and hot links.

CollegeSelect
www.cyber-u.com

CollegeSelect provides finaid and registration information for four-year U.S. colleges. You must register to use the search engine and EFC calculator.

Department of Education, Office of Postsecondary Education
www.ed.gov/offices/OPE/Students

This government site allows you to file your FAFSA online. It gives awesome, step-by-step instructions on how to begin your quest for college money and what to do if your student loan goes into default, plus a bonus compilation of finaid basics. The site is tricked out with directories and links to colleges listed by type.

EASI — Easy Access for Students and Institutions
www.easi.ed.gov

EASI neatly organizes all the major federal loans and grants into a concise list with links to their respective sites. The site exposes you to details that finaid seekers commonly overlook. EASI covers what to do after college when you start giving back loan money.

Ecola Directories College Locator
www.ecola.com/college

This site contains more than 2,500 links to colleges and universities, including their libraries and alumni pages.

Educaid
www.educaid.com

This site guides you on loans and gives behind-the-scenes info on finaid resources and loan programs.

Elm Resources
www.elmresources.com

This site offers online access to loan information, providing numbers for loan amounts and disbursements. The site does not require you to submit personal financial information.

ExPAN Scholarship Search
www.collegeboard.org/fundfinder/bin/fundfind01.pl

ExPAN is an online version of the College Board's FUND FINDER scholarship database. After you enter information about yourself, the search returns scholarships that you're eligible for. This service is *gratis* (free) and includes thousands of colleges.

FAFSA Express
www.ed.gov/offices/OPE/express.html

This cutting-edge site allows you to download, complete, and electronically submit the FAFSA form. You must still print out the signature sheet and snail-mail it back; the application only gets processed when the U.S. Department of Education gets your signature; schools get the results 72 hours later.

fastWEB
www.fastweb.com

fastWEB has a huge database of scholarships, fellowships, grants, and loans. On this site, you can set up a personalized mailbox and have customized finaid info mailed directly to you. You enter gobs of information about yourself when you apply for a mailbox (things like ethnicity, religion, desired major, age, veteran status, and so forth); for your efforts, fastWEB mails you contact info and requirements for new scholarships that best match your information.

FinAid — The Financial Aid Information Page
www.finaid.org

This site is a major financial aid information page on the Net. No other site even comes close to having the massive amount of guidance that this site provides. On this page, you can use finaid calculators, look up laws and lenders, find specialized scholarships, or browse top-drawer links to other terrific sites.

Financial Aid Professional Associations
www.finaid.org/finaid/faa/assocs.html

This site links you to professional associations for finaid administrators and related disciplines. Here's a good place to give your finaid administrator's practices the once-over.

Financial Aid Newsgroup
www.soc.college.financial-aid

Network and discuss financial aid issues on this newsgroup. The newsgroup often provides contacts and insider information that you can't find anywhere else on the Internet.

Independence Federal Savings Bank
www.ifsb.com

This site offers comprehensive information on bank's loans and answers important FAQs about finaid.

KapLoan
www.kaploan.com

KapLoan presents well-organized information about loans for parents or students and an online form to request more information about specific finaid. Free software calculates your expected family contribution. (See the software section later in this chapter.)

MOLIS Scholarship Search
www.fie.com/molis/scholar.htm

Designed especially to help major minority groups find and get scholarships, MOLIS has a straightforward search engine to find all the scholarships that match your race, gender, age, and location.

NACAC — National Association of College Admissions Counselors
www.nacac.com

This site provides useful, behind-the-scenes info on finaid issues and developments in the field.

Peterson's Education Center
www.petersons.com/resources/finance.html

Peterson's is famous as one of the best sites on the web. Its finaid section is on par with the rest of the site, having extensive financial aid info for beginners and experts alike. This site also provides an admissions calendar so you can synchronize with the rest of the finaid world.

The Princeton Review
www.review.com/College/Find/index.html

This site provides a very basic, step-by-step explanation of procedures and forms you must complete to get finaid. The site has a kickin' tutorial on the many types of loans and how to get them.

PHEAA (Pennsylvania Higher Education Assistance Authority)
www.pheaa.org

At this site, find finaid resources, advice on mapping your future, and info on institutions.

RSP Funding Focus
America Online: keyword **RSP**

This site has a searchable database of finaid sources; in its Money Trail Message Center, chatters discuss nonprofit fundraising, business ventures, and so on.

Sallie Mae
www.slma.com/xalternate.html

This site offers a hard-core look at the ins and outs of loans, lenders, and repayment. It provides several calculators for interest, repayment, and more. You can even transfer values from calculator to calculator as you work out the numbers. Downloadable versions are available. (See the software section later in this chapter.)

Scholarship Resource Network TM., Daigle and Vierra, Inc.
www.rams.com/srn

This site offers a free scholarship search service and information for students; it also links to a loan forgiveness directory.

Special Operations, The Warrior Foundation
www.specialops.org

This site advertises the foundation's own heavy-duty finaid and offers thorough advice on financing and entering college.

Student Services
www.studentservices.com/search

This site offers an impressive, searchable database of more than 180,000 finaid sources, concentrated in private sector funding for U.S. college students. It requires on-site registration.

The Student Guide
www.ed.gov/prog_info/SFA/StudentGuide/1997-8

This yearly service provided by the U.S. Department of Education tells you all about eligibility, deadlines, and mounds of information on government grants and loans. All of the information is current and accurate.

U.S. Bank
www.usbank.com/personal/index.html

This site helps answer serious questions about attending college and taking and applying for loans. It also offers a list of hot links on related topics.

U.S. Department of Education
www.ed.gov/offices/OPE/Students/index.html

This government site offers a range of full-on information and advice, including new procedures used in awarding aid.

U.S. News.Edu
www.usnews.com/usnews/edu

This *U.S. News and World Report* site gives the latest stats and rankings of fields and schools, helping you make serious choices about them.

Yahoo!'s Financial Aid Search
www.yahoo.com/Education/Financial_Aid/

This site allows you to locate online finaid and provides a long link-list of college finaid offices listed alphabetically by college.

Finaid Telephone Numbers

Telephone these agencies for a variety of financial aid services.

Financial aid applications

Call these offices for information about applying for aid.

✔ **California Student Aid Commission (Cal Grants)** 916-445-0880

✔ **College Scholarship Service (CSS)** 609-771-7725

✔ **Questions about Financial Aid PROFILE** 800-778-6888

✔ **Federal Student Aid Information Center (U.S. Department of Education)**

- Federal Financial Aid 800-433-3243

  The government provides this toll-free number to provide you information about federally subsidized loans, grants, and scholarships. Operators are on hand to answer questions about your FAFSA or a particular school's loan interest rates.

- Fraud/Waste/Abuse of Federal Student Aid Funds 800-647-8733 (press 3)

- Immigration and Naturalization Services (INS) 800-870-3676

- Internal Revenue Service (IRS) 800-829-1040

- Duplicate/ Missing Student Aid Report (SAR) 319-337-5665

  You can find out your SAR's status or request a copy of your Student Aid Report (SAR).

✔ **National and Community Service Program (AmeriCorps)** 800-942-2677

✔ **Selective Service** 847-688-6888

✔ **Social Security Administration** 800-772-1213

✔ **State Student Assistance Commission of Indiana (SSACI)** 317-232-2350

✔ **National Council of Education Opportunity Association** 202-347-7430

Included here are TRIO Programs — Upward Bound, Student Support, Talent Search, Educational Opportunities, and Ronald E. McNair Post-baccalaureate Achievement. Representatives can direct you to colleges and programs in your state.

Information hotlines

Call these numbers for the hottest finaid information around.

✔ **College Answer Service (Sallie Mae)** 800-222-7182 or 800-239-4211

You can call this hotline to receive brochures about how to pay and borrow for college.

✔ **College Savings Bank** 800-888-2723

- ✔ **College Scholarship Service** 609-771-7725 or for PROFILE 800-778-6888
- ✔ **Educaid — The Student Loan Specialists** 800-776-2344
- ✔ **FAFSA Express Questions** 800-801-0576
- ✔ **fastWEB** 800-327-8932
- ✔ **Federal Student Aid Hotline** (U.S. Dept of Education) 800-433-3243
- ✔ **Kaplan Student Loan Information Program** 888-527-5626

Direct loans

Direct Loans are serviced by the U.S. Department of Education.

- ✔ **Direct Loan Origination Center** (Applicant Services) 800-557-7394
- ✔ **Direct Loan Origination Center** (Consolidation) 800-557-7392
- ✔ **Direct Loan Servicing Center** 800-848-0979
- ✔ **Direct Loan Servicing Center Consolidation Department** 800-848-0982
- ✔ **Direct Loan Servicing Center** (Collections) 800-848-0981
- ✔ **Direct Loan Servicing Center** (Debt Collection Service) 800-621-3115
- ✔ **Direct Loan School Relations** (Origination & Servicing) 800-848-0978

Loan programs

Loan programs are available from the following banks and other institutions:

- ✔ **Access Group** 800-282-1550
- ✔ **American Express College Loan Program** 800-814-4595
- ✔ **Bank of America**
    - Bank of America National Student Lending 800-344-8382
    - Bank of America (Texas Student Loan Center) 800-442-0567
    - Bank of America (loans in Idaho, Seattle, and Washington) 800-535-4671
- ✔ **Bank of Boston** 800-226-7866
- ✔ **Bank One Educational Finance Group** 800-487-4404
- ✔ **Chase Manhattan Bank Educational Loans** 800-242-7339
- ✔ **Citibank Student Loan Corporation** 800-692-8200

- Commerce Bank 800-666-3910
- Connecticut Student Loan Foundation (CSLF) 860-257-4001, ext. 470
- Crestar Bank's Student Lending Department 800-552-3006
- EduServ Technologies 800-445-4236
- Eduserve's ConSern Loans for Education 800-732-2178
- Extra Credit Extra Time 800-874-9390
- First Union Education Loan Services 800-955-8805
- Fleet Education Finance 800-235-3385
- GATE Student Loan Program 800-895-4283
- Heal Loans (Medical — graduate) 301-443-1540
- Independence Federal Savings Bank 800-824-7044
- KeyBank USA 800-539-5363
- Law-Access Group 800-282-1550
- Massachusetts Educational Financing Authority 800-842-1531
- MBA Loans (Graduate students) 888-440-4622
- MED Loans 800-858-5050
- Mellon Bank EduCheck 800-366-7011
- Nellie Mae (Excel and Share Loan Programs) 800-634-9308
- Norwest Student Loan Center 800-658-3567
- PHEAA (Graduate Loan Center, division of Pennsylvania Higher Education Assistance Agency) 800-446-8210
- Sandy Spring National Bank 301-774-8488
- Sallie Mae (College Answer Service) 800-239-4211
- Signet Bank Educational Funding 800-434-1988
- TERI Supplemental (The Educational Resources Institute) 800-255-8374
- United Student Aid Funds (Option 4) 800-635-3785

Loan processing centers

These agencies clear the loans for disbursements. If you want to know what's happened to your loan application, these agencies can tell you:

- ✔ **American Student Assistance** 800-999-9080
- ✔ **New York State Higher Education Services Corporation (HESC)** 800-642-6234
- ✔ **PHEAA (Pennsylvania Higher Education Assistance Authority)** 800-692-7392
- ✔ **Texas Guaranteed Student Loan Corporation (TGSLC)** 800-845-6267
- ✔ **United Student Aid Funds** 800-824-7044

Loan consolidation

The following let you consolidate your loans into one manageable monthly payment:

- ✔ **Nellie Mae** 800-634-9308
- ✔ **PHEAA (Pennsylvania Higher Education Assistance Agency)** 800-692-7392
- ✔ **Sallie Mae Educational Loan Center** 800-524-9100

Loan forgiveness program

Call the **National College Scholarship Foundation** at 301-548-9423 for information about its loan forgiveness program.

Tuition payment plans

Tuition payment plans are available through the following organizations:

- ✔ **Academic Management Services (AMS)** 800-635-0120
- ✔ **EduServ Tuition Installment Plan (TIP)** 800-445-4236
- ✔ **FACTS Tuition Management System** 800-624-7092
- ✔ **Key Education Resources and Knight College Resources Group** 800-225-6783
- ✔ **Tuition Management Systems, Inc. (TMS)** 800-722-4867

College saving programs

Call these numbers for information about baccalaureate accounts:

- ✔ **College Board** 212-713-8000
- ✔ **College Savings Bank** 800-888-2723

State prepaid tuition plans

These states have prepaid tuition plans. Call for more information:

- ✔ **Alabama** 800-252-7228
- ✔ **Alaska** 907-474-7469
- ✔ **Colorado** 800-478-5651
- ✔ **Florida** 800-552-4723
- ✔ **Indiana** 317-232-6386
- ✔ **Kentucky** 800-928-8926
- ✔ **Louisiana** 800-259-5626 x1012
- ✔ **Maryland** 800-903-7875
- ✔ **Massachusetts** 800-449-6332 x1

- ✔ **Michigan** 800-243-2847
- ✔ **Mississippi** 800-987-4450
- ✔ **New Jersey** 800-792-8670
- ✔ **Ohio** 800-589-6882 or 800- 233-6734
- ✔ **Pennsylvania** 800-440-4000
- ✔ **Tennessee** 888-486-2378
- ✔ **Texas** 800-445-4723
- ✔ **Virginia** 888-567-0540
- ✔ **Wisconsin** 888-338-3789

Benefits grow for state tuition plans

Until now, families could contribute to qualified state-sponsored prepaid tuition plans for expenses that cover tuition, fees, books, supplies, and required equipment but not room and board. The new tax law changes this by allowing prepayment of reasonable room and board costs of a student enrolled at least half-time. The contributions on the account are not taxed. The (interest) gain on the account isn't taxed until withdrawals to pay for school; you can apply your Hope or Lifetime Learning credits to the gain. Get details from your state's prepaid tuition plan.

Miscellaneous

These groups can provide information about more finaid opportunities:

- ✔ **American Association of University Women Educational Foundation** 319-337-1716

- ✔ **Academic Common Market** 410-974-2750

- ✔ **Council of Better Business Bureaus** 703-276-0100

- ✔ **Institute of International Education** 212-883-8200

- ✔ **National Association for College Admissions Counseling** 703-836-2222

- ✔ **Americorps National and Community Service Program** 800-942-2677

- ✔ **USA Group** 800-562-6872

- ✔ **U.S. Department of Education, Inspector General Hotline** 800-647-8733

- ✔ **Western Interstate Commission for Higher Education** 303-541-0210

Free Software

Take advantage of the free software offered by the following groups:

- ✔ **Apply Technology**
  www.weapply.com

  Software, links, and awesome electronic applications to 500 colleges.

- ✔ **CollegeCalc** by Sallie Mae

  A hardcore collection of calculators and information. In this free package, you receive calculators for loan repayment, future college costs, expected family contribution, accrued interest, and estimated borrowing needs. You also get information about specific loans and procedures.

- ✔ **ExPAN** — The College Board, 800-223-9726

  Ask — no, beg — your school for this comprehensive information delivery system that links schools, colleges, students and parents. ExPAN software offers a searchable database with more than 3,200 two- and four-year colleges plus graduate and professional schools, electronic application forms, financial planning and FUND FINDER, a financial aid tutorial with college cost data and 3,300+ scholarships verified annually. (ExPAN isn't a product for home use but is available at high schools throughout the United States and many locations abroad.)

✔ **John Hancock Financial Aid Software** 800-633-1809

Software that helps you plan your college education. Number-crunches your estimated future tuition and room and board at more than 1,500 public and private schools. Available for Mac and Windows.

✔ **KapLoan Financial Contribution Estimator**
www.kaploan.com/software.html

Though it looks like a calculator, this handy software helps you totally simplify the college aid process. After you enter your income, assets, and other variables, the program displays your Expected Family Contribution. Available for download in Mac or Windows format on KapLoan's Web site (mentioned in "Internet Resources" earlier in this chapter).

Keeping Ahead of the Information Age

As we often say, we've checked and rechecked these resources into oblivion, but things electronic change quickly, so periodically, we update this list on the ...*For Dummies* Web site: www.dummies.com (click on *College Financial Aid For Dummies*).

Chapter 13

Just the FAQs: Dr. Davis Answers Your Questions

*F*amilies with college-bound students have turned to Dr. Herm Davis for guidance for more than 25 years. Students and parents have asked questions and received answers about virtually every aspect of the financial aid system. Here are *FAQs* (frequently asked questions) from Dr. Davis's vast data bank that answer many of your nagging, unsolved mysteries:

  ✔ The first FAQ group addresses an assortment of nitty-gritty concerns, including panic-buttons for all students when it's time to pay tuition and you don't have dollar one.

  ✔ The second FAQ group deals with emergency funding.

  ✔ The third FAQ group discusses independent student status.

  ✔ The fourth FAQ group covers transfer students' problems.

Nitty-Gritty FAQs

Among the thousands of questions he has fielded, these are evergreens. They turn up again and again.

How long do I have to wait for a response from the finaid office? What should I do if I sent my FAFSA and have no response after six weeks?

First, call the FAFSA information center at 319-337-5665.

The odds are that your FAFSA has been processed and for one reason or another your SAR (see Chapter 3) was lost in the mail. Second, call your college's financial aid office to see if they have received the results of your FAFSA. Let your finaid counselor know that you did file on time and that, even though you don't have your copy of the SAR, you are on the ball and taking the responsibility for your documentation.

Now go the extra mile. Tell your finaid counselor that you are sending a copy of your FAFSA, federal tax Form 1040 for parents and yourself, and W-2 forms for parents and yourself to the finaid office by certified mail. In essence, you are doing the financial aid counselor's job for him or her. This approach wins you friends in the finaid office.

Send your refiled FAFSA by regular mail. Don't send your refiled FAFSA by certified mail because it goes to a post office box, where no one signs for it.

If the FAFSA information center personnel asks you when you filed your FAFSA and you say "nine weeks ago," they'll say it must have been lost in the mail and you should refile. Do so.

Will half-time status lessen my chances of winning financial aid?

Many private and school-awarded scholarships are for full-time students only. Of those that are not, you are likely to receive the amount proportional to being a half-time or three-quarters-time student.

If I submit my FAFSA with the wrong Social Security number, how can I correct my mistake?

If you identified this error early in the processing year (January or February), complete a new FAFSA and resubmit it with the correct Social Security number. You'll then get a control number that matches your Social Security number.

But if you found your goof late in the process, you should correct your SAR and mail it in with your correct Social Security number. Unfortunately, the control number on your SAR will remain that of the wrong Social Security number. The good news is that the correct Social Security number will be read at college financial aid offices even though the control number is not changed.

Why shouldn't you submit a new SAR with the right number so that everything is neat and orderly? Some state scholarship boards and some colleges award funds based on the date that the FAFSA was submitted. Your original FAFSA has seniority and also confirms that you met all deadlines for all awards.

If my family qualifies for the simplified needs test, should I still fill out Section G on the FAFSA?

Section G is the student and parental asset area. If a parent can file a 1040A or EZ tax form and earns less than $50,000 annually, the parents do not have to fill out Section G listing assets to receive federal aid.

But some states and most private colleges require the asset information in Section G so they can estimate their own finaid awards. This information won't affect your eligibility for federal finaid. In general, include the information even if none of your schools of choice request it.

In short, completing Section G doesn't hurt your chances.

If my parents are divorced or separated, who fills out the FAFSA?

The *custodial parent* (the parent with whom you've lived with the most for the past 12 months) fills out the FAFSA. If you haven't received support from either parent during the past 12 months, use the most recent calendar year for which you received some support from a parent or lived with a parent.

When determining household size, list those who live with the parent who continually provides more than half of your support. Oddly enough, even if the custodial parent provides less than half of your financial support, she or he can also list you as a member of his or her household.

Note that the child support must be included on the FAFSA.

Am I sunk if my divorced mother cannot get her ex-husband (my natural father) to complete a divorced/separated statement that is required by a high-cost private college?

You could be. Some private colleges are adamant about receiving information on both of the natural parents before they consider your file complete. In essence, these colleges want to financially remarry the natural parents to see if, as a family unit, they can support your college expenses.

If your father has remarried and has started a new family, colleges may be more lenient on this requirement. When you can document that the couple has been separated or divorced for a relatively long period of time, the college is probably going to be lenient. If the natural father has been making reasonable child support payments and has indicated that he is willing to pass those payments through to the college while you're enrolled, the college becomes downright agreeable.

The bottom line is that high-cost colleges expect natural parents to help support your college education.

Bear in mind that this problem applies only to private colleges and does not affect your FAFSA for federal funds.

What if I have been awarded finaid but the college tuition bill arrives before the aid shows up on my student account at college?

At most colleges you must pay bills when they are due or risk losing your classes. You may request a deferment if you have proof of your finaid award (for example, an award letter).

Contact the college financial aid office to ask if your award letter has been processed. Request a faxed copy of that letter for your records. If your tuition bill doesn't show your finaid award, return the bill to the student billing office with a copy of your award letter. Include a check for the difference and a note that asks the student billing office staff to credit your award money toward the bill. Follow up this mailing with a call to the student billing office asking if your action is all that is required.

If you must ask for a deferment, realize that even deferments are temporary. A loan from a relative, friend, or institution may keep you in good standing while you await the finaid award or loan. Most colleges accept credit cards.

If I temporarily leave school, does loan repayment begin immediately? What happens to my finaid if I withdraw?

Most loans provide a grace period before repayment begins. Some even wait to bill borrowers (for the principal, interest, or both) until they have an income if a *forbearance* has been arranged in advance(see Chapter 23).

If you plan to return to school, many loans stall repayment or only require that you pay the interest. Consult your loan agreement or lender for specific limitations, as some loans defer for limited time periods, while others require documents from you or your college verifying your intent to return to school.

You'll probably need to fill out some forms for the school's financial aid or registrar's office that formalize your withdrawal. Most schools have their own policies for refunding tuition and reimbursing finaid funds. Typically, colleges do not refund money to students after the established refund period — the first three or four weeks — has passed.

Are my parents responsible for loans in my name?

The Federal Perkins, Federal Stafford, and Direct Student loans do not require a co-signer or endorsement from parents. Your parents are responsible only for Federal PLUS loans and other loans taken out in their name(s). If your parents want to help pay off your loan, they can ask your lender to automatically deduct monthly payments from their bank accounts. But if they forget a payment, the problem is yours.

Q If I were awarded aid as an early decision student and I change my mind about attending the school, what happens?

The early decision process normally only affects elite colleges, and their policies vary. No regulations or rules cover early decision changes. If it happens to you, you'll have to deal with it on an individual-case basis. Best advice: Get in touch with the financial aid counselor at the new school as quickly as possible.

Q Must I report outside scholarships to my school's financial aid office?

Yes, you are supposed to report all sources of aid. Scholarship checks usually are written to the college you designate; if a strange award turns up in your name, you lose credibility. Although finaid administrators must adjust your award accordingly, some universities use outside scholarships to reduce the amount of self-help or loan aid they award.

You can negotiate the issue of having your school aid reduced by the amount you win in an outside scholarship. Some colleges encourage students to bring in outside awards, and may match the funds rather than take money away. For negotiating hints, see Chapter 9.

Q What if my family didn't earn enough to pay the expected contribution?

Contact your school finaid counselor. Inform the counselor of the special circumstances that kept your family from earning what you anticipated. Your loan or other finaid may increase due to the cutback; many offices require that your family document the shortfall in writing.

Q My family bought a tuition prepayment plan for me. Must the plan be reported as an asset on my FAFSA?

No. Tuition prepayment plans are excluded from being reported as an asset on the FAFSA.

Q I have a trust fund split between my mother and myself. Do I have to report this as an asset on my FAFSA?

Yes. A trust fund in the name of a specific person should be reported as that person's asset on applications for aid. When the trust is owned jointly, the value is split for reporting purposes unless the terms of the trust specify another method of dividing the money.

An exception is when you have a large savings account or trust because of a car accident. A court probably restricted the trust to pay for future medical bills. When a trust is restricted by court order, do not report it as an asset.

Panic-Button FAQs

These questions focus on urgent and immediate needs for cash to pay for college.

School opens next month. What should I do if I have no finaid and the semester is about to begin? What if I miss the application deadline?

If you haven't yet applied for finaid, contact your college's financial aid counselor instantly to find out what you must do to apply. Some offices may accept a copy of your FAFSA and do some preliminary calculations while they await the official copy.

If you qualify, you probably still have a shot at the Federal Pell grant and/or the Federal Stafford Student Loan. Financial aid officials normally will extend credit up to the amount of the unsubsidized student loan.

All parents who have good credit are eligible to participate in the Federal PLUS loans, which you'll remember, is not based on demonstrated need.

Some colleges offer low-interest *bridge loans* to cover student emergency needs. These 90-day loans bridge your financial gap until other funds can be rounded up.

You've probably missed deadlines for state aid, college scholarships, and private gift programs. You may have to ask for a 30-day extension to pay your account.

Here's a neat move: Charge your tuition, especially at high-cost colleges, to a credit card that rewards plastic spending with free airline mileage. Then quickly switch the high-interest credit card tab with a lower-cost, long-term loan.

Loan and credit applications take about five to ten working days to process; add delays related to enrollment verification and miscellaneous information processing, and even the fastest loan application may take up to 20 days.

If you win no financial aid, you'd probably need a loan anyway; if you do win finaid, you may be able to reshuffle your budget and pay off loans pronto.

Better luck next semester when you meet deadlines.

If you've already applied but received no response, ask your finaid office for a status report on your application. Financial aid offices are so busy that they rarely have the time to call applicants who may have omitted crucial information or documents. If your award has come through, ask when it will be *reconciled* (posted) to your student account.

Q **The school won't take credit cards, and the bill isn't paid. What now?**

Register for the minimum hours of enrollment to be eligible for financial aid, which is half-time or six semester hours, and add credit hours when funds are forthcoming.

Q **What other payment options are available in an emergency?**

Most colleges offer a tuition installment plan through which you can pay off your student bill with a number of payments within a specific time period, typically the semester.

The tuition installment plans require a maximum of three or four installment payments at no interest or market-rate interest. Colleges charge a small administrative fee for handling the paperwork, but such a plan may buy time for getting your financial aid award cleared up.

Another variation: tuition payment plans. These plans are sponsored by your college or by a third-party agency (contractor) that has been authorized by the college to administer the program on its behalf. Repayment schedules for these plans vary, ranging from ten months to years to pay off four years of a college education.

Independent Student FAQs

Students on their own — not supported by families — have a smaller income and thus qualify for higher amounts of financial aid.

Q **What are the requirements to become an independent student?**

You are considered independent if you are 24 years old. Otherwise, you must meet one of the following criteria:

- ✔ You are a veteran of the U.S. Armed Forces.
- ✔ You are an orphan or ward of the court.
- ✔ You have legal dependents (children) other than a spouse.

✔ You are married.

✔ You are a graduate or professional student (your parents may be able to claim you as a U.S. tax exemption for the years you are in graduate or professional school if you qualify under IRS guidelines).

 My parents want me to pay my own way, but their income kept me from earning adequate finaid. Am I out of luck?

Just about. Financial aid administrators generally don't award aid or declare students independent simply because their parents won't foot the tuition bill. They usually measure your family's ability to pay for college, not its willingness. The ugly truth is that if your parents don't cooperate, you will have to pay your own way or win the lottery. If you have good grades, seek merit-based finaid and consider working part-time while attending school half-time.

Call or write to your finaid office explaining your situation. Ask your finaid counselor for suggestions. The school may accept a notarized statement of parent nonsupport as proof that you are independent, if you can show that you have reasonable income and expense receipts that prove you have been supporting yourself.

A financial aid counselor can override students' dependency status, case-by-case, using his or her *professional judgment*. If your parents are incarcerated, or you can document an adversarial relationship (letters from your counselor or social worker, a protection-from-abuse order, or a restraining order, for example), the financial aid counselor may declare you independent.

Two more ideas: Apply for a job at the college human resource office; at some colleges, employees get free or reduced tuition. Or attend night school, which may be less expensive than day school.

Transfer Student FAQs

A *transfer student* ends enrollment in one institution and subsequently enrolls in another, usually with *advanced standing credit* (meaning credits earned at one college transfer to another so that the student doesn't have to start over from scratch).

The term is sometimes allied to students who transfer from one college to another within an institution. A popular transfer is from a two-year community college to a four-year institution. But as an undergraduate, a transfer from one college to another is possible at any time before the senior year of college.

Transfer students make their moves either in the fall at the beginning of the academic year, or by mid-year, at the beginning a new semester or quarter.

Can transfer students get financial aid?

Yes. Students must reapply annually for aid, which levels the playing field every year for everyone. Financial aid counselors see little difference between a transfer student's application for aid and a continuing student's.

Must I have a financial aid transcript?

Yes. You need a financial aid transcript (FAT). Even if you never applied for aid, the transfer college needs to document that fact. Secondly, you may be able to transfer any private scholarship aid you're currently receiving at your original institution to the transfer institution. Finally, if you don't submit this document, your application may sit under a paperweight for months while others fly past on the assembly line towards the finaid finish.

What should I do if I'm transferring, have never applied for finaid, and don't know the routine. What do I need?

Collect your and your parents' tax forms and W-2s. Most colleges also require the FAT (financial aid transcript), even if you've never applied for financial aid. Obtain the FAFSA form at your new or old school, complete it, and ask the financial aid office at the new college if special documentation is required.

What paperwork should I do to apply for finaid if I'm transferring?

If you've already completed your FAFSA and SAR for your present college, call the FAFSA information center at 319-337-5665 and ask them to send the SAR to your new college. You'll need the PIN number on the SAR to make this request. Otherwise, correct Part II of your SAR (naming colleges you plan to attend) and add your transfer school. Some colleges to which you're transferring take the initiative by using the Federal Electronic Data Exchange to instantly update your record.

Whom should I notify if I transfer?

Notify the student billing office at both the old and the new college and your lender(s), and scholarship providers. Advise your new financial aid office as well.

If I transfer mid-semester and apply for finaid last-minute, what finaid can I expect?

If you're applying mid-year, you're probably too late to receive priority for institutional aid because college funds are committed early in the awarding season. You may win a combination of federal grants and loans plus state and outside private scholarships. If you already receive outside private aid through your original college, you may be able to transfer that aid; your new college finaid office can evaluate this possibility.

Is it better to apply for finaid at the end of the academic year?

No. You should apply as early in the financial aid season as possible, right after January 1.

Transfer students applying at the beginning of the academic year usually receive the same privileges as other returning students and have the same shot at federal and state funds as anyone else. Some colleges entice transfer students with generous financial aid.

Additional reading

For more information about transferring, see the following resource:

The Transfer Student's Guide to Changing Colleges by Sidonia Dalby and Sally Rubenstone; 1993; Macmillan/Arco/Prentice Hall; 800-858-7674.

Part III
Finaid Planning for the Long Haul

The 5th Wave   By Rich Tennant

"I really can't have a relationship now –
I'm afraid it might impact my
'needs analysis form'."

In this part ...

You wouldn't try rock climbing unless you were in the best of shape. For that matter, you probably wouldn't try a mountain hike without conditioning your body. You spent a lot of time preparing for college, hoisting loads of homework and power-lifting late into the night for exams. So what makes you think you can enter the college finance championships without stretching a financial muscle or two?

You understand that financing higher education takes preparation, or you wouldn't be reading this book. This part conditions you closer to financial fitness with detailed examinations of savings and borrowing strategies and efficient ways to save money, and helps you warm up for the next four years and beyond.

Chapter 14

Choosing a College Financial Aid Planner

*M*eet a new arrival on the college scene: the college financial aid planner, an expert who leads families through the Byzantine aid process, designs strategies on how to fill out forms to attract the maximum gift aid, and teaches poker-playing techniques for smartly handling your finaid hand of cards.

College financial aid planners cost money but save more. At least, that's how their service is supposed to work. Over a four-year period, expert planners can save you thousands of dollars.

Payment ranges from hourly charges, often $125 per hour, to package prices of more than $500 for a year's service. The size of a reasonable fee depends upon the level of service you need.

Suppose you only want your FAFSA completed. Are your financial affairs simple or complex? If your money matters are uncomplicated and you hired a tax preparer to complete a short form 1040A or 1040EZ, you probably paid about $50. Expect to pay approximately the same amount for your rudimentary FAFSA.

If, however, your fiscal situation is complex enough to require a 1040 long form, you probably paid a tax preparer up to $200 to fill it out. Expect to pay a finaid broker in the same neighborhood for a comparable task.

Finaid planners: What's in a name

Private financial aid experts are also called:

- College specialists
- Financial aid consultants
- CPAs
- Financial planners
- Financial aid brokers

Their services are often called:

- College aid advising
- College-bound financial planning services
- College financial services
- Education credit company
- Independent college counseling
- Educational consulting
- Financial aid and admissions consulting
- College funding
- Financial services

Should a college financial aid planner's charges ever be higher? Yes, when you are middle-income and need to learn about alternative loans, state residency requirements, institutional policies on award packaging, financial aid appeal processes, or future financial aid award structuring. In this situation, it may be well worth investing as much as $300 to $500 per year with a college financial aid planner.

Still higher? Probably not.

Avoid planners who hit high-C-notes, charging up to $1,500 per year. The more you pay for services *does not* mean the more you'll save in financial aid.

Choosing Experts, Not Hustlers

Anyone can hang out a finaid shingle. No certification, degree, or license requirement exists for an individual to open a financial aid service and charge a fee for consulting.

Like many other consultants, financial aid professionals come in three basic groups: *experts, incompetents,* and *hustlers*.

Experts have special knowledge derived from training or experience. Many, perhaps most, financial aid experts have worked as financial aid counselors on a college campus. Sometimes, they later were hired by banks or loan agencies and delivered education loans to college students and their families. A few who have professional counseling degrees worked first for foundations or private financial aid family services.

Experts have been in the field and know the process from inside out:

- ✔ They know which regulations are changing and who will be affected by the changes.

- ✔ They have returning clients from across the United States who consistently feed them with information from the finaid trenches.

- ✔ They place themselves on call throughout the financial aid process to keep their clients from freaking out with worry.

- ✔ They know which appeal letters work with which colleges.

- ✔ They know which out-of-state public universities award only loans and jobs and no gift aid.

- ✔ They are willing to certify on the FAFSA that they assisted in preparing the FAFSA as required by federal regulation.

In one way or the other, the real experts are deep inside the financial aid system.

Incompetents may have exhaustive knowledge of taxes or other financial planning strategies but lack detailed, up-to-date knowledge of local state educational grants, specific scholarships, or effective ways to deal with the financial aid structure at various institutions. They crunch numbers and hopes.

Hustlers are entrepreneurs who usually have superficial if any knowledge, recommend unethical strategies, guarantee results, overcharge, or do a number of other numbers on you. Stay clear of these folks. It's all pain and no gain for you.

A Guide to Finding Experts

To protect yourself, a few guidelines are in order.

Get recommendations

Referrals from satisfied clients work best. Also call your high school guidance counselor and colleges' financial aid counselors. The expert will be recommended; the incompetent or hustler will not.

Hustlers and incompetents know they're recommendation-free, so they use smoke and mirrors to look reputable. They claim that they belong to a local better business bureau, a state professional financial aid association, or even the National Association of Student Financial Aid Administrators. They may, in fact, be members. Anyone can become a member of these organizations by paying membership dues.

Seek emphasis on four-year planning

The expert cares enough about your four-year financial aid plan to develop long-range designs that accommodate the multitude of documents, regulations, and college inquiries. The expert does all this work without compromising ethics or breaking rules or regulations.

The incompetent focuses on paying for a single year and rarely focuses on a comprehensive plan.

The hustler calls you nightly with a sales pitch about how cleverly the hustler can fill out the FAFSA (which, you may notice, warns that lies can bring $10,000 fines and/or a jail sentence).

Hustlers have been known to direct parents to keep two sets of forms, one for the IRS and the other for the completion of the FAFSA — this duplicity may be discovered if a college asks for a signed waiver to obtain tax records from the IRS.

Another hustler-special is the so-called *Grannie Loan.* Hustlers frequently tell families to lower the Expected Family Contribution by claiming that family assets belong to others. They even advise clients to write letters claiming that the family home has been sold to the grandparents for $50 or so with certain stipulations. The asset disappears because, in theory, it's now in the grandparents' hands. College officials aren't fooled by this subterfuge.

Expect a place of business

The expert asks you to come to his or her office, which may be a residence, because that's where the professional resources are located to assist in setting up a financial aid plan. The incompetent may also invite you to an office. The hustler comes to your house with a three-ring binder promising you great results no matter what college you pursue.

Anticipate issues to be discussed

The expert discusses such topics as

- ✔ **Family structure:** The parental legal status: married, separated, thinking about separation, divorced, single, or widowed (some colleges require a separated or divorced statement)

- ✔ **Home equity:** The family's equity in its primary home (to anticipate possible effects on other forms and documents required by a college)

- ✔ **Retirement accounts:** The history of retirement accounts (these funds must be reported on some college applications)

- ✔ **Employment history:** The parents' job record (some colleges require business and farm supplemental documents) and similar subjects

The incompetent or hustler probably won't know about these issues and is unlikely to bring them up or answer a question intelligently.

Avoid influence peddling

The expert never promises to slip in a college's side door to intercede with the financial aid office on behalf of a client. The expert knows that the college's financial aid counselor has high legal exposure if student confidentiality is breached. Influence peddling doesn't happen among reputable professionals, including incompetent planners.

The hustler, by contrast, pretends to have connections with college financial aid counselors that make a gift award "a sure thing."

Pay only for services rendered

The expert charges either by the hour or by the year. Ditto the incompetent but honest broker.

The hustler wants to be paid up-front for four years. If you quit school before graduation, don't expect a refund. The hustler never gives money back.

Expert Planners Put Money in Your Bank

Question: Can you do everything for yourself for free that a college financial aid planner does for a fee?

Answer: Yes.

Better question: Can you do so as cheaply?

Answer: Probably not.

From Dr. Davis's files, here are three case histories that show how a financial aid planner can win you more than his or her fee while your do-it-yourself approach may cost you a modest fortune:

- ✔ **$50,000 Savings:** Paul wanted to become an aeronautical engineer to launch a career as a commercial airline pilot. Dr. Davis advised Paul to price the program at the University of North Dakota (UND), where the cost was less than half that of Embry-Riddle Aeronautical University in Florida. Plus, UND offered more financial aid. The net saving to the student and his family exceeded $50,000.

- ✔ **$30,000 Savings:** Harry, a Maryland resident, narrowed his choice of engineering schools to Virginia Polytechnic Institute, which offered out-of-state students only self-help (loans and work).

    Upon Dr. Davis' recommendation, Harry then applied to Texas A & M and its militaristic Cadet Corps. Acceptance into the Cadet Corps carries a $2,000 scholarship; when an out-of-state student is accepted and also wins an outside scholarship of at least $1,000, that student is allowed to enroll at in-state-resident rates which, at this writing, are less than $1,800 per year. In brief, Harry got a full ride at Texas A & M, resulting in a net savings for Harry's family over the next four years in excess of $30,000.

- ✔ **$8,000 Savings:** Terry received an immediate $2,000 increase in finaid on the telephone (even before the documentation was submitted) when Dr. Davis helped her document her appeal to Syracuse University. This single act saves Terry $8,000 over the next four years of school.

An expert college financial aid planner looks around financial corners, anticipating problems and solving them before they explode into major obstacles that prevent you from getting the best values in finaid.

Chapter 15

Please Save for My College Education

*ear Parents,*

I am writing to you from my book-crammed college dormitory to thank you for thinking ahead. Studies are demanding and parties are fewer than I expected. But I really can't complain — I love what I'm learning!

Recruiters already collected resumes on career day and one even asked me to call her when I graduate. I didn't understand what that "long-term planning" was all about; as a matter of fact, I thought you guys were total scrooges when you put away that $500 that could have bought me that 10-speed I wanted in eighth grade. But now I understand: I may have never had the chance to attend college if you hadn't saved like crazy.

I don't have to work full-time to pay for college, but many of my class-mates do — they're doing everything from making cafe mochas 40 hours a week to writing other people's term papers with every spare minute, and lots of them had to drop out altogether to save up tuition money. Most of them say their parents can't help them! Thanks to your thinking ahead, I feel very lucky to devote my time to studying and work that's more related to my studies than to my bills. I was just sitting here, thinking about you, and wanted to say thanks for planning ahead.

Love,

Rickie

Not every family gets letters like this — many, in fact, get short e-mails like,

```
Mom: please send money! My credit cards are maxed and I
owe Penn State $900! :-) Allison
```

If your kids could talk at birth, they'd coo, or maybe scream:

"Folks, please save for my college tuition." Because language skills come a few years later, we stand in to proclaim, "It's never too soon to start saving for your child's education."

Ever since Americans realized how much a college degree improves job prospects and, often, income, they've begun saving up for their kids' tuition. Like most college-minded families, you're wondering:

What will college cost when my child's ready for college; what will four years of college cost? How much should I start saving, and when? Where's the money going to come from?

Most middle- to upper-income families' answers lie in long-term savings — they start socking away money in stocks and bonds even before their children utter their first words. Financial wizards call this *long-term planning*. They also recommend all kinds of detailed financial asset reshuffling just two years before anyone goes collegiate — this is called *short-term planning*.

College costs are big enough to wear most people down before you even begin the long run. But instead of breaking a sweat just trying to keep up, use the tips in this chapter to swiftly fund your child's (or your own) education to the finish.

Are you a sucker for saving?

You've heard horror stories about prudent, dutiful parents who worked hard and sacrificed to save for their children's college and lost out on financial aid to people who didn't save a dime? We've heard them too.

Because nonsavers do get rewards, we emphasize legitimately shifting assets during the two years before college.

Plus, remember that financial-aid formulas give more weight to your income than your assets. On average, the first $40,000 of assets are forgiven when the system assesses need. Now that loans are the leading method of paying for college, more cash in hand means less debt for you. With the exception of gift money, someone has to pay the bills sooner or later.

For Parents: Saving Intelligently for the Distant Future

This section is dedicated to parents because saving for a student's education starts long before the student has a chance to participate. Thanks to declining financial aid for college, parents, states, colleges, and private organizations have been forced to turn to intricate savings strategies to pay for a higher education. Investments for long-term planning can be safe or high-risk.

Rule of thumb: The more risk, the greater the return on your investment.

Consider the long-term savings methods in the following sections to master that looming tuition bill.

Tuition Prepayment Programs

Tuition prepayment programs are available in many states. In addition to tuition prepayment plans, other long-range savings plans can help you meet skyscraping costs of higher education. Check with your state's Department of Education to see what's offered.

Bonds

Bonds are basically IOUs — from corporations or the state or government to you the buyer. Otherwise known as municipal bonds (or *munis),* state- or local-government-issued bonds earn you tax-exempt interest. U.S. government-issued bonds (*Treasury bonds)* are both state-tax-exempt and relatively risk free. (Nothing is totally risk free, but these are about as low risk as you can get.)

High-risk bonds offer no guarantees that they'll grow or survive. All bonds normally pay more in returns than bank savings or money market mutual funds, but they tend to risk more investment money. Consider the following college savings options.

U.S. Series EE Savings Bonds

If you've little to invest, these bonds may be your best strategy because they can cost as little as $25 or as much as $5,000 each. The most you can buy in any one year is $15,000 worth. Call 202-377-7715 for more information.

U.S. bonds guarantee earnings with their fixed interest rate, but on the downside, they return less than other savings tools. Nevertheless, U.S. savings bonds do have some advantages over other types of long-range saving:

- Bonds are purchased for half their worth — for example, if you want to buy a $1,000 savings bond, you'll pay $500 for it.

- Bonds can be redeemed after six months in return for the exact purchase price plus any interest earned.

- The coupon rate is reset every six months, resulting in little risk of losing interest and no risk of losing the capital investment. The original purchase price (or capital outlay) will never go down, and its interest will always be a plus — not high, but not zero.

- Taxes on the interest earned are deferred until the bond is cashed, as long as the bond is held for a minimum of five years.

- Taxes on the interest earned are forgiven if you cash in the bonds to pay for college fees and tuition. (*Note:* These bonds depend upon the parents' income; as this book goes to press, a combined parents' income when redeeming a bond can't exceed $91,850; this level adjusts annually according to inflation. The Technical and Miscellaneous Revenue Act of 1988 — P.L. 100-647 — mandates that no interest be charged on earnings from EE bonds purchased after 1990 if they're withdrawn to pay for college.)

U.S. Treasury bonds (T-bills or T-notes)

Just as secure as savings bonds, T-bills require you to accept the feds' IOU for a longer period of time. But the longer you sit on T-bills, the more they're worth.

Don't buy Treasury bonds that exceed ten years because other investments will probably earn you more over such a long period.

To purchase Treasury bonds, contact your nearest Federal Reserve Bank branch. Although Treasury bonds may not be your lifelong best buddies, they have redeeming qualities worth considering for college financing:

- Earnings are exempt from state and local taxes.

- T-bills have virtually no credit risk (as long as the U.S. government is sound, these bills are sound).

- T-bills are more liquid than some other investments, such as CDs.

- T-bills can be cashed in any time without penalty — after the maturity date.

✔ T-bills can be purchased at maturity dates that coincide with college bills.

✔ T-bills can be withdrawn at any time (before maturity) to pay for college without penalty fees. However, if interest rates rise, you will get less money back if you sell before maturity.

On the downside, T-bills normally have lower returns than other investments, and there are limits to how much you can purchase at any one action.

Municipal Bonds (Munis)

City, county, and state governments, agencies with a public purpose such as electric utility companies, hospitals, and universities issue municipal bonds. Municipal bonds have the following features:

✔ Interest rates are lower than other investments because you don't have to pay taxes on the interest you pull on your investment.

✔ Munis (and tax sheltered retirement accounts) generally help parents in tax brackets higher than 31 percent to cover college expenses far better than bonds that require taxable interest.

✔ Interest is exempt from federal and state taxes.

✔ Munis are low risk so long as credit rating on bond is good.

✔ Munis are redeemable before date of maturity

State college savings (Tuition) bonds

More than 20 states sponsor programs to finance higher education that are modeled after Illinois College Bonds. Parents can buy state-sponsored college bonds (state versions of U.S. Series EE Bonds) at extremely high discounts. Because the bonds serve as a college savings vehicle, they are sometimes referred to as *baccalaureate bonds*.

States issue these bonds as a way for families to save for future education expenses. Called *zero-coupon* bonds, these instruments allow you to buy a highly discounted bond with high interest and begin collecting interest only once the bond reaches maturity (instead of gradually collecting lower interest).

Like U.S. savings bonds, baccalaureate bonds sell for less than their face value and pay no interest until maturity. States use the proceeds from college savings bonds to meet the cost of building projects targeted by the state. State College Savings Bonds cost about $1,000 to $5,000, with maturities between 5 and 20 years. For college planning, the bond should mature the same year the student goes to college.

Following are some features of tuition bonds:

- Minimum bond amount: $1,000
- Purchased at high discount
- Low credit-risk
- Interest earned is tax-exempt (federal and state — for residents of the issuing state)
- Pay no interest until maturity
- Can be used for any college — even out of state
- Available for purchase anytime.

In some states, tuition bonds can't be included in the college financial aid assessment. Although marketed as a means for saving for college, no requirements obligate you to use them for college tuition (although Illinois pays a bonus if the bonds are used to pay for college). You don't even have to designate a beneficiary, such as a college.

Student Savings and Investment Accounts

Although savings in the student's name typically subtract from finaid eligibility, some tax breaks and earned interest plans *may* make up for the loss. For example, if the parent or grandparent zaps money into a trust account for the student under the UGMA (Uniform Gifts to Minors Act) or the UTMA (Uniform Transfers to Minors Act), the IRS provides some tax breaks on the earned interest.

Although the parent remains custodian of the account until age of majority (meaning the student can't arbitrarily opt to buy a jet ski instead of the first semester of tuition), the parent can't take back the money to cover a vacation or add a new room to the family home. These limitations can be helpful or harmful depending on your situation.

Advantages:

- First $650 in earned interest is exempt from federal income tax.
- Second $650 of earned interest gets taxed at the student's tax rate, which could be next to nothing if the student earns nearly zilch.
- Earned interest above $1,300 gets taxed at the parents' rate until the student turns age 14.
- Funds can only be withdrawn for education and specific reasons until the student reaches and age between 18 and 21 (it varies with the state).

Disadvantages:

✔ Funds can be withdrawn for any use — but only once the student reaches between ages 18 and 21 (depending on the state). The money belongs to the student and until that age, must cover education costs, health, security, and welfare.

✔ The student might decide not to attend college, or might need less money than the amount saved. The student gets the cash — a frightening possibility if your child's greatest aspiration is to sleep on the beach and live on berries and saltwater.

✔ The funds saved in the child's name do subtract heavily — to the tune of 35 percent of the amount saved annually — from the student's finaid eligibility.

CollegeSure Certificates (A Private Plan)

The College Savings Bank
5 Vaughn Drive
Princeton, NJ 08540-6313
800-888-2723

Unlike other savings plans tied to the prime rate (the rate at which the Federal Reserve System loans money to banks), this in the only plan that depends on college costs' growth. Introduced in 1987 to help parents meet new increases in education costs, the CollegeSure CD (certificate of deposit) allows a variable rate of return based on the inflation of college costs (rate based on expense budgets at 500 select, private, independent colleges identified as the College Board's Independent College 500 Index). Each July 31, interest rates reset (at 1.5 % below the rate of annual inflation in college costs for the index). Though the CollegeSure CD interest rate parallels inflation nicely, it's hardly perfect.

Advantages:

✔ If tuition suddenly skyrockets, this CD could protect the long-range saver from the decreasing purchasing power of inflation.

✔ The minimum deposit is $1,000.

✔ It's insured by the FDIC (Federal Deposit Insurance Corporation) up to $100,000.

Disadvantages:

✔ Interest earned is taxable.

✔ CollegeSure is less profitable when tuition inflation is low.

✔ The plan lacks significant long-term growth potential such as can be derived from stocks.

What will happen to the stock market next?

If you're new to the market of investments, you're probably nervous about the risks of chucking your money into an invisible investment that may seem as iffy as your chances of winning the office football pool.

You notice that people who invest regularly and patiently over a long time realize serious wealth, whether the stock market crashes or soars. Veteran investors say you've little to worry about if your investment methods are rock-solid, and they've proven two basic principles for steadfast investing.

Lesson one: Focus on long-term returns, not immediate gains. Shares bought when prices are high average out shares bought when prices are low. Slowly, steadily reinvest everything possible from your salary and investments. Historically, the longer you follow this policy, the more compounding will kitty up for you.

Lesson two: Diversify your collection of investments to guard yourself against losses in individual areas.

For Everyone: Saving for College in the Next Two Years

Because college fees approach so terribly soon, don't even think about chucking money into an obligation of any kind — and avoid risking it in unstable investments. Maybe you or your parents couldn't start a fancy savings plan 20-odd years ago. Maybe you already spent everything you'd saved in undergraduate school, or you spent all your scrimps on your children and now want to return to college yourself.

Money-market mutual funds

These set-ups allow short-term investments while holding onto the cash you'll need for college. Money-market mutual funds slot money into government and corporate bonds. You can collect a fair amount of interest off these shortest of short-term bonds. Although not insured by FDIC, these funds provide low-risk investments with fairly high returns. Consider the following:

- ✔ The best money market mutual funds provide higher yields than bank savings accounts.

- ✔ Money market mutual investments tend to involve little risk — they typically plug your investment money into low-risk, government securities, commercial certificates from well-established corporations, and bank certificates.

College saving is for everyone, anytime

Many major banks and lending institutions offer college plans (the major undergrad programs are listed in the chart at the end of this chapter). Additionally, college lenders and other private organizations offer plans of similar convenience. Even if you've spent your savings or never had extra money to save, you're not dead in the water. These plans may not be your best bet financially, however. Other ways to save and invest give you more bang for the buck with less bucks for the bank.

✔ You can write checks from the account.

✔ The fund draws interest until the moment you withdraw.

✔ The funds are liquid, with no penalty for withdrawal.

Tuition-freeze programs

More than 500 colleges have adopted these tuition discount programs; a *tuition freeze* allows you to prepay four years of college. In return, you pay the present tuition price, not the increased fee you'd pay later when the student attends college. See Chapter 16 for more about Tuition-freeze programs.

Home equity loans

If you own a home, you can save yourself the trouble of seeking an outside line of credit based on your financial pretty face. You can use the interest you've paid on your equity loan as a tax deduction, so you may as well use that home equity to get a college loan of credit too. Both an equity loan and an equity line of credit will win you tax deductions, but their differences may help you decide which one is best for you. See Chapter 16 for more about equity loans and lines of credit.

Federal Parent Loans for Undergraduate Students (FPLUS)

Provided by the feds (the U.S. Department of Education), this program allows parents who have good credit to borrow as much money as they need to fill the gap between the cost of education and the finaid the student has already garnered. For more information, see Chapter 7.

Educational Savings Accounts

Starting in 1998, parents and grandparents can put away as much as $500 a year for any child younger than 18. That's a total of $500 from all sources. You pay into these accounts with after-tax dollars, meaning you get no tax deduction. As long as you spend the money on education, you can withdraw the (interest) gain tax-free.

Most parents and gramps qualify. You can make the full contribution if you're single with adjusted income no higher than $95,000 or, if married, up to $150,000. The benefit phases out at higher incomes: $110,000 for singles and $160,000 for marrieds.

Analysts say the ESA option is not necessarily a good deal. For example, if your kid receives 15 years' savings at $500 a pop, with interest, you may wind up with $15,000 — way short of what you'll need.

Suppose you live in one of the 18 states that operate a state prepaid tuition plan (see Chapter 12) and want to participate in it. You cannot put money in your child's ESA in any year you contribute to that child's state prepaid tuition plan.

Nor can you use your Hope or Lifetime Learning credits (see the Introduction) in a year in which you spend ESA funds to pay for school.

✔ If available, choose your state's prepaid tuition plan instead of an ESA. You can stash larger chunks of money each year in a state plan.

✔ If your child is very young and you decide on an ESA, fund it religiously and plant the money in a high-yield investment. Spend every cent in your child's first year of college. When you've emptied your child's ESA, turn to the Hope and Lifetime Learning credits (see the Introduction) for tax relief.

Additional reading

✔ *Personal Finance For Dummies*, 2nd Edition, and *Investing For Dummies*, both books by Eric Tyson; 1997; IDG Books Worldwide; order through 800-762-2974 or through your local retailer.

✔ *Paying For College*, by Gerald Krefetz; 1995; The College Entrance Examination Board, Box 886, New York, NY; call 212-713-8165 for further information.

Chapter 16

Becoming an Educated Borrower

. . . .

. . . .

So you filled out every form in the financial aid office and wore rags hoping to demonstrate financial need, but somehow the financial aid administrator couldn't find enough money to fill the gaping holes in your pockets. It happens — especially now that some financial aid cups are turning up dry as the aid-thirsty lines stretch longer at the financial aid office.

Not enough money! You're so discouraged that you're now considering a life of degree-less manual labor. Don't. You may have already guessed the reason: In today's job market, the fittest survive thanks largely to their college education.

In a number of the most attractive fields, professional status begins with master's and doctoral degrees. For example, highly competitive fields like psychology treat a basic baccalaureate like a birth certificate.

But the school's proposed aid package doesn't go far enough, and you've already negotiated as recommended in Chapter 9. What do other students do when standing in your shoes? They and their families get loans — federal and private loans. The smart ones become educated borrowers.

Choosing the Best Loan

Many lenders offer carefully designed programs that allow borrowers to pay less when they earn less. Many programs even defer those payments for several years if the payments pose undue hardship. Some employers offer loan repayment assistance as one of their benefits. The possibilities lending institutions offer have made many students' education possible.

Choosing the right loan (or combination of loans) makes all the difference. College-minded families should factor in the following as they examine educational loans:

- Who must repay the bulk of the loan (student or parents)?
- How *little* can the family afford to borrow?
- How *much* the family can afford to repay (estimate monthly payments)?
- How much can the graduate expect to earn upon graduation?

Before you sign on the dotted line and split to the bank with the refund check, don't hesitate to bug lenders with questions about every nook and cranny of repayment. So what if you drive them around the bend — you've got to get it straight. Banks, the loan service bureaus such as Sallie Mae, United Student Aid Funds, PHEAA, and others including lending institutions provide information both in hard copy and on the Web describing the many options that students have for paying back their loans.

Review the rules for repaying your loan with a magnifying glass. For instance:

- What happens to the debt if the borrower becomes permanently disabled, or dies?
- In what circumstances and how should you apply for deferment or forbearance?
- If both parents assume a joint loan, who pays how much if they divorce?
- Can you begin repaying even before interest accrues?

Loans usually require payment of such charges as loan, origination and insurance fees — all this in addition to interest. Students are given options to stretch out payments over 30 years. But remember, the longer you stretch out loan repayment, the more you have to pay in interest. A better idea: Get three jobs if necessary and limit your repayment to 10 years.

Don't know where to start? The following sections describe types of loans to help you decide which is the least painful method of going into debt.

The first group of resources in "Primary Wellsprings of Loan Money" revisits two kinds of federally guaranteed loans and offers two examples of direct state loans. This group also looks at borrowing on family equity and at borrowing to pay for four tuition-frozen years of college.

Keep those cards and calls coming

However distant a relationship may seem between you and an organization to which you owe major money, forge a close relationship immediately and constantly. Don't be shy. Organizations indeed may be lending money strictly for altruistic reasons, but commercial lenders earn profits, and colleges want to insure that they have the means to keep attracting top students.

Make a habit of communicating with your college loan lender just like you would a credit card company — call them to inform them of these changes:

- ✔ Changes in your finances
- ✔ Changes in name, address, employment
- ✔ Withdrawal from school, failure to enroll in the specified period, or less than half-time attendance

Primary Wellsprings of Loan Money

If you are not eligible for subsidized Federal Stafford Loans, then start by looking at the Unsubsidized Federal Stafford Loans and the Federal PLUS loans (see Chapter 7), because they're the biggest loan programs. Ordinarily, these two classes of loans are the cheapest, but some private and commercial loans have a lower interest rate than the government's loans (which we identify later in this chapter). First, an instant replay of the federal offerings.

Unsubsidized Federal Stafford Loans
U.S. Department of Education
Federal Student Aid Information Center
P.O. Box 84
Washington, DC 20044-0084
800-433-3243

- ✔ **Loan limits:**

    - Dependent students

        $2,625 (1st year), $3,500 (2nd year), $5,500 (3rd , 4th, or 5th year). Aggregate for undergraduate school is $23,000.

    - Independent students

        $6,625 (1st year), $7,500 (2nd year), $10,500 (3rd, 4th, or 5th year). $18,500 (each year of graduate school). Aggregate for independent undergraduate student loans is $46,000.

    - Graduate or professional students

        The graduate debt limit including undergraduateFederal Stafford Loans may not exceed $138,500.

✔ **Interest rate:** Variable rate based on 91-day T-bill +2.5 percent while the student is in school. Variable rate based on 91-day T-bill +3.1 percent when in repayment period. Loan is capped at 8.25 percent with rate being adjusted annually. These rates apply to loans made after July 1, 1995

✔ **Fees:** 3 percent origination fee and a 1 percent guarantor insurance fee for Federal Stafford Loans; 4 percent origination fee for Federal Direct Loans

✔ **Deadline:** Recommended to apply at least 60 days before school starts so as to allow the college and the lender to process the application.

✔ **Features:** Unsubsidized Stafford/Direct loans are available to students who do not qualify for need-based loans. *Unsubsidized* means that the federal government doesn't pay the interest while the student is in college the student pays the interest. Payments can be deferred under some conditions. Repayment of principal follows a six-month grace period after the student is no longer enrolled half-time. Loans may be repaid early with no penalty. Loans do not require a credit test and do not require need.

This loan is available to you the student as long as you are in school at least half time. You get better loan terms than your parents, and you can let your poor ol' folks off the hook and repay the loans yourself after you graduate. You can put off repayments until six months after graduation and take up to 10 years to pay under the Standard Repayment Plan.

Most loan service groups and lenders will reduce your interest rate by two percentage points if you pay the first 48 payments on time, plus a whiff of a discount for using electronic banking transfer.

Federal Stafford Loans come from financial institutions such as banks and credit unions under the Federal Family Education Loan Program or by the Department of Education under the Federal Direct Loan Program.

Federal PLUS Loans
U.S. Department of Education
Federal Student Aid Information Center
P.O. Box 84
Washington, DC 20044-0084
800-433-3243

✔ **Loan limits:** Up to cost of education minus any student financial aid

✔ **Interest rate:** Variable rate based on 52-week T-bill + 3.1 percent with a 9 percent cap. Rate is adjusted annually.

✔ **Fees:** 3 percent origination and 1 percent guarantor fees for Federal PLUS Loans; 4 percent origination fee for Federal Direct loans.

✔ **Deadline:** Recommendation is to submit the application at least 60 days prior to the start of the academic year to allow for school and lender processing.

✔ **Features:** Parent(s)/guardian of the student is eligible to apply. The FPLUS requires a credit check.

A parent cannot be turned down for having no credit history — only for having an adverse one. If the parent(s) doesn't pass the credit check, the parent may still be able to receive a loan if someone, such as a relative or friend who is able to pass the credit check, agrees to co-sign the loan. The parent does not have to complete a FAFSA to qualify for this loan (unless the school requires a completed FAFSA). Eligibility does not depend on demonstrated need. Checks are made payable to the school, and disbursements are made two or more times during the year. Parents do not make payments on the loan until 60 days after the final disbursement of the loan. Interest begins to accrue on the day the loan is disbursed. Parents have up to 10 years to repay the loan.

Your parents can borrow all of your education costs, minus any other financial aid. If your total college costs are $10,000 and you have already borrowed $4,000 on a Federal Stafford or Federal Direct loan, your folks can borrow another $6,000 on an FPLUS. Banks and other financial institutions usually furnish the cash. Your folks have to repay, without any grace period, almost as soon as school starts and normally take 10 years to retire the loan. However, parents may consolidate loans and receive a longer repayment period option.

MASSPlan (State Loan)

Massachusetts Educational Financing Authority
125 Summer Street, 14th Floor
Boston, MA 02110-9740
800-449-6332
www.mefa.org

✔ **Loan limits:** $2,000 up to cost of education less any student financial aid

✔ **Interest rate:** Fixed interest rate at 7.50 percent (or) variable interest rate at 6.57 percent, interest reset annually

✔ **Fees:** 3.75 percent origination fee

✔ **Deadline:** Open

✔ **Features:** The MASSPlan allows the borrower 15 years to repay the loan. You have no prepayment penalty and no application fees. The borrower, usually the parent or guardian, must be creditworthy and the student must sign the loan. Repayment begins a month after the loan is made. Loans are available to Massachusetts residents and out-of-state residents pursuing an education at any of the participating institutions of higher education in the state.

At the request of Massachusetts college and universities, the Massachusetts Educational Financing Authority was established in 1982 under Massachusetts general law to assist families, colleges, and universities in financing the cost of higher education.

Keystone Rewards Stafford Loan (State Loan)
Pennsylvania Higher Education Assistance Agency (FA)
1200 North Seventh Street
Harrisburg, PA 17102-1444
(717) 720-2509

✔ **Loan limits:** (1st) $2,625 (2nd) $3,500 (3rd & 4th) $5,500

✔ **Total Fees:**

- **Guarantee Fees:** 0 percent vs 1 percent for all other Stafford and Direct loans

- **Origination Fees:** 2 percent vs 3 percent for all other Stafford and Direct Subsidized loans

✔ **Interest rate:** May not exceed 8.25 percent

- **Fee Savings on $16,000:** $320 on subsidized loans; $160 on unsubsidized loans

- **Interest savings:** 2 percent interest rate reduction after 48 consecutive on-time monthly payments; .25 percent interest rate reduction for electronic debit.

  Total interest rate savings on $16,000 would be $1,255

✔ **Restrictions:** Program is available for all PA residents to attend in-state or out-of-state colleges and nonresidents attending college in PA.

Home-equity line of credit or loan

The next stop on your loan shopping list should be a home-equity line of credit or loan. You can deduct the interest on a home-equity loan of as much as $100,000 on your federal tax return. For middle- and upper-middle income families, the after-tax cost of home equities is attractive.

Both an equity loan and an equity line of credit win you tax deductions, but differences exist between the two. An *equity loan* requires you to pay interest on the full amount; you must repay it within a negotiated period, at a fixed or variable rate. You may end up paying higher interest on money that you don't need immediately — for example, if you borrow $100,000, you'll pay interest on that entire amount even if you only use $25,000 in the first year. Look at an equity loan as a second mortgage.

An *equity line of credit* allows you to negotiate for the maximum line of credit possible based on the equity in your home. But you only make payments on the funds you withdraw on that line of credit. If you're only using the funds for college tuition, this option may be smarter and less expensive than the equity loan.

Either program of credit obligations can negatively affect your credit report, because most credit institutions estimate your eligibility by examining your debt-to-income ratio. An $80,000 debt, for example, may disfigure an otherwise attractive, middle-income profile.

Features of these loans include

- Equity lines are less expensive because you won't immediately pay interest on entire college cost.
- If you itemize your tax deductions, both types of credit are tax deductible.
- Equity loans are established at a fixed interest rate.
- Equity lines are often established at a variable interest rate.

Contact your bank or mortgage company for more information.

401 (k) and other retirement accounts

Should your parent(s) borrow from themselves by dipping into their retirement account? They can, but if they don't repay in five years they're in tax deep-guacamole. If a parent changes jobs or gets fired, the money's due right now. Another problem: The missing money slows down a retirement fund. Overall: Not such a hot idea.

Tuition-freeze programs

Next on the borrowing billet: Should your folks take a loan to buy a guaranteed tuition price for four years?

More than 500 colleges have adopted tuition discount programs, a tuition freeze that allows you to prepay four years of college. In return, you pay the present tuition price, not the increased fee you'd pay later when college rolls around.

Colleges can even loan you the money if you don't have an extra $60,000 or more sitting around. If your college of choice offers such a program and its tuition is skyrocketing, maybe you should jump on this opportunity to save big bucks. Or maybe not, depending upon tuition inflation rates compared to your family's financial status. In a negative example: If tuition is only increasing at an average rate (6 percent) and the usual interest charge on the loan is increasing to 9 percent , prepayment will cost you 3 percent overall.

If you have $20,000 in bank savings paying 3.5 percent interest and take an unsubsidized loan that charges 8 percent interest, you'll come out ahead by 5 percent .

Features of the tuition-freeze program include

- ✔ Your family is spared tuition increases while you're in college.

- ✔ If you take a loan approved as an equity line of credit, your federal and state tax bills will be reduced (but you have no guarantee that you'll profit from the program).

- ✔ Interest on loans may cost more than the discount you'll get for paying early.

For more information, contact the financial aid office at your colleges of choice.

Loans from and for Specific Groups

These loans are from private-sector educational, service, professional, or membership organizations and loans from philanthropic foundations, many of which are targeted at specific groups.

Albert Baker Fund
5 Third St. #717
San Francisco, CA 94103
415-543-7028

- ✔ **Loan limits:** $1,600-$2,500

- ✔ **Interest rate**

- ✔ **Deadline:** July 1

- ✔ **Eligibility:** Students must be active Christian Scientists and members of the Mother Church (First Church of Christ Scientist in Boston). Foreign students must have a U.S. resident as a co-signer. The fund places no restrictions as to field of study.

American Occupational Therapy Association (AOTA)
P.O. Box 31220
Bethesda, MD 20824-1220
301-652-2682

- ✔ **Loan limits:** $2,000

- ✔ **Interest rate**

- ✔ **Deadline:** Open

- ✔ **Eligibility:** Female members of AOTA who have a B.A. degree and who are pursuing a graduate or advanced degree in occupational therapy education may apply. U.S. citizenship is a prerequisite.

American Society of Mechanical Engineers (ASME)
345 East 47th St.
New York , NY 10017-2392
212-705-7375

- ✔ **Loan limit:** Up to $2,500, maximum $5,000

- ✔ **Interest rate:** 7.5 percent

- ✔ **Deadline:** April 15 (for summer and fall); Oct. 15 (for winter and spring)

- ✔ **Eligibility:** Graduate or undergraduate students majoring in mechanical engineering or engineering technology who are members of ASME may apply. Graduate students must have a 3.2 GPA; undergraduates must have a minimum of 2.2 GPA. U.S. citizenship is a prerequisite.

Delaware Academy of Medicine
1925 Lovering Ave.
Wilmington, DE 19806
302-656-1629

- ✔ **Loan limit:** $1,000-$3,000

- ✔ **Interest rate:** Non-interest bearing while in college

- ✔ **Deadline:** May 15

- ✔ **Eligibility:** Graduate and professional students must be majoring in allied health fields, medicine, or dentistry and be residents of Delaware who are enrolled in full-time study and have financial need. U.S. residency or permanent residency is a prerequisite.

Emanuel Sternberger Educational Fund
P.O. Box 1735
Greensboro, NC 27402
910-275-6316

- ✔ **Loan limits:** $1,000 (first year), $2,000 (succeeding years)

- ✔ **Interest rate:**

- ✔ **Deadline:** April 30

- ✔ **Eligibility:** Residents of North Carolina who are juniors, seniors, or graduate students may apply. Loans may be used at any accredited institution. Eligibility is determined by grades, need, references, and credit rating.

Field Co-Operative Association
P.O. Box 5054
Jackson, MS 39296-5054
601-939-9295

- **Loan limits:** $2,000

- **Interest rate:** 6 percent

- **Deadline:** Open

- **Eligibility:** Only third-year undergraduate or graduate students who are Mississippi residents may apply for this loan. Students must have demonstrated need. U.S. citizenship or permanent residency is a prerequisite.

Franklin Lindsay Student Aid Fund
c/o Texas Commerce Bank
P.O. Box 550
Austin, TX 78789
512-479-2634
512-479-2656 (Fax)

- **Loan limits:** Up to $3,000 per year (aggregate of $12,000)

- **Interest rate:** Non-interest-bearing while in college; 6 percent after non-attendance

- **Deadline:** Open

- **Eligibility:** Students who have completed one year of college with a 2.0 GPA may apply for this loan. Proceeds of the loan disbursement must be used to attend an accredited postsecondary institution in Texas.

Hattie M. Strong Foundation
1620 Eye St. NW, Rm. 700
Washington, DC 20006
202-331-1619

- **Loan limits:** Up to $3,000

- **Interest rates:** None

- **Deadline:** January 1 — March 31

- **Eligibility:** Students must be U.S. citizens attending undergraduate or graduate school. Eligibility is based on merit. This loan is only for the final year of college for students pursuing a baccalaureate degree or higher.

Jewish Family and Children's Services
1600 Scott St.
San Francisco, CA 94115
415-561-1226

- ✔ **Loan limits:** $5,000 aggregate

- ✔ **Interest rate:** 80 percent of prime

- ✔ **Deadline:** Open

- ✔ **Eligibility:** Available to college students of the Jewish faith who are U.S. citizens living in the San Francisco Bay area.

Knights Templar Educational Foundation
5097 N. Elston, Suite 101
Chicago, IL 60630
312-777-3300

- ✔ **Loan limits:** $6,000 aggregate

- ✔ **Interest rate:** 5 percent

- ✔ **Deadline:** Open

- ✔ **Eligibility:** Payments and interest are deferred until student is no longer enrolled in college. Students who are in their junior, senior, or graduate year may apply, as well as vocational-technical student enrollees. U.S. citizenship or permanent residency is a prerequisite.

Lemberg Scholarship Loan Fund
60 East 42nd St., Suite 17
New York, NY 10165

- ✔ **Loan limits:** Vary

- ✔ **Interest rate:** None

- ✔ **Deadline:** April 1

- ✔ **Eligibility:** Loans are available to Jewish men and women for undergraduate, graduate, or professional study. Loan repayments commence after graduation with a 10-year repayment period.

Pickett & Hatcher Educational Fund, Inc.
1800 Buena Vista Road
P.O. Box 8169
Columbus, GA 31908-8169
407-327-6586

- ✔ **Loan limits:** maximum of $3,000 per year

- ✔ **Interest rate:** 6% after leaving college; 27% while in school

- ✔ **Deadline:** May 15 (funds awarded first-come, first-served)

- ✔ **Eligibility:** Applicants must be residents of and attend colleges in one of the following states: Alabama, Florida, Georgia, Kentucky, Mississippi, North Carolina, South Carolina, Tennessee, or Virginia. Students majoring in law, ministry, or medicine are not eligible.

Six good commercial loan providers

Here is a selection of the best private commercial loans.

Achiever Loan
Knight College Resource Group
855 Boylston Street
Boston, MA 02116
800-225-6783

- ✔ **Loan limits:** Up to the cost of education per annum, unlimited aggregate

- ✔ **Interest rate:** 3 wk T-Bill + 3.95 to 4.5%

- ✔ **Fees:** 3-4% Loan origination fee plus $35 application fee

- ✔ **Deadlines:** Open

- ✔ **Features:** This loan requires a credit test, but the loan is not based on need. The loan has a deferment period while the student is in college but the interest is capitalizing. Students have up to 15 years to repay with no penalty for early repayment of the loan.

ENGLoans
United Student Aid Group Loan Service
1100 USA Parkway
Fishers, IN 46038
317-951-5600 or 800-538-8492

- ✔ **Loan limits:** Up to the cost of education, unlimited aggregate

- ✔ **Interest rate:** Prime rate plus 3.65%

- ✔ **Fees:** 6% while in college and 7.5% during repayment

- ✔ **Deadlines:** Open

> ✓ **Features:** These loans are for engineering majors only. A credit test is required but no demonstrated need must be met. The loan is deferred while the student is in college, but the interest is capitalizing on the loan. The grace period includes nine months after non-enrollment. Fifty dollars is the minimum payment on the loan, or the regular payment as established by the payment schedule. Students have up to 15 years to repay with no penalty for early repayment.

Excel Program
Nellie Mae
50 Braintree Hill Park, Suite 300
Braintree, MA 02184
800-634-9308

> ✓ **Loan limits:** $5,000 for freshmen/sophomores; $7,500 for juniors/seniors, up to cost of education less any student financial aid

> ✓ **Interest rate:** Prime + .5 percent for 1st year of college, prime + 1 percent thereafter; 7 percent guarantee fee

> ✓ **Deadline:** Open

> ✓ **Features:** A credit test is required to be eligible for the loan. This loan is not based on demonstrated need. The student has 20 years to repay the loan with no penalty for early repayment. The loan program allows the student to defer the loan payments while in college, but the interest is capitalizing.

PLATO Loan
University Support Services
205 Van Buren Street, Suite 200
Herndon, VA 22070
800-467-5286

> ✓ **Loan limits:** $1,500 up to cost of education not to exceed $25,000 per year; $100,000 aggregate

> ✓ **Interest rates:** Fixed rate of 7.9 percent for first 12 months; thereafter variable of prime + 2-6 percent

> ✓ **Fees:** 8.2 percent origination fee

> ✓ **Deadline:** Open

> ✓ **Features:** The borrower has up to 15 years to repay the loan. Deferred payments are allowed while the student is in college, with interest capitalizing. Payments on principal and interest commence after the six-month grace period. No penalty for early repayment. May be used for purchase of computer equipment.

SHARE Loan
Nellie Mae
Private Loan Processing
50 Braintree Hill Park, Suite 300
Braintree, MA 02184-8753
800-634-9308

✔ **Loan limits:** $2,000 up to cost of attendance, less other financial aid received.

✔ **Interest rate:** Choose one of two options:

- Monthly variable: prime + .0 percent in 1st year and prime + 0.25 percent in subsequent years

- One year renewable: prime + 2-3 percent fixed rate

✔ **Fees:** 5 percent guarantee fee; no origination fee

✔ **Deadlines:** Open

✔ **Features:** Borrowers do not need to complete the FAFSA to apply for a SHARE loan. Loan can be pre-approved by phone. Repayment options include the ability to pay interest-only while student is in school or make monthly payments of principal and interest. Borrower must be creditworthy. SHARE allows the borrower up to 20 years to repay with no penalty for early repayment.

TERI Loan
The Education Resources Institute
P.O. Box 312
330 Stuart Street, Suite 500
Boston, MA 02117-9123
800-255-8374

✔ **Loan limits:** $2,000 up to cost of education less financial aid; unlimited aggregate

✔ **Interest rate:** Variable not to exceed prime +2 percent

✔ **Fees:** 5 percent guarantee fee

✔ **Deadlines:** Open

✔ **Features:** The Teri loan requires a credit check but no demonstrated needs test. Loan deferment is available while the student is in college, but the interest on the loan is capitalizing. The loan has a 45 day grace period after the student is no longer enrolled in college. The loan requires a minimum payments of $50 or payments as established by the payment schedule with 25 years allowed to repay the loan. There is no penalty for early repayment.

CitiAssist Undergraduate
Citibank Student Loan Corporation
Citibank (New York State)
P.O. Box 22945
Rochester, N.Y. 14692-6805
716-248-7672
800-692-8200
www.citibank.com/student/assist.htm

- ✔ **Loan limits:** $10,000 per year with an aggregate of $50,000

- ✔ **Interest rate:** Prime + 1 percent

- ✔ **Fees:** None

- ✔ **Deadlines:** Open

- ✔ **Features:** Student borrowers may defer the loan while in college. Interest capitalizes only once at the start of repayment. Loan allows for a six-month grace period after separation from the institution. Students are allowed up to 10 years to repay the loan with $50 minimum monthly payments. Loans are available for full, half-time, or part-time study. Loans may be available for international students with a U.S. citizen's co-signature. For four year institutuions and graduate schools only.

Commercial lenders offer varying policies. Simplify your life by sticking with one lender whenever possible. This policy, of course, doesn't apply to direct loans made only by the federal government or loans from nonprofit organizations and foundations.

Hold borrowing to a college yell

When you attend a formal loan entrance interview, you'll likely get a long lecture on the evils of unpaid debt — you may even have to watch a video about making calls when you need deferment or forbearance. Though such warnings may seem ritualistic and arcane, they're not to be ignored.

Loan default or a poor payment record gets on your credit report, and scars it so deeply (for up to seven years) that you may not be able to get other loans, credit cards, mortgages, or even an apartment lease. In addition, your wages or income tax returns may be garnisheed, your assets may be attached, your professional licenses may not be renewed or granted, or you may end up in court. Increased interest, late fees, and court and attorney fees may be added to your unpaid total.

Chapter 17

Can You Smile and Salute?

"*H*ello sailor, buy you an education?" That question could be asked of anyone serving in any branch of the U.S. Armed Forces. If you say "yes," you'll be surprised at how much in financial aid resources are related to serving in the U.S. armed forces and how widely college study is supported via several channels of funding.

Four populations of people get dollars for school when a family member serves in a military service. These populations are the following:

- College student on active duty
- College student who is a veteran
- College student who is a veteran's dependent
- College student who will become a veteran

Four funding sources service these four populations. These funding sources are the following:

- Federal government
- State governments
- Colleges
- Private organizations and agencies

This chapter examines each student population and itemizes funding sources that service it.

College Student on Active Duty

Who says you can't suit up in uniform and bolster your education at the same time? The possibilities are nearly endless.

Federal

As an active military member, you can attend college on a part- or full-time basis.

- **What the military wants.** The Department of Defense (DOD) pays the tuition to upgrade your skills in your military occupational specialty. On your military employer's time — on-duty hours — you probably won't be able to select the education or training you prefer but will be assigned to learn skills that your service needs.

- **What you want.** On your own time — off-duty hours — the U.S. Department of Veterans Affairs (VA), under the Montgomery GI Bill (see below), pays for you to learn subjects of your choosing. For example, more than 20,000 military personnel around the world study everything from American history to economics in courses taught by the University of Maryland, the largest provider of higher education to the armed forces. The University of Maryland's yearly catalogues list hundreds of courses offered at military sites. Just about every subject taught domestically is also taught somewhere overseas.

A U.S. Department of Veterans Affairs publication, *Summary of Educational Benefits, VA Pamphlet 22-90-2,* describes details of higher education that you choose. If you want a copy, or have questions, contact a VA office at the addresses listed in Table 17-1.

Table 17-1	Regional Veterans Administration Offices
Region Address	*States in Region*
EASTERN REGION VA Regional Office P.O. Box 4616 Buffalo, NY 14240-4616 800-827-1000	Connecticut, Delaware, Maine, Massachusetts, New Hampshire, New Jersey, New York, Ohio, Pennsylvania, Rhode Island, Vermont, West Virginia
SOUTHERN REGION VA Regional Office P.O. Box 54346 Atlanta, GA 30308-0346 800-827-1000	Alabama, Arkansas, District of Columbia, Florida, Georgia, Louisiana, Maryland, Mississippi, North Carolina, Puerto Rico, South Carolina, Tennessee, Virginia, Foreign Schools

Region Address	States in Region
CENTRAL REGION VA Regional Office P.O. Box 66830 St. Louis, MO 63166-6830 800-827-1000	Colorado, Illinois, Indiana, Iowa, Kansas, Kentucky, Michigan, Minnesota, Missouri, Montana, Nebraska, North Dakota, South Dakota, Wisconsin, Wyoming
WESTERN REGION VA Regional Office P.O. Box 8888 Muskogee, OK 74402-8888 800-827-1000	Alaska, Arizona, California, Hawaii, Idaho, New Mexico, Nevada, Oklahoma, Oregon, Philippines, Texas, Utah, Washington

You are considered to be on active duty if you attend one of the federal military academies. For more information, contact the academy admission offices listed in Table 17-2 or your Congressional Representative or Senator.

Table 17-2   U.S. Military Academy Program Directory

U.S. Air Force	U.S. Army	U.S. Coast Guard	U.S. Merchant Marine	U.S. Navy/ Marines
ADMISSIONS DIRECTOR HQ USAFA/RRS	ADMISSIONS DIRECTOR U.S. MILITARY ACADEMY	ADMISSIONS DIRECTOR U.S.C.G. ACADEMY	ADMISSIONS DIRECTOR U.S.M.M. ACADEMY	ADMISSIONS DIRECTOR U.S.N. ACADEMY
2304 Cadet Drive Ste. 200 USAF Academy, CO 80840-5025 719-333-2520	2304 Cadet Drive Ste. 200 West Point, N.Y. 10996-1797 914-938-4041 800-822-USMA	606 Thayer Rd. New London, CT 06320-4195 860-444-8503 800-883-8724	15 Mohegan Ave. Kings Point, NY 11024 516-773-0000 800-732-6267	117 Decatur Rd. Annapolis, MD 21402-5018 410-293-1858 800-638-9156

Academy dropouts have safety net

Suppose you campaign for and win a seat in one of the military academies, a seat that some observers say is worth $250,000 including its full-ride tuition and monthly pay.

Then suppose you discover that the military life just isn't for you. If you withdraw under honorable conditions, you're still ahead in the financial aid process. That's because you automatically become an *independent student,* which generally results in maximum eligibility for federal student aid. Your pay as a former cadet is not counted and neither is your parents' income.

College Student Who Is a Veteran

Now that you're out of uniform and into the civilian higher education scene, check out ways you can wind up with money to pay your way through school.

Federal

Uncle Sam and Aunt Feddie channel your scholarly benefits through the U. S. Department of Veterans Affairs. Most veterans attending college are funded under the *Montgomery GI-Bill*, also known as *Chapter 30* by the U.S. Department of Veterans Affairs Regulations.

The Montgomery GI-Bill applies to those who enter active duty for the first time after June 30, 1985. Active duty for benefit purposes includes full-time National Guard duty performed after Nov. 29, 1989. An honorable discharge is required. To receive maximum benefits, you must serve continuously on active duty for three years — or two years' active duty plus four years in the Selected Reserve or National Guard. The top dollars are $427.87 a month for 36 months, with annual adjustments for inflation.

What if you don't finish your stretch? Those who enlist and serve for less than three years receive $347.65 per month.

Questions? Check with your VA Regional Office listed back in Table 17-1.

State

Most states give qualified veterans free or reduced tuition at any state four-year public institution. Details? Ask your state scholarship administration, which is listed in a directory included in Chapter 8.

Colleges

Most colleges have an Office of Veterans Affairs whose employees have responsibility for coordinating the paperwork for the federal VA office. Additionally, this office helps you with loans and study programs, including providing extra tutoring money if you need it. In essence, Veterans Affairs staffers are supposed to smooth your pathway through college and keep you from blowing your great educational opportunity.

Student Who Is a Veteran's Dependent

A grateful nation provides for the children and spouse of veterans who have paid a heavy price to serve their country.

Federal

VA educational assistance benefits are available to the children and spouses of

- ✔ Veterans who died or are permanently and totally disabled as the result of a disability arising from active service in the Armed Forces
- ✔ Veterans who died from any cause while rated permanently and totally disabled from a service-connected disability
- ✔ Veterans who are missing in action or captured in the line of duty by a hostile force
- ✔ Veterans who are presently detained or interned in the line of duty by a foreign government or power

Monthly benefits are paid at the rate of $427 per person for up to 45 months. You usually must be between the ages of 18 and 26. Benefits to a spouse end ten years from the date the VA notifies the spouse of eligibility. In addition, a spouse can apply for VA education loans.

State

Most states honor with education benefits their former residents who joined the Armed Forces and paid a stiff price in the course of duty. The service members honored are those who became prisoners of war (POW), were classified as missing in action (MIA), died or became disabled.

The states award education benefits to the veterans themselves or to their dependents in varying degrees. Some states, for example, do not include benefits for the spouse, while others generously reward the entire family. Table 17-3 offers a sampling of key benefits, whether they are administered by a veterans' affairs or higher education agency. To get the entire scope of veterans' education benefits for your state, consult the relevant state office.

Table 17-3	Veterans' Benefits for Dependents and Spouses of MIA/POW/Disabled/Deceased Veterans				
State & Address	*Tuition*	*Fees*	*Books*	*Stipend*	*Comments*
ALABAMA State Dept. of VA P.O. Box 1509 Montgomery, AL 36102l 334-242-5077	Free	Free	Free	No	
ARKANSAS Contact college's financial aid office	Free	Free	No	No	
CALIFORNIA State Dept of VA Div. of Veterans Svcs. P.O. Box 942895 1227 O St., Rm. 101 Sacramento, CA 95813 916-653-2573	Free	Free	No	No	Cal. State Univ. System, U. of California, Cal. Comm. Colleges
COLORADO CO Commission on Higher Education 1300 Broadway, 2nd Fl. Denver, CO 80203 303-866-2723	Free	No	No	No	
CONNECTICUT CN Dept. of Higher Ed. Ed. Information Ct. 61 Woodland St. 3rd Fl Hartford, CT 06105-2391 860-566-3910	Free; also for Veteran	No	No	No	
DELAWARE DE Higher Ed. Comm. 820 North French St. Carvel State Bldg. 4th Fl Wilmington, DE 19801 302-577-3240	Free	No	No	No	Dependents only; Spouse excluded
FLORIDA Contact college's financial aid office	Free	Free	No	No	
GEORGIA	Pending	Pending	Pending	Pending	

State & Address	Tuition	Fees	Books	Stipend	Comments
ILLINOIS IL Dept. of VA P.O. Box 19432 833 So. Spring St. Springfield, IL 62794 800-827-1000	Free; also for Veteran	No	No	No	
INDIANA IN Dept. of VA Attn: Education Div. 302 West Washington St. Room E-120 Indianapolis, IN 46204 317-232-3910	Free or Partial related to cost of the college	No	No	No	Up to 4 years at any postsecondary institution
IOWA IA Comm. of VA Camp Dodge Office 7799 NW Beaver Dr. Bldg. A6A Johnston, IA 50131-1902 515-252-5331	$600 up to $3,000	No	No	No	Dependents only; Spouses excluded
KANSAS KS Comm. of VA Jayhawk Towers, 700 SW Jackson Rm 701 Topeka, KS 66603-3150 913-296-3976	Free	No	No	No	Dependents only; Spouses excluded
KENTUCKY KY Vet. Dependents Ed. Assistance KY Ctr for VA 545 So. 3rd St., Rm 123 Louisville, KY 40202 502-595-4447	Free	Free	No	No	Up to 36 months or until age 23
LOUISIANA Local Parish Vet. Svcs P.O. Box 94095 Capitol Station Baton Rouge, LA 70804-9095 504-922-0500	Free	Free	No	No	

(continued)

Table 17-3 *(continued)*

State & Address	Tuition	Fees	Books	Stipend	Comments
MAINE ME Vet. Benefits Ofc. State Ofc. Bldg., Stn 117 Augusta, ME 04333 207-626-4464	Free	No	No	No	Up to $300 per year may be used towards expenses at any private college
MARYLAND MD State Scholarship Board 16 Francis St. Annapolis, MD 21401 410-974-5370	Free	No	No	No	Tuition benefits may be used at any college in-state, not to exceed tuition at Univ. Maryland
MASSACHUSETTS MA State Scholarship Office 330 Stuart St. Boston, MA 02116 617-727-9420	Free; Depend-ents only	No	No	No	Tuition benefits may be used at any college in state, not to exceed tuition at a public college
MICHIGAN MI Vet Trust Fund 611 West Ottawa Lansing, MI 48913 517-373-3130	Free	Free	No	No	Dependents only; Spouse excluded
MINNESOTA Dept. of VA Veterans Svc. Bldg. 20 West 12th St St. Paul, MN 55155 612-296-2562	Free except for the U. of MN	See Note	See Note	See Note	**NOTE:** Eligible students may receive up to $350 in any one year to be used for expenses
NEBRASKA Dept. of VA 301 Centennial Mall, So. P.O. Box 95083 Lincoln, NE 68509-5083 402-471-2458	Free	No	No	No	Includes state colleges, U of NE, and technical colleges
NEVADA Contact the College Admissions Office	No	No	No	No	Out-of-state tuition is waived for all veterans

State & Address	Tuition	Fees	Books	Stipend	Comments
NEW HAMPSHIRE *To attend: 4 yr. College* contact U. System of NH Durham, NH 03824 *To attend: 2 yr college* contact: NH Dept. of Ed. Concord, NH 03301 603-271-2257	Free	No	No	No	Dependents only; Spouse excluded
NEW JERSEY NJ Dept. of VA Eggert Crossing Rd CN 340 Trenton, NJ 08625-0340 609-989-6120	Free	No	No	No	Dependents of MIA/POWs from Southeast Asia conflict only
NEW MEXICO NM Vet. Svc. Comm. P.O. Box 2324 Santa Fe, NM 87504 505-827-6300	Free	Up to $600	No	No	Dependents of deceased parents only
NEW YORK NY State Higher Ed. Washington Ave., Albany, NY 12255 518-474-8615	No	No	No	No	Award is $450 per year regardless of income, tuition, or costs
NORTH CAROLINA NC Div. of VA Albemarle Bldg Ste 1065 325 No. Salisbury St. Raleigh, NC 27603 919-733-3851	Free *$1,200 to $3,000	Free	Free	Free	*Students attending 2-yr.colleges or private college may receive this benefit.
NORTH DAKOTA ND Dept. of VA P.O. Box 9003 Fargo, ND58106-9003 701-239-7165	Free	Free	No	No	Dependents only; Spouse excluded
OHIO Ohio Student Aid Commission 309 South Fourth P.O. Box 182452 Columbus, OH 43218 614-466-1190	Free	No	No	No	Dependents only; Spouse excluded

(continued)

Table 17-3 *(continued)*

State & Address	Tuition	Fees	Books	Stipend	Comments
OKLAHOMA Contact college's financial aid office	Free	No	No	No	Dependents of POWs or MIAs only; spouse excluded
PENNSYLVANIA (1)PHEAA 1200 No. 7th. St. Harrisburg, PA 17102 800-692-7435 (PA Only)	(1)Up to $2,600 or $800 out of state	No	No	No	Veteran benefit for bona fide PA residents.
(2)PA Dept. of VA Fort Indiantown Gap Bldg 5-0-0-47 Annville, PA 17003-5002 717-861-8901 800-54PAVET	(2) Up to $500	No	No	No	Dependents only; Spouse excluded
TEXAS TX Veterans Comm. P.O. Box 12277 Austin, TX 78711 512-463-5538	Free	Free	No	No	Includes Texas Nat'l/Air Nat'l Guard
VIRGINIA Commonwealth of VA Dept. of VA 270 Franklin Rd. SW Poff Fed. Bldg.Rm1012 Roanoke, VA 24011 540-857-7101	Free	No	No	No	Dependents only; Spouse excluded
WEST VIRGINIA WV Div of VA 1321 Plaza East, Ste. 101 Charleston, WV 25301 304-558-3661	Free	Up to $500	Up to $500	Up to $500	Dependents only; Spouse excluded
WISCONSIN WI Dept. of VA P.O. Box 7843 30 West Mifflin St. Madison, WI 53707-7843 608-266-1311	Free Also, free veteran (Part-time study only)	Free	Free		Tuition exemption for non-resident veterans; Ed. Loans up to $4,500 at 6%

State & Address	Tuition	Fees	Books	Stipend	Comments
WYOMING WY Dept. of VA 2360 E. Pershing Blvd Cheyenne, WY 82001 307-778-7396	No	No	No	No	Monthly stipends only.

Private Organizations and Agencies

Need more help in finding scholar dollars generated by military service for yourself, child or spouse. The following organizations can provide or help you track down the information you need. With the exception of the American Legion, which covers a wide range of benefits for former members of all military services, you can guess from the organization's name the type of assistance it provides.

American Legion
P.O. Box 1055
Indianapolis, IN 46206
W: www.legion.org

Air Force Sergeants Scholarship Program
P.O. Box 3111
Northbrook, Il 60065

Disabled American Veterans' Scholarship Program
P.O. Box 14301
Cincinnati, OH 45250-0301

Non-commissioned Officers Association Scholarship Program
NCOA Scholarship Foundation
P.O. Box 33610
San Antonio, TX 78265

Retired Officers Association Scholarship Foundation
Scholarship Loan Program
201 North Washington Street
Alexandria, VA 22314

Student Who Will Be a Veteran

Study now, pay your dues later! The money's good while you're in school, and you pay up in labor (yours) after graduation.

Federal

The U.S. government operates several scholarship programs for students who are willing to serve their nation in return for the scholarship funds.

Reserve Officer's Training Corps (ROTC) offers scholarships that cover as much as 100 percent of tuition, fees, textbooks, plus a $100 monthly stipend for four years of college. If you wait to join until you're in the upper-division ROTC program (junior and senior years of college) you'll receive less aid — only a $100 monthly stipend, but your service obligation is also less.

Each branch of the military operates ROTC offices. For information, contact the branch of your choice:

- ✔ **U.S. Air Force ROTC,** HQ AFROTC/RROO, 551 East Maxwell Blvd., Maxwell AFB, Al 36112; 334-953-2091

- ✔ **U.S. Army ROTC,** Gold Quest Center, PO Box 3279, Warminster, PA 18974; 800-USA-ROTC

- ✔ **U.S. Marines ROTC,** Command General Recruiting Command, Code MRON, 2 Navy Annex, Washington, DC 20380; 703-614-8541 x-1356

- ✔ **U.S. Navy ROTC,** Navy Opportunity, Information Center, PO Box 9406, Gaithersburg, MD 20898; 800-327-NAVY.

State

Each state maintains a National Guard for the Army and Air Force, providing a little known avenue of educational funding.

- ✔ **Montgomery GI Bill:** You can use the GI Bill to pursue an undergraduate or a graduate college degree as a member of the Army National Guard. If you attend a school approved by the U.S Department of Veterans Affairs, you'll receive a monthly check each month you're in school. As a full-time student (12 or more hours), you'll receive $203.24 per month for 36 months; as a three-quarter-time student (9 to 11 hours), $152.43 per month for 48 months; and as a part-time student, $101.62 per month for 72 months or $50.81 per month for 144 months. After graduation, you must have served, or agree to commit yourself, for six years of service in the Selective Reserve.

- ✔ **Enlistment Bonus:** If you have a skill the Army National Guard wants, you can get an enlistment bonus of $2,500 for choosing a designated military occupational specialty (MOS). See your Army National Guard recruiter for more information.

✔ **Student Loan Repayment Program:** If you qualify when you join the Army National Guard, you can get a big assist in paying back your college federally insured or guaranteed loans of up to $10,000. See your Army National Guard recruiter for more information.

✔ **Tuition Assistance (TAP) — Army Continuing Education System (ACES)** This program that pays for part-time undergraduate or graduate study is available to all members of the Army National Guard. The rules limit payment to 75 percent of tuition charges for a maximum of $1,000 per semester. Books or other fees are not reimbursed. Undergraduate studies are limited to 12 semester hours per fiscal year; graduate studies are limited to six semester hours per fiscal year. Payment for undergraduate studies at a four-year college is limited to a semester-hour cap of $85.00; payment for graduate studies is restricted to a semester-hour cap of $150.

Because the National Guard passage to college financial aid is unfamiliar to most students, Table 17-4 lists what we believe to be the first National Guard Directory with finaid contact information, scholarship programs, and tuition waivers.

Table 17-4	State National Guard Directory	
State National Guard/ Education Offices	**State Tuition Waiver**	**Scholarship Programs**
ALABAMA Education Services Office Military Dept. P.O. Box 3711 Montgomery, AL 36109-0711 334-271-7200	TAP-ACES only	Alabama Nursing Scholarship Program
ALASKA Education Services Office Education Officer P.O. Box 5800 FT. Richardson AK 99505-5800 907-428-6844	TAP-ACES	None
ARIZONA Education Services Office 5636 East McDowell Road Phoenix , AZ 85008-3495 602-267-2885	TAP-ACES AZ reimburses up to $250 per year	None
ARKANSAS Education Services Office N. Little Rock, AR 72118-2200 501-212-4021	TAP-ACES only	$1,000 Enlistment Scholarship

(continued)

Table 17-4 *(continued)*

State National Guard/ Education Offices	State Tuition Waiver	Scholarship Programs
CALIFORNIA Department of Air Force Education Services Office 77th MSS/DPEE 5146 Arnold Ave., Ste 2 McLellan AFBCA 95652-1079 916-643-4776	TAP-ACES CA reimburses up to 75% of tuition	None
COLORADO Education Services Office Public Affairs Officer 6848 So. Revere Parkway Englewood, CO 80112-6703 303-340-9431	TAP-ACES CO reimburses up to 75% of tuition	None
CONNECTICUT Education Services Office National Guard Armory 360 Broad Street Hartford, CT 06105-3795 860-524-4953	TAP-ACES CN pays up to 100% of tuition at any state-supported college, university, or community College	None
DELAWARE Education Services Office First Regiment Road Wilmington, DE 19808-2191 302-326-7001	TAP-ACES DE pays up to $1,000 per year for any state-supported institution	None
DISTRICT OF COLUMBIA Education Services Office National Guard Armory 2001 East Capitol St. Washington, DC 20003-1719 202-433-4960	TAP-ACES DC pays up to 75% of tuition not to exceed $1,000; 15 sem. hrs. maximum per year	$1,000 per semester
FLORIDA Education Services Office P.O. Box 1008 St. Augustine, FL 32085-1008 904-823-0350	TAP-ACES FL has legislation pending for potential state assistance	None

State National Guard/ Education Offices	State Tuition Waiver	Scholarship Programs
GEORGIA Education Services Office GA Dept. of Defense P.O. Box 17965 Atlanta, GA 30316-0965 404-675-5331	TAP-ACES only	None
GUAM Education Services Office 622 E. Harmon Industrial Park Rd. Fort Juan Muna Tamuning, GU 96911-4421 011-671-475-0803	TAP-ACES	None
HAWAII Education Services Office 3949 Diamond Head Rd. Honolulu, HI 96816-4495 808-733-4133	TAP-ACES HI state program varies based on funding	None
IDAHO Education Services Office 4040 W. Guard Street Boise, ID 83705-5004 208-422-3761	TAP-ACES only	None
ILLINOIS Education Services Office 1301 N. MacArthur Blvd. Springfield, IL 62702-2399 217-761-3782	TAP-ACES IL provides 100% tuition for any state-supported institution	Illinois National Guard Scholarship
INDIANA Education Services Office Adjutant General of IN ATTN: MDI-AG, 2002 South Holt Road Indianapolis, IN 46241-4839 317-247-3502	TAP-ACES IN provides 100% tuition at any state-supported college or univ. in Indiana as of 7/1/97	None
IOWA Education Services Office 7700 N.W. Beaver Drive Camp Dodge Johnston, IA 50131-1902 515-252-4414	TAP-ACES only	10-15 $500 NG scholarships are awarded annually

(continued)

Table 17-4 *(continued)*

State National Guard/ Education Offices	State Tuition Waiver	Scholarship Programs
KANSAS Education Services Office 2800 S.W. Topeka Blvd. Topeka, KS 66611-1287 913-274-1081	TAP-ACES KS provides 100% tuition for any new enlistment or reenlistment	ROTC scholarship is available up to four years in return for four years' service to KSNG
KENTUCKY Education Services Office Bldg 100-100 Minuteman Pkwy Frankfort, KY 40601-6168 502-564-8550	TAP-ACES KY provides 100% tuition at any state-supported postsecondary institution	None
LOUISIANA Education Services Office Headquarters Building Jackson Barracks New Orleans, LA 70146-0330 800-899-6355	TAP-ACES LA provides 100% tuition at any state-supported postsecondary institution	None
MAINE Education Services Office Military Bureau Hdqtrs. Maine National Guard Camp Keyes Augusta, ME 04333-0033 207-626-4370	TAP-ACES pays tuition for four seats per campus at six Maine Technical Colleges	None
MARYLAND Education Services Office 5th Regiment Armory Baltimore, MD 21201-2288 410-576-1499	TAP-ACES MD provides 25-50% tuition at any public institution	None
MASSACHUSETTS Education Services Office MA National Guard 50 Maple Street Milford, MA 01757 508-233-6552 617-944-0500 Ext. 2254	TAP-ACES MA provides 100% tuition at any state-supported institution in MA	Adjutant Scholarship Program at Norwich U(3 @ $1,000); Nat'l. Guard Asc. of MA Scholarship
MICHIGAN Education Services Office 2500 So. Washington Ave Lansing, MI 48913-5101 517-483-5519	TAP-ACES only Association of Michigan Scholarships	National Guard

State National Guard/ Education Offices	State Tuition Waiver	Scholarship Programs
MINNESOTA Education Services Office Dept., Military Affairs 4th Fl. Veterans Services Bldg. 20 West 12th Street St. Paul, MN 55155-2098 612-282-4591	TAP-ACES MN provides 50% tuition at any state-supported institution in MN; or at private or out-of-state colleges not to exceed 50% cost at U of MN	None
MISSISSIPPI Education Services Office P.O. Box 5027 Jackson, MS 39296-5027 601-973-6300	TAP-ACES only	None
MISSOURI Education Services Office 2302 Militia Drive #DPP-I Jefferson City, MO 65101-1203 573-526-9537	TAP-ACES only	Missouri National Guard State Sponsored Scholarship
MONTANA Education Services Office 2475 Broadway St. Helena, MT 59604-4789 406-444-2260	TAP-ACES Bill proposed; pending approval for state benefits	None
NEBRASKA Tuition Assistance Office 1300 Military Road Lincoln, NE 68508-1090 402-471-7170	TAP-ACES NE provides for 50% tuition assistance at any state-supported school in NE	None
NEVADA Nevada Air National Guard State Headquarters Education Services Office 2525 South Carson Drive Carson City, NV 89701-5502 702-887-7288	TAP-ACES NV provides up to 50% reimbursement at any state-supported college in Nebraska	None
NEW HAMPSHIRE Education Services Office #1 Airport Road Concord, NH 03301-5353 603-228-1135 x1550	TAP-ACES NH provides 100% tuition at any state-supported institution of higher education in NH	None

(continued)

Table 17-4 *(continued)*

State National Guard/ Education Offices	State Tuition Waiver	Scholarship Programs
NEW JERSEY Education Services Office New Jersey Department of Military and Veterans' Affairs Eggert Crossing Rd., CN 340 Trenton, NJ 08625-0340 Education Services Officer 609-562-0668	TAP-ACES provides 100% tuition at state-supported institutions of higher education in NJ	None
NEW MEXICO Education Services Office 47 Bataan Boulevard Santa Fe, NM 87505 505-474-1245	TAP-ACES only	None
NEW YORK Education Services Office 330 Old Niskayuna Road Latham, NY 12110-2224 518-786-4937	TAP-ACES NY recruitment/ retention incentive program provides for 100% tuition only, not to exceed cost of attending SUNY	Yes; contact Capt. Gallerie for details of each service's scholarship program
NORTH CAROLINA Education Services Office 4105 Reedy Creek Road Raleigh, NC 27607-6410 919-664-6194 or 800-621-4136	TAP-ACES NC provides up to $1,000 per state fiscal year toward tuition and fees; $4,000 over Guard career	North Carolina National Guard Association Scholarship
NORTH DAKOTA Education Services Office P.O. Box 5511 Bismarck, ND 58506-5511 701-224-5903	TAP-ACES ND provides 100% tuition at any state-supported institution in ND	None
OHIO Education Services Office Tuition Grant Program 2825 West Dublin-Granville Rd Columbus, OH 43235-2789 614-889-7032	TAP-ACES OH provides 60% tuition at any state-supported institution; private schools receive an avg. grant based on OU's tuition	None

State National Guard/ Education Offices	State Tuition Waiver	Scholarship Programs
OKLAHOMA Education Services Office 3501 Military Circle Oklahoma City, OK 73111-4398 405-425-8322	TAP-ACES OK provides 100% tuition at state-supported institution up to Bachelor's degree	None
OREGON Education Services Office Oregon Military Dept. P.O. Box 14350 Salem, OR 97309-5047 503-945-3816	TAP-ACES	None
PENNSYLVANIA Education Services Office Tuition Assistance Office Fort Indiantown Gap Annville, PA 17003-5002 717-861-8536	TAP-ACES provides from $1,200 to $2,400 per school year	None
PUERTO RICO Education Services Office P.O. Box 3786 San Juan, PR 00904-3786 787-289-1416	TAP-ACES TAG-PR provides 100% tuition not to exceed $75 per credit for maximum of 6 credit hours for post-graduate and doctorate courses, or 9 credits at U of PR	Military dependents; program defrays tuition costs up to 100% for 12 credits or less, not to exceed $20 per college credit for undergraduate school; or 50% for up to 6 credits, not to exceed $25 at master's level
RHODE ISLAND Education Services Office 645 New London Cranston, RI 02920-3097 401-457-4309	TAP-ACES	None
SOUTH CAROLINA Education Services Office #1 National Guard Road Columbia, SC 29201-4766 803-806-4253	TAP-ACES legislation pending regarding additional tuition benefits; estimated to be $1,000 per year	None

(continued)

Table 17-4 *(continued)*

State National Guard/ Education Offices	State Tuition Waiver	Scholarship Programs
SOUTH DAKOTA Education Services Office 2823 West Main Rapid City, SD 57702 605-399-6729	TAP-ACES only	Partial state tuition and textbook reimbursement
TENNESSEE Education Services Office Houston Barracks P.O. Box 41502 Nashville, TN 37204-1502 615-313-0594	TAP-ACES only	Yes; scholarships available through the Enlisted Association and the Officers' Association
TEXAS Education Services Office ATT: AGTX-PAE P.O. Box 5218, Camp Mabry Austin, TX 78763-5218 512-465-6024 or 512-465-5515	TAP-ACES only	RSVP Scholarship plus GI provides nearly $5,000/year
UTAH Education Services Office 12953 S. Minuteman Dr. AOPCA-ESO Draper, UT 84020-1776 801-576-3614	TAP-ACES only	None
VERMONT Education Services Office Green Mountain Armory Camp Johnson Colchester, VT 05446-3004 802-654-0348	TAP-ACES only	None
VIRGINIA Personnel Services Office 600 East Broad Street Richmond, VA 23219-1832 804-775-9226	TAP-ACES VA provides 50% tuition not to exceed $500 per semester and $1,000 per year	Scholarships up to $2,000

State National Guard/ Education Offices	State Tuition Waiver	Scholarship Programs
VIRGIN ISLANDS Education Services Office 4031 La Grande Princess Lot 1B Christiansted, VI 00820-4353 809-712-7758	TAP-ACES	None
WASHINGTON Education Services Office Camp Murray, Building 1 Tacoma, WA 98430-5000 206-512-8899	TAP-ACES WA provides 75% tuition, based on space availability at selected colleges	None
WEST VIRGINIA Education Services Office 1703 Coonskin Drive Charleston, WV 25311-1085 304-341-6335	TAP-ACES	None
WISCONSIN Education Services Office P.O. Box 8111 Madison, WI 53708-8111 608-242-3448	TAP-ACES provides 50% tuition based on undergraduate admissions at UW-Madison; Legislation in place July 1 for 100% tuition	None
WYOMING Education Services Office 5500 Bishop Boulevard Cheyenne, WY 82009-3320 307-772-5262	TAP-ACES provides $3,000 per year credit for nonresidents attending University of Wyoming	None

Be Glad You Wear Army Boots

You don't need a drill sergeant to scream that no matter which branch of the military you select, going to school in or out of uniform is a lot cheaper than hoofing it on your own.

Additional reading

Need A Lift? The American Legion's annual college scholarship and financial aid guide for veterans and their families is a true public service. Send $3 to: Need A Lift, P.O. Box 1050, Indianapolis, IN 46206.

Chapter 18

Planning for Graduate and Professional Study

*F*ewer than half of all graduate students receive any financial aid, but in the humanities, about six out of ten graduate students are on their own and in the social sciences, seven out of ten graduate students receive no finaid dollars.

Graduate student support is more abundant in the science and engineering precincts, but even there some graduate and professional students are financially flying solo.

Other than gifts from Aunt Sue and working, what resources are left? In a word, loans. In fact, *loans are the chief source of funding* for most students who pursue graduate and professional study.

Graduate students acquire loans and grants from many of the same places that undergraduate students do. In addition, institutions award money to graduate students for fellowships and teaching assistantships, which carry teaching or research responsibilities.

Climbing a Mountain of Debt

Rosa and her husband, Dan, recently graduated together from a private law school. If you hyperventilate easily when you think about big numbers, catch your breath before you read the next paragraph.

Because they'd financed most of their entire education with borrowed money, the newly minted professional couple now owes $220,000 in education loans and it's payback time. Dan and Rosa can expect to keep sending fat checks to loan providers long after the dust settles on their law degrees. Payments will be roughly $2,000 monthly for both. That's $24,000 a year — gadzooks!

Rosa and Dan's mix of madness and money are hardly rare. As tuition for advanced education climbs and the government and private lenders pass out loans by the fistful, futurologists predict that the $3.3 billion increase in graduate/professional loans in the last four years will continue rising rapidly. For example, the government's Federal Stafford loan (see Chapter 7), which covers most medical studies, raised its annual limit to $18,500 per student, not to exceed an aggregate of $138,500 for all years of college.

Terrifying, isn't it? Especially when you consider the entry-level salary you can expect in the first few years after you graduate.

The race to gain an advanced education and pay for it is like trying to run a marathon wearing leg-irons. If you decide to enter the race, you have to take the attitude that the odds are merely formidable, not insurmountable.

A question of degree: Terms for advanced education

The term *advanced study* describes both graduate and professional study.

Graduate study means study that follows a bachelor's degree in a given academic field, such as history, chemistry, or literature. The Ph.D. is a graduate degree, as is the Master of Arts.

Professional study describes the practical application of knowledge and skills such as in business, law, architecture, and medicine. JD (for *juris doctor*) is a first professional law degree, not a doctorate in law.

In everyday usage, the term graduate degree is often substituted for the correct term of advanced degree when referring to both graduate and professional degrees.

Then again, some debt burdens do seem insurmountable, such as a newsmagazine report of a husband and wife who graduated from medical school last year owing almost $500,000 in student loans. (Quick! The smelling salts!)

The insanity of borrowing a debt load that may have you looking over your shoulder for bill collectors most of your life is not going to go away. A frightening career uncertainty has slithered into the work world, and smart first-time and returning students alike are in the educational trenches, taming the serpentine beast by earning imposing professional degrees.

Whether you're a dedicated scientist in the making or a hard-core numbers-cruncher, your future's far more alluring when you have a competitively-edged degree in hand. You know that! What you may not have focused on so clearly is the financial aid planning and sacrifice needed to cushion your landing when you must repay all those loans.

As you consider borrowing for graduate education, anticipate what the monthly cost to repay the loans will be, especially if you have a spouse, kids, pets, a mortgage, two autos, and a boat to support. Table 18-1 shows a 10-year monthly repayment schedule that gives you clues to what debt burdens you face in the future for jumbo loans at 8%, 9%, or 10% amounts up to a quarter of a million dollars.

Table 18-1	10-Year Monthly Repayment Plan		
Amount Borrowed	*8%*	*9%*	*10%*
$75,000	$910.50	$950.25	$991.50
$100,000	$1,214.00	$1,267.00	$1,322.00
$125,000	$1,517.50	$1,583.75	$1,652.50
$150,000	$1,821.00	$1,900.50	$1,983.00
$175,000	$2,124.50	$2,217.25	$2,313.50
$200,000	$2,428.00	$2,534.00	$2,644.00
$225,000	$2,731.50	$2,850.75	$2,974.50
$250,000	$3,035.00	$3,167.50	$3,305.00

Source: Sandy Springs National Bank of Maryland

When you weigh the cost of graduate or professional study, give your imagination something positive to play with: The U.S. Census Bureau finds that over a lifetime, those with *professional degrees* earn $3 million on average; those who have a baccalaureate, $1.4 million.

The payoff for professional degrees is especially high in technology, law, medicine, and business. Janice, for example, a new biomedical Ph.D., landed a plummy job at a biomedical firm in San Diego. The job pays enough to cover a new car payment, rent, a comfortable lifestyle, and her $850 monthly education-loan payments.

Graduate Loans for Fields with High Earnings Potential

Students who pursue professional degrees are granted larger loans than those who go after graduate degrees in academic fields such as biology or English. That's because lenders expect doctors, lawyers, and MBAs to outearn lab workers and English teachers, placing them in a better position to pay off their loans. Table 18-2 compares typical loan limits for programs funding advanced degrees and notes the various disciplines that apply. The data on this chart was verified in mid-1997. Things change. Always recheck the particulars of any loan program in which you are interested.

Legend for Table 18-2

wic = while in college

woc = while out of college

wcs = with co-signor

wocs = without co-signor

* = Requires credit test

† = Need-based loan (parents' and/or student's income)

Source of data for Table 18-2: Dr. Herm Davis

Table 18-2   **Comparison of Loan Programs for Graduate and Professional Study**

Loan Programs	Annual Loan Limit	Maximum Loan Limit	Interest Rate	Fees- (Guarantee, Organization, Insurance)	Deferment	Grace Period	Repayment Calendar	Minimum Monthly Payment
Federal Subsidized † **Stafford (or) Direct Loan** [800-433-3243]	$8,500	$65,500	Variable not to exceed 8.25%	4%	Yes, while in college (wic)	6 months after non-enrollment	Up to 10 years* to repay	$50
Federal Unsubsidized † **Stafford (or) Direct Loan** [800-433-3243]	$18,500	$138,500	Variable not to exceed 8.25%	4%	Yes, wic; interest is capitalizing	6 months after non-enrollment	Up to 10 years to repay	$50
Health Education † **Assistance Loan** **(HEAL) †** [301-443-1540]	$12,500-$20,000	$50,000-$80,000	Variable 91-day T-Bill +3%	Yes Yes Av. 8%	Yes- maximum of 4 years enrollment	9 months after non-	Up to 25 years to repay	$50
Signature Health Loan* [888-888-3461]	Cost of education		7.5% wic 7.85% woc	7% wic+ 2% woc	Yes- wic Yes- 2 years woc	Yes- 24 months	Up to 25 years to repay	$50 per schedule
Primary Care (Medical) **Loan (PCL)** [301-443-1540]	$2,500 plus tuition and fees	None	5%	No	Yes- while in college/	12 months after non-residency	Up to 10 years* to repay enrollment	$15
MEDLOANS and **Alternative Loans** **Program (ALP)*** (Medical only) [202-828-0400]	$30,000	$120,000 (aggregate debt of education loans)	Variable 91-day T-Bill +2.7%	8% Maximum	Yes 3-4 yrs postgrad training	No	Up to 10 years to repay	Per schedule
Medical Access Loans (Medical only) * [.....SL]	Cost of education	$165,000 (aggregate debt of educational loans)	Variable 91-day T-Bill+2.75%	6.5% +2.0% at repayment	Yes- wic; interest is capitalizing	9 months after non-enrollment	Up to 20 years to repay	$50 Per schedule

(continued)

Table 18-2 (continued)

Loan Programs	Annual Loan Limit	Maximum Loan Limit	Interest Rate	Fees- (Guarantee, Organization, Insurance)	Deferment	Grace Period	Repayment Calendar	Minimum Monthly Payment
MED/DENT EXCEL (Medical and Dental only) [800-634-9308]	$20,000 wocs Up to cost of education wcs	$90,000-wocs $120,000-wcs (with cosigner)	Prime+.5%	Yes	Yes- wic; interest is capitalizing			Per schedule
LawLoans (LSL) * [800-948-1090]	Minimum $500 up to cost of education	$125,000-wocs $150,000- wcs	Variable 13-wk T-Bill +3.25% wic & 3.5% woc	6.5% wcs or +5.75 wocs (won't exceed 9.25%)	Yes- wic; interest is capitalizing	9 months after non-enrollment	Up to 15 years to repay	Per schedule
Law Access Loan (LAL) * [800-282-1550]	Cost of education	$120,000 (aggregate debt of education loans)	Variable 91-day T-Bill +3.25%	7.0% +4.0% at repayment	Yes- wic; interest is capitalizing	6 months after non-enrollment	Up to 20 years to repay	$50 Per schedule
LawEXCEL * [800-634-9308]	$15,000 wocs Up to cost of education wcs	Unlimitied-wcs $80,000 wocs	Variable Prime +.5% maximum	9% wocs 6% wcs [+2% fee for capitalization]	Yes- wic; interest is capitalizing	6 months after non-enrollment	Up to 20 years to repay	$50 Per schedule
MBAEXCEL * [800-634-9308]	$15,000 wocs Up to cost of education wcs	$80,000 with a cumulative debt	Variable Prime +.5% Maximum	8% wocs 5% wcs [+2% fee for capitalization]	Yes- wic ; interest is capitalization	6 months after non-enrollment	Up to 20 years to repay	$50 Per schedule
Business Access * Loan Program [800-282-1550]	Cost of education	$120,000 (aggregate debt of education loans)	Variable 91-day T-Bill +3.25%	6.5% +2% at time of repayment	Yes- wic; interest is capitalizing	9 months after non-enrollment	Up to 20 years to repay	Per schedule

Loan Programs	Annual Loan Limit	Maximum Loan Limit	Interest Rate	Fees- (Guarantee, Organization, Insurance)	Deferment	Grace Period	Repayment Calendar	Minimum Monthly Payment
MBA Tuition Loans * [888-440-4622]	Cost of education	Unlimited	Variable 91-day T-Bill +3.25%	7.5%	Yes- wic; interest is capitalizing	6 months after non-enrollment	12-15 years to repay	$50 Per schedule
MBA Loan * [888-440-4622]	Cost of education Minimum $500 minus other aid	Unlimited	Variable 13-wk T-Bill +3.25% or fixed 4.5%	6% wcs or up to 7% wocs	Yes- wic; interest is capitalizing	6 months after non-enrollment	Up to 15 years to repay	$50 Per schedule
Professional Education Plan (PEP) * [800-243-8886]	$2,000- $12000 wocs $2,000- 20,000 wcs	Unlimited	Variable not to exceed prim plus of 4%	5%guarantee fee	Yes- wic; interest is capitalizing	6 months after non-enrollment	Up to 20 years to repay	$50 Per schedule
Graduate Access Loans (All Graduate Majors) * [800-282-1550]	Cost of Education	$120,000 (aggregate debt of education loans)	Variable 91-day T-Bill +3.4%wocs or +3.0%wcs	7.0% +3.0% at repayment	Yes- wic; interest is capitalizing	9 months after non-enrollment	Up to 20 years to repay	$50 Per schedule
GradSHARE * [800-634-9308]	$12,000 wocs Up to cost of education	$52,000 cumulative debt $60,000	Prime rate plus 3% is maximum	6.0% wcs 8.0% wocs [+2% at repayment	Yes- wic; interest is capitalizing	6 months after non-enrollment	Up to 25 years to repay	$50 Per schedule
Option 4 Loan Program * [800-635-3785]	$15,000	$60,000	Variable 91-day T-bill +3.5%		Yes- wic; interest is capitalizing		Up to 15 years to repay	Per schedule
ENGLoans (Engineering) [800-255-8374] *	Cost of education	Unlimited	Prime rate plus 3.65%	6% wcs 7.5% at repayment	Yes- wic; interest is capitalizing	9 months after non-enrollment	Up to 15 years to repay	$50 Per schedule
EXCEL (All Majors) [800-634-9308]	Cost of education	Unlimited	Prime +WSI +.5%	7%	Yes- wic ; interest is capitalizing		Up to 20 years to repay	

(continued)

Table 18-2 (continued)

Loan Programs	Annual Loan Limit	Maximum Loan Limit	Interest Rate	Fees- (Guarantee, Organization, Insurance)	Deferment	Grace Period	Repayment Calendar	Minimum Monthly Payment
Achiever Loan * (All Majors) [800-225-6783]	Cost of education	Unlimited	13 wk t-Bill +3.95-4.5%	3-4% Loan Fee + $35 Application Fee	Yes- wic; interest is capitalizing		Up to 15 years to repay	
Signature Loan * (All Majors and non citizens wcos) [888-888-3461]	Cost of education	$100,000	91-day T-Bill +3.10%	6%	Yes- wic; interest is capitalizing	6 months after non-enrollment	Up to 15 years to repay	$50 per schedule
PLATO * [800-467-5286]	Cost of education $25,000 maximum	$100,000	fixed 7.9% (or) Prime +2-6%	7%	Yes- wic; interest is capitalizing	6 months after non-enrollment	Up to 15 years to repay	
CitiAssist Graduate [800-692-8200] All grad programs — full, half, or part-time study	$15,000 ($20,000 medical)	$110,000 ($135,000 medical)	Prime = 1%	None	Yes - interest capitalizes only once at start of repayment	6 months after separation (6 months after residency for medical)	15 years (20 years for medical)	$50 standard; lower graduated payments may be available
TERI Alternative LOAN [800-255-8374]	Cost of education	Unlimited	Varies, not to exceed prime +2%	5%-6% fully deferred	Yes - interest is capitalized	45 days after non-enrollment	Up to 20 years to repay	$50 per schedulle

Graduate/Professional Private Loans

Federal Stafford and Direct Student Loans
(for graduate students in any discipline)
U.S. Department of Education
Federal Student Aid Information Center
P.O. Box 84
Washington, DC 20044-0084
800-433-3243
http://www.ed.gov

Health Education Assistance Loan (HEAL)
(for medical students only)
Division of Student Assistance
HEAL Branch
Parklawn Building, Room 8-37
5600 Fishers Lane
Rockville, MD 20857
301-443-1540

Signature Health Loan
(for allopathic medicine, dental, optometry, osteopathic medicine, pharmacy, podiatry, and veterinary medicine only)
Sallie Mae
1050 Thomas Jefferson St. NW
Washington, DC 20007-3871
888-888-3461

Primary Care Loan (PCL)
(See HEAL Loan Program)

MEDLOANS and Alternative Loan Program (ALP)
(for medical students only)
Association of American Medical Colleges
2450 N. Street, NW
Washington, DC 20037
202-828-0400

Medical Access Loans
(for medical students only)
The Access Group
P.O. Box 7430
Wilmington, DE 19803-0430
800-282-1550

MEDSHARE
(for medical and dental students only)
The New England Loan Marketing Association
Nellie Mae
50 Braintree Hill Park, Suite 300
Braintree, MA 02184
800-634-9308

LawLoans (LSI)
(for law students only)
Sallie Mae
P.O. Box 59023
Panama City, FL 32402-9023
800-282-1550

Law Access Loan (LAL)
(for law students only)
The Access Group
P.O. Box 7430
Wilmington, DE 19803-0430
800-282-1550

LawSHARE
(for law students only)
The New England Loan Marketing Association
Nellie Mae
50 Braintree Hill Park, Suite 300
Braintree, MA 02184
800-634-9308

MBASHARE
(for business students only)
The New England Loan Marketing
Association
Nellie Mae
50 Braintree Hill Park, Suite 300
Braintree, MA 02184
800-634-9308

Business Access Loan Program
(for business graduate students only)
The Access Group
P.O. Box 7430
Wilmington, DE 19803-0430
800-282-1550

MBA Loans and Tuition Loan Plan
(for business graduate students only)
(contact the financial aid office)

Professional Education Plan (Pep)
*(for graduate and professional students
including but not limited to chiropractic,
osteopathic, optometric, veterinary,
physical therapy, physician's assistant,
nursing, or occupational therapy fields)*
The Education Resources Institute
(TERI)
330 Stuart Street, Suite 500
Boston, MA 02116-5237
800-243-8886

TERI Alternative Loan
800-255-8374

Graduate Access Loans
(for graduate students in any discipline)
The Access Group
P.O. Box 7430
Wilmington, DE 19803-0430
800-282-1550

GradSHARE
(for graduate students in any discipline)
The New England Loan Marketing
Association
Nellie Mae
50 Braintree Hill Park, Suite 300
Braintree, MA 02184
800-634-9308

Option 4 Loan Program
(for graduate students in any discipline)
USA Funds
P.O. Box 6198
Indianapolis, IN 46206-6198
800-635-3785

ENGLoans
(for engineering students only)
United Student Aid Group
P.O. Box 6182
Indianapolis, IN 46206
800-255-8374

EXCEL
Nellie Mae
50 Braintree Hill Park, Suite 300
Braintree, MA 02184
800-634-9308
info@nelliemae.org

Achiever Loan
Key Bank Education Resources
17 Corporate Woods Blvd
Albany, NY 12211
800-540-1855

Signature Education EducationLoan
Sallie Mae
1050 Thomas Jefferson St. NW
Washington, DC 20007-3871
888-888-3461

PLATO
(for graduate students in any discipline)
The Classic Student Loan
205 Van Buren St., Suite 200
Herndon, VA 20170-5336
800-467-5286
703-709-8609 fax

CitiAssist
(for graduate students in any discipline)
Citibank Student Loan Corporation
99 Garnsey Road
Pittsford, N.Y. 14534
716-248-7672
800-692-8200

Other Resources for Graduate School

The GEM Ph. D. Science Consortium
(National Consortium for Graduate Degrees for Minorities in Engineering and Science)
1118 N. Eddy St.
Notre Dame, IN 46556
219-631-7771

National Health Service Corps Scholarship
2070 Chain Bridge Road
Vienna, VA 22182
800-221-9393

National Science Foundation
Oak Ridge Assoc. of Universities
4201 Wilson Blvd.
Arlington, VA 22230
703-306-1234

Sallie Mae
(loan consolidation)
Attention CMIS
P.O. Box 1304
Merrifield, VA 22116
800-524-9100

USA Group
(repayment counseling)
P.O. Box 6180
Indianapolis, IN 46206-6180
800-448-3533

National College Scholarship Foundation
(national loan forgiveness data base)
P.O. Box 8207
Gaithersburg, MD 20898-8207
301-548-9423
ncsf@aol.com

Fellowships and Assistantships: Finaid for Advanced Study

Only advanced study offers the form of financial aid known as fellowships and assistantships.

Fellowships

Most fellowships are outright awards that require no service in return. Fellowships often provide the cost of tuition and fees, plus a stipend to cover bare-necessity living expenses. They may be based primarily on demonstrated need, or on academic merit, or on a combination of need and merit.

Both university and foundations provide fellowships. Most often the fellowships sponsored by universities are merit-based because the schools wants students whose accomplishments add to their institutional prestige.

The awards often must be renewed annually. Fellowships attract graduate to post-doctoral students with sterling academic records; the competition is fierce, but the rewards are tremendous and prestigious.

Assistantships

First-year graduate students often become teaching assistants (TA), research assistants (RA), or administrative assistant (AA). Some universities provide financial support in the form of a project assistantship (PAship). Most schools reduce or waive tuition fees for assistants.

TAs pursuing an advanced degree in a subject taught at the undergraduate level (arts and sciences, for example) typically work 20 hours a week as a teacher-in-training. You may give lectures, grade papers, correct classwork, and advise students. TAs receive salary. This type of finaid comes from academic departments, not the university's financial aid office.

RAs assist a faculty member in research these and positions go to the most promising students, but usually not before the second year of advanced study. Hours vary. The appointment pays a salary.

AAs toil 10 to 20 hours each week in an administrative office of the university. Some administrative assistantships pay a salary, others provide a tuition waiver, and still others provide both.

By riding the coattails of a faculty member as an assistant, you earn not only money and maybe tuition, but you also gain crucial experience for your first after-graduation job.

Conditional trades

Designed to recruit good people for understaffed areas, some scholarships and grants are really loans in that recipients agree to return the value of the education in work, usually with a specific employer or in a specific career or geographic area.

A student physician, for instance, in return for a medical education may agree to work at a medically-underserved rural area for four years; a nurse whose training costs were paid by the federal government may agree to serve in a military service for four years.

If a recipient chooses not to make good on the promise, the award generally must be repaid in full.

Employer-Aided Study in Selected Fields

Employers are another alternative to loans (see Chapter 2). A number of current and future employers give special financial assistance to students in specific fields. The examples of business and engineering follow.

Business Administration

Employers often help cover the expenses of students pursuing an MBA (Master's in Business Administration) degree. For example, a prospective employer may cover the costs of a second-year business school student who looks like a hot hire. Another popular approach is for employers to help pay the costs for current employees enrolled in part-time MBA programs.

An MBA who has consulting capabilities and a degree from a top school can look forward to a starting salary of more than $76,000 — an income that more than compensates for pregraduation expenses. Management consulting (especially the type that helps trim overstretched companies), finance, marketing, and management information systems are promising employment spots in the new millennium.

Engineering

The National Research Council says that only four out of ten engineering students who receive a Ph.D. are in debt at graduation — meaning that the majority of engineering doctoral candidates obtain enough grants and fellowships to stay virtually debt-free. At private universities, annual costs sometimes exceed $30,000 per year; at public universities, about $18,000.

The tax man biteth

Graduate-level tuition reimbursement from employers used to be tax-free, but it is currently treated as taxable income. Because graduate-level education is increasingly seen as important for mid-career professionals who want to change jobs or be promoted, as well as for younger graduate students, lawmakers will be urged by many voters to reconsider the issue. Maybe in the next Congress, the tax man goeth. Watch the news.

In the meantime, anticipate a bite out of your paycheck when you create your educational financial plan.

Engineering and scientific fields are generally big on grants because the government has set up several funds to encourage technological growth. Current grants come especially easy to females and minority group members who are currently underrepresented in the technical and engineering fields.

After receiving their advanced degree, graduates can look forward to eager employers. Computer science and engineering Ph.D.s are rewarded with an average starting salary of more than $56,000.

When compared to repaying jumbo loans, employer-paid alternatives are appealing alternatives.

As a rule of thumb, you can find out what free money is available in a profession by quizzing the relevant professional organizations, which you can find online by using the organization's name in a keyword search, or by looking in such references as the *Encyclopedia of Associations*.

With effort, most students can scarf up some form of aid besides loans. If you choose the right field, your feverish finaid quest will pay off later when you have a fast-track future. But only if you complete the degree.

Too many graduate students leave school with what amounts to a partial degree, which can be a liability. Some employers interpret unfinished education as evidence of an inability to stick with a project to completion or a lack of passion for the work.

Don't let money worries bog down your education; apply your study skills and energy to finding the finaid that can help you complete that degree.

Additional reading

Dan Cassidy's Worldwide Graduate Scholarship Directory, 4th Edition; National Scholarship Research Service, Santa Rosa, CA

The College Blue Book — Scholarships, Fellowships, Grants and Loans, 24th Edition; Huber William Hurt, Harriet-Jean Hurt, and Christian E. Burckel, Macmillan Publishing Company, 1996

Fellowships and Grants for Training and Research, Social Science Research Council, New York

Financing Graduate School, Patricia McWade, Petersons Guides, Princeton, NJ, 1996

Foundation Grants to Individuals, 9th Edition, Carlotta R. Mills (ed.), Foundation Center, New York

The Road to Graduate School: Selection, Admissions, Financial Aid, Dianne Lake, Bantam Doubleday Dell Publishers, New York, 1996

Scholarships, Fellowships and Loans, Gale Research Inc., Detroit, 1997

Part IV
Filling Out Forms and Other Fine Print

The 5th Wave   By Rich Tennant

"Our plan is to buy the rest of it when we pay off our college loan."

In this part ...

The innocuous statement "read instructions and complete this form" may seem simple. The hundreds of blanks in the typical finaid application may even seem harmless. But one false move and your chances for finaid could crash down on hard earth. This part helps you jack up your aid by correctly filling out need analysis forms. You also learn in plain English how to understand your award letters and when you get your first check. These chapters give line-by-line tips on every blank, from the no-brainers to the tricky questions.

Chapter 19

Blooper-Proof These Lines

. . . .

. . . .

*T*he previous chapter discussed serious pitfalls to avoid on financial aid application forms. This chapter focuses on what should be no-brainers.

Many of the questions on the Free Application for Federal Student Aid (FAFSA) seem easy — too easy. Just because the form asks for information you can recite in your sleep doesn't mean you can't bollix it up.

You, the student, should fill out the FAFSA. But most often, put off by the myriad blanks and lines and requests for numbers, the future college student freaks out and passes the work on to Mom or Dad.

Finaid-hungry applicants all over the country are blemishing their applications at this very moment due to pure carelessness. Don't join the bumbling throngs. As you, or your folks, gingerly print in your information, tend to the tips that follow.

Lines 8 and 9: What's Your Number?

When well-meaning moms or dads fill out the FAFSA, sometimes they get so intense that they give their own Social Security number when the form asks for the student's. The same dear parents can be so consistent that they give their own dates of birth as well.

The joke's on the student when the application reviewer looks at the age listed and classifies the student as an independent student.

Line 17: Are you married?

This question asks if the student is married; parents filling out this form may mistakenly answer "yes" — which means the typically single student is instantly married in the finaid reviewer's eyes.

Not so funny, because the rest of the answers on the form won't make sense and will confuse the federal processor. This puzzler can cause the form to be questioned, delayed, and even rejected before it is finally processed.

Line 19: A diploma is not a degree

This question asks if students will have a first bachelor's degree by July 1 before entering college in September. Students have been known to confuse a diploma with a degree, and answer "yes." Oops.

With this bubble-headed clowning, students become seriously ineligible for the major federal grant programs (Pell, SEOG) and most state scholarship programs. The bulk of grant programs crusade to assist students towards their first degree. Graduate finaid usually comes from loans or work-study. See Chapter 18 if you need graduate finaid assistance.

Line 29: Staying on course

This question asks students for their course of study. Greenhorns commonly list law or medicine, when in fact, these are long-haul hopes. Their present course of study should be listed as liberal arts, social studies, science, nursing, and so forth. Listing the wrong course of study can disqualify bungling blank-fillers from aid related to their immediate course of study.

Line 37: Dependents

This question asks for the number of dependents for which the student will pay childcare. The parent who is dutifully completing this FAFSA is likely to list the number of children (including the student) in the entire family. However, newly sprung college hopefuls are usually without dependents.

Line 46: Apart is separate

This question asks the parents' current marital status. Students normally get more aid if the parent is single, separated, or divorced. However, many parents do not consider themselves separated because they are not "legally" separated. In other words, faced with a formal form, they get overly particular for their own good. Legal separation isn't required for this question. If the parents are living apart for the purpose of eventually becoming divorced, answer the question "separated." Complete the rest of the form using the information about the parent with whom the student chiefly lives or who provided the most financial support during the last 12 months.

Line 50: Anybody else in school?

This question asks for the number of people in the family who will be attending an eligible college program at least half time while the student attends college. The more people in college, the more eligible the student is for finaid. However, many parents don't include themselves, because their employer pays for the parent's tuition. Who picks up the tuition tab is irrelevant for this question.

Line 52: Use the short form

This question asks for U.S. income tax figures reported on the parents' income tax form. Historically, parents and tax preparers in this situation use the long-form 1040. But if parents make less then $50,000 and have large assets, they will always be more eligible for aid if they file the U.S. IRS short form 1040A or 1040EZ. If they use the short form and net less than $50,000, they're exempt from completing section G on the FAFSA, which counts up family assets.

Line 77: No student assets

This question asks the value of the student's assets. Many parents continue to build up this account thinking that it will get the student more money. Wrong way to go. Students are penalized 35 cents on the dollar, or 35 percent, for their assets. Parents who leave money in their own asset accounts always do their children's finances a full-on favor.

Nominees for Best Blooper Award

The SAR (Student Aid Report) is where the rubber meets the road in the race for financial aid. That's when blundering students discover they goofed in filling out their FAFSA (Free Application for Federal Student Aid). The SAR goes to the student and the information on the SAR goes to the colleges that the student designates.

As discussed in Chapter 3, colleges receive the SAR information via electronic transmission. However, students are supposed to either update, correct, or submit unamended copies of their SARs in hard-copy form to colleges' financial aid office, as required by the institution.

In the process that starts with filling out the FAFSA and ends with receipt of the SAR, lots of room for calamity is present. One of the authors, Dr. Davis, knows this well because he has counseled thousands of finaid-seeking students in his private practice — sometimes after the fact, when the student needs help to straighten out a financial aid disaster.

From Dr. Davis's file of best blunders, here are true stories of finaid crashes that could have been avoided with an information infusion. To protect the formerly unaware, we don't use real names.

The case of too many zeros

When Roger received his SAR, he was surprised to see that he and his family had an EFC (expected family contribution) of 00000. Roger often received grades of F in school, which was probably the reason Roger thought the string of zeros meant he had failed and wasn't eligible for aid of any kind. Roger thought about those zeros. He decided he could never attend college because he wasn't eligible for financial aid and joined the Navy. In fact, however, the zeroes meant that his family needed to contribute nothing to his education as he was eligible for aid for the total amount.

They jumped to the wrong conclusion

Jonathan had his heart set on attending the college where all his friends were going — good old State U. When Jonathan's SAR came back, it reflected the fact that his family's EFC was too high to make him eligible for a Federal Pell grant, a grant reserved for low-income families. Jonathan's SAR included this specific message: "Based on the information given us, you are not eligible for a Federal Pell grant."

Jonathan's family misinterpreted the message to mean he was ineligible for any financial aid and stopped applying for it. Good old State U. was out the window. Too bad. Jonathan was eligible for institutional aid, state aid, and private aid; he would have received enough funding to cover tuition, fees, and room and board, although none of the money would have come from the Federal Pell grant program.

The moral to this story: Never assume, always ask.

When forms collide

Lauren is reminded of the old complaint about bureaucracies — *The left hand doesn't know what the right hand is doing* — each time she remembers Question 52, not a trick question, but one with costly consequences when answered incorrectly.

The more family members in college at the same time, the more finaid each receives. Lauren would join several siblings who were already enrolled in college. They'd all be attending at the same time. But Lauren didn't know how the system worked and almost lost out because of Question 52.

FAFSA Question 52, (now Question 50), asks for "Number of college students in household in (YEAR) attending college." But the SAR Question 52 changes the wording to say "Parent(s) number in college in (YEAR)."

When Lauren's family received the SAR, they changed the number on Question 52 to "0" because no parent was going to college. When the number on Question 52 is changed to zero, the system assumed that only one person would be in college, drastically lowering Lauren's financial aid.

Because Question 52 on the SAR is incorrectly stated, many students who actually have multiple family members in college lose out because the system thinks they are the only student in the family.

Wiser but poorer by $3,500

Maryann's parents were married when she submitted her original FAFSA. They separated in December. The mother, a stay-at-home mom, didn't have an income to report.

The bungle: Maryann's mom didn't bother to correct her SAR because she thought they'd have to wait until the next school year. If only mom had refiled, Maryann would have been eligible for a Pell grant retroactive to the beginning of the school year, which, with the other aid the refiling would trigger, would have saved the family $3,500.

Two cannot pay as cheaply as one

Sonny's parents had been separated for more than three years, although they continued to file joint income taxes. Sonny lived with his mother — the custodial parent. Only the custodial parent has to include his or her taxable and untaxable (child support) income and assets on the FAFSA.

Unaware of that fact, Sonny's parents reported both parents' income and resources. This miscalculation was an expensive one: Sonny lost $4,200 in financial aid funding. That's one mistake they won't make again.

Dollars short and days late

Rebecca missed the finaid boat because she missed the deadline for filing for aid from her state and her college. She wasn't forgetful, she just thought she had to be accepted by a college before asking for financial aid. No, no, no. Not so.

She did manage to apply in time for a Pell grant and Federal Stafford loan, which she received, but Rebecca's loss of free money was $5,000. Ouch.

The next year she knew better than to wait — she made all her deadlines and is decidedly richer for her promptness.

Twins who made the same mistake twice

Allison and Emily are twin sisters in a family of six, none of whom had ever attended college. The family income is under $45,000. When Allison filled out her FAFSA for the fall semester, she was the only one who was college-bound. Her request for a Pell grant was a near-miss but she did receive state aid and a subsidized student loan.

Emily, seeing how well Allison was doing in school, decided to enroll as a full-time student in the nearby community college.

Allison didn't think to refile her SAR with the new information (two in college), a failing that denied her a full Pell grant, which would have canceled out her student loans.

Even worse, Emily never applied for aid for the second semester, causing the proud parents to take out an equity loan to help pay Emily's tuition. Emily would have been eligible for a full Pell grant for the second semester.

Because each twin failed to let their college financial aid teams know both sisters were in college, the twins lost more than $5,000.

Lined Up and Ready to Go

Knowing the right ways to fill out your forms, as discussed in Chapter 20, and the wrong ways that are discussed in this chapter, you're all set to move ahead. Figure 19-1 is a handy checklist you can photocopy to keep track of your forms and applications.

Figure 19-1:
Lasso those forms and applications on your newly created paper ranch by keeping good records of deadlines, when you meet them, and what you send.

Dr. Davis's Checklist for Forms and Apps								
Key: #1 = Date institution must have forms						#2 = Date you sent forms		
Name of College	A		B		C		D	
Date	#1	#2	#1	#2	#1	#2	#1	#2
Admission								
H.S. Transcript								
College Transcripts								
Recommendation Letters								
Other								
1.								
2.								
3.								
Financial Aid								
Application								
FAFSA								
PROFILE								
Divorced / separated statement								
Business / farm statement								
Parent's 1040								
Parent's W-2								
Student's 1040								
Student's W-2								

Chapter 20

The Lines That Cross Up Your Finaid Chances

. . . .

In This Chapter

▶ Anticipating your estimated family contribution

▶ Answering the most important questions on the form correctly

▶ Including unusual circumstances in the usual blanks

. . . .

*I*n the ivy-covered financial aid processing building at the University of California in Berkeley, a team of financial and legal specialists pieces together applicants' futures — they flip through applications and charts, run sophisticated computer software, and determine how much money Jean Moore, a journalism hopeful, needs to pay for school and to survive in the expensive San Francisco Bay area.

Moore won't be able to attend college unless her parents win the lottery . . . or she completes her Free Application for Federal Student Aid (FAFSA) carefully and wins financial aid. But financial and legal specialists aren't the only people who affect Moore's finances. Moore and her parents can improve her chances by filling out this important application with care and concentrated attention to detail.

Yes, you have the power to improve your financial aid package yourself. Use the following, line-by-line instructions to ace this daunting task. And focus on the fine print until you're cross-eyed — these are the little lines that can trip you up big-time. If you don't provide financial aid processors the correct information in the correct form, you can lose all chances at free money and loans.

Calculating Your Need

The formula for calculating your need is as follows:

Total college cost budget for example:	$16,000
(–) Expected family contribution (EFC) for example:	$ 9,500
(=) Demonstrated financial need:	$ 6,500

The college financial aid need (level of eligibility) in this model is under $6,500 and may include self-help funds — loan and/or work and some gift money (grant and/or scholarship).

You don't have to wait for your Student Aid Report form or the ever more elusive response from your chosen college. If you're not a numbers-cruncher, determining your own financial need may seem absolutely alien. But you can easily estimate your Estimated Family Contribution ahead of time on the Web at www.finaid.org. (See the Tools listing on that Web page.) After you know how much colleges will expect you to shell out, you can start scrimping — or not scrimping. Simply enter your financial data next to the mathematical symbols in each box. Using the symbols, calculate figures until you reach the final boxes, which estimate the student's and parents' contributions (divided by the number of family members in college).

Understanding and reading your SAR

Eligibility for all federal grants, work study, and subsidized loans is based on a need analysis system: the Federal Methodology need analysis system. To get the best results, use the following advice as you fill out the FAFSA. When you send your FAFSA to your designated federal processor, he or she will determine the Expected Family Contribution (EFC), and mail you a Student Aid Report (SAR).

The SAR forms (usually, blue, pink, green, or some other pastel color) contain the official EFC, which appears on Part I below the date of processing and will look like the following example:

EFC: 03535

It resembles a serial number. But if you exchange the first zero for a dollar sign, it will have greater meaning:

EFC: $3535

Another need analysis system, Profile, required by some colleges, gives you a Profile acknowledgment. Although you won't see your own EFC anywhere, Profile sends your need analysis to colleges that will in turn decide how to treat the results. This practice is known as *Institutional Need Analysis Methodology*. After you've estimated your family contribution, call your financial aid administrator and ask how the finaid office plans to treat the results of the Profile.

Use the following advice to complete each blank of the FAFSA and effortlessly turn the base metal of your financial information into educational gold.

Instructions for Completing the FAFSA

If you don't file either the FAFSA or the Renewal FAFSA, you won't get any federal or state finaid. Most state institutions and all two-year colleges and trade schools use only this form. Some colleges require additional documentation. Check with each college you apply to.

Preparation

Locate the following records to simplify the process:

- ✔ 1997 federal income tax form for both the student and parent(s)

- ✔ 1996 federal income tax forms — to estimate 1997 income in lieu of a 1997 federal income tax form

- ✔ W-2 Forms and other records of money earned in 1997

- ✔ Copy of last payroll stub that may give an indication of the year-to-date earnings for estimating annual income in lieu of the 1997 federal income tax form

- ✔ Untaxed income records such as welfare, Social Security, AFDC, ADC, voluntary contributions to tax-deferred income programs such as annuity programs, IRA, KEOUGH, 401(k), and the like, and housing allowances

- ✔ Business and farm records

- ✔ Records of stocks, bonds, and other investments for parent and student

- ✔ Student's Social Security and driver's license numbers

More preparation

Use a black or dark ink pen or a #2 pencil. Blue ink will not scan the information as well.

- ✔ Print carefully — others need to be able to read your writing.

- ✔ When marking the ovals, keep the ink inside the ovals. (Scanners get confused when the markings are outside of the ovals.)

✔ Do not use a special handling mail service if you're preparing your forms late. Special mailing only delays the process because this form goes to a P.O. Box and no one can sign for delivery.

✔ Do not enclose, attach, or staple any documents with the FAFSA. They will only be thrown away and will slow down forms processing.

✔ Use numbers or a zero to respond to questions. Do not use responses such as N/A, —, or leave a question blank.

✔ Round off all figures to the nearest dollar.

✔ Use numbers to reflect dates (for example, 11-10-98).

✔ The term *school* relates to the postsecondary institution (college, university, two-year college, career school, or trade school) that you plan to attend.

✔ Make copies of all documents that you prepare.

Start Form-Filling!

The following sections explain what you need to know to fill the FAFSA completely and correctly. An error in this form could sink your chances of qualifying for needed aid. Check the boxes at left as you fill them out in the form.

Section A, Questions 1-19 — Personal background

This section pertains only to the student applicant.

❑ **Lines 1-3:** Use your proper name — no nicknames.

❑ **Lines 4-7:** Use a permanent mailing address; processors use this address to communicate with you.

❑ **Line 8:** A Social Security number is required for this form to be processed. If you do not have one, apply for one as soon as possible. This form won't be processed without one. (The SSN question has one of the most frequent error rates and is among the main reasons students lose eligibility.) To order a new or replacement Social Security card call 1-800-772-1213.

❑ **Line 11:** State abbreviation: Use the state of permanent residence — not the state of college residence. (If you're planning on living in the state after graduation, find out how to become a state resident and qualify for lower tuition fees and state scholarships.)

❑ **Line 12:** Date of legal resident status. If you were born in the state, use your date of birth. If you move to the state of residence, give the month and year.

❑ **Lines 13-14:** List driver's license number. If you don't have one, write **none**.

❑ **Lines 15-16:** Mark the appropriate box for citizenship status.

❑ **Line 17:** Marital status — respond to questions as appropriate.

❑ **Line 18:** ⭘ Month ⭘ Year

Write date of marriage, separation, divorce, or widowhood.

❑ **Line 19:** ⭘ Yes ⭘ No

If you will receive a high school diploma or a GED before the first date of your enrollment, ink in the correct response.

❑ **Line 20:** ⭘ Yes ⭘ No

Note: A college transcript that reflects two years of college credit towards a baccalaureate degree is equivalent to a high school diploma. If you have one of these, respond with a yes.

Check No if you don't have a bachelor's degree and/or won't have one by July 1, 1998. Check Yes if you already have a bachelor's degree or will have one by July 1, 1998.

If you have a degree from another country equal to a bachelor's degree, check Yes.

If you already hold a bachelor's degree, you won't qualify for a Pell grant (free money), a Federal Supplemental Educational Opportunity grant (free money), or some state grant and scholarship programs.

❑ **Lines 21-22:** ⭘ Father ⭘ Mother

Write the number from the following chart representing the highest educational level or grade level your father and mother completed.

(1) Elementary school (K-8)   (3) College or beyond

(2) Secondary school (9-12)   (4) Unknown

Section B, Questions 23-37 — Your plans
❑ **Lines 23-37:** Complete the FAFSA questionnaire as requested.

Section C, Questions 38-43 — Student status
The questions in this section determine your eligibility for aid as an independent or dependent student. An independent student can normally qualify for more aid. However, the main criterion for establishing independent status while attending undergraduate school is age. The magic age is 24. A student 24 years of age or born before January 1, 1975, automatically qualifies for independent status. However, some institutions may require further criteria for independent status before qualifying the student for institutional aid.

❑ **Line 38:** ○ Yes ○ No

Were you born before January 1, 1975?

❑ **Line 39:** ○ Yes ○ No

Are you a veteran? Answer Yes if you have engaged in active service in the U.S. Army, Navy, Air Force, Marines, or Coast Guard; or are not a veteran now but will be one by June 30, 1999.

Note: If you've attended any U.S. Military academy and were dismissed for any reason but dishonorable discharge, answer Yes and you qualify as an independent student.

❑ **Line 40:** ○ Yes ○ No

Will you be enrolled in a graduate/professional program (beyond a bachelor's degree) in 1998-1999?

❑ **Line 41:** ○ Yes ○ No

Check Yes if you're married as of today or if you are separated. You're still considered married until officially divorced. If you're divorced and less than 24 years of age, you may be considered a dependent student and may have to list your parents' assets. Complete this FAFSA and submit it to your college financial aid officer to review your circumstances and certify you as an independent student [page 4 after Section I: (School Use Only) is for the financial aid officer to determine your dependence status].

D/O means *dependency override*. If this financial aid counselor agrees that you are independent, the consultant will certify you as such and submit your data as an independent student.

❑ **Line 42:** ○ Yes ○ No

Are you an orphan or a ward of the court, or were you a ward of the court until age 18? Check Yes if

- You're currently a ward of the court or were until age 18.

    or

- Both of your parents are deceased and you do not have an adoptive parent or legal guardian. (*Legal guardian* is defined as a person appointed by a court to be your legal guardian in a legal relationship that will continue after June 30, 1999, and who is directed by a court to support you with his or her own financial resources.)

❑ **Line 43:** ○ Yes ○ No

Do you have legal dependents (other than a spouse)? Check Yes if

- You have any children who get more than half their support from you.

or

- Other person(s) (not your spouse) live with you and get more than half of their support from you and will continue to get that support during the 1998-1999 school year.

  Note: This person does not necessarily have to be claimed on the IRS Form1040, but you must be able to document that you provide at least half of his or her support.

Section D, Questions 44-45 — Household Information

This section (gray area) pertains to student and spouse (independent students only).

✔ If you answered *Yes* to any of the questions in Section C, respond to Questions 44-45. Be sure to answer questions 1-45, 51-62, and 90-108 for you and/or your spouse.

✔ If you answered *No* to any of the questions in Section C, skip Questions 44-45 and go to Question 46. You and your parents must answer questions 1-43, 46-74, and 90-108.

Note: Graduate health profession students applying for federal aid under the Public Health Service Act — Title VII programs must also complete all questions on the form for your parent(s) as well as for yourself. Why? Because these funds are regulated under different federal authorization, which legislates that the parents' income and assets must be factored into the need analysis formula. Check with your financial aid office to verify the institution's policy. Otherwise, complete the **blue, gray,** and **white** areas.

❑ **Line 44:** Write in the number of your household.

The following persons may be included in the household size of independent students:

- Yourself.

- Your spouse, exclude a spouse if not living in the household as a result of death, separation, or divorce.

- Your dependent children, if they received or will receive more than half their support from you between July 1, 1998, and June 30, 1999.

- Your unborn child, if that child will be born before or during the award year and you will provide more than half the child's support from the projected date of birth to the end of the award year.

- Other persons, if they live with you and receive more than one half of their support from you at the time of application and will continue to receive that support for the entire 1998-1999 award year (July 1, 1998, through June 30, 1999).

❑ **Line 45:** Write the number of household members reported in Line 44 who'll be attending college at least half-time (6 credit hours) in 1998-1999. This response must always be at least one (1).

The following are the definitions that apply:

- ✔ **Enrollment Period:** July 1, 1998 to June 30, 1999

- ✔ **College:** Any accredited post-secondary institution

- ✔ **Enrollment:** Registered for at least half-time for one term in a degree or certificate program.

- ✔ **Half-time:** six semester hours or 12 clock hours per week.

- ✔ **One-term:** One quarter, one semester, and so on.

Section D, Questions 46-50 — Household Information

This section (blue area) pertains to parents.

If you answered *No* to each of the questions in Section D, you will be considered a dependent student, and your parent(s) must complete Questions 46-50.

Note: The level of financial aid eligibility is largely determined on how you answer the next five questions.

❑ **Line 46** List your parents' marital status using the following codes:

Single (1), Married (2), Separated (3), Divorced (4), Widowed (5)

Definition of "Parent"

- **Adoptive Parent:** Considered same as natural parents.

- **Foster Parent:** Not considered a parent of the student.

- **Grandparent:** Not considered student's parent. Grandparents' income can't be reported on the FAFSA unless the grandparents are court-appointed legal guardians or have legally adopted the student. (When in doubt, contact the finaid office.)

- **Legal Guardian:** Considered same as natural parents if the legal guardian is appointed by a court that will continue after June 30, 1999, and who is directed to support you with his or her own financial resources.

- **Stepparent:** Considered same as a natural parent. Stepparent's income and assets are treated same as natural parent's even if no adoption takes place. Prenuptial agreements are disregarded for FAFSA. (*Note:* If natural parent has died and stepparent survives, the student is independent unless stepparent legally adopts student.)

- **Married:** Natural parents remain married (or) have remarried; in either case the answer is **married.**

- **Separated:** Parents are separated and getting an eventual divorce. Separation doesn't have to be "legal or formal," but it must be a reality even if it is a trial separation.

- **Divorced:** Natural parent that student lives with is divorced and a single head of household. If the parent is now remarried, respond to Question 46 as **married.**

❑ **Line 47:** Your parents' state of legal residence abbreviation. Parents may have dual residence, as in the case of military personnel or when parents pay state income tax in different states. The FAFSA document only allows for listing one state of residence. "Residence" is your parents' true, fixed, and permanent home.

❑ **Line 48:** (/) Month and year when your parents became state residents. If they were born in the state of residence, give their date of birth. Use the older of the parent(s) information used to complete this form.

❑ **Line 49:** Number of persons in your parents' household in 1998-1999. Include all persons who live in the household for whom your parent or guardian provides at least half their support and will continue to do so from July 1, 1998, to June 30, 1999.

Note: For the purpose of including children in household size, the *support test* is used rather than *residency test* due to divorce and separation situations. In such cases, the parent who provides more than half of the child's support may claim the child in household size even if this person does not live in the same domicile. The following persons may be included in the household size of the dependent student:

- The student

- The student's parent(s), excluding a parent not living in the household as a result of death, separation, or divorce

- The student's siblings, if they received or will receive more than half their support from the student's parent(s) between July 1, 1998, and June 30, 1999.

- The student's children, if they received or will receive more than half their support from the student's parent(s) between July 1, 1998, and June 30, 1999.

- The student's parents' unborn child and/or the student's unborn child, if that child will be born before or during the award year (July 1, 1998, through June 30, 1999) and the student's parent(s) will provide more than half the child's support from the projected date of birth until the end of the award year.

- Other persons, if they live with and receive more than one-half their support from the student's parent(s) at the time of application and will continue to receive that support for the entire 1998-1999 award year (July 1, 1998, through June 30,1999).

Financial need is based on household size and not on the exemptions on the IRS Form 1040. The larger the size of the household, the more need can be demonstrated.

❑ **Line 50:** Number of college students in household in 1998-1999.

From Line 49 determine how many household members will attend college (any postsecondary institution) for at least 6 semester hours in one term or 12 clock hours per week and will be working towards a degree or certificate leading to a recognized education credential at a college that is eligible to participate in any of the federal student aid programs, even though they do not complete a term.

Remember that the answer to this question must be at least one; the applicant student is included.

Note: Applicants who are required to register for college credit to renew their professional certificates (for example: teachers' professional certificates or nurses' certificates) to be employed aren't required to be enrolled in certificate or degree-seeking programs.

Question 50 is considered to be one of the most important questions on the FAFSA. Why? Because the Federal Methodology divides the parents' contribution by the number of family members attending college during the same academic year. For example, if this formula calculates that after looking at all of the responses, the parents' contribution is $12,000 for one family member in college, then the amount would be approximately $6,000 for two in college, $4,000 for three in college, and so on.

In cases where a parent has remarried and the new parent is paying at least 50 percent of support for a child living at the other residence, the parent should list the child living at another residence as part of the family size on Line 49. More importantly, if any of these children are attending college and meet the definition of enrollment, then they should be listed on Line 50 as college students.

If graduate students meet the definition of family members to be included in Line 49, include them in Line 50. However, a financial aid counselor may use "professional judgment" and disqualify the graduate student as a family member or member of the family attending college. Always include the graduate student as a family member in college and personally discuss the entry with the appropriate financial aid office.

Section E, Questions 51-74 — 1997 Income, earnings, and benefits

❑ **Lines 51 and 63:** Forms filed to complete this questionnaire:

	Student		Parent
1997 completed IRS 1040A/EZ	O	1.	O
1997 completed IRS 1040	O	2.	O
1997 estimated IRS 1040A/EZ	O	3	O
1997 estimated IRS 1040	O	4.	O
Will not file a 1997 U.S. income tax return	O	5.	O

Note: You will normally get special consideration for lowering the assessment on your assets if your income is less than $50,000 and you are able to file an income tax Form 1040A or 1040EZ. Even if you filed or will file an IRS Form 1040, if you were eligible to file the 1040A or 1040EZ, check the above box for 1040A or 1040EZ. Why? Because if you can file your tax returns by using either of these forms, you don't have to list any of the parents' or student's assets in Section G.

❑ **Lines 52-74 (Taxable Income):**

	Student		Parent	
	Student		*Parent*	
1997 Total number of exemptions	52.	[#]	64.	[#]
1997 Adjusted Gross Income (AGI)	53.	[$]	65.	[$]
1997 U.S. income tax paid	54.	[$]	66.	[$]
1997 Income earned from work	55.	[$] (student)	67.	[$] (father)
1997 Income earned from work	56.	[$] (spouse)	68.	[$] (mother)
Earned Income Credit	57.	[$]	69.	[$]

Social Security Benefits (SSB) that parents collect on behalf of the student should be reported under parents' income. Most stop at age 18, which will normally come in the 1998 calendar year. Many college financial aid officers will disregard the applicants' SSB reported on Line 58 because they won't be continuing while the student attends college. You may wish to contact the financial aid office to discuss this concern.

	Student	Parent
Social Security Benefits	58. [$]	70. [$]
Aid to Families, Dependent Children (AFDC/ADC)	59. [$]	71. [$]
Child support received for all children	60. [$]	72. [$]

Child Support Payments (CSP) received in 1997 should be reported in terms of the annual amount. Most CSP stop when the applicant reaches age 18, which will be in 1998 for most students. You may wish to notify each school's financial aid office and appeal for applicant's CSP to be disregarded because those funds won't be available during the year of aid.

❑ **Lines 57-74:**

	Student	Parent
Other untaxed income and benefits	61. [$]	73. [$]

Other untaxed income and benefits are associated in the following areas:

• Tax-deferred pension/savings plans payments made directly or withheld from earnings and reported on the W-2 Form (for example: 401(k) and 403(b) plans)

• Welfare benefits (except AFDC or ADC reported on Line 59 or 71)

• Workers' Compensation

• Veterans' noneducation benefits such as Death, Pension, Dependency and Indemnity Compensation (DIC), and so forth

• Housing, food, and other living allowances (excluding rent subsidies for low-income housing) paid to members of the military, clergy, and others, including cash payments and cash value of benefits)

• Money paid on student's behalf, not reported elsewhere on form

• Any other untaxed income and benefits, such as Black Lung Benefits, Refugee Assistance, or untaxed portions of Railroad Retirement Benefits

- Wages from international organizations that are exempt from inclusion on the U.S. Federal Income Tax Form 1040

  Do not include money received from the following sources as other untaxed income:

- Social Security

- Money from student financial aid

- Food stamps

- State payments for foster care and adoption assistance, under title IV-A or IV-E of the Social Security Act.

- Gifts/support, other than money, received from friends/relatives

- "Rollover" pensions

- Veterans' educational benefits

- JTPA benefits

- Contributions to, or payments from, flexible arrangements, such as cafeteria plans

- Any income reported elsewhere on the form

❑ **Lines 62 and 74:**

	Student	*Parent*
1997 Exclusion Income	62. [$]	74. [$]

Definition of exclusion income (to the applicant's advantage) includes

- Income reported on IRS Form 1040 from scholarships or grants received that are in excess of tuition, fees, books, and supplies.

- Taxable earnings from Federal Work-Study or other need-based work programs.

- Allowances and benefits received under the National and Community Service Trust Act of 1993 (AmeriCorps awards).

- Child support "paid" by the student, spouse, or by the parent(s) whose income is reported on this form related to a divorce or separation. (Do not include support for children living in home.)

Section F, Questions 75-89 — Asset Information

Pay attention to the following information:

- ✔ If the student applicant did/will submit an IRS Form 1040A or EZ and earns less than $50,000, skip the student's portion of Section F.

- ✔ If the parent(s) whose information is used on this form did/will file an IRS Form 1040A or EZ, and if the AGI is less than $50,000, skip the parent(s)' portion of Section F.

Otherwise, complete Section F as directed.

❑ **Lines 77-91:**

The following asset values should be estimated as of the time you complete the form:

	Student		Parent	
• Cash, saving, and checking accounts	75.	[$]	83.	[$]
• Other real estate and investments value (do not include home)	76.	[$]	84.	[$]
• Other real estate and investments debt (not home)	77.	[$]	85.	[$]
• Business value	78.	[$]	86.	[$]
• Business debt	79.	[$]	87.	[$]
• Investment farm value (don't include a family farm)	80.	[$]	88.	[$]
• Investment farm debt (don't include a family farm)	81.	[$]	89.	[$]

Section G, Questions 90-105 — Release and Signatures

Be especially careful in completing Section G. If you use the wrong codes, list the wrong schools, or forget to sign and date the form, you subtract from your aid amount.

❑ **Lines 90-101:** The FAFSA results (shown on the Student Aid Report — these are blue paper forms for 1998-99) will be sent to each of the six colleges you list. State scholarship agencies consider the college you write on the first line (90) when determining their state aid awards. Doing so assures that they can use an institution-specified budget to assess your need.

Except for a few state scholarship programs, a student cannot use a state award at a college outside of the student's state of residence. Ask your state scholarship agency if your state has reciprocity agreements with other states. State scholarship agencies are listed with contact information in Chapter 8.

Note: A common mistake in this section is failure to complete the Housing Code column, Questions 91-101. This code is very important because it tells the college financial aid officer which budget to use. If you don't list a housing code, the college will most likely use the lowest budget, and you won't receive the maximum award. On-campus budget codes tend to result in more aid than off-campus or living-with-parent codes.

Special note: If you are applying to more than six colleges, you may wish to prioritize these with the earliest deadlines.

Here's how to have information sent to more than six colleges:

- ✔ Don't write the name of more than one college per line. Doing so only delays the process. You will receive a Student Aid Report (SAR) about four weeks after submitting the FAFSA to the processing center.

- ✔ When you receive your SAR (the colored-paper forms) you can deliver or send a photocopy of your SAR to a new college.

- ✔ You can write a letter to your assigned FAFSA processor requesting that information be sent to new colleges.

- ✔ You can add new colleges on Part II of the SAR and return Part II to the address provided on the SAR.

- ✔ Additional colleges can be added by telephone: Call the U.S. Department of Education at 319-337-5665, have the PIN available (found on the blue SAR)

❑ **Lines 104-105:** Sign and date this document.

Remember the following caveats:

- ✔ Do not mail the FAFSA to the processor before January 1st.

- ✔ Do not attach or include other documents or paper with the FAFSA.

- ✔ Do not mail by special delivery — doing so slows up processing.

Student Aid Report (SAR)

The colored-paper forms that make up the Student Aid Report (SAR) are the secret to receiving financial aid — the end result of submitting the FAFSA. After the FAFSA is submitted to the federal central processor, the student receives a SAR about four to six weeks after submission. The SAR has two parts. Part I restates everything you submitted on the original FAFSA. Part II allows you to make revisions. Review all data for accuracy.

For example, the first time you submit the FAFSA, you provide estimated income to meet deadlines. Now that you have the SAR, hold onto it until you've completed all federal income tax forms. When the new income forms are complete and ready for submission, transfer the new information to the SAR, Part II. Resubmit Part II of the SAR to the federal central processor in the enclosed self-addressed envelope to update original information. Each college listed on the SAR receives the new information.

The SAR's main purpose is to show the expected family contribution (EFC). The EFC is in the upper right-hand corner of the SAR under the processed date. Remember, the mission for completing all documents is to arrive at a low EFC. The EFC appears as a five-digit number without the dollar sign (place a $ sign before the number to better understand what it means).

Remember, the cost of the college (minus the EFC) is your demonstrated need. To receive the maximum financial aid, you need a low EFC. By following all the preceding suggestions, you'll greatly improve your odds for earning college money.

Chapter 21

Figuring Out Your Best Deal

- -

In This Chapter
▶ Sample award letters
▶ Tips on comparing awards
▶ Your awards comparison chart

- -

*B*e happy when your award letters arrive. Then be critical. Analyze each letter and try to figure out its bottom line. How good is the deal you're being offered?

In case you've never seen an award letter, we reprint four letters (with student identities deleted) on the following pages.

As we mention in Chapter 3, award letters are kicked out by computers programmed with specific criteria. College financial aid counselors may not have reviewed each one before mailing the letters, especially at large institutions where the reading task is formidable.

Because the letters come off an assembly line, you should go over yours with a fine-toothed mental comb. You are trying to find both your best deal among the various awards and reasons to appeal for even more gift aid.

Immediately accept each part of each award. You're keeping your options open. Even if you turn down a particular school and its award later, you want to be sure that the school doesn't give your aid to someone else while you're making up your mind. You need a little time to sort things out, to compare competing offers.

After you finally decide which school and aid offer to accept, notify the financial aid offices of the rejected schools as quickly as possible. Your thoughtfulness allows the spurned schools to offer the vacated admission set to another student and to free up money for students on the award waiting list.

What if the offer you finally select contains a job or a college work-study position, and you don't want to be employed — at least, not during your first year when you're uncertain how much time you'll need for studies?

You can turn down work opportunities and accept only the gift aid if you wish. But you may make a big mistake if you do so. As we comment in Chapter 11, employers hiring new graduates consistently favor applicants who gained work or internship experience during college years. Furthermore, working improves your time management skills, which will prove to be a blessing throughout your entire life.

If you're really a marginal student who needs every free hour to study, perhaps you shouldn't work during your undergraduate years. The conventional wisdom, however, says that a job will not interfere with your college education experience as long as you don't toil beyond 14 hours a week.

Another reason to turn down a work-study position or campus job is that you're already in the workplace as an adult student who has a job. If you decide to turn down the work portion of the award, however, the financial aid counselor may bounce the money-gap ball back to your court, leaving you on your own to solve the shortage of funds.

Letter 1 Bentley College

Note that this letter offers a sholarship (gift aid) from the Admissions Office, and the scholarship will become part of a financial aid letter that will come from the finaid office at a later date. The award becomes firm once you sign and return the obligatory paperwork.

Letter 2 American University

An excellent award, but one that leaves a substantial gap. A definite candidate for negotiation (see Chapter 9). Notice that the Direct Loan origination fee is deducted from the amount shown prior to payment into your account; this is a standard deduction with all schools.

Letter 3 University of Colorado

The award letter gives good consumer information; however, Step 3 does not give a clear picture of the true balance to be paid by the family. To arrive at the true EFC, you should add up the Pell grant ($1,500), CU-Boulder grant ($1,000), and the Subsidized Stafford/Ford loan ($2,620), which total $5,120. Subtract this amount from the expenses ($12,409-$5,120), and the balance is the cost to you — the expected family contribution — in this case, $7,739. In this award document, the college is offering a PLUS loan of $7,730 to meet the EFC. This is a common practice and one that is very helpful to assist the family with its cash flow. The base award is well balanced, with the grant (gift aid) and student loan (self-help) being almost equal in meeting the student's demonstrated need.

BENTLEY

	Bentley College	Office of the President
		175 Forest Street
		Waltham, Massachusetts
		02154-4705

June 23, 1997

617.891.2101
617.891.2569 FAX

Dear

Congratulations on your acceptance to Bentley College! I am delighted to inform you that you have been named a President's Scholar in recognition of your academic achievements. The discipline, leadership and motivation you have demonstrated during your high school years attest to your ability to achieve future goals.

As a President's Scholar, you will receive a $5,000 academic scholarship for the 1997-98 academic year. This scholarship will be automatically renewed for an additional three years at Bentley provided that you are a full-time student and that you maintain a 3.25 cumulative grade point average. Overall, you will be eligible to receive $20,000 in President's Scholarship funds during your four years of enrollment at Bentley College. Your award may be used toward tuition at Bentley during the nine-month academic year (September through May). If you have applied for financial assistance, a financial aid notification letter will be mailed to you under separate cover.

I am proud to honor you with this special award and hope that it will help to make Bentley College a reality for you. If you have any questions about this scholarship or the financial assistance process, I encourage you to contact our Office of Financial Assistance at (617) 891-3441. I look forward to welcoming you to the Bentley community in September.

Sincerely,

Joseph M. Cronin
President

JMC:ctd

cc: Office of Financial Assistance

AMERICAN UNIVERSITY

W A S H I N G T O N , D C

ADMISSIONS AND FINANCIAL AID

March 28, 1997
SSN: (F)

American University is pleased to inform you of your eligibility for the 1997-98 Financial Aid Award detailed below. The amount awarded is based on an estimated cost of attendance of $27,655. Please read the award very carefully. Accept or Decline each award by indicating with an (X). Sign and date one copy and return it to the Financial Aid office by May 1 or within three weeks of receiving this award (whichever is the later date).

AWARD	FALL	SPRING	SUMMER	ACCEPT	DECLINE
FEDERAL PERKINS LOAN	$ 600	$ 600	$ 0	( )	( )
PELL GRANT (EST.)	$ 925	$ 925	$ 0	( )	( )
AU GRANT	$ 5,795	$ 5,795	$ 0	( )	( )
FEDERAL DIRECT LOAN*	$ 1,313	$ 1,312	$ 0	( )	( )
FEDERAL WORK STUDY**	$ 750	$ 750	$ 0	( )	( )
Total Estimated Award	$ 9,383	$ 9,382	$ 0		

* All Direct Loans require a 4% origination fee which is deducted from the amount shown above prior to payment into your account.

** A Work Study award is not credited to your account, but is earned by you in a Work Study job.

By signing below, I certify that: 1) I have read and understand the "Conditions of Award" detailed on the back of this letter; and 2) I understand that this is a **tentative** award which will not become final until the Financial Aid office receives all documents requested for verification purposes.

Student Signature: _____   Date: _____

Please list below any financial aid or scholarship assistance which you expect to receive, which is not listed above.

Award Name	Fall	Spring	Summer
_____	_____	_____	_____
_____	_____	_____	_____

OFFICE OF ENROLLMENT SERVICES
4400 MASSACHUSETTS AVENUE, NW   WASHINGTON, DC 20016-8001   202-885-6000   FAX: 202-885-1025

UNIVERSITY OF COLORADO AT BOULDER
1998-99 AWARD OFFER

Sample Student
1560 Main Street
Anytown USA 00000

Date: February 1, 1998
SID: 999-99-9999

STEP 1: Estimate your total expenses for one entire academic year (9 months) for each college or university

	CU-BOULDER	Institution B	Institution C
ESTIMATED EXPENSES			
Resident Tuition/Fees	3335		
Room/Board	4545		
Books/Supplies	649		
Expenses Dependent on Life Styles:			
Personal	1730		
Transportation	1075		
Medical	1075		
TOTAL ESTIMATED EXPENSES	$ 12409	$	$

STEP 2: Estimate the total amount of financial aid available to you from each college or university

	CU-BOULDER	Institution B	Institution C
FINANCIAL AID			
Scholarships:			
Grants:			
Pell	1050		
CU-Boulder Grant	1000		
Work-Study:			
Loans:			
Subsidized Stafford/Ford	2620		
Parent PLUS Loan	7730		
TOTAL FINANCIAL AID	$ 12400	$	$

STEP 3: Subtract "Total Financial Aid" from "Total Expenses" to determine the cost to you for each college or university

	CU-BOULDER	Institution B	Institution C
EXPENSES MINUS FINANCIAL AID	$ 9	$	$

See reverse side for explanation of terms

The University of Colorado at Boulder is an equal opportunity/affirmative action institution that does not discriminate on the basis of race, color, national origin, sex, age, disability, creed, religion, or veteran status.

MACALESTER

Admissions Office   MACALESTER COLLEGE. 1600 Grand Avenue. Saint Paul. Minnesota 55105-1899   Telephone 612-696-6357

March 14, 1997

Dear Meg:

Congratulations! You have been chosen as a recipient of the Catharine Lealtad Scholarship. You will receive a $5,000 scholarship for each of your four years at Macalester.

Dr. Catharine Lealtad '15 was Macalester's first African American graduate. Our multicultural population has increased in the last eighty years and, with it, our commitment to provide excellent educational programs for students of color. Dr. Lealtad's lifetime of service to the medical profession and her community reflect Macalester's traditions of academic excellence and service to others. It is to honor her achievements that a scholarship program exists in her name today.

You have been honored as a Lealtad Scholar for your achievements in high school, as demonstrated by your transcript and your contributions to school and community activities. You have shown by your past accomplishments a dedication to excellence. This scholarship is in recognition of both your demonstrated achievement and expected success at the college level.

The Admissions Committee congratulates you again on this honor. We hope to see you on campus in the fall, if not before.

Sincerely,

William M. Shain
Dean of Admissions

P.S. If you have applied for additional need-based financial aid through Macalester's Financial Aid Office and your aid application is complete, you should receive a financial aid package in the next several days. Your scholarship will be incorporated into your financial aid award.

Letter 4 Macalester College

This letter is not a full-spectrum financial aid package award, but notification of a handsome single award designed for African-American students.

Comparing Your Awards

Jot down the data about each award on *Dr. Davis's Awards Comparison Chart*. (We give you your own blank copy later in this chapter.) Then compare each category of an award with its equivalent on other awards.

Study Table 21-1, which compares the awards of *College USA* vs. *Ivy Green*, to quickly see the value of making standard comparisons.

Table 21-1	Dr. Davis's Awards Comparison	
Factors to Consider	*College USA (Example)*	*Ivy Green (Example)*
1. Total tuition, room, board, fees (Hard costs) $	$27,000.00	$29,000.00
2. Total costs (hard + soft costs) (books, supplies, transportation, and so on)	30,130.00	32,000.00
2A Expected family contribution	1,200.00	1,200.00
2B Student's financial need	28,930.00	30,800.00
GIFT AID (free money)		
3. Scholarship (#1)	8,000.00	4,000.00
4. Scholarship (#2)	0.00	2,000.00
5. Federal Pell grant	2,700.00	2,700.00
6. Federal SEOG grant	800.00	400.00
7. State grant	1,000.00	00.00
8. Merit grant	0.00	00.00
9. Need grant	0.00	00.00
10. TOTAL AMOUNT FREE MONEY (gift awards)	12,500.00	9,100.00
11. (lines 1 – 10 = Best gift aid)	14,500.00	15,900.00
SELF HELP (loans and jobs)		
12. Federal Perkins student loan	1,500.00	1,000.00
13. Subsidized Stafford/Direct Student Loan	2,625.00	2,625.00
14. Other student loan	0.00	4,000.00
15. Campus job/ federal work-study	1,400.00	3,000.00
16. Other	00.00	00.00

(continued)

Table 21-1 *(continued)*

Factors to Consider	College USA (Example)	Ivy Green (Example)
17. TOTAL SELF HELP (loans and jobs)	5,525.00	10,625.00
18. TOTAL FINANCIAL AID AWARDED (award package) (Lines 11 + 17 = award offer)	18,025.00	19,725.00
Best awards can be assessed on one of the following factors:		
A. Ratio of gift aid to self help	$12,500/5,525	$9,100/10,625
B. Gap between awards and demonstrated need	(gap) $10,905.00	(gap) $11,075.00
C. Money you need to pay for college after awards are made	$12,105.00	$12,275.00

Chart Source: Dr. Herm Davis

Comparing the gift aid awarded by each school, College USA offers this student $3,400 more free dollars than does Ivy Green. Assuming the college's awards remain constant over the next four years, College USA will fork over $13,600 more cash that does not have to be repaid than will Ivy Green.

In looking at loan awards, you see that College USA gives this student $4,125 the first year. Ivy Green awards $7,625. The net difference for one year is $3,500 more money that this student has to pay back. Assuming each college increases the Federal Stafford/Direct Student loan to the maximum to make up the difference in the increased cost of education, Ivy Green saddles this student with $14,000 more in loans to repay than does College USA, as Table 21-2 illustrates.

Table 21-2   Comparing Gift Aid

College	Year	Perkins	Stafford	Other	Total
USA	1	$ 1,500	$ 2,625	$ 0,000	$ 4,125
IVY	1	$ 1,000	$ 2,625	$ 4,000	$ 7,625
USA	2	$1,500	$3,500	$0,000	$5,000
IVY	2	$1,000	3,500	$4,000	$8,500
USA	3	$1,500	$5,500	$0,000	$7,000
IVY	3	$1,000	$5,500	$4,000	$10,500
USA	4	$1,500	$5,500	$0,000	$7,000
IVY	4	$1,000	$5,500	$4,000	$10,500

College	Year	Perkins	Stafford	Other	Total
USA	Total	$6,000	$17,125	$0,000	$23,125
IVY	Total	$ 4,000	$ 17,125	$ 16,000	$ 37,125

[$37,125 - $23,125 = $14,000]

When adding up the difference in grants of $13,600, plus not having to pay back an additional $14,000 in loans, you see that one of the two colleges offers a clear financial advantage. By selecting College USA, this student will be ahead $27,600 in real money after graduation.

Additionally, when comparing money awarded from work, College USA asks this student to work an average of 10 hours per week, about one third of the 28 weekly hours programmed by Ivy Green.

As soon as your award letters come in, record them on your own copy of Dr. Davis's Awards Comparison Chart shown in Table 21-3 and figure out your best deal!

Table 21-3	Dr. Davis's Awards Comparison Chart			
Factors to Consider	*(School Name)*	*(School Name)*	*(School Name)*	*(School Name)*
1. Total tuition, room, board, fees (Hard costs) $				
2. Total costs (hard + soft costs – books, supplies, transportation, and so on)				
2A. Expected family contribution				
2B. Student's financial need				
GIFT AID (free money)				
3. Scholarship (#1)				
4. Scholarship (#2)				
5. Federal Pell grant				
6. Federal SEOG grant				
7. State grant				
8. Merit grant				
9. Need grant				

(continued)

Table 21-3 *(continued)*

Factors to Consider	(School Name)	(School Name)	(School Name)	(School Name)
10. TOTAL AMOUNT FREE MONEY (gift awards)				
11. (lines 1 – 10 = Best gift aid)				
SELF HELP (loans and jobs)				
12. Federal Perkins student loan				
13. Subsidized Federal Stafford/ Direct Student Loan				
14. Other student loan				
15. Campus job/ federal work-study				
16. Other				
17. TOTAL SELF HELP (loans and jobs)				
18. TOTAL FINANCIAL AID AWARDED (award package)				
(Lines 11 + 17 = award offer)				
Best awards can be assessed on one of the following factors:				
A. Ratio of gift aid to self help				
B. Gap between awards and demonstrated need				
C. Money you need to pay for college after awards are made				

Chart Source: Dr. Herm Davis

The College Business Office and Your Account

Once you've made your final selection of a college and finaid award, the college financial aid office notifies the business office of your awarded funds.

Don't worry about the colleges you initially accepted and later rejected; the paperwork on your account will be canceled.

The funds described in your award letter (except for the work funds that you have not yet earned) are credited to your account, which is also called *the student bill.*

When you receive your student bill, the financial aid funds show a credit against your expenses. You are responsible for paying any outstanding balance on your bill.

Table 21-4 is an example of how a student bill shows a financial aid credit.

Table 21-4	Example of Student Bill at New College		
(FOR FALL SEMESTER- 1998)			
07-01-98	*Debit*	*Credit*	*Balance*
Tuition	$5,850.00		
Fees-Student Activities	200.00		
Fees-Lab	125.00		
Housing	1,250.00		
Board- Plan II	1,400.00		
Advance Deposit		$ 300.00	
Fed. Stafford Loan-Sub.		1,650.00	
Fed. Perkins Loan .		1,000.00	
Fed. Pell Grant		1,350.00	
Fed. Supplemental Grant		400.00	
State Incentive Grant		950.00	
P.T.A. Scholarship		1,200.00	
Fed. PLUS		2,500.00	
Balance	**$8,825.00**	**$9,350.00**	**+ $525.00**

(The balance of $525.00 will be refunded to you within 15 working days from the date of this invoice)

The credit will be refunded to this student in about three or four weeks after school starts. At that time, the student can spend the excess funds on personal maintenance, off-campus housing, books, supplies, and other school-related costs. The funds also can be used to repay bridge loans (to keep you financially alive) made by parents or others when school first begins.

Affordability as a Value

In earlier generations, factors for choosing a college clustered around these kinds of values: intellectual challenge, a nurturing environment, geographic location, family tradition, good party school, and probability of acceptance. The cost of the school was usually "something to be worked out" — the equivalent of "We'll worry about that later; just get in."

Although these values are still intact, we observe that today's students are far more apt to enroll in a particular school for two reasons more closely aligned to a changing economy and a revalued cost/benefit ratio:

- The school's reputed ability — curriculum, prestige of degree, and contacts — to prepare its graduates for the best jobs
- The cost of the school

Affordability, while always of some concern, has now raced to the head of the values parade when students and families decide which institutions they'll attend.

Part V
It's Payback Time — Or Is It?

The 5th Wave

By Rich Tennant

©RICHTENNANT

$(a+5)^9 =$

$\int x\, dx = \partial^{2}\!/_{2}$

$:= xe(\div x)$

"It's part of my employer tuition assistance agreement with the 'Pizza Bob' corporation."

In this part ...

Years or months from now, you graduate. Big sigh of relief, you think you've just crossed your biggest hurdle — completing a degree. But one potentially high-priced milestone lies ahead if you're in debt: repayment. These chapters help you look around expensive corners to see the best ways to handle your student loan repayment, including jobs that bring loan forgiveness. Whether you're terrified of hefty debt now or later, read these essential tips to plan your financial survival.

Chapter 22
Can Your Loans Be Forgiven?

Six out of ten college students go to school on borrowed money. They borrowed more than $21 billion in 1994, the most recent year tallied by the U.S. General Accounting Office. Those who've already been through the debt gauntlet wonder:

Where will I get the money to repay my share of those billions of dollars?

Because loans often seem more like Monopoly paper than real money, you may not take the certainty of repayment seriously when you borrow. And then comes the shock: As you begin or recharge your adult life, you owe a lot of money!

If you're an average borrower, you'll owe $17,000 when you complete four years of college, and you'll pay back about $200 per month for ten years thereafter — an unappetizing total of $24,000. Each ten years of repayment gets closer to being equal to the amount of the original loan. The lesson? Shed the loan fast. Some lenders are "generous" enough to allow you 30 long years to repay, at interest rates high enough to *triple* your loan by the time you finish paying it off.

Everywhere you look, college students are stacking up debt. Using New York as a single illustration, student loans at that state's universities increased by 65 percent in a mere five years, from 1990 to 1995. How did that happen? New York state budget cuts slashed other types of finaid and school funding, tuition fees exploded to help schools fill yawning budgetary gaps, and students found themselves clamped in an either-or situation: they could take out loans or quit school.

Sallie Mae, one of the biggest cash-cows in the loan pasture, gobbles up most student loans by buying them from banks and other financial institutions.

A little background about Sallie Mae can help you understand the student loan business. Congress established Sallie Mae (officially known as the Student Loan Marketing Association) as a quasi profit/nonprofit agency to buy student loan paper from lenders, thus replenishing the supply of money to make new student loans.

Suppose a bank starts out with $10 million to lend to students; the bank has the students sign all of the promissory notes and related statements, and then it sells the loan paper to Sallie Mae and gets another $10 million to circulate.

Sallie Mae, as well as all its customers who lent the money in the first place, receive a cost allowance referred to as a *special allowance*. This fee adds up to substantial profits for the banks and other financial institutions. Even Sallie Mae was approved by Congress to revise its charter and become a for-profit company because it wants to provide additional profit-making services.

Perhaps because the student-loan/banking complex wants you to borrow, borrow, borrow, it's not surprising that neither Sallie Mae nor its participating lenders have developed a program for loan forgiveness. It's pay all the way.

But other nonprofit entities, including government agencies, have discovered that it pays to reward graduates for putting their education to use to serve society by granting partial-to-full loan forgiveness. Nellie Mae, for instance, which is the largest nonprofit provider of student loans nationally, is considering starting a loan-forgiveness program for its employees. This chapter illustrates the forgiveness principle.

Wipe Out Debt: Volunteering and Working

The following programs provide partial or complete loan forgiveness for people who volunteer to help others or who work under special circumstances.

AmeriCorps

AmeriCorps is a program of volunteer service in return for help with college tuition. Participating states have programs that reward 12 months' volunteer service with up to $7,400 in stipends plus $4,725 that can be used to pay educational loans. You can collect that $4,725 only twice, although volun-teering is unlimited. Call AmeriCorps at 800-942-2677 or visit the AmeriCorps Web site, which contains details about loan repayment and positions available in every state at: www.cns.gov/americorps.html.

The Perkins Loan

Established under the Eisenhower administration, the National Defense Student Loan (now called the Perkins Loan) encouraged students to become math, science, and foreign language teachers. The National Defense Educa-tion Act rewarded new teachers for arming the population's minds by forgiving their loans.

Today, the Perkins Loan may forgive all of your loan if you teach full-time in an elementary or secondary school that serves students from low-income families. It forgives 15% of your loan for the first and second years of ser-vice, 20% for the third and fourth, and 30% for the fifth. Teachers should contact their personnel offices for the list of eligible schools in their district.

Military service

See Chapter 17 for information about loan forgiveness available through Army Reserve and National Guard programs in each state.

Peace Corps

Volunteering in the Peace Corps as a student can cancel up to 70% of your loan and defer the remaining balance while you are in service. The Peace Corps offers a wide variety of positions, training, and overseas experiences, and may pay you back with skills as well as loan cancellation. Contact the Peace Corps at 1990 K Street, NW, Washington, DC 20526, 202-606-3730 or 800-424-8580.

VISTA (Volunteers in Service to America)

Volunteering for this part of AmeriCorps may cancel a good chunk of your loan. You can participate in private, nonprofit, community development, anti-poverty, anti-hunger, anti-homelessness, and health or literacy-related organizations at the local, state, or federal level in return for an allowance and a stipend at the end of service.

Members who volunteer for 1,700 hours can receive an education award of $4,725 for one year of service. A relocation allowance is also available. This award accompanies a living allowance, health coverage, and special non-competitive eligibility for other federal employment — some VISTA positions require some college education or a bachelor's degree. Contact VISTA at 202-606-5000 or 800-942-2677.

Uncommon Ways to End Debt

The following are some special programs that reward achievement with loan forgiveness.

For good grades and teaching in Mississippi: The **William Winter Teacher Scholar Loan** is for students who meet academic requirements and are education majors. After receiving this loan and teaching in Mississippi for one year, one year of loan will be forgiven. If you teach in a shortage area, you are eligible for two years of loan forgiveness for one year of service. Contact the Mississippi Office of State Student Financial Aid, 3825 Ridgewood Road, Jackson, MS 39211-6453, 601-982-6663.

For graduation from Baker University: Baker University provides a loan-forgiveness program for students who complete a bachelor's degree at **Baker University's College of Arts and Sciences**. Contact Baker University, P.O. Box 65, Baldwin City, KS 66006-0065; 913-594-6451

For Alaska State Troopers: The **Michael Murphy Loan Program** allows students who receive this loan in college and major in law enforcement, law, probation and parole, penology, or other related fields to work it off, one-fifth per year, as full-time law enforcement (or related field) employees in Alaska. Contact Alaska State Troopers, Director's Office Scholarship Fund, 5700 East Tudor Road, Anchorage, AK 99507; 907-269-5511.

For Maryland state and local government employees: If you work in Maryland and earn an annual gross salary that is less than $40,000, you may be eligible for this loan-repayment-assistance program for the fields of study of law, nursing, physical and occupational therapy, social work, and teachers of mathematics, science, and special education. Contact Maryland State Scholarship Administration, 16 Francis Street, Annapolis, MD 21401; 410-974-2971(x146).

Law Students' Loan Forgiveness

Because law graduates often owe an excess of $80,000 (if they went to a public college) or $125,000 (if they went to a private college), we thought these resources would be especially helpful. The National Association for

Public Interest Law and the American Bar Association developed *An Action Manual for Loan Repayment Assistance* to encourage states, colleges, and private groups to support loan-forgiveness programs. Maryland offers such a program and gives lawyers priority.

More than 30 law schools forgive students' loans if they serve in public interest or in nonprofit positions. Among them are Loyola University, Stanford University, University of California, University of San Diego, University of Southern California, Georgetown University, American University, Chicago-Kent College of Law, Northwestern University, University of Chicago, University of Notre Dame, Valparaiso University, University of Minnesota, Brooklyn University, Cornell University, Fordham University, New York University, Hofstra University, Duke University, Temple University, Brown University, Southern Methodist University, University of Virginia, Washington and Lee University, and the University of Washington.

Contact the Director of Financial Aid or National Association for Public Interest Law, 1666 Connecticut Avenue, Suite 424, Washington, DC 20009, 202-265-7546 or check out the National Association for Public Interest Law's Web site at, www.napil.org/.

Healthcare Students' Loan Forgiveness

Every medical student knows that the usual six years' study at an expensive program runs up quite a tuition tab. But not every future white-coat knows that alternatives to major repayment exist. If you take the maximum Federal Stafford loans for six years' medical education, you're looking at $111,000 in debt. If you attend a public school, add $50,000 in other loans. If you attend a private school, add a mega-debt of $120,000 in additional loans.

Medical school students

Several programs may take the bitterness out of med school debt. For example, California State University offers a loan-forgiveness program to applicants who will be new or continuing students in full-time, accredited universities anywhere in the U.S. Applicants aren't required to have attended a California State University or to have been accepted to a doctoral program at time of application.

Other states offer comparable programs sponsored by the National Health Service Corps or programs that recruit primary care physicians to practice in medically underserved areas, like the doctor in Alaska on the television show *Northern Exposure*. Award recipients get an annual salary plus payments for medical school loans and costs, but must commit to a minimum number of years of practice, depending on the state.

Contact the State Loan Repayment Program, Primary Care Resources and Community Development Division, Office of Statewide Health Planning and Development, 1600 Ninth Street, Room 440, Sacramento, CA 95814, 916-654-1833, `www.oshpd.cahwet.gov`/or a comparable agency in your state. See also the state finaid agencies listed by state in Chapter 8.

Occupational and physical therapy students

Since licensed/certified occupational and physical therapists remain a rare species, many hospitals and private health-related organizations use student loan forgiveness fringe benefits as a recruitment tool. Wherever you apply in these fields, ask how the employer's loan forgiveness package compares to those of other employers.

For example, the Florida Department of Education pays up to $2,500 per year on undergraduate loans and up to $5,000 for graduate loans for licensed occupational and physical therapists. You're eligible for this tantalizing program if you're a licensed therapist (valid temporary permit is okay) who's worked full-time in Florida public schools for one year and you declare your intent to work for Florida public schools for at least three years. Contact the Florida Department of Education, Bureau of Education for Exceptional Students, 622 Florida Educational Center, Tallahassee, Florida 32399-0400.

For general resources on loan forgiveness in the occupational or physical therapy biz, contact

- **American Physical Therapy Association**
  1111 North Fairfax Street
  Alexandria, VA 22314-1488
  800-999-2782

- **National Clearinghouse, Professionals Information Center Council for Exceptional Children**
  1920 Association Drive,
  Reston, VA 22091
  703-264-0476 or 800-641-7824

- **American Occupational Therapy Association**
  P.O. Box 31220
  4720 Montgomery Lane
  Bethesda, MD 20824-1220
  301-652-2682

COLLEGE MYTHS

Myths about loan forgiveness

The following myths about lifestyle and professional issues relate to a specific healthcare forgiveness program in the State of Washington and are debunked by the Higher Education Coordinating Board in Olympia.

They do not apply across-the-board to all forgiveness programs but are useful as a guide to know what questions to ask about conditions in specific programs. The Web sites noted in this chapter may answer your questions.

Myth: Recruits cannot choose their sites.

Choice abounds. Program participants are allowed to choose from among areas designated by the Washington Department of Health that have a broad range of options and great need. Vacancy lists are available.

Myth: All clinic conditions are terrible.

Not so. At a minimum, all sites must provide a system of care with referrals and backup procedures in place, as well as accept Medicaid and Medicare beneficiaries, and have the funds to pay the provider's (healthcare professional who is working out a loan) salary and benefits. Site visits are always recommended to prevent unwelcome surprises.

Myth: You'll be all by yourself.

Providers are seldom placed in solo practices. Group practices are the norm rather than the exception. Most practices are community based and employ two or more providers.

Myth: You won't have a life outside of work.

Even rural areas provide opportunities for community involvement from volunteer fire departments, churches, and schools, to recreational resources.

Myth: You work in rural areas — "out in the sticks."

Many sites are in rural areas; however, most are located within short driving distances of large cities or within proximity to scenic National Parks. And there are many openings in urban underserved areas.

Additional reading

For more about loan forgiveness, send for *The Student Loan Forgiveness Directory* by Dr. Herm Davis and the National College Scholarship Foundation; 1996; 54 pages. This resource is available only by mail for $22, postage included, from NCSF, Box 8207, Gaithersburg, MD 20898.

Other healthcare programs

Listed below are national agencies in occupations that have a shortage of applicants to fill their needs. Use these contacts to hunt down employers with the best loan-forgiveness options.

- **Midwifery or Nursing**

  Disadvantaged Health Professions Students
  National Institutes of Health
  Division of Student Assistance
  Rockville, Maryland 20850
  301-443-1748

- **Nursing**

  National League for Nursing
  350 Hudson Street
  New York, NY 10014
  212-989-9393 or 800-669-1656

Expanded Loan Forgiveness Plus No Taxes

When a school debt is canceled (forgiven) you usually must report the cancellation as income on your tax return. The 1997 tax law made changes in this requirement.

Until now, when a loan was forgiven, to escape taxes the loan had to have come from the U.S. government, a state government, or a tax-exempt public benefit corporation (like a charity). Loans made with private funds didn't qualify for the tax break.

From now on, in addition to forgiveness jobs with those employers, you can avoid income taxes if you take a loan-forgiveness job with an educational institution, even when the money that funded the loan came from nongovernment sources.

To qualify, you must take a community service job that addresses society's unmet needs for a specified period of time.

Chapter 23

Drowning in a Sea of Debt

. . . .

In This Chapter

▶ SOS moves when you're in money trouble

▶ Staying out of money trouble

▶ Painlessly chipping away at a debt

. . . .

Do you feel like you're about to go underwater for the third time with debt? Then you and hundreds of thousands of other grads who are in deep water with student loans may find this chapter to be the life preserver you need.

Two Debtors Up a Creek

A college borrower we'll call Dale graduated with a degree in marketing five months ago. With one more month of grace period, he's still job hunting and waves of loan repayment are rising. After he careens into repayment, he has two chilling options — sink or swim.

His college buddy, Diana, graduated with a liberal arts degree last year, and she's already sunk in debt's deep waters. Before she could find a well-paying job, she was caught up in $206 monthly loan payments, $300 monthly car payments, and $1,200 rent and utilities payments; she was living on her credit cards. Within the first 12 months of repayment, she had already *defaulted* (failed to pay her loans) and waterlogged her once-buoyant credit.

Diana is no oddball. Nearly a million people are defaulting on their student loans. The default rate peaked at 22.4 percent in 1990. In response, the feds cracked down and today the default rate has shrunk to about 11 percent. Paying back student loans is more important to your future than ever before. If you default on your loans, you can sink your credit, lose your ability to finance your home, car, or savings, and even part of your wages. Diana's tax refund went straight to Uncle Sam's Treasury, no questions asked.

Diana's mistakes, all too common among new grads, taught Dale how to avoid hitting bottom. No stranger to carefully crunched numbers, Dale realized he'd have to waterproof his financial future fast. But how could he take the helm of his finances and steer a steady course when he was already way out to sea?

Find out who's making waves

Dale's first worry was how his lender expected him to repay his whopping $17,125 loan. Because he'd never kept records of his loans during his college years, he had no idea to whom he would be paying his loan or what storms his lender would raise if he couldn't pay. Dale forgot the first rule of borrowing: Know thy lender.

Dale first decided to read the only book specifically written to deal with his problem — *Take Control of Your Student Loans* by Attorneys Robin Leonard & Shae Irving (see the sidebar, "Additional resources" at the end of this chapter). He then rooted through all his financial aid records for any old paperwork, receipts, promissory notes, check stubs, or award letters — documents that often list the name(s) of your original lender and any loan guarantee agencies.

But Dale had inadvertently trashed everything but his loan checks, which went straight to his school. Even current, written material on student loans from the U.S. Department of Education couldn't clear Dale's clouded waters; the mix of repayment options and even names of loans had changed since Dale took his first loan.

Playing the probabilities couldn't help disorganized Dale. Although federally sponsored education loans account for nearly 60 percent of all student financial aid (see Chapter 7 for more on federally sponsored loans), students may also receive loans from a variety of sources, including private loan programs offered by banks, schools, and state agencies. Federal laws specify the terms for buying, selling, collecting, and repaying Federal Stafford and other federal education loans. Policies for repayment of non-federal loan programs can vary from lender to lender.

Even when he received his first bill, Dale couldn't figure out whose money he would be paying off or who should be called if he needed mercy. So Dale asked for help from his school's financial aid office. (Some finaid offices can find out who carries your loan for you; others can connect you with your state's loan guarantee agency) or nonprofit organization that guarantees your loans. Guarantors can help you locate your lender or loan servicer.

Lenders are required by law to clue in borrowers (not in default) when selling loans or hiring a servicer to collect and process loan payments. If you didn't save all such documents and if you think you're in default, contact your college or the U.S. Department of Education Debt Collection Services for Student Loans at 800-621-3115.

Words to know in debt management

Knowing these terms will help you navigate your sea of debt.

- **Anticipated Graduation Date:** The date you expect to graduate; your school must verify this date on your loan application to determine when you must begin repayment.

- **Capitalization of Interest:** The practice of adding interest to the principal amount rather than making interest payments. This method increases both the total amount you owe and your monthly payments.

- **Consolidation:** The practice of combining loans into a single loan. Federal consolidation loans may include a variety of federal loan programs.

- **Delinquency:** When loan payments are late or missed. After 180 days of delinquency, the loan goes into default. Delinquency gets reported to credit bureaus and can limit your ability to obtain credit.

- **Forbearance:** Temporary postponement or reduction of your loan payments. During forbearance, interest continues to accrue.

- **Guarantee Fee:** A fee paid to the state agency or nonprofit organization that guarantees a Stafford or PLUS issued by a private lender under the Federal Family Education Loan Program (FFELP). The guarantee protects lenders against the risk that a loan will not be repaid due to a default, bankruptcy, death, disability, or school closure.

- **Half-time:** Federal rules generally require that you enter repayment six months after you leave school or drop below half-time enrollment, which is usually at least 6 semester hours or 9 quarter hours per term; 12 semester hours or 18 quarter hours per year; or 12 hours per week. Some schools may set higher requirements for half-time enrollment.

- **Origination Fee:** A charge that helps defray the feds' cost for subsidizing federal education loans.

- **Prepayment:** Making your loan payments ahead of schedule. For federal education loans, you may prepay your debt in full or in part at any time without any penalty.

- **Principal:** The total balance of your loan on which interest is charged.

- **Repayment Agreement:** A form lenders provide that arranges repayment. The form lists the amount borrowed, the amount of monthly payments, and the date payments are due.

- **Servicers:** Some lenders, including many colleges and universities, pay these organizations to collect and process loan payments. Unless you're in default, your lender will tell you if your loan gets transferred to a servicer. Your payments go to the servicer, but are otherwise unchanged. Inform your servicer of any change in address.

- **Secondary Market:** Some lenders sell their loans to secondary markets that have authorization to participate in student loan programs. Your loan may be sold without your permission or prior notification, but your lender will inform you after the transaction. Nothing on your end changes except that you send payments to and communicate with the secondary market or its loan servicer. If you want additional loans, however, contact your original lender.

- **Tax Offset:** When defaulted borrowers lose their state or federal income tax refunds.

- **Variable Interest:** Interest rates that change according to a market-sensitive index.

Test repayment plans before you jump in

After contacting his servicer, Dale found out he had several types of loans and a number of options for reducing his monthly payments. With his future in the balance, he decided to compare these options as carefully as the stocks he'd studied in college. Until he eyed the fine print in each option, he'd always assumed he was doomed for giant payments for as far as he could see. Before he jumped into repayment waves over his head, he tested the water. Following are the plans he had to choose from.

The Cannonball: Standard payment method

If your income can stand the cold, full-body slap of standard plan payments, you'll save long-run money. While a standard plan carries the highest monthly payment, you can overcome your debt faster and pay less in interest. You may pay a fixed amount for up to ten years; payments on loans with variable interest rates may fluctuate.

The Swan Dive: Graduated payment method

If your starting income is relatively low but expected to increase on a regular basis, this more graceful method may ease your payment pangs. Payments start low and increase every two to three years for the next 10 to 30 years. Interest charges, which are based on the outstanding principal, will remain high for the first few years, so you'll pay more total interest over the life of your loan.

Federal education loans, including Stafford, SLS, PLUS, HEAL, Federal Consolidation Loans, and HEAL loans, as well as some private loans, offer graduated repayment terms, which can vary from lender to lender. Some lenders, including Sallie Mae, let you make interest-only payments for the first two to four years; after that period, you must pay principal and interest.

Wading in: Long-term repayment method

If all you can afford is a tiny monthly payment, an extended, get-used-to-it payment plan may be your only option. The feds and other lenders allow you to extend payments from 12 to 30 years, and even offer plans that combine graduated repayments with an extended schedule. Although your monthly payments may be low, you could end up paying twice the original amount of your loan.

Water wings: Income-based repayment plans

If your income bobs up and down unpredictably, or can't keep you above water, choosing an income-based repayment plan may keep you afloat. This option is available for both Federal Direct and guaranteed loans.

The *income-contingent repayment plan* offered by the Federal Direct loan program lets you base your payment on your annual income, the amount you owe, and other factors such as family size. The monthly installment amount cannot exceed 20 percent of your discretionary income, which is defined as the adjusted gross income (AGI) you report on your federal tax return minus the poverty income for your household size as determined by the U.S. Department of Health and Human Services. If you are married, you must report the income for your spouse. Every five years, you must sign a waiver allowing the Internal Revenue Service to disclose your AGI to the U.S. Department of Education. The direct loan servicer will send you an authorization form that you must sign and return.

Under direct loan rules, your repayment may be less than the accruing interest. Unpaid interest, subject to a limit equal to 10 percent of your initial loan balance, can be capitalized (that is, added to your principal balance), requiring you to pay interest on interest. Any additional unpaid interest will be added to your total loan balance. If you have any leftover debt after 25 years, the federal government will forgive the remaining balance, but under current law will tax the amount forgiven as if it were regular income.

The guaranteed loan program offers an income-sensitive repayment option that also bases the monthly payment on the borrower's income. Repayment schedules vary from lender to lender, but many plans typically set the maximum payment at 4 percent of your monthly income, as long as that payment amount covers the accruing interest. No loan forgiveness is available, and the lender does not need to access your tax return.

New! Paying back student loans at less cost

You or your family can take a tax deduction for interest paid on your student loan in the first 60 months of repayment, which need not be consecutive months. Maximum deductions: $1,000 in 1998, $1,500 in 1999, $2,000 in 2000, and $2,500 in 2001 and beyond. Income adjusted limits for individuals: $40,000, phasing out at $55,000; for families: $60,000, phasing out at $75,000. Good for most educational loans with interest paid starting in 1998 (the loans themselves can be older). Check the tax law's fine print on this one.

Consolidation: A Life Preserver

As Dale surveyed his options, he realized that he had such a collection of loans that he could end up mailing four different checks a month — for a lead weight total of $1,189 a month. As with many GenerationX grads, Dale's debt was so high he had to minimize early payments. According to some statistical estimates, roughly 1.176 million graduates consolidated their debts in 1997. Treading water in his young, uncertain career, Dale found the option of tying all his loans into one and making lower payments instantly appealing.

After you graduate, you should consider consolidation as an option. Consolidation plans allow you to pay off your balance (depending on its size) between 10 and 30 years. Consolidated loans are available for both Federal Direct and guaranteed loans and are eligible for equal-installment, graduated, and income-based repayment outlined earlier in this section. Examine the pluses and minuses Dale factored into his decision to consolidate.

Consolidation can help when

- ✔ Your payments overstress your bare-bones budget, even under the preceding payment plans.
- ✔ You are trying to pay off the balance on your credit cards, which charge higher interest rates.
- ✔ You are trying to save money to start a business or return to school.

Consolidation can hurt, however. When you consolidate just to lower your payments you end up paying quite a bit more in interest over the life of your loan. For example, a $49,000 loan paid off in ten years could total $71,341.20, assuming an interest rate of 8 percent; but paid off in 25 years, it could total $113,457.00.

Many debtors consolidate to avoid keeping track of multiple loans. If you choose consolidation for its simplicity, plan to pay off the debt within ten years or expect to pay up to three times the amount of your loan. Consider these alternative conveniences:

- ✔ Authorize lenders to withdraw monthly payments from your checking account; Sallie Mae discounts .25% off your interest for this authorization.
- ✔ Make at least 48 on-time loan payments; USA Group Secondary Market Services, Sallie Mae, and others will lower your interest rate on eligible Federal Stafford loans.
- ✔ Ask a lender to buy your loans and combine the payments without changing their terms. However, lenders are not required to buy or sell your loans for this purpose.
- ✔ Ask your loan servicer to coordinate payment due dates.

Loans you can consolidate

If you're certain about consolidating your loan after considering the additional expenses, make sure that your loans qualify for consolidation. Normally, you must leave school to consolidate federal loans. The following types of loans may be consolidated:

- **Federal loans**

    - Federal Family Education Loans: Stafford, PLUS, and/or SLS

    - Federal Insured Student Loans (FISL)

    - Federal Perkins Loans

    - Health Professional Student Loans

    - Nursing Student Loans (NSL)

    - Health Education Assistance Loans (HEAL)

- **Defaulted loans**

    Certain federal loans such as Guaranteed Student Loans and Direct loans may be consolidated if the borrower meets the terms and conditions for doing so.

Caveats for consolidation loans

Think twice about consolidating subsidized Federal Stafford Loans with other loans, including unsubsidized Federal Stafford, SLS and Plus loans. Doing so will sacrifice potential interest subsidy benefits on your subsidized Stafford loans should you later decide to return to school or seek a deferment.

Avoid consolidating Perkins loans as well, and keep the low 5% interest rate, unless lenders can promise you that it will pull down the total interest rate on your consolidation loan. If you consolidate the Perkins loan with other loans, including subsidized Federal Stafford loans, you lose all subsidies.

The following are your best bets for obtaining loan consolidation:

- **Sallie Mae;** www.salliemae.com; **800-524-9100:** Sallie Mae consolidates most types of federal loans; its Web site has debt management software, including a calculator that estimates monthly payments under different plans.

- **USA Group, Inc.;** www.usagroup.com; **800-382-4506:** USA Group will help you arrange a consolidated loan providing that at least one of your current loans is guaranteed by its affiliate, USA Funds. Their Web site offers a calculator to assess payments.

✔ **Citibank; 800-967-2400; 800-845-1297 (TDD):** Citibank will consolidate your loans if the bank has made at least one of them.

✔ **Federal Direct Consolidation Loan Information Center;** `www.ed.gov/offices/OPE/DirectLoan`**; 800-557-7392.**

✔ **Department of Health and Human Services; 301-443-1540:** Call for information about consolidating HEAL loans.

After you've consolidated, you have 180 days to add other loans (taken before the consolidation) to your loan package.

Come Up for Air, Defer, or Forbear

With all the naysaying surrounding loan debt, you'd think no reprieve existed. But think again: Many loans and laws show mercy through deferment and forbearance when the situation is truly out of your hands. Be aware that some borrowers may not be eligible for some deferment options because eligibility is related to the history of the borrower's participation in a particular loan program.

Deferments and forbearance may be granted for the following:

✔ Temporary disability

✔ Rehabilitation programs for individuals with disabilities

✔ Unemployment

✔ Economic hardship

✔ Parenting young children

✔ School enrollment

✔ Teaching or servicing underserved populations

✔ Membership in a uniformed service

✔ Community service

✔ Working in healthcare

✔ Law enforcement

Most private, state, and university loans can be deferred while you're in school or in your grace period (typically six to nine months). After you enter repayment, deferment becomes much harder to get, unless you're a medical student completing an internship or residency. Because provisions for deferment vary among schools, contact your school's financial aid office or your state loan servicing center. If you have other loans, such as federally sponsored loans, contact your loan holder for information about canceling or deferring payments.

How do you get deferment?

- **Filling out the right forms.** Even if you meet all the requirements for deferment, you must still request it. Lenders defer payments only if you're not in default, so do your best to keep making payments while you await deferment. Some lenders even provide retroactive deferment to cover past-due payments in lieu of default. Contact your loan holder and ask for deferment forms. The representative you speak with should note in your file that you've requested such documents, in case your bills become due while you await deferment.

  Once you have your deferment request forms, read and complete them carefully and in entirety — don't skip the fine print. Attach all documentation required to verify your eligibility.

- **Saving copies of all correspondence to your lender.** A few weeks after you send your request, contact your lender to double-check that it arrived and is being processed. Ask when to expect a response. Most deferment applications take between four and six weeks to process.

- **Recertifying deferments:** Some types of deferments require borrowers to reapply every six to twelve months. For example, borrowers may need to recertify a deferment granted for a temporary disability. Ask your lender, loan servicer, financial aid counselor, or guarantor for details on how to maintain your deferment.

Even if you don't qualify for deferment, some lenders will *forbear* your payments — they will postpone or temporarily lower them, but your interest will continue to build up. Forbearances can last as long as three years; ask your lender how long you can forbear.

To come up for air when you feel like you're drowning financially, request forbearances on low-interest loans first. Forbearance request forms (available from your lender) typically require information about your income and expenses. Remember, forbearances are generally granted at the lender's discretion.

Lenders must allow forbearance if your loan payments exceed 20 percent of your monthly income, and in cases of natural emergencies and disasters. Borrowers' poor health, personal problems, or financial hardship are normally causes for forbearance.

In the Eye of the Storm: Surviving Default

Diana couldn't take it any more. She'd lost her credit, her car, and her tax refund. She had spent her savings and was living on credit cards that were almost maxed, and after phone calls, letters, and e-mails from her lender, a collection agency was after her in court and billing her.

Dale didn't have a steady job yet, and the only positions open paid just enough to finance a comfortable lifestyle — without Dale's tsunami-sized loan payments. But he learned from Diana's mistakes how to survive and escape a default disaster.

Legend has it that comedian Dennis Leary's student loans never came past due until he appeared on national television. In an interview, he confessed his surprise when he received a slew of collection calls and notices after years of anonymity. His escape from college debt wasn't so surprising years ago; avoiding debt these days is about as easy as escaping hounds on your scent.

When you're delinquent on payments

If you haven't requested forbearance, deferment, or cancellation, expect phone calls and notices demanding payment in a timely fashion. Collectors may also contact local credit bureaus and report your delinquency, thus

Life preservers at debt counseling firm

Dale's worries about repayment were nothing compared to the troubles of debtors already in a lurch. His friend Diana owed $8,000 on roughly 20 credit cards when she found help balancing loan payments, default penalties, and credit card bills. Her eddying credit cost her a chance at a home loan, a new car lease, and early retirement savings. Fortunately, a nationwide agency tossed her an affordable life preserver.

The National Association for Consumer Credit oversees more than 1,300 offices nationwide. If you're having difficulty budgeting or negotiating

with creditors, contact your local Consumer Credit Counseling Service (see resources cited in the sidebar, "Additional reading and resources"). For a small fee, these nonprofit groups can help you negotiate with creditors and can set up your monthly budget.

When Dale's debt-loaded friend Diana visited the debt counseling service, she discovered that she qualified for a break from loan payments. Even if she couldn't completely escape her debt, she got time to save money, pay off outstanding debts, and reshuffle her budget.

glitching your efforts to obtain more credit, rent an apartment, or make large, financed purchases. In other words, even minor sluffing on payments can keep you from your dream home, your ideal car, or a new pair of jeans. Unless you know you've already dug your own hole, request forbearance or deferment pronto.

Letters are promises

If you've seriously shirked on student loan payments, expect collection letters (otherwise known as *dunning letters*) and phone calls from a collection agency. The first letter usually arrives one to 45 days after you're already in default; the second through the fourth will arrive between 46 and 180 days after default. These letters announce that your nonpayment of debt has been reported to national credit bureaus and reiterate the demands of previous letters. For federal loans, lenders, guarantors, and collection agencies are required to follow federal regulations when pursuing defaulted borrowers.

Promises come true

If you don't respond to this trail of verbal and written notices, your income tax refunds or wages may be siphoned off, or you may be sued. If collectors or guarantee agencies don't have your correct address, they will contact relatives, friends, references, landlords, or employers listed on your loan application. They may also check with the post office, the department of motor vehicles, voter registrations, utility companies, banks, credit bureaus, or federal government records. This is called *skip tracing* as required by federal law. And, you have given them permission to use these references for the tracing of your whereabouts.

The ugly truth about credit reports

Credit bureaus make a profit from reporting your financial history to every company that wants to pay a small fee. They maintain files on your personal identification numbers, location, monthly account activity, legal history, who has inquired about your credit, and your defaults. They sell credit files to financial institutions, retail stores, landlords, insurance companies, and employers. The three major bureaus are *Experian* (formerly TRW), *Equifax*, and *Trans Union*.

Because your livelihood and credit hang in the balance, we suggest you work to protect both. Default reports on your credit tell an ugly truth that may prevent you from getting anything from a simple credit card to a job. Lenders may report any default over $100 at any time. Federal law requires that defaulters be reported to credit bureaus.

The last life preserver: reasonable and affordable repayment plan

Under the reasonable and affordable repayment program, you can ask that loan holders temporarily reduce your payments so they reflect your finances. Collectors must consider your obligatory and living expenses, but the feds haven't established a formula for calculating payments. However, collectors can't demand the same minimum amount from all applicants. If collectors allow you to pay less than $50 per month, they must document for the feds why you're entitled to such small payments.

Call *and* write your loan holder to request a reasonable and affordable repayment plan, and ask what documentation the loan holder will need to process your request. If you make six payments under the new plan, you become eligible once again to apply for federal loans and grants. Your loan comes out of default after you make twelve consecutive payments; it then gets sold to a loan holder. At that point, arrange for one of the flexible payment options discussed in the section "Test repayment plans before you jump in," earlier in this chapter.

Failure to pay costs money

Collection fees are paid for by the defaulter — you. These agencies may collect interest on the added amount due plus other charges, such as for mail and phone expenses, credit reporting expenses, bank charges, and even file maintenance fees.

To avoid sinking yourself even deeper into the debt quagmire, contact the holder of your loan immediately and negotiate a reasonable and affordable repayment plan. If you can offer to repay your balance in a lump sum or over a few months, your collector may let up.

Guarantors help identify borrowers who are in default, and the federal government receives the money via the IRS offset. The IRS applies the refund monies against the amount owed by the borrower. If your loan is in default, the lender is paid an insurance claim and effectively is out of the picture.

If the U.S. Department of Education, a collection agency working for that department, or a guarantee agency holds your loan, your tax refund may go straight to them. If you owe $25 or more and have made no payment in the last 90 days, the collector can notify the IRS that your loan is in default, and the IRS may decide to keep part or all of your refund to apply to the debt that you owe.

For the 20 days following this notice, you can request (in writing) copies of your loan documents and payment records. For the following 65 days, you can request a repayment schedule or review of your file (an in-person or telephone review is possible). To halt an intercept of your return, present any of the following evidence:

- ✔ You've repaid the loan.
- ✔ You're making payments according to an agreement you made with the collector.
- ✔ You're in deferment or forbearance.
- ✔ You filed for bankruptcy and the case remains open.
- ✔ Your loan was discharged due to bankruptcy.
- ✔ You meet any of the aforementioned criteria for loan cancellation.
- ✔ The loan is not yours.
- ✔ Your signature on the loan was forged.
- ✔ You dropped out of school and are awaiting a refund.
- ✔ Your school closed or the loan was falsely certified.

When you're headed for court, contact an attorney immediately; regulations for collecting debts vary by state. Just like any other debt, college loan default can mean that you lose your property if the judgment is against you.

Additional resources

- ✔ *Take Control of Your Student Loans*, by attorneys Robin Leonard and Shae Irving. NoloPress, 1997; $19.95; bookstores or call 800-992-6656.

- ✔ *Direct Student Loan Consolidation.* Order this free booklet from U.S. General Services Administration, Consumer Information Center. S. James Consumer Information Center - 6C, P.O. Box 100, Pueblo, Colorado 81002, or online, www.pueblo.gsa.gov. Ask for publication number 509C.

- ✔ *Paying for College.* Order this free booklet from U.S. General Services Administration,

Consumer Information Center. S. James Consumer Information Center - 6C, P.O. Box 100, Pueblo, Colorado 81002, or online, www.pueblo.gsa.gov. Ask for publication number 589C.

- ✔ *Knee Deep In Debt.* Order this free publication from the Federal Trade Commission's Public Reference Branch, Room 130, 6th Street and Pennsylvania Avenue, N.W. Washington, D.C. 20580.

- ✔ To locate the *Consumer Credit Counseling Services* office nearest you, contact the national office: telephone 800-388-2227; online www.nfcc.org.

When you can get a compromise

After all the notices and warnings from collectors, can you possibly get them to compromise? Yes! If you agree to certain payments, loan holders may forget about your collection costs and up to 30 percent or more of the principal and interest with approval from the agency's director.

How To Talk To Your Lender

To: Lender Name _____

        Lender Address _____

        City, State, Zip _____

Date:

Please note the following changes in your record(s) on my student loan:

____ My address has changed. New address is listed below.

       Address: _____

____ My graduation date has changed.

       The new date is: _____

____ My enrollment status became less than half-time effective (date) ____

____ I have transferred to a different school effective (date) _____

       My new school is: _____

____ I have changed my name.

____ My new name is: _____

____ Other (describe): _____

       _____

Borrower Name: _____

Social Security Number: _____

Address: _____

Phone Number: _____

Type of Loan: _____ (GSL, PLUS, SLS, other)

School Name _____

Part VI
The Part of Tens

The 5th Wave   By Rich Tennant

"and here's our returning champion, spinning for her 3rd & 4th year college tuition..."

In this part ...

A *...For Dummies* book without a Part of Tens is like a software company without a home page. This part sums up ten tips for just about every stage of the finaid process — locating and winning aid, cutting expenses, uncovering well-kept secrets about finaid application, avoiding pricey mistakes, using computerized scholarship services, and avoiding finaid scams. Use this important information to get every last finaid cent.

Chapter 24

Ten Ways to Grow Your Own Opportunities

In This Chapter

▶ Making your own breaks

▶ Aiming local spotlights on you

▶ Turning good works into good money

*T*his chapter focuses on individual actions you can take and choices you can make to grow free-money crops on the fields of financial aid. Perhaps none of these ten suggestions are startling news, but a timely reminder to plow, seed, and water your chances can't hurt.

Raise your class rank

Recognition for reaching the top of your class is nice . . . but money gets you through school. Sources aplenty automatically award finaid to classroom achievers whose rank in class is as high as an elephant's eye. A few examples follow:

- ✔ **Bard College,** Annandale-On-Hudson, New York, gives first-year students in the top 10 percent of their high school class a tuition discount.

- ✔ **The North Dakota Merit Scholarship Program** provides tuition scholarships to in-state students who rank in the top 20 percent of their high school class. Contact your high school counseling center for more details and an application.

- ✔ **The State of Iowa Merit Scholarship Program** gives financial assistance to Iowa seniors who rank in the upper 15 percent of their class and have strong SAT scores.

- ✔ **The Whiteside Scholarship Fund Trust** in Duluth, Minnesota, rewards Duluth students who rank in the top 10 percent of their high school class with scholarships.

Cultivate good grades

Granted, other criteria can win you college funds, but without a stellar grade point average, you'd be ineligible for programs like these.

- ✔ **The National Honor Society Scholarship Awards Program,** sponsored by the National Association of Secondary School Principals in Reston, Virginia. This program requires candidates to meet national minimum requirements to qualify for membership to their local high school National Honor Society. Each school may nominate two chapter members who've demonstrated that they have outstanding scholarship, among other requirements. The 250 award recipients receive $1,000 each.

- ✔ **The Education Foundation of the National Society of Professional Engineers Regional Scholarships** in Alexandria, Virginia. This program awards scholarships to students who'll study engineering in college who sport a 3.0 GPA during their last two years of high school, among other requirements. Awards vary between $1,000 per year to four-year, full-tuition scholarships.

Test your test-taking skills

If you're not the type to blank out under pressure, test your mettle for money in academic competitions. Many merit-based scholarships consider test scores, but this one bases eligibility on them.

The National Merit Scholarship Program is the largest academically competitive scholarship program in the United States. Each year, more than 3,000 scholarships are awarded among 5,000 finalists and an additional 650 scholarships go to African-American students who compete for African-American colleges. Fifteen hundred of these awards are one-timers of $1,000; 1,500 are four-year awards for the same amount.

Competition's abundant, but if you win, your harvest is more abundant than the $1,000 awards. As we noted in Chapter 10, schools that value lustrous reputations lure National Merit winners with a bumper crop of finaid awards.

To qualify, take the Preliminary Scholastic Aptitude Test (PSAT) or the National Merit Scholarship Qualifying Test (NMSQT), usually given in your junior year of high school. Ask your high school guidance counselor for details. Finalists are chosen based on scores. Go study your head off.

Plant career seeds in high school

You'd never guess that acting in school plays or painting still-life oils could be a cash cow grazing in your future. But interests you develop during your high school years that cast light on what you want as a college major or career may lead to scholarship dollars. Following are three examples:

- **Communicative Arts (theater, film, speech, radio, television, broadcasting, music, and dance)** scholarships are sponsored by the Educational Theater Association/International Thespian Society. You need a 2.7 GPA but your academic record doesn't count in the judging. Criteria include acting, interviewing with the judges, and activities with your thespian club in high school. Each year about ten scholarships worth $1,000 each are awarded.

- **Graphic Arts (design and illustration)** scholarships are offered by the National Scholarship Trust Fund of the Graphic Arts. This program offers awards to high school students and college undergraduates who wish to pursue a career in graphic communications. Finalists are selected based on SAT/PSAT scores, transcripts, recommendation letters, and the application and materials. In excess of 160 awards ranging between $500 and $4,000 go to winners annually.

Rake in contest cash

Millions of dollars go out sponsors' doors each year to students who have honed their hobbies, activities, and talents to a competitive level. Check out this sampling of rewards that students can win for having fun:

- **The American Legion National High School Oratorical Contest** yields good money for students who can think and speak well. You must pen an essay and present it in several levels of competition. Regional level winners receive $1,000 each. National winners receive $18,000 for first place, $16,000 for second place, $14,000 for third place and $12,000 for fourth place. Contact your local Legion Post or your state's department headquarters of the American Legion.

- **Guideposts Youth Writing Contest** is a nonfiction contest that pays better than many professional writers earn for similar work. Sponsored by *Guideposts* magazine, the rules invite high school juniors and seniors to write about their most memorable and inspiring true experience. The judges assess the originality of the writing, sincerity of the author, and the values of kindness, spirituality, fairness, and morality. Annually, 30 students win between $1,000 and $4,000. No pulp fiction in this award.

✔ **The Voice of Democracy Audio-Essay Contest** is sponsored by the Veterans of Foreign Wars of the United States and its Ladies Auxiliary, in cooperation with the National Association of Broadcasters. Thirty winners each year take home awards ranging from the first prize of $20,000 to finalists who receive $1,000 each. A different patriotic theme is selected each year and assigned to contestants who broadcast the theme and move up through a series of competitive tiers, ending in a big, flashy finale in Washington, D.C.

Dig in your backyard

A lot of cash for your college stay is buried in your own home town, county, or state. Create your own version of going native by making a list of local sources you can hit up for scholarships, such as

✔ Trusts

✔ Philanthropic organizations

✔ Service clubs

✔ Civic groups

✔ Chambers of commerce

✔ School boards

✔ Immigrant rights groups

✔ Religious organizations

✔ Youth organizations

✔ Professional organizations

Sometimes you can get money chiefly for living in the chunk of geography you call home! Your school guidance counselor and librarian should be able to give you a big assist in this effort.

After a thorough scouting of what's lurking around your neck of the woods, you'll find sources like these that other students may not have noticed:

✔ The **California Masonic Foundation** hands out more than $200,000 to Californians in undergraduate programs.

✔ The **Chautauqua Region Community Foundation Inc.,** bestows finaid to residents of Allegheny, Chautauqua, and Cattaragus counties, New York.

✔ The **Colorado Masons Benevolent Fund Association** awards scholarships to Colorado high school grads who'll attend in-state colleges.

- The **Ebell of Los Angeles Scholarship Endowment Fund** allots grants to students from Los Angeles county who reside in and attend college in the county.

- The **Horace Smith Trust Fund** rewards students who've graduated from high school in Hampden County, Massachusetts.

- The **Jennie G. and Pearl Abell Education Trust** helps out students who are Clark County, Kansas, residents and graduates of Clark County high schools.

- The **Paul Stock Foundation** sponsors students who live in the Cody, Wyoming, area with grants to attend college.

Till the vineyards of volunteerism

While doing good works through volunteering in community service activities, you build career skills and leadership experience. As if that's not enough, a number of organizations return the favor with scholarships toward your education. Let these several examples inspire you to get in touch with your finer feelings:

- **Soroptimist Foundation's Regional Youth Citizenship Awards** chooses scholarship recipients on the basis of service, dependability, leadership, and sense of purpose. Academic criteria (grades, test scores) aren't considered. The foundation gives over 50 scholarships worth several hundred dollars each, plus one $2,000 international award.

- **Tylenol Scholarship Fund** recognizes students who provide leadership in community and school activities. What counts? School awards, academic record, activities, and honors are considered. Each year, 500 scholarships worth $1,000 each and ten $10,000 awards are passed to upstanding students.

- **U.S. Senate Youth Program, William Randolph Hearst Foundation** acknowledges students who have been elected to leadership offices in their high school student governments. This program distributes 104 awards annually at $2,000 each.

- **The Toyota Community Scholars Program** recognizes 100 students each year who show dedication to community service as well as academic leadership. This award was launched in 1997 with a bang of big bucks: The four-year awards range from $10,000 to $20,000. To be considered, you must have initiated or been actively involved in a service program that addresses a school or community need.

Sprout a job in the school finaid office

A part-time, student assistant job in the school financial aid bank vault can expose you to how awards are figured and how students win them. Just by working in this office you pick up nuances you may otherwise miss. Your close contact with the office's inner workings can unveil the perfect finaid for you.

Land a job in the alumni office

The alumni office offers student assistants opportunities to find out which alumnus are helping financially-strapped students complete their education. As an added benefit, you can get to know alums, who, scouting their alma maters for talent, may offer you a job after graduation.

Spread the word you need a sponsor

Are you a pleasant, sincere, hard-working, deserving person? If so, you may be able to find yourself a sponsor who will pay part or all of your way through college.

You think such generosity doesn't happen? Multimillionaire Eugene Lang is well known for backing, not just a single student but entire classes with his "I Have a Dream Project," which has now spread to more than 20 cities. Lang began with sixth-grade students at a Harlem school in New York City, promising that he'd take care of college if they graduated from high school.

To find your own sponsor, you can't be shy bout asking teachers, friends, professionals, and community leaders to recommend potential sponsors and, if possible, introduce you to them.

A Washington D.C. student whom Dr. Davis counseled turned sponsor search into an art by passing out self-marketing packets containing a transcript, recommendation letters and awards letters to potential sponsors. The student received several partial sponsorships.

If you are lucky enough to find a sponsor, be sure to keep in touch and say thanks.

Chapter 25

Ten Strategies for Cutting College Costs

*I*f you would welcome the gift of a financial chain saw to cut down tall college costs, cast your eyes on the approaches identified in this chapter. Some of these strategies require a financial or academic about-face, while others call for minor changes in lifestyle.

Study in bulk

Most students finish school in four or five years, but Bill Thomas, a Pennsylvania State veteran, graduated in three. How? He carried 20 hours per semester and attended summer and winter school. Even though summer and winter tuition cost more per unit, his total tab was below the usual four-year bill. Thomas entered the job market ahead of his class and found an entry-level administrative job that helped him pay off his loan debt fast. Consider overloading courses if your school allows it.

Double up high school and college

Your high school may allow you to take as many as 12 semester hours of college-level courses before you graduate from high school. You may have to meet certain selection criteria or your hours of attendance may be limited. The most popular money-saving route is to enroll in a community or public college and build up units that can transfer to any university.

Swap AP courses for college classes

If you score a 3.0 or better in Advanced Placement (AP) courses, the credits usually substitute for first-year general education courses at the vast majority of U.S. colleges. You must pass an Advanced Placement test in the subject, administered by the Education Testing Service of Princeton, NJ; the tests are given throughout the U.S. By replacing first-year courses that count towards a college degree with AP courses, you can save $10,000 to $12,000 at a public college and $24,000 to $30,000 at a private college.

Get a bargain at two-year colleges

Two-year community colleges are among the best buys in higher education. Their courses cost about half those of four-year institutions, and the first two years of general education courses are roughly the same no matter where you attend college. All in all, when money's a problem, beginning your studies at a community college is your best answer.

Note: Most community colleges coordinate their curriculum with senior institutions, but check that your four-year college or university will accept the credits you earn at a two-year institution. The question to ask an admissions counselor at a four-year institution (from which you plan to graduate one day) is which of your two-year courses will transfer for full credit. Get the counselor to sign the agreed-upon list of transferable courses. Students have been known to accept a verbal agreement that certain courses would transfer for credit, only to find out later that the courses would not transfer and the authorizing college official had left the institution.

Choose a lower-cost school

Okay, we admit the pedigree from a prestigious university such as Sarah Lawrence and Brandeis looks pretty slick on your wall, but you should realize that you're paying for a brand name and the contacts you make on campus.

Magazines such as *Money* and *U.S. News & World Report* annually report on bargain schools — such as Berea College in Kentucky, Missouri Southern State, and Cooper Union in New York — where tuitions are free or modestly priced and the educational standards are high.

Work at co-op education

Wouldn't you love some hands-on experience so you can use your learning and not be considered a raw rookie after you graduate? Cooperative education programs allow you to do just that. You study some, work some, and study some more throughout your college experience. You earn money as you go. More than 900 colleges operate cooperative education programs that typically take five years to complete undergraduate degrees. For more information, read *A College Guide to Cooperative Education,* free from the National Commission for Cooperative Education, 360 Huntington Avenue, Boston, MA 02115.

Old Faithful: Get a job

Granted, working part-time and attending college can take all your energy and time — but more students than ever must choose between doubling up work and school or financially doubling over in pain. If you think that idea is exhausting, hear this: Countless students, many of whom are parents, hold full-time jobs and study at night school or through distance education programs. For more information, see the section on distance education later in this chapter and Chapter 11 for more about jobs.

Test out or get credit for life experience

Many schools spare you a pile of course work if you can prove you know the material well enough not to need the course. Ask at your college admissions office about obtaining credits for passing tests or relevant life experience.

For example, you could escape a $600 computer competency course if you can get life experience credit (such as job experience or military service using computers) or take the school's computer competency exam.

Information for Candidates, a free booklet, explains testing out. Order from College-Level Examination Programs, The College Board, Box 886, New York, NY 10101.

Consider low-cost distance learning

Many online and study-at-home courses cost as much as on-campus studies. But persistent research can connect you to reputable classes for pennies on the dollar. Harvard College, for example, in its distance education program, offers an online college-level calculus course for under $100. Such a deal! Are you a self-starter?

Quell spending urges

College students tend to ease bookworm stress with shopping sprees. Well-meaning parents spring for new wardrobes, cars, and dorm supplies, forgetting that materialistic trappings rarely improve higher learning. The rule of thumb: Don't buy anything until you know you need it.

- **Clothes:** Until you see what your classmates are wearing, don't make over your closet. A surprising amount of money is wasted on a new college wardrobe only to have a parent drag it home to store. The best wardrobe investments you'll make during college will be the graduation cap-and-gown and the suits you'll need to go on job interviews.

- **Textbooks:** Don't automatically believe the book list; talk to your instructor long before the first day of class and find out which books you should have first. College bookstores often have exclusives on assigned textbooks, so try to buy them used. If a course requires an especially pricey book and you don't expect you'll ever read it after this semester, see if you can borrow it from the library. Sell back any textbooks you don't plan to use again.

- **Transportation:** Some college towns are so well designed that you won't need a car most of the time. A friend's car, a bus, a subway, or a taxi can come in handy occasionally, but the expense of purchasing, maintaining, parking, and fueling your own car can eat up sparse dollars. Consider saving your money — perhaps for your dream car much, much later.

- **Living expenses:** Limit long-distance calls and air travel and watch for special deals during off-hours or off-season. Washington University in St. Louis, for instance, has established an airline travel service to help any student in the U.S. save money — Air & Sea Travel, 800-330-3400.

Watch for student discounts on everything, including movie tickets. Put every practical need (like socks, bookshelves, umbrellas) on a wish list and share it with relatives near major holidays. Check for special discounts for low-income families from utilities companies.

If you're as preoccupied as most students, you may think that take-out food costs the same as grocery store food and saves you all the prep time. But $8 meals twice a day add up to $448 per month — and that's skipping a meal! Buy staples in bulk when they're on sale, and use an electric frying pan for quick feeds. Save your money for when you need the positive reinforcement you get from occasionally dining out.

Chapter 26

Ten Facts That Finaid Counselors Don't Tell You

*I*f you thought that you solved the finaid enigma but somebody came up with an answer you didn't like, it's probably because you're missing a piece of the aid puzzle that no one told you existed. Here are ten points you may have overlooked.

Zero aid now, zero aid later

If you don't win finaid your first year, you may not win any later. Many private colleges' policies stipulate that first-year aid winners get priority at reapplication time. Leftover funds go to new incoming students — which means that those unlucky enough not to win finaid during their first year are completely out of the finaid loop. If your school emphasizes first-year finaid over all other levels of aid, throw extra energy and time into finding finaid from the get-go.

Fine print: Oops, money is missing

Many colleges advertise that they meet 100 percent of need; what they don't tell you is that they do so by packaging in parent loans to meet the gap between need and the award.

Some colleges keep mum on what's called a *gapping policy* — a harmless-looking term that means they don't meet 100 percent of your need; instead, they award part of it but leave a gap that they expect your family to fill. Gapping doesn't seem so harmless any more. For example, assume the college annual cost is $26,000 and your demonstrated need is $18,000. Suppose you receive an award package of $14,000. You're left with a need gap of $4,000, which is filled with PLUS loans to parents (see Chapter 7) or cash out of thin air. Your parents must begin repayment on loans after you're in school a couple of months.

State colleges keep gift aid at home

The gift aid (that need not be repaid) pouring forth from some state colleges' financial aid offices seems to have in-state residents' names on it. The type of aid awarded to out-of-state students tends to be limited to self-help (loans and jobs) unless the student is eligible for a Federal Pell Grant.

Note that this trend applies only to financial aid office largesse, not to special scholarships awarded by departments in the colleges. Department faculty are more likely to aim for excellence without regard to whether you're an in-state or out-of-state student.

You can't win without losing

If you win finaid from outside your institution, expect to lose some of your school's award. Although your dear alma mater may not publish policies about third-party awards, as soon as your financial aid office hears of one, they are likely to deduct at least some of that amount from the college award.

After you notify your financial aid office (and yes, you must), negotiate to keep both awards. If they must deduct some money, ask that the amount be subtracted from your college loan or work-study, not from free money.

ROTC meets IRS: The pleasure's not yours

Reserve Officers' Training Corps tuition benefits — which may pay up to 100 percent of college costs — are viewed by schools as an outside scholarship (see Chapter 17). If you receive another outside scholarship that totals more than the cost of tuition, fees, and books and supplies, the excess is taxable income. College finaid personnel aren't obligated to tell you that you can't have it all.

Psst! Top secret: Make deadlines or else

Some finaid counselors don't post deadlines in giant neon letters. Don't hesitate to ask about deadlines. A priority deadline translates as first-come, first-served. If you miss the deadline, you'll be lucky to catch leftover crumbs, and some private schools are super-strict about their deadlines. Most second-semester deadlines hit around mid-November. Call your financial aid office often to check priority deadlines, even if they give you the "don't call us, we'll call you" line.

If you're applying for second (spring) semester, apply as if you were also seeking aid for the fall semester; after you receive the award, only accept the aid for the spring semester.

Student loans beat folks' bad credit

Mom and Dad don't qualify for a Federal PLUS loan because of their credit rating; big bummer. But the finaid office may not tell them that you, their child, can still qualify for an additional, unsubsidized Federal Stafford loan with a lower interest rate — up to $4,000 for each of the first two undergraduate years of college, and $5,000 for each of the second two undergraduate years. Apply for this low interest loan in your name for better cash flow and a longer grace period between graduation and repayment.

More info requested? Watch what you say

The finaid office requests additional information to measure your ability to qualify for institutional aid. You thought you'd filled out all the forms, but your financial aid office asks you to fill out one more, "for their records." But the questions seem far too detailed to be simply FYI.

- What is the equity on the parents' home?
- In the event of a separation or divorce, what is the noncustodial parent's income, assets, and debts?
- Will the noncustodial parent help with college expenses?
- How many cars do the parents own? (Including year, model, value, and debt.)
- Will the student drive to school? If so, how much is the car worth?
- How much of the student's college expenses will the parents cover?
- What is the cash value of the parents' life insurance policies, retirement accounts, and so forth?

✔ Are any siblings holding any money in their accounts for the student?

✔ How much money will the student earn during the summer after graduating from high school?

What they're not telling you is that they may adjust your EFC based on internal guidelines that assume additional funds are available for college based on the value of assets not used in the Federal Methodology formula. Don't hesitate to ask what the information will be used for so you can target your responses to their queries.

Finaid folks push the override button

Though nobody behind the financial aid office desk wants to admit it, finaid directors have unadvertised powers to make what is called a *professional judgment* in the event of additional facts and conditions.

Because of this leeway, new, documented information on employment, income, assets, and other variables that can seriously affect your family's ability to pay college expenses may change your award for the better. Don't hesitate to send letters of appeal along with hefty documentation (see Chapter 9).

If your college uses the College Scholarship Services Profile, the finaid counselor can still make their own judgment calls as they evaluate family assets. For example, some colleges assess 35 percent of the value of the car the student drives to school as an increase in the Expected Family Contribution (EFC). If the student's income tax form shows interest income, even if you don't list assets on the finaid form, some finaid offices figure you made an investment somewhere big enough to make that much interest. Some finaid offices consider part of the family's retirement account as available assets that could pay for college.

Three weeks to live aidless

Even if you win pocket money, don't expect to pick up your check and buy books, supplies, or food the first day of school. Many schools disburse living expense funds after the third week of school, or after the last day you can ask for a refund.

Bring enough cash to cover books (prices are usually available through the bookstore's book list), supplies, food, housing, and transportation.

Chapter 27

Ten Common Goofs That Can Cost You Money

*T*wo wrongs are only the beginning. That rewritten adage is certainly true for the millions of students who go tearing down the yellow brick finaid road only to bounce around in its countless potholes.

You can enjoy a much smoother journey by avoiding any and all of the following ten goofs.

Waiting until you're enrolled to ask for aid

For any college you are even thinking about favoring with your presence, ask about financial aid policies BEFORE you apply.

Don't hang back waiting to be admitted to a college before filing your financial aid request forms. Too many beginners make this mistake.

One explanation may be that students worry that the money-first, enrollment-second formula is asking for rejection. Maybe so if you're applying to the small but growing number of financially stretched colleges where paying customers get the sunny front rooms while finaid basket cases get the gate.

By contrast, most schools still look at other factors — the whole you — before finding out if you come with cash batteries included.

Another reason not to wait for admission before pursuing financial aid is that a college's admission timeline and its financial aid timeline are not necessarily entwined.

- For payment purposes, obtain financial aid information and respond on the financial aid timeline.
- For enrollment purposes, obtain admission information and respond on the admission timeline.

Refusing to spend cash on the Profile

The Profile application form that many select private colleges require you to fill out before they'll award financial aid is described in Chapter 3. Even when you're tired of scribbling on forms, the request for Profile data is one you can't afford to ignore.

Typically, expensive schools require the Profile. It costs you about $20 to provide a Profile application to each school you select that uses this form. So, if you apply to six high-cost schools, you pay about $120 for Profile application processing.

When they hear the cost, students may say they can't pay the processing fee, so they don't apply to the Profile-requiring schools. Big mistake in flashing lights and buzzing bells. If payment is a problem, ask your guidance counselor for a fee waiver for at least one of the schools of choice. Then pay the processing fees and get on with the task of looking for college money — you'll get a gigantic return on your investment. If any one of the Profile-using colleges comes through for you, you're looking at a swap of about $120 for a return of more than $25,000 for a year's tuition, or more than $100,000 for a degree.

Think of it this way: One Profile fee is the cost of two big pizzas. Don't eat pizza this month.

Applying too late for mid-year aid

When you plan to start college in mid-year or to transfer in mid-year, apply for financial aid as if you are starting in the fall semester. Reasons:

- You must meet deadlines; January to April deadlines won't reopen to accommodate your later start.
- You must reserve money before it's all given away for the year.

When you receive an award letter, all you need to do is indicate you are accepting for the mid-year term. If you wait until the fall to apply for the spring or mid-year, you'll probably only get federal loan money and perhaps a Pell grant. You may not get free money from your state, your college, or private scholarships.

Misunderstanding your SAR

Part I of your Student Aid Report (SAR) contains a letter explaining what you need to do to receive aid. Often, the SAR says, "Based on this information, it appears that you are not eligible to receive a Federal Pell grant."

This is the point at which some students go wrong. They interpret the sentence to mean "...it appears that you are not eligible to receive financial aid for college." Nope, that's not what it means.

Think of a suit with lots of pockets. The correct interpretation of the SAR statement is that you cannot receive aid out of the Pell grant "pocket." You may be able to receive aid from the state pocket, the college's pocket, the federal government's loan pocket, or some other pocket. You just won't get money out of the pocket marked "Federal Pell grant."

Not bringing your SAR up to par

Dragging your feet on reviewing your SAR for errors — especially your Social Security number, correct listing of colleges, and the first bachelor's degree statement causes lots of problems.

- ✔ Start with your Social Security number. If it's wrong on your SAR, you'll be missing in action in a college's financial aid office because that's how the offices keep track of you. If the office can't find you on the computer, you don't exist on campus.

- ✔ Make sure that all colleges you've targeted are listed on your SAR. If a school is missing, call the federal student aid information center (319-337-5665) to report the omission. The center will ask for your SAR's PIN number, so have it ready. If a school doesn't get your SAR, you don't get the money at that school.

- ✔ Review to see if you made a mistake by saying that you did "receive your first bachelor's degree." Amazingly, many students think that a high school diploma is a first bachelor's degree. If you already have a first bachelor's degree, you automatically become ineligible for Federal Pell grants, Federal Supplemental Educational Opportunity grants, and most state grants. Wow, what a mistake!

Correct your SAR and get the aid for which you qualify.

Skipping verification paperwork

Colleges, by federal regulation, are required to verify by random sample the eligibility for 30 percent of the students filing for aid.

That's why students are sent a standard verification form that requires them to identify each family member listed as a household resident and any untaxed income, as well as submit the student's and parents' tax forms and W-2 statements.

Many families pitch a fit because they believe they are being audited in the same way that the IRS audits taxes. Wrong. A verification is not an audit, but an effort to provide quality control to the financial aid process.

Not infrequently, the student or parents did err in completing their paperwork with the outcome that they become more, not less, eligible for aid.

Don't sweat verification. You can't prevent it, and it may actually do you some good. On the downside, if you fail to respond to the verification process when asked, you can kiss your federal aid goodbye.

Mixing up transcripts

Still another federal regulation can pop up and bite you in the aid. College financial aid offices can't award federal money to students who have previously attended a postsecondary institution until the FAT (financial aid transcript, described in Chapter 3) is received from the previous college(s). The FAT is required even if you never received financial aid in the past.

When a student with selective listening skills hears the question, "Have you submitted your financial aid transcript," that student may hear only the word "transcript." The student says, "Sure, I had the registrar at my last school send that already," when what was really sent was the academic transcript.

An academic transcript reports grades; a financial aid transcript reports money.

Realize that your aid is being held for ransom until your financial aid transcript(s) is received.

Not saying yes to all colleges

Accepting or regretting college offers is not akin to accepting or regretting social invitations. You are polite when you quickly turn down parties you're pretty sure you won't attend. You are foolish when you quickly turn down colleges you're pretty sure you won't attend.

Say yes to all offers. Yes, *all* offers! You can sort them out later. You may have to appeal for more aid later, but right now, accept what the school has offered.

You need time to sit back, weigh your offers, and make your decisions. Saying no too quickly leads to aid gone astray because someone else received the money you threw away.

Taking automatic renewal for granted

It took you a whole year to get all the kinks out of your understanding of financial aid, and now it's time to start again for the second year.

Too bad — but financial aid, unlike admissions, is not automatically renewed. Financial aid is an annual event.

Pick up financial aid packets from your college's financial aid office to continue or initiate awards for next year. A number of colleges do in fact initiate aid renewals automatically, but they have no responsibility if your renewal slips between the cracks.

One lucky little reminder: The federal government sends out renewal FAFSAs (which are really SARs from the previous year in disguise) to cue you that the time is here to start the process all over again. Flash — renewal FAFSAs will be available on the Web in January 1998.

Not reapplying after a turn-down

Just because you didn't get federal money or a state scholarship one year does not mean you are ineligible forever. Eligibility can boomerang as a result of changes in income, parents' marital status, revisions in assets and savings, fresh money in a college's resources, and even because the student and parents have learned to play the finaid game better.

Don't confuse advice to keep trying for federal and state aid with the advice in Chapter 26: "zero aid now, zero aid later." This observation relates to the college's own aid. For institutional scholarships, you may not get aid after your first year if you weren't awarded aid as an incoming student.

Different strokes for different folks.

Chapter 28

Ten Tips on Hiring a Computer to Help Find Aid

● ●

In This Chapter
▶ Characteristics of good computerized services
▶ Spotting bum information
▶ Questions you must ask to get value

● ●

*1*f your family is racing to send you off to college, researching finaid may seem like a time-hogging task. You feel as though you don't have two minutes to rub together when — bingo! — you spot an ad that shrieks *Money for College — Results Guaranteed!* Such seductive ads are run by firms that claim to tailor a computerized scholarship search to your individual needs for a fee.

What a temptation! Why not let a computer help pay tuition bills? Maybe you should, but then again, maybe you shouldn't.

Computer-based research companies that do the legwork for you at a modest price can be a quick fix in a time-crunch for private scholarships. But only a few scholarship search firms provide serious returns. We identify some of the best of the breed at the end of this chapter.

The unhappy truth is that some computerized search firms have proven to be borderline fraud cases, and taint the entire industry with a bad odor. Some were such rip-offs that in recent years the Federal Trade Commission, state attorneys, and other government scam squads shut them down.

But other computer-based scholarship search firms, neither corrupt nor competent, continue to take advantage of time- and tuition-short students and their families.

This chapter identifies hallmarks of a good scholarship search firm.

A top-quality operation run by pros

Find out who operates the commercial database:

- ✔ Is the owner a financial aid professional (a veteran of the schools or college financial aid services) who is concerned about the quality of the scholarship database and whether the referrals meet each student's requirements?

- ✔ Or is the owner an entrepreneur with virtually no experience in education who looked around for a business opportunity, stumbled onto the business of student financial aid, thought it sounded like a winner, found a supplier for a finaid database, and set off to resell the database — having no idea whether the research that built it is superficial and full of mistakes?

Anyone can become a scholarship search licensee and retail someone else's database. If you are told that the scholarship firm has its own research staff, ask to speak to a research analyst, using the concerns listed in the sidebar, "Five questions to avoid duds."

A good scholarship search firm invests energy in maintaining its product quality as a selling point. It does not try to sell you information about federal and state programs for which you are considered at no charge through the regular financial aid application process.

Scholarships without application fees

Does applying for scholarships listed in the service's database cost money? A good service deletes scholarships that require a fee to apply because many such scholarships are money-making schemes in disguise.

A good scholarship search firm bans application-fee scholarships.

Basic search fees under $50

You can usually get free finaid information at your school or on the Web. That's why most commercial computerized search firms now cap their searches at $50.

A good search firm can use your characteristics to retrieve many private scholarships for $50 or less.

Short-term service

Some persuasive entrepreneurs claim that for a one-time fee — ranging from $300 to $1,000 — they'll set your finaid research up for the next four years. Many of these firms last only a few months before disappearing. Moreover, anyone familiar with college life knows that few students know how long they'll be in school. You're wiser to use the college finaid office's free resources.

A good scholarship search firm allows you to pay as you go, one hour, one week, one month, or one year at a time.

Coordination with college calendars

Search firms that advertise their services after April through July to find money for the fall don't realize that most scholarship sponsors stop taking applications in March. They must not understand the finaid system.

A good scholarship search firm advertises for customers early enough to make scholarships' usual deadlines in March or before.

Pledge of confidentiality

Some reputable firms offer their search free over the Internet. They can do so because the service is advertising-driven. What that means to you is that they sell your name and contact information to mailing list houses to use for direct mail promotions and telemarketing solicitations. Because schools don't monitor the quality of online financial aid searches, the results of your search may disappoint you.

If privacy is a concern, ask if the service keeps your information confidential. A good scholarship search firm can be for fee or for free, but it does not sell your name without your permission.

Savvy research methods

The quality of the scholarship database is all-important. You need accurate, current information that matches your criteria. A superior service maintains its own research staff and updates regularly. Ask the service's research analyst how frequently the service updates its database.

Scholarship criteria change from year to year. Researchers who know their business are knowledgeable enough to update their information only after the sponsor's board of directors has met to determine the ground rules for next year's awards. Normally, the boards meet between March and August. To merely verify on an arbitrary date is useless; for instance, verifying in January results in simply repeating last year's data. Experienced researchers know when the boards meet because it's their business to know — they ask and note the dates in their working files.

Some scholarship search firms advertise that they update every quarter. This claim is marketing hype. Scholarship rules don't change with the seasons — they change once a year. A good scholarship search firm updates its database annually, using savvy research methods.

Portable and targeted finaid

Ask what percentage of the service's database consists of portable awards. You want finaid you can take to any college or to any group of colleges that participate in a specific scholarship award, such as the National Merit Scholarship Program.

Find out if you'll be told about scholarships for which you're ineligible. A good scholarship search firm doesn't try to stick you with scholarships specific to geographic regions or colleges you're not considering or scholarships for groups of people to which you don't belong.

Realistic database growth

Ask how large the database is and how much it has grown in the past two years. A typical size is a couple of hundred thousand scholarship sources. Hypesters claim that their databases balloon by the hundreds per day or week. Genuine services admit that although they constantly add new sources, deleting outdated information keeps total tallies low.

Be wary if you see more than 500 new portable scholarships added from one year to the next. And definitely sneeze with suspicion if a search firm claims to be adding more than 10 or 20 new portable scholarships a day.

A good scholarship search firm doesn't oversell the size of its database from year to year. A smaller database with high-quality scholarships can prove far more valuable than a large one with the kitchen sink thrown in. One search firm, for instance, will not include any scholarship in its database that awards less than $1,000 per student. Another search firm, however, incorporates scholarships as small as $50 book awards.

Printed publications

Don't mistakenly assume that any computer search, no matter how credible the firm or reliable the data, can do all the heavy lifting for maximizing your college money. Look at printed publications that list sources of financial aid.

Your high school guidance office, college financial aid office, and libraries offer materials to conduct searches for finaid at no cost.

A good scholarship search firm doesn't pretend that it has all the answers.

Five questions to avoid duds

When you're paying for a financial aid computer search, get answers to these five important concerns. Even when the search is free, you can waste time and money by using bum information.

✔ **Ask about advertising claims.** If the firm says that large amounts of aid currently are not being used, what proof is offered? Are the unused funds locked in employee tuition plans for which you have no chance?

✔ **Ask about refunds.** Will the firm refund your fee if the search does not produce leads to private scholarships appropriately matched to your qualifications? To get a refund, do you have to submit a rejection letter from every lead that the search firm generated for you? If so, you're in scam territory, because you can be certain that not all scholarship sponsors will send you a rejection letter. If, for instance, you apply for 30 scholarships and only have 18 rejection letters because you never heard from the other 12 sponsors, you can't get a

refund and the firm has lived up to its "guarantee."

In the same vein, ask how long the firm has been in business and if it can offer references and success rates.

✔ **Ask about database quality.** How many financial aid scholarship sponsors exist in the company's computer? Does the firm maintain its own database of scholarships, or does it use the database of another company or service? How often does the database get updated? If the firm says it continually updates, ask how often they verify their data by mail.

✔ **Ask about database content.** Are jobs, loans, contests, and government aid excluded? (The database should contain only private scholarships that can be used at any college or university.)

✔ **Ask about timeliness.** How long will you have to wait for the information? Will you get the information before deadlines have passed?

Dr. Davis's recommended computer sources

Which are the top financial aid computer search services in the business? Here are Dr. Davis' recommendations:

National Scholarship Research Service (NSRS), a division of Cassidy Research Corporation, 2280 Airport Blvd., Santa Rosa, CA 95403; 707-546-6777; www.800headstart.com

Peterson's Education Center, 202 Carnegie Center, P.O. Box 2123, Princeton, NJ 08543; 609-243-9111; www.petersons.com

Scholarship Resource Network (SRN), Daigle and Vierra, Inc., 555 Quince Orchard Road, Ste. 200, Gaithersburg, MD 20878; 301-670-1281; www.rams.com/srn

The College Fund Finder, The College Board, 45 Columbus Ave., New York, NY 10023; 800-323-7155; www.collegeboard.org

Wintergreen/Orchard House, PO Box 15899, New Orleans, LA 70175; 504-866-8658; www.wgoh.com

While we believe these recommendations are reliable, they are not guaranteed. You should evaluate each one for yourself before you buy or use their services.

Chapter 29

Ten Ways to Avoid Finaid Fakes and Frauds

. . . .

In This Chapter

▶ Spotting the biggest, baddest scams

▶ Believing "free money" promises can cost you

▶ When families cheat

. . . .

*B*ased on information from the Federal Trade Commission, we estimate that a minimum of 10,000 questionable financial aid search services annually sucker some 300,000 college families out of millions of dollars.

Most phony finaid operators are true scam artists, but a few may just be seriously incompetent entrepreneurs who mean well but victimize you with their ineptitude (see Chapter 14). No matter, these tricksters fool even the smartest people with a rich variety of come-ons, including the "satisfied customer" testimonial that invites you to get yours. Like this:

> *Ann Smith won $499,000 in scholarships; so can you!*

Who is Ann Smith? Ann Smith may be a figment of the scam artist's imagination. Or Ann Smith may be the lead charlatan's kid sister. Don't be taken in by the testimonial fakery of finaid fraud artists who promise collegiate versions of get-rich-quick schemes.

Their scams pull in large fees that range between $5 and $1,500 for information — often worthless — that you can get for free.

Undeniably, finding money to help you pay for college does cost something, if only postage and paper and your Internet bill. Nevertheless, you shouldn't need financial aid just to apply for financial aid. To help you spot the differences between legitimate services and bottom-feeders, we've compiled this list of ten scams and signs of scams.

Recognize low-life lingo

Knowing finaid frauds' hallmark jargon can spare you a wasted expense. Examine the service's sales pitch for any version of

> ✔ *We just need your credit card or bank account number to hold this award.*
>
> ✔ *Just give all your information; we do all the work.*
>
> ✔ *I can get anyone financial aid.*
>
> ✔ *You can't get this information anywhere else.*
>
> ✔ *Act now; awards are disappearing fast.*
>
> ✔ *$6.6 million in scholarship funds go unused each year.*

The last claim about unused scholarships has a kernel of truth. The problem is that unused scholarships are usually reserved for children and/or employees of a given corporation or some other requirement — like being a left-handed, Irish-Mexican, first son whose major is Russian literature at an Ivy League university — that you can't fulfill.

Rate returns in computer search

As discussed in Chapter 28, a computerized scholarship search can be very helpful or virtually useless depending on several factors.

Almost anyone can get into a handful of national finaid databases for a small annual fee. Some are sold by sales people while others are advertised on the Internet. Even if the scholarship service waves a flashy World Wide Web page in your face and claims to have access to more finaid sources than anyone else, first try the free services available at high schools and colleges.

Another point of caution: Some online databases reside on computers that require long-distance telephone calls. Other computerized scholarship tricksters don't tell you the call isn't free, directing you to 900-number calls that cost $3, $4 a minute or more. While you calmly peruse an incredibly long list of scholarships that coincidentally don't seem to fit your situation, your telephone bill corkscrews sky-high.

Further, many computerized search services, however well-wired, don't update their data often enough to pay back your investment. Not only will you waste your time, but their scholarship resources are so old they have moss hanging off them. Your time and application efforts are squandered.

Pay an application fee? For what?

Some scholarship programs charge an application fee. Avoid these people.

Paying money to get money usually means no money.

Scholarship swindlers pull a disappearing act once they've skimmed enough money, but long before they've accumulated a significant number of complaints with a local Better Business Bureau. Others get your bank account or credit card number, lay low, and make an unauthorized withdrawal when you're not looking.

Say phooey to phony processing fees

Frauds may require a "set-up" fee to process your loan application. Real loan providers charge origination and insurance fees at the time you get their money, not before. They often deduct those charges from your award.

Duck dubious guarantees

Tricky scholarship peddlers often "guarantee" their services, claiming you'll win a scholarship or get your money back. (They don't say what year you'll get it back.) They usually get you to okay some fine print that only promises to *match* you to finaid sources — the rest is up to you.

Some "guarantees" are even more fraudulent. The guarantee promises you $100 to $3,000 or a U.S. Savings Bond providing you can *prove* you were turned down by every scholarship address the search service provides.

No matter how good the database, it is virtually unheard of for a consumer to hear back from each scholarship sponsor to which the consumer wrote for an application. Add the no-reply factor to the probability that many of the addresses are bad to begin with, and you'll understand why a consumer can never prove he or she was turned down by 100 percent of the potential scholarship givers.

When a third party claims it can guarantee someone else's money, this is the very first sign of a scam. The only person or group that can guarantee anything is the person or group that is giving away the money.

Don't ring costly 900 numbers

The prefixes 900 and 976 cost you dollars per minute just for talking — or listening to some scammer's long-winded spiel. Legitimate programs typically have a toll-free 800 or 888 number or a straightforward telephone number beginning with the area code.

Even a few supposedly toll-free 800 or 888 numbers are programmed to switch you over to a fee-charging 900 number after you're connected; the law requires that the caller be notified when this happens, so listen carefully to what is said when you call an 800 or 888 number.

One more comment about 800 or 888 numbers that really are toll-free: Don't assume an 800 number is a sign of a reputable scholarship service. Anyone can arrange for an 800 or 888 line.

Avoid quirky contests

Some scammers publicize contests that exact an entry fee. Others require specific research or information as an entry requirement for a chance to win a scholarship, such as demanding a law essay which is a cheap way to collect legal documentation. Another example: A new magazine asks students to submit articles for its first issue on speculation. The purpose is to avoid paying for freelance work. Adding insult to injury, the magazine charges each entrant $15 for the submission.

Don't pay for free information

Some tricksters get you to pay for access to finaid databases you can get for free in high school counseling offices and college financial aid offices. For example, California college finaid offices connect students with a Pell grant database; some proprietary services, however, try to charge you for this access.

Many schools offer services like The College Board's Fund Finder, which may give you more listings than you'll ever have time to write to.

Upshot: Private financial aid services that claim to link you to private organizations have the same access to the same databases as your school guidance or finaid office.

Spot phony finaid consultants

A real dramatist, this fraud peddler poses like a real expert, charges you a consulting fee, and offers you empty advice. See Chapter 14 for ways to scope out the real experts.

Heed these Red Flags

Any of the following red flags may be the tip-off to a less-than-honest organization. The more signals you get, the more tightly you should hold onto your wallet.

The mail-drop address. Good private financial aid counselors usually list a street address on their letterhead. Some tricksters try to disguise a box number as a suite number. Although using a mailbox address admittedly is a common practice among small businesses, this masquerade could be the tip-off to a fraud.

Official looking name or logo. Take notice of official-looking promotional literature. The organization or implied government agency may not exist. A flyer for "The National Federation for Free Money," complete with a federal-like insignia and seal, could be too good to be true. In fact, we made up the name. This is an old scam but it pops up every few years.

Notification by telephone or e-mail. Beware the telephone call or e-mail message urging you to apply for a given scholarship. There's usually a catch that costs. Real scholarship providers are so swamped with requests that they don't have the time or need to contact potential recipients who have not applied.

A super-easy entry. One scam organization mailed thousands of postcards to senior high school students, promising free money. The scammers also pulled most of the other fake deals mentioned in this chapter.

The scammers' real agenda was to obtain credit card and checking-account numbers from money-hungry students, who bit on the fraud and expected financial aid checks in return for handing over their fiscal information.

What the students actually received — if anything at all — was a hodgepodge listing rife with out-dated, misaddressed, and nonrelevant organizations plus a whopping $175 in credit charges.

Never believe a hoaxer who claims landing financial aid is so easy that simple contact information will be enough to make a total stranger hand you greenbacks. Scholarship sponsors always want specific and personal data, such as hobbies, memberships, fields of study, personal statements, achievements, and honors.

Check it out

When you have doubts about an offering, you can check it out with:

National Fraud Information Center
Address: NFIC, P.O. Box 65868,
Washington, DC 20035
Telephone: 800-876-7060 or 202-835-0159
Fax: 202-835-0767
e-mail: nfic@internetmci.com
Web page: www.fraud.org/

Council of Better Business Bureaus
Address: 4200 Wilson Blvd, Suite 800
Arlingotn, VA 22203
Telephone: 703-276-0100 or 703-525-8277
e-mail: bbb@bbb.org

Federal Trade Commission "Scholar Scam"
Address: P.O Box 99-6
Washington, D.C. 20050
email: consumerline @FTC.gov

Don't think you're too smart to get fooled

Strangely enough, despite all the good-sense that a search service is a con game, hundreds of intelligent — even — brilliant — students each year get taken in. They miss the red glags and obvious scams because they're desperate to enter college or pay off debts.

Angela (not her real name), a Washington, D.C. graduate English student, confessed that when she was a month away from her baccalaureate *(cum laude) with a specialty in critical thinking,* she handed over 50 hard-earned dollars to a complete stranger who promised her substantial graduate grants. She never heard from the stranger again — and she learned a critical lesson in thinking.

Resource Guide

*O*nce upon a time in a decade far, far away, the 1980s, Mike Hayes graduated from Rochelle (Illinois) High School wondering how he could come up with the $28,000 he needed to attend four years at the University of Illinois.

Then Mike had a brainstorm — why not go after 2.8 million pennies from heaven? Why not just ask people around the country to each send him a penny? Mike wrote a syndicated newspaper columnist asking the columnist to publish a nationwide plea for one-cent donations. Readers responded with vigor — some even sent donations up to $100. When the story appeared in *People* magazine, Mike had received more than 77,000 letters containing in excess of $26,000.

The idea probably wouldn't work the second time around, so don't try it. Go after free money scholarships instead!

Scholarships by the Score

As you review the following scholarships, refer to your *Personal Financial Aid Inventory* (see Chapter 10) to make sure that you don't have to pinch pennies because you missed a money tre tree.

The following awards are only a fraction of the nation's 300,000 scholarship pool. But they are substantial and worth going after. They are listed by the following categories.

- ✔ Academic achievement
- ✔ College major or career objective
- ✔ Organizations (whose members are students or parents)
- ✔ Individuals with disabilities
- ✔ Graduate students

✔ Heritage

✔ International students

✔ Military

✔ Minorities

✔ Religious affiliations

✔ Women

ACADEMIC, MERIT, LEADERSHIP

Elks National Foundation

2750 North Lakeview Avenue
Chicago, IL 60612-1889
V: 773-929-2100
F: 773-929-9670
No. Awards: over 2,000
Award Amount: National: two $20,000;
two $12,000; two $8,000; 494 $4,000
State: 1,585 $800 (renewable for all four
years)
Deadline: January 16
Features: High school seniors who are U.S.
citizens and have an interest in furthering
their education. Must have financial need.
Applicant must be in the top 5 percent of
senior class. Based on leadership abilities.

International Brotherhood of Teamsters (See Organizations)

Jostens Foundation Leader Scholarship Program

Citizen's Scholarship Foundation of
America
P.O. Box 297
St. Peter, Minnesota 56082
V: 507-931-8034
No. Awards: 200
Award Amount: $1,000
Funds Available: $200,000
Deadline: Dec. 10
Features: Graduating high school seniors
who demonstrate good leadership
abilities. Also open to students in U.S.
territories and Department of Defense
schools.

National Honor Society

National Association of Secondary School
Principals (NASSP)
Department of Student Activities
1904 Association Drive
Reston, VA 22091
No. Awards: 250
Award Amount: $1,000
Funds Available: Approximately $250,000
Deadline: January 30
Features: High school seniors who are
members of NHS. Must have high class
rank and GPA. Applicant must also send
transcript, writing sample, and recommen-
dations with application. Scholarship
packets are mailed to NHS Adviser in
November. National Selection Committee
convenes in April, and winners are
announced in May.

Principal's Leadership Award (PLA)

National Association of Secondary School
Principals (NASSP)
Department of Student Activities
1904 Association Drive
Reston, VA 22091
No. Awards: 150
Funds Available: $1,000
Deadline: December 12
Features: One student from the senior
class of each school is nominated by the
principal. All school winners receive a
certificate of merit and are considered
semifinalists. At the national level, school
winners compete on the basis of their
application. Scholarship packets are
mailed to principal in October. National
Selection Committee convenes in February
and winners are announced by NASSP in
April in conjunction with National Student
Leadership Week.

Meliora Grant (See Local)

Long and Foster Scholarship Program

Long and Foster Real Estate, Inc.
11351 Random Hills Road
Fairfax, VA 22030
V: 703 359-1500
No. Awards: 50
Award Amount: $1,000
Funds Available: $50,000
Deadline: March 1
Features: Applicants must be high school seniors and U.S. citizens who are preparing to attend four-year colleges or universities. Any area of academic study is acceptable. Students should be academically strong and have records of participating in school activities as well as having held positions of leadership and responsibility. All applicants must document their demonstrated financial need. Students should develop listings of participation in community service groups and work experiences. Limited to students living in Virginia, Maryland, and Washington, D.C.

The Toyota Community Scholars Program

Toyota Motor Sales, USA Inc.
19011 South Western Avenue
P.O. Box 2991
Torrance, CA 90509-2991
V: 310-618-4459 or 310-618-6799
F: 310-618-7816
No. Awards: 100
Award Amount: $10,000-$20,000, renewable
Deadline: December 16
Features: High school applicants should have a consistent record of academic excellence, be active in school programs, and be recognized as a leader by his/her peers and instructors. Applicants must be actively involved in a service program that addresses a school or community need. This is a merit scholarship and demonstrated financial need is not a prerequisite. Notification is made in April.

Urban League Scholar

University of Rochester, Director of Admissions
Rochester, NY 14627
V: 716-275-3221
F: 716-461-4595
W: http://www.rochester.edu
E: jmejia@admissions.rochester.edu

No. Award: varies
Award Amount: $6,000 or greater, depending on demonstrated need
Features: This scholarship is offered through the local Urban League Community offices. Applicants must be nominated by the local Urban League members. The award can be used only at the University of Rochester.

U.S. Senate Youth Program

The William Randolph Hearst Foundation
90 New Montgomery St., Suite 1212
San Francisco, CA 94105-4504
V: 415-543-0400
T: 800-841-7048
No. Awards: 2 or more per state for a total of 104
Award Amount: $2,000
Funds Available: varies
Deadline: Sept./Oct., but actual date varies by state
Features: High school junior or senior elected to a student office. Must attend public or private school in state where parent or guardian legally resides. Permanent residents of the United States only. Also open to U.S. students attending Department of Defense schools overseas. This scholarship is based on leadership abilities.

AGRICULTURE

California Farm Bureau Federation (See Local)

Cargill Community Scholarship

Cargill, Inc.
P.O. Box 9300
Minneapolis, MN 55440
V: 612-742-6201
F: 612-742-7224
No. Awards: 150
Award Amount: $1,000
Funds Available: $150,000
Deadline: Feb. 15, postmarked
Features: High school seniors who are U.S. citizens and are enrolling for two to four years in vocational schools, universities, and colleges. Students must live within communities where Cargill has a facility. Recipients of this scholarship get $200 for their school library.

Cargill Scholarship for Rural America

Cargill, Inc.
P.O. Box 9300
Minneapolis, MN 55440
V: 612-742-6201
F: 612-742-7224
No. Awards: 250
Award Amount: $1,000
Funds Available: 250,000
Deadline: Feb. 15, postmarked
Features: High school seniors who are U.S. citizens from farm families. Applicant must be enrolling in two- or four-year colleges or vocational schools.

Moorman Scholarships in Agriculture

Moorman Manufacturing Company (MMC)
Contact the Dean's office at your university or College of Agriculture
No. Awards: 93
Award Amount: $1,000, renewable
Funds Available: varies
Deadline: varies with each college
Features: Applicant must be interested in pursuing careers in agriculture.

National Council of State Garden Clubs Scholarships

National Council of State Garden Clubs, Inc.
4401 Magnolia Avenue
St. Louis, MO 63110-3492
V: 314-776-7574
F: 314-776-5108
No. Awards: 32
Award Amount: $3,500
Funds Available: over $112,000
Deadline: March 1
Features: Applicants must be junior or senior undergraduates and graduate students majoring in horticulture, floriculture, forestry, landscape design, botany, biology, plant pathology, agronomy, environmental concerns, city planning, land management, and/or allied subjects. Applicants must apply through state where they are permanent residents. Students must be nominated by home state's Garden Club and enrolled at a four-year institution, maintaining a minimum 3.0 GPA.

ANIMALS/WILDLIFE

Delta Waterfowl and Wetlands Research Station Summer Field Assistantships

Delta Waterfowl Foundation
RR #1, Box 1
Portage la Prairie
Manitoba, R1N 3A1 Canada
V: 204-239-1900
F: 204-239-5950
E: dw4ducks@portage.net
No. Grants: 25
Award Amount: Average award is $1,000
Funds Available: $80,000
Deadline: Oct. 25 for graduate students and Jan. 30 for undergraduate students
Features: Must attend accredited university in North America or field stations in North Dakota, U.S.A., and or Manitoba, Canada, study conservation and renewable natural
resources or ecology with an emphasis on waterfowl and wetlands ecology. U.S. nationals abroad and foreign national residents may apply. Supports undergraduate student to work as field assistant with graduate students.

Lindbergh Grants Program

Charles A. and Anne Morrow Lindbergh Foundation
708 South 3rd Street, St. 110
Minneapolis, MN 55415-1141
V: 612-338-1703
F: 612-338-6826
W: http://www.mtn.org/lindfdtn
No. Awards: 10
Award Amount: up to $10,580
Deadline: June 3

Features: Applicants must be interested in research in area addressing balance between technological advancement and preservation of human/natural environment. Open to all nationalities. This is not a scholarship for school. Rather, it is a grant given for research. Please send a self-addressed, stamped envelope.

Rockefeller State Wildlife Scholarship (See Local)

APPLIED SCIENCES/ AUTOMOTIVE

Automotive Educational Fund

Automotive Hall of Fame, Inc.
PO Box 1727
Midland, MI 48641-1727
V: 517-631-5760
F: 517-631-0524
No. Awards: varies
Award Amount: $250-$2,000
Deadline: June 30
Features: Applicants must be in under-graduate degree programs and sincerely interested in pursuing automotive careers. Scholarships are awarded to candidates who are at least sophomores in college, although they may apply in their freshman year. Students must be enrolled full-time (minimum of 12 credit hours per term) for the full year. Financial need is considered but is not necessary. Students may apply for a scholarship at any time after January 1. Only one graduate scholarship is available at the University of Michigan. Most of the available scholarships are designated for undergraduate upper-classmen.

DeVry Bachelor's Degree Scholarships

Contact the director of Admissions at the nearest DeVry Institute
No. Awards: 36
Award Amount: up to $14,510, renewable
Deadline: continuous

Features: Applicants must be students who have completed associate's degree to begin study at DeVry. Students must be enrolled in technical institutions and maintain a minimum GPA of 3.3. For study in electronic engineering technology, technology management, computer information, business, telecommunications, or accounting. Open to non-U.S. citizens.

DeVry Scholarships

Contact high school guidance counselor or the director of Admissions at the DeVry Institute you plan to attend.

No. Awards: 120
Award Amount: $8,263-$29,685, renewable
Deadline: March 18
Features: Applicant must be a high school graduate and begin studies at a U.S. DeVry Institute the same year. Student must be a U.S. citizen or permanent resident. Minimum SAT scores is 530 Math and 270 Verbal. Minimum ACT score is 22.

Fred Duesenberg Memorial Scholarship (Car Restoration)

McPherson College
McPherson, KS 64460
V: 316-241-0731
No. Awards: varies
Award Amount: varies
Features: Contact the college department of restoration technology for dates and criteria for this new scholarship program created by TV personality Jay Leno. McPherson College is the only four-year college in the U.S. that offers an associate degree program in car restoration technology.

ARTS

Arts Recognition and Talent Search (ARTS)

National Foundation for Advancement in the Arts
800 Brickell Avenue, Suite 500
Miami, FL 33137
V: 305-377-1140
T: 800-970-ARTS
F: 305-377-1149
W: www.nfaa.org
E: nfaa@nfaa.org
No. Awards: varies
Award Amount: varies
Funds Available: scholarships totaling approximately $3 million; cash awards totaling approximately $300,000 (1st Place: $3,000; 2nd Place: $1,500; 3rd Place: $1,000)
Deadline: June 1, early; October 1, regular deadline
Features: High school seniors or 17- or 18-year-olds as of December 1 of the year of application. U.S. citizens or permanent residents only (except for ARTS Jazz applicants, who are accepted internationally.) Open to U.S. citizens studying

abroad. Based on dance, music, music/jazz, theater, visual arts, writing, photography, and voice. Applicants who are in the advanced level will attend a final judging session in Miami, Florida, at all expenses paid.m

Association/International Thespian Society

Director of Festival and Convention
International Thespian Society
3368 Central Parkway
Cincinnati, OH 45225-2392
V: 513-559-1996
No. Awards: 10
Award Amount: $1,000
Funds Available: $15,000
Features: Scholarships are sponsored by the Educational Theatre Association. The scholarship is based on the applicants' thespian ability including acting, interviewing with the judges, and activity with a thespian club while in high school. A GPA of 2.7 is required for entry, but academic record is not part of the judging.

The Elizabeth Greenshields Grants

The Elizabeth Greenshields Foundation
1814 Sherbrooke Street West, Suite 1
Montreal, Quebec H3H 1E4 Canada
V: 514-937-9225
No. Awards: 40-50
Award Amount: $10,000 Canadian funds
Funds Available: Approximately $500,000
Deadline: none

Features: The purpose of the Foundation is to aid talented artists in the early stages of their careers. Awards are limited to candidates working in the following: painting, drawing, printmaking and/or sculpting — abstract or non-representational art is precluded by the terms of the Foundation's charter. Applicants must have already started or completed training in an established school of art and/or demonstrate, through past work and future plans, a commitment to making art a lifetime career. Open to nationals of any country, without regard to age, sex, color, religion, or ethnicity. The foundation is not a school and does not conduct any classes. Applicants

may write or call. This scholarship is worldwide and there is no age limit.

Longy Scholarship

Longy School of Music
One Follen Street
Cambridge, MA 02138
V: 617-876-0956 ext. 144
F: 617-876-9326
E: music@longy.edu
W: www.longy.edu
No. Awards: approximately 75, (which is about 80% of the students who apply)
Award Amount: $1,000-full tuition
Funds Available: $350,000
Deadline: April 15

Features: Applicant must be a full-time degree or diploma student (undergraduate or graduate) at the Longy School of Music aiming to study composition, orchestral instruments, piano, organ, early music. Based on financial need, audition, performance experience, and academic background. Nationality and residency unrestricted.

National Scholarship Trust Fund of the Graphic Arts

Graphic Arts Technical Foundation
200 Deer Run Drive
Sewickley, PA 15143
V: 412-741-6860
F: 412-741-2311
No. Grants: 300
Award Amount: $500-$1,500, renewable
Deadline: March 1 for high school students, April 1 for undergraduates
Features: Full-time students who are U.S. citizens and are interested in graphic arts careers; minimum GPA 3.0.

ATHLETICS/GOLF

FINA/Dallas Morning News All-Texas Scholar-Athlete Team Scholarship

FINA Oil and Chemical Company
P.O. Box 2159
Dallas, TX 75221
V: 214-750-2584
F: 214-890-1876
No. Awards: 12-28
Award Amount: $500-$4,000

Funds Available: $48,000
Deadline: Dec. 15
Features: The purpose of this scholarship is to honor Texas high school students who excel in athletics, academic achievement, and leadership qualities, and who participate in other school and community activities. Candidates should be seniors in Texas high schools who have lettered in varsity sports. Anyone may nominate an eligible senior. To become finalists, applicants must have been varsity letter winners in a UIL approved sport, have a high school average of at least 90 percent, and be in the top 10 percent of the graduating class. This scholarship is based upon academic achievements and honors, community service, and leadership. Forty finalists are chosen. Contact high school coaches, principals, or counselors, or call or write for application forms.

Francies Ouimet Scholarship Fund

190 Park Road
Weston, MA 02193
V: 617-891-6400
No. Awards: varies
Award Amount: $500-$5,000
Funds Available: varies
Deadline:
Features: This four-year renewable scholarship is for students who work three years in Massachusetts as caddies, or in pro shops or golf course operations. This scholarship is not for persons who are golfers. Applicants who do not meet the basic criteria for eligibility as described will not be given a reply.

Gloria Fecht Memorial Scholarship Fund (See Women)

GCSAA Legacy Award

Golf Course Superintendents Association of America
1421 Research Drive
Lawrence, KS 66046-3859
V: 913-832-4445
No. Awards: 10
Award Amount: $1,500
Funds Available: varies
Deadline: April 15
Features: Applicants must be children or grandchildren of GCSAA members who have been active for five or more consecutive years. Students must be studying a field unrelated to golf course management. Applicants must be enrolled full-time at an accredited institution of higher learning, or in the case of high school seniors, must have been accepted at such an institution for the next academic year.

GCSAA Scholars Program

Golf Course Superintendents Association of America
1421 Research Drive
Lawrence, KS 66046-3859
V: 913-832-4445
No. Awards: varies
Award Amount: $1,500-$3,500
Funds Available: varies
Deadline: June 1
Features: Applicants must be outstanding undergraduate students who are planning careers as golf course superintendents. Applicants must be enrolled in a recognized undergraduate program in a major field related to golf/turf management. Undergraduate applicants must have successfully completed at least 24 credit hours or the equivalent of one year of full-time study in an appropriate major.

GCSAA Watson Fellowships

Golf Course Superintendents Association of America
1421 Research Drive
Lawrence, KS 66046-3859
V: 913-832-4445
No. Awards: varies
Award Amount: $5,000
Funds Available: varies
Deadline: Oct. 1
Features: Applicants must be aiming towards master's and doctoral degrees in fields related to golf course management. The goal of this program is to identify tomorrow's leading teachers and researchers.

The Scotts Company Scholars Program

Golf Course Superintendents Association of America
1421 Research Drive
Lawrence, KS 66046-3859
V: 913-832-4445
No. Awards: varies
Award Amount: $2,500
Funds Available: varies
Deadline: March 8
Features: Students are selected for paid

summer internships and an opportunity to compete for a limited number of financial aid awards. Applicants must be pursuing careers in the green industry and be graduating high school seniors, or collegiate freshmen, sophomores, or juniors who have been accepted at an accredited university, college, or junior college for the next academic year. Candidates from culturally diverse backgrounds receive initial consideration in judging and are strongly encouraged to apply.

BUSINESS

Appraisal Institute Education Trust Scholarship

Appraisal Institute Education Trust
875 North Michigan Avenue, Suite 2400
Chicago, IL 60611-1980
V: 312-335-4100
F: 312-335-4200
W: www.realworks.com/ai
No. Awards: 30
Award Amount: $2,000-$3,000
Deadline: March 15
Features: Applicants must be graduate or undergraduate students majoring in real estate appraisals, land economics, real estate, or allied fields. Minimum 3.5 GPA required. Applicant must be enrolled at a two-year or four-year institution. U.S. citizens only. Applicants may reapply.

Arthur H. Carter Scholarship Fund

c/o Cummings and Lockwood
P.O. Box 120
Stamford, CT 06904
V: 203-327-1700 or 203-351-4296
No. Awards: varies
Award Amount: varies
Funds Available: $100,000
Deadline: April 1
Features: Students who have completed two years of accounting to pursue further undergraduate and graduate studies in accounting.

Avon Products Foundation Scholarship Program for Women in Business (See Women)

John L. Carey Scholarship

American Institute of Certified Public Accountants

1211 Avenue of the Americas
New York, NY 10036
V: 212-596-6221
F: 212-596-6292
W: http://www.aicpa.rg
E: lromeo@aicpa.org
No. Awards: 5
Award Amount: $5,000
Funds Available: $25,000
Deadline: April 1
Features: Liberal arts seniors and undergraduates and accepted, or in process of applying, to graduate program in accounting that will allow them to take CPA examination at an institution where the business administration program is accredited by the American Assembly of Collegiate Schools of Business. Renewable for one year, provided satisfactory scholastic progress is maintained.

Duracell Scholarship and Internship Program (See Minorities)

Executive Women International Scholarship Program

Executive Women International
515 South 700 East, Suite 2E
Salt Lake City, UT 84102
V: 801-355-2800
F: 801-355-2852
No. Awards: 130
Award Amount: up to $10,000
Deadline: March 1
Features: Applicants must reside within the boundaries of one of the 34 participating chapters, enter that local contest, and be available for interview. Applicants must be high school juniors enrolling at a four-year institution. Students must be planning careers in any business or professional field of study that requires a four-year degree. Include self-addressed, stamped envelope for application forms.

Harry A. Applegate DECA Scholarship Award

Distributive Education Clubs of America (DECA)
1908 Association Drive
Reston, VA 22091
V: 703-860-4013
F: 703-860-4013
No. Awards: 4
Award Amount: $5,000
Deadline: 2nd Monday of March of each year

Features: Active DECA member pursuing full-time, two- or four-year study in marketing, merchandising, or management in an accredited institution offering those programs of study. This scholarship is based on merit.

IMA/Stuart Cameron and Margaret McLeod Scholarship

Institute of Management Accountants
10 Paragon Drive
Montbale, NJ 07645-1760
V: 210-573-0550
T: 800-638-4427
F: 201-573-9000
No. Awards: 18
Award Amount: $2,000
Features: Applicants must have junior, senior, or master's degree enrollment status majoring in financial management, management, or accounting.

Minority Scholarship Program (See Minorities)

National Society of Public Accountants Scholarship Foundation

1010 North Fairfax Street
Alexandria, VA 22314
No. Awards: 26
Award Amount: $500-$1,000, renewable
Deadline: March 10
Features: Applicant must enroll in college as an accounting major. U.S. or Canadian citizens must be enrolled in a U.S. school. Maintaining a B average is prerequisite for scholarship renewal.

State Farm Companies Foundation Exceptional Student Fellowship

State Farm Companies Foundation
One State Farm Plaza, SC-3
Bloomington, IL 61710-0001
V: 309-766-2311
No. Awards: 50
Award Amount: $3,000
Deadline: Feb. 15
Features: At time of application, student must be enrolled full-time in college with junior or senior status. Applicants must be majoring in a business-related discipline or computer science with a GPA of 3.60. Applicants must be U.S. citizens who are nominated by the head or dean of the department or school. Application requests should be made between November 1 and February 1.

COMMUNICATIONS

Academy Foundation of the Academy of Motion Picture Arts and Sciences

Academy of Motion Picture Arts and Sciences Student Academy Awards
8949 Wilshire Boulevard
Beverly Hills, CA 90211-1972
No. Awards: up to 12
Award Amount: $1,000 - $2,000 non-renewable
Deadline: April 1
Features: Applicants must be majoring in communications or film-making. Eligible applicants must have made a dramatic/documentary/or animated film of up to 60 minutes within the structured curriculum of the accredited college or university.

The American Legion National High School Oratorical Contest

National Americanism Commission
P.O. Box 1055
Indianapolis, IN 46206
V: 317 630-1200
F: 317-630-1223
No. Awards: 63
Award Amounts: (51) $1,000. State, county, and local scholarships, (one) $18,000; (one) $16,000; (one) $14,000; (one) $12,000; (eight) $3,000;
Funds Available: $138,000
Deadline: Nov. 30
Features: Students in 9th-12th grades who are less than 20 years of age (as of the national contest date); U.S. citizens only. Also open to U.S. students studying abroad (in some locations). Students must demonstrate great public speaking abilities and prepare speeches. Students should contact the local American Legion post or the above address.

Asian-American Journalists Association Scholarship (Non-Members)

Scholarship Committee
Asian-American Journalists Association
1765 Sutter Street
San Francisco, CA 94115

V: 415-346-2051
F: 415-346-6343
W: www.aaja.org
No. Awards: approximately 15
Award Amount: up to $2,000
Deadline: April 15
Features: Applicant must be high school senior, undergraduate student, or graduate student pursuing a news media career. Based on scholarship, goals, journalistic ability, financial need, and commitment to Asian-American community. A work sample may be required. Applicants must be enrolled at a two-year or four-year institution and must be pursuing photography, print, broadcast, or news media. Please send a self-addressed, stamped envelope for application forms.

Broadcast Education Association

1771 N. Street NW
Washington, DC 20036-2891
V: 202-429-5354
W: www.usu.edu/~bea or fweaver@nab.org
No. Awards: 14
Award Amount: $1,250 to $3,000, not renewable
Deadline: January 16
Features: Applicants must be full-time college students ready for the junior, senior, or graduate level and enrolled at accredited colleges or universities where at least one department is a BEA institutional member. Students must show potential to be outstanding media professionals and make superior academic progress. Awards must be used exclusively for college costs. Winners are announced each spring.

Community College Scholarship (See Local)

Cox Enterprises Scholarship

National Association of Hispanic Journalists
1193 National Press Building
Washington, DC 20045
V: 202-662-7178
F: 202-662-7144
No. Awards: 6
Award Amount: $1,000
Funds Available: $6,000
Deadline: Feb. 28
Features: Full-time student with academic excellence and a demonstrated interest in journalism career. Open to high school seniors, undergraduates, and graduate level students pursuing careers in journalism.

Editing Intern Program

Dow Jones Newspaper Fund
P.O. Box 300
Princeton, NJ 08543
V: 609-452-2820
W: www.dowjones.com/newsfund
E: newsfund@wsj.dowjones.com
No. Awards: up to 100
Award Amount: Summer wages plus $1,000
Funds Available: varies
Deadline: Nov. 15
Features: U.S. citizen who is or will be full-time college junior, senior or graduate student to work as copy editors at daily newspapers, on-line newspapers, and financial news services. Applications are available Aug. 15 through Nov. 1.

Editing Programs

Dow Jones Newspaper Fund
P.O. Box 300
Princeton, NJ 08543
V: 609-452-2820 or 800-DOW-FUND
F: 609-520-5804
W: www.dowjones.com/newsfund
E: newsfund@wsj.dowjones.com
No. Awards: up to 100
Award Amount: paid internship plus $1,000 scholarship to students returning to full-time college studies.
Deadline: Nov. 15
Features: Must be college sophomores or juniors in writing field. Applicants must have interests in newspaper editing, online editing, real-time financial information, and/or business reporting. Business reporting is open only to minority sophomores and juniors. All other internships are open to all students. U.S. citizenship is required. Application forms are available only September 1 to November 1.

Harold E. Ennes Scholarship Fund

Society of Broadcast Engineers, Inc.
8445 Keystone Crossing, Suite 140
Indianapolis, IN 46240
V: 317-253-1640
F: 317-253-0418
W: www.sbe.org (click on ennes button)
E: lgodby@sbe.org
No. Awards: up to 2

Award Amount: up to $1,000
Funds Available: varies
Deadline: July 1
Features: Applicants must have a career interest in the technical aspects of broadcasting and must be recommended by two members of the SBE. Preference will be given to members of SBE. Send a self-addressed, stamped envelope for application forms.

Harold E. Fellows Scholarship

Broadcast Education Association
1771 N Street, NW
Washington, DC 20036
V: 202-429-5354
No. Awards: 8
Award Amount: $1,250
Deadline: Dec. 16
Features: Full-time student able to show evidence of superior academic performance with the potential to be an outstanding media professional.

Institute for Humane Studies

Humane Studies Fellowships
Institute for Humane Studies
4084 University Dr. Suite 101
Fairfax, VA 22030-6812
V: 703-934-6920
F: 703-352-7535
W: http://www.osf1.gmu.edu/ihs/
E: ihs@gmu.edu
No. of Awards: approximately 60
Award Amount: up to $18,500
Deadline: December 31

Features: Applicants may be enrolled in undergraduate or graduate studies majoring in communication, economics, history, humanities, literature, English, writing, political science, or social sciences. Only applicants enrolled at a four-year institution are eligible. U.S. citizenship is not required.

National Scholarship Trust Fund Program

National Scholarship Trust Fund of Graphic Arts
200 Deer Run Road
Sewickley, PA 15143
V: 412-741-6860
F: 412-741-2300
W: http://www.gatf.lm.com
E: info@gatf.lm.com
No. Awards: 300

Award Amount: $500-$1,000 renewable
Deadline: March 1 for high school students; April 1 for undergraduate students
Features: Applicants must be High school seniors or first, second or third-year college students, enrolled full-time in a two- or four-year college and aiming for a career in graphic communications. U.S. citizenship plus 3.0 GPA required.

Optimist International Oratorical Contest, (The)

Contest Project Coordinator
Optimist International
4494 Lindell Boulevard
St. Louis, MO 63108
V: 314-371-6000 x224
F: 314-371-6006
No. Awards: 108
Award Amount: (54) $1,500 (male students) and (54) $1,500 (female students)
Funds Available: $162,000
Features: This scholarship is based on the applicant's ability to prepare and present a speech within a timed period. Contestants must speak about the official oratorical contest subject which is **"My Vision of Tomorrow's World"** for 1998-1999. The contest year is October 1 to the next September 30.

Harry S. Truman Scholarships

Harry S. Truman Scholarship Foundation
712 Jackson Place, NW
Washington, DC 20006
V: 202-395-4831
W: http://www.truman.gov
No. Awards: 75 to 85
Award Amount: $30,000 per year for graduate studies
Deadline: Jan. 24
Features: Awarded to college juniors who wish to pursue a career in government or public service. Applicant must attend a four-year institution and be a U.S. citizen. The student must be nominated by a college or university faculty or administrative staff person.

Voice of Democracy Program

VFW National Headquarters
406 West 34th Street
Kansas City, Missouri 64111
V: 816-756-3390
F: 816-968-1157
W: www.vfw.org

No. Awards: 55
Award Amount: (one) $20,000; (one)
$15,000; (one) $10,000; (one) $6,000; (two)
$5,000; (one) $4,000; (one) $3,000; (one)
$2,000; (seven) $1,500; (thirty-nine)$1,000
Funds Available: up to $119,500
Deadline: Nov. 1
Features: High school students in grades
10-12 who are U.S. citizens. Applicant must
prepare a short speech. Scholarship is
based on public speaking abilities. The
theme is different each year. Also open to
American students studying abroad.

ENGINEERING

AT&T ESP Scholarships (See Minorities)

Business & Professional Women's Foundation (See Women)

Duracell Scholarship and Internship Program (See Minorities)

Electronic Industries Foundation Scholarship Program (See Minorities)

General Emmett Paige Scholarship (See Organizations)

General John A. Wickham Scholarship (See Organizations)

Nancy Lorraine Jensen Memorial Scholarship Fund (See Organizations)

National Society of Professional Engineers—Regional Scholarships

NSPE Education Foundation
1420 King Street
Alexandria, VA 22314-2794
V: 703-684-2800 or 703) 684-2830
F: 703-836-4875
W: www.nspe.org
No. Awards: varies
Award Amount: $1,000-$2,000
Deadline: Dec. 1
Features: High school seniors who are U.S.
citizens and are interested in studying
engineering. This scholarship program is
handled by each state organization.
Student applicants must contact the state
office for specific information.

NSA Undergraduate Training Program

National Security Agency
9800 Savage Road, Suite 6840
Attn: 5232-UTP
Ft. Meade, MD 20755-6840

V: 410-859-4590
T: 800-962-9398
No. Awards: varies between 5-25
Award Amount: Pays tuition and fees for
four years; provides summer work, year-
round salary and a job upon graduation.
Deadline: Nov. 30 of student's high school
senior year
Features: Must be high school senior
entering first year of college, U.S. citizen;
minimum SAT 1,200, minimum ACT 27.
Studying electrical engineering, computer
engineering, computer science, mathematics, Slavic languages, Asian languages, or
Middle Eastern languages. Must demonstrate leadership. Minorities are encouraged to apply. Minimum GPA 3.0. Call for
applications.

The SPE Foundation Scholarship Fund

The SPE Foundation
14 Fairfield Drive
Brookfield, CT 06804
V: 203-740-5434
F: 203-775-8490
No. Awards: Varies
Award Amount: Up to $4,000
Deadline: Dec. 15
Features: Full-time undergraduate
students at two- or four-year college or
technical schools and have demonstrated
interest in plastics industry. Must be
majoring in or taking courses beneficial to
career in plastics industry which would
include but not be limited to plastics
engineering, polymer science, chemistry,
physics, chemical engineering, mechanical
engineering, industrial engineering, and
business administration.

Undergraduate Scholarship Program (See Minorities)

FOOD SERVICE

IFT Freshman Scholarship

Institute of Food Technologists
221 North LaSalle Street, Suite 300
Chicago, IL 60601
V: 312-782-8424
F: 312-782-8348
E: pgpagliuco@ift.org
No. Awards: 16
Award Amount: approximately $1,000
Funds Available: $16,000
Deadline: March 1

Features: Based on academic merit. Must be high school senior or graduate entering college for the first time in a program in food science/technology that meets IFT undergraduate curriculum minimum standards. Nationality unrestricted. Notification is made in April. Applicant must be enrolled in an IFT approved food science program.

IFT Graduate Scholarship

Institute of Food Technologists
221 North LaSalle Street, Suite 300
Chicago, IL 60601
V: 312-782-8424
F: 312-782-8348
E: pgpagliuco@ift.org
No. Awards: 39
Award Amount: $1,000-$5,000
Funds Available: $96,000
Deadline: Feb./March

Features: Applicant must be graduate student in food science related research. Based on academic merit. Nationality unrestricted.

IFT Junior/Senior Scholarship

Institute of Food Technologists
221 North LaSalle Street, Suite 300
Chicago, IL 60601
V: 312-782-8424
F: 312-782-8348
E: pgpagliuco@ift.org
No. Awards: 65
Award Amount: $1,000-$2,000
Funds Available: $72,000
Deadline: Feb. 15
Features: Applicant must be junior or senior in college studying food science/technology that meets IFT undergraduate curriculum minimum standards. Based on academic merit. Nationality unrestricted. Notification April 15. Applicant must be enrolled in an IFT approved food science program.

IFT Sophomore Scholarship

Institute of Food Technologists
221 North LaSalle Street, Suite 300
Chicago, IL 60601
V: 312-782-8424
F: 312-782-8348
E: pgpagliuco@ift.org
No. Awards: varies

Award Amount: approximately $1,000
Funds Available: varies
Deadline: March 1
Features: Applicants must be sophomore in college studying food science/technology that meets IFT undergraduate curriculum minimum standards. Based on academic merit. Nationality unrestricted. Notification is made in April. Applicant must be enrolled in a IFT approved food science program.

ProManagement Scholarship

Educational Foundation of National Restaurant Association
250 South Wacker Drive, Suite 1400
Chicago, IL 60606
V: 312-715-1010
No. Awards: Approximately 40-50 (Up to 5 recipients per school)
Award Amount: $850
Deadline: Nov. 1 and May 1
Features: Applicant must be enrolled in a ProManagement Partner School or in home-study ProManagement course and have successfully completed at least two ProManagement. courses. Applications available at school in September and February.

Undergraduate Scholarship

National Restaurant Association Education Foundation
250 South Wacker Drive, Suite 1400
Chicago, IL 60606
V: 312-715-1010
No. Awards: Not specified
Award Amount: Average award $1,000
Deadline: March 1

Features: Applicant must study food service/hospitality/culinary arts program. Undergraduate full-time student working toward either an associate's or bachelor's degree. Nationality and residency unrestricted. Must have taken four management development courses and demonstrated commitment to the industry. Essay on career goals in the industry required. Announcement of award recipients are made in July.

United Food & Commercial Workers International Union Scholarship

United Food & Commercial Workers
International Union
1775 K Street, NW
Washington, DC 20006
V: 202-223-3111
No. Awards: 7
Award Amount: $1,000 renewable for four years
Funds Available: $7,000 for four years (totaling $28,000)
Deadline: March 15, postmarked
Features: Must be high school graduate, U.S. citizen, under age 20, and member or child of member of UFCW in good standing for one year. Minimum GPA: 3.5 on a 4.0 scale. Deadline to request applications is Dec. 31.

GRADES/CLASS RANK

Bard College

Annandale-on-Hudson, NY 12504
V: 914-758-6822
No. Awards: varies
Award Amount: varies
Deadline: Open
Features: Bard college will give first year students who rank in the top ten percent of their high school class a discount on tuition. These students will be charged only as much tuition as they would have paid had they gone to their state-supported school. Each student must maintain a "B" average in college.

Duluth Superior Area Community Foundation (See Local)

National Honor Society Scholarship Awards Program

National Association of Secondary School Principals
National Honor Society
Office of Student Activities
1904 Association Drive
Reston, VA 22091
V: 703-860-0200
No. Awards: 250
Award Amount: $1,000
Funds Available: $250,000

Features: Students must meet national requirements to qualify as a member of their local high school National Honor Society. From membership in National Honors Society, each high school may nominate two chapter members who have demonstrated that they have outstanding leadership, scholarship, character, and a history of providing service.

North Dakota Merit Scholarship Program (See Local)

State of Iowa Merit Scholarship Program (See Local)

HEALTH

AACN Educational Advancement Scholarships for Undergraduates

American Association of Critical-Care Nurses
101 Columbia
Aliso Veijo, CA 92656-1491
V: 714-362-2000
F: 714-362-2020
E: educ@iqnow.com
W: pveml14f@vta.net
No. Awards: varies
Award Amount: $1,500
Funds Available: varies
Deadline: May 15

Features: Applicants must be current AACN members, licensed as registered nurses, enrolled in NLN-accredited baccalaureate degree program in nursing with junior status, have a cumulative GPA of 3.0, and currently work in a critical-care unit or have worked in a critical-care unit for at least one year in the last three years. Previous recipients are eligible to reapply, but may receive no more than a total of $3,000. Members of the Board of Directors, Education Committee, and AACN staff are ineligible. Different awards are available for graduate and BSN students.

AAPS-GLAXO-AFPE Gateway Scholarship Program

American Foundation for Pharmaceutical Education

One Church Street, Suite 202
Rockville, MD 20850
V: 301-738-2160
F: 301-738-2161
No. Awards: 4
Award Amount: $4,250
Funds Available: $17,000
Deadline: Jan. 28
Features: Undergraduate in last three
years of a B.S. or Pharm. D. program in
accredited college of pharmacy or a
baccalaureate degree program in a related
scientific field of study with at least one
full academic year remaining.

AAPS-GLAXO-AFPE Gateway Scholarship Program

GLAXO-WELCOME-AFPE First Year
Graduate Scholarship
One Church Street, Suite 202
Rockville, MD 20850
V: 301-738-2160
F: 301-738-2161
No. Awards: up to 8 first year graduates
Award Amount: $5,000
Deadline: varies
Features: Final year of pharmacy college
degree program or recent pharmacy
college graduate and continuing pursuit of
graduate or professional degree (not
Pharm. D) in pharmaceutical sciences
(Ph.D.) but also business administration,
law, public health, engineering, and related
areas. Applicants must be U.S. citizens or
have permanent resident status.

AMBUCS Scholarships

P.O. Box 5127
High Point, NC 27262
V: 910-869-2166
F: 910-887-8451
W: www.ambucs.com
E: AMBUCS@hte.infi.net
No. Grants: Over 400
Award Amount: $500-$2,500, renewable
Funds Available: varies
Deadline: April 15
Features: Applicants must be enrolled in
accredited programs in physical therapy,
music therapy, occupational therapy,
speech-hearing, therapeutic recreation.
For upperclassmen or graduate students in
good scholastic standing (at least 3.0 GPA)
who plan to enter clinical therapy in the
U.S.; U.S. citizens only; financial need

required. Send a self-addressed stamped
envelope for application forms. Applications will be sent after December.

American Business Club Living Endowment Fund

P.O. Box 5127
High Point, NC 27262
V: 910-869-2167
No. Awards: varies
Award Amount: $500-$6,000
Funds Available: $250,000
Deadline: April 15
Features: Applicants must be college
juniors, seniors, or graduates in physical
therapy, occupational therapy, music
therapy, speech and hearing, or recreational therapy. Students must be U.S.
citizens with a GPA of at least 3.0. Awards
are based on financial need, commitment
to local community, demonstrated
academic accomplishment, compassion
integrity, and career objectives. Applications are mailed to students in December
upon request with a self-addressed
stamped envelope. Award winners are
announced in June.

Dental Assisting Scholarship Program (See Minorities)

Dental Hygiene Scholarship Program (See Minorities)

Dental Laboratory Technology Scholarship (See Minorities)

Dental Student Scholarship Program

ADA Endowment and Assistance Fund, Inc.
211 East Chicago Avenue 17th Floor
Chicago, IL 60611
V: 312-440-2567
No. Awards: Up to 25
Award Amount: $2,500
Deadline: June 15
Features: Entering second year and
attending dental school accredited by
Commission on Dental Accreditation. A
cumulative GPA of 3.0 in required. Must
show minimum financial need of $2,500.
Notification of scholarship awards is made
in the fall.

Albert W. Dent Student Scholarship (See Minorities)

Gina Finzi Memorial Student Summer Fellowships for Research

Research Grants Program
Lupus Foundation of America, Inc.
1300 Piccard Drive, Suite 200
Rockville, MD 20850
V: 301-670-9292
F: 301-670-9486
No. Awards: 10
Award Amount: $2,000
Funds Available: $20,000
Deadline: Feb. 1
Features: The purpose of these awards is to foster an interest in lupus erythematosus through the conduct of basic, clinical, or psychosocial research under the supervision of any established investigator. Undergraduate, graduate, and medical students are eligible to apply. However, preference is given to students with a college degree. All applicants will be reviewed by the LFA Medical Council. Each research fellowship will be competitively reviewed NIH-style and ranked by a member of the Peer Review Committee. Notification of the award is expected in April.

Foundation of National Student Nurses Association (See Minorities)

Foster G. McGaw Student Scholarship

Foundation of American College Healthcare Executives
1 North Franklin Street, Suite 1700
Chicago, IL 60606
V: 312-424-2800
F: 312-424-0023
No. Awards: varies
Award Amount: $3,000
Deadline: March 31
Features: Applicant must be U.S. or Canadian citizen and a Student Associate of the American College of Healthcare Executives; enrolled full time and in good standing in graduate program in healthcare management accredited by any regional accrediting association. Applicant must not be a previous recipient.

Irene and Daisy MacGregor Memorial Scholarship

National Society, Daughters of American Revolution
1776 D Street NW
Washington, DC 20006
V: 202-879-3292
No. Awards: varies
Award Amount: $5,000, renewable
Deadline: April 15.

Features: Applicants must be U.S. citizens and obtain a letter of sponsorship from a local DAR chapter. Applicants must be students who have been accepted into or who are pursuing an approved course of study either in psychiatric nursing (graduate level) or studying to become a medical doctor (pre-med does not qualify) at accredited medical schools, colleges, or universities. This application is conducted without regard to race, religion, sex, or national origin. Men also qualify. Send a self-addressed, stamped envelope for application. Only completed applications submitted in one package will be considered. No records are returned. Annual transcript required for renewal. Notification is made in June.

New York Life Foundation Scholarship for Women in Health (See Women)

NSNA Frances Tompkins Breakthrough to Nursing Scholarship for Ethnic People of Color (See Minorities)

NSNA Frances Tompkins Specialty Scholarships

The Foundation of the National Student Nurses' Association, Inc.
555 W.57th Street, Suite 1327
New York, NY 10019
V: 212-581-2215
F: 212-581-2368
W: nsna@nsna.org
No. Awards: varies
Award Amount: $1,000-$2,000
Deadline: Jan. 31, postmarked
Features: Applicants must be currently enrolled in state-approved school of

nursing or pre-nursing program leading to an associate or baccalaureate degree, diploma, or a generic doctorate or master's degree. Some area of specialty must also be acknowledged. Awards are based on academic achievement, financial need, and involvement in nursing student organizations and community activities related to health care. All factors are equally weighed. Students must submit copies of their recent nursing school and college transcripts or grade reports and a $10 processing fee along with completed applications. NSNA members must submit proof of membership. Application forms are available from September through January by sending a self-addressed, legal-size envelope with 52 cents postage. Recipients are notified by March.

Physician Assistants Foundation Scholarship

American Academy of Physician Assistants Foundation
950 N. Washington Street
Alexandria, VA 22314-1552
V: 703-836-2272
No. Awards: 40-50
Award Amount: $2,000, 3,000, or $5,000
Funds Available: varies
Deadline: Feb. 1
Features: Any AAPA student member attending a physician assistant program accredited by the Commission on Accreditation of Applied Health Education Programs (CAAHEP), or its predecessor, Committee on Allied Health Education Accreditation (CAHEEA), is eligible to apply (includes provisional accreditation). Students may apply for AAPA membership at the same time of scholarship application. If applicants are unsure if their programs are accredited by CAHEEA/ CAAHEP, they should consult the program director. No exceptions are made on this requirement. Applications are judged on the basis of financial need, academic record as a PA student, extracurricular activities, and future goals. All applicants are notified in May of the status of their application. The official announcement of recipients is made at the Annual PA Conference.

Procter & Gamble Oral Health/ADHA Institute Scholarship Program

ADHA Institute Scholarship Program
444 North Michigan Avenue, Suite 3400
Chicago, IL 60611
V: 312-440-8900
No. Awards: 25
Award Amount: $1,000; includes tuition
Funds Available: $25,000
Deadline: June 15

Features: Applicant must be a full-time, first-year dental-hygiene student in the U.S. and show evidence of community service and leadership. Applicant must have a minimum cumulative GPA of 3.3. Nationality and residency are unrestricted. Notification is in September.

Research Grants Program

Lupus Foundation of America, Inc.
1300 Piccard Drive, Suite 200
Rockville, MD 20850
V: 301-670-9292
F: 301-670-9486
No. Awards: varies
Award Amount: $15,000/year for two years
Deadline: April 1

Features: Applicants must be junior investigators (Ph.D.s and M.D.s with assistant professor and below rank, if in academic medicine) to support biomedical research related to finding the cause(s) and/or cure for lupus erythematosus. Each research grant proposal will be competitively reviewed NIH-style and ranked by members of Peer Review Commit-tees, including members of the LFA Medical Council and/or outside experts in the field of proposed study. Award date is late June.

Alice W. Rooke NSDAR Scholarship

National Society, Daughters of the American Revolution
1776 D Street NW
Washington, DC 20006-5392
V: 202-879-3292
No. Awards: varies
Award Amount: $5,000
Deadline: April 15

Features: Applicants must be U.S. citizens and attend an accredited college or university in the U.S. All applicants must obtain a letter of sponsorship from a local DAR chapter. Applicants must be accepted into or already pursuing an approved course of study in medicine (pre-med does not qualify) at an approved, accredited medical school, college, or university. This application is conducted without regard to race, religion, sex, or national origin. Men also qualify. Send a self-addressed stamped envelope for application. Only completed applications submitted in one package will be considered. No records are returned. Annual transcript required for renewal. Notification is made in June.

Undergraduate Scholarship Program (UGSP) for Individuals from Disadvantaged Backgrounds

National Institutes of Health (NIH)
Grants Information Office
Division of Research Grants/NIH
Westwood Building, Room 449
Bethesda, MD 20892
V: 301-402-0912
T: 800-528-7689
No. Awards: 10-15
Award Amount: up to 20,000
Deadline: March 10
Features: Applicants must be individuals from disadvantaged backgrounds planning to pursue undergraduate degrees in the biomedical/behavioral sciences. Must be U.S citizens, nationals, or permanent residents. Must work for NIH for 12 months for each year awarded. Applicants must be full-time students enrolled at accredited four-year institutions and interested in biology, biophysics, nursing, nutrition, pre-medicine, psychology, biochemistry, chemistry, or chemical engineering. This program is highly competitive.

Wyeth-Ayerst Scholarship for Women in Grad Medical (See Women)

LEADERSHIP/ COMMUNITY ACTIVITIES

Soroptimist Foundation's Regional Youth Citizenship Awards

1616 Walnut St.
Philadelphia, PA 19103-7508
V: 215-557-9300
No. Awards: 50 (regional awards), (one) international award
Award Amount: $1,250 (one) International award is $2,000.
Funds Available: $60,000 (projected)
Features: Students are selected who have been recommended for this award based on the student's service, dependability, leadership, and sense of purpose. Academic criteria such as grades, SAT scores, class rank, or GPA are not considered for this award. Revisions to program will be published in summer 1997.

Tylenol Scholarship Program

Tylenol Scholarship Fund
Citizens Scholarship Foundation
of America, Inc.
1505 Riverview Rd., P.O. Box 88
St. Peter, MN 56082
V: 507-931-8034
No. Awards: 510
Award Amount: (500) $1,000, (10) $10,000
Funds Available: $600,000
Features: The awards are given to undergraduates who are first-year students, sophomores, and juniors or who will be enrolled at an undergraduate institution in the fall of 1998. Students must be U.S citizens or permanent residents. These scholarships are awarded based on transcript, academic achievement, school and community leadership activities, and personal statement.

U.S. Senate Youth Program, William Randolph Hearst Foundation

90 New Montgomery St. #1212
San Francisco, CA 94105
V: 415-543-0400
No. Awards: 104
Award Amount: $2,000
Funds Available: $208,000

Features: The foundation awards scholarships to students who have served in elected leadership offices in high school student government. Each student must attend high school in the state where his or her parent or legal guardian also resides.

LOCAL RESOURCES

Jennie G. and Pearl Abell Education Trust

717 Main St.
P.O. Box 487
Ashland, KS 67831
V: 316-635-2228
No. Awards: varies
Award Amount: varies
Features: The Abell Trust awards numerous grants to Clark County, Kansas, high school senior students in varying amounts. Kansas college and university budgets are used as a basis to determine the awards. The student must show demonstrated need. The funds can be used at any school of higher education in the United States. The student must maintain 12 semester hours of study with a GPA of 2.0. Awards are renewable each year for four-or five-year programs.

Abraham Burman Charity Trust

P.O. Box 608
Dover, NH 03820-4103
No. Awards: varies
Award Amount: varies
Funds Available: $30,000
Features: This local trust provides grants to students who reside in the New Hampshire community.

California Farm Bureau Federation

C.F.B. Scholarship Foundation
1601 Exposition Boulevard
Sacramento, CA 95815
V: 916-924-4052
No. Grants: approximately 27
Award Amount: $1,500-$2,000, renewable
Deadline: March 1
Features: California residents who are U.S. citizens and are planning to study agriculture at a four-year California college or university can apply.

California Masonic Foundation

1111 California Street
San Francisco, CA 94108-2284
V: 415-776-4702
No. Awards: varies
Award Amount: $2,000
Funds Available: $200,000
Deadline: February 28
Features: This foundation awards college scholarships to high school seniors who are U.S. citizens and residents of California. Students must have a GPA of 3.0 or higher. The application must be requested in writing.

Bright Futures Scholarship Program

Florida Department of Education
Office of Student Financial Assistance
325 West Gaines Street
Tallahassee, FL 32399-0400
V: 888-827-2004
Features: This new program is beginning for the 1997-1998 school year. Students with high school GPAs of 3.0 to 3.5 will receive $1,500 per year. Students who have attained GPAs above 3.5 will receive $2,000 per year plus $600 for textbooks. Students must be Florida residents and must attend a state university, college, or vocational school.

Chautauqua Region Community Foundation Inc.

21 East 3rd Street
Jamestown, NY 14701
V: 716-661-3390
No. Awards: varies
Award Amount: $100 to $1000
Features: The Foundation awards grants to residents of Allegheny and Chautauqua Counties, New York. Awards are renewable each year.

Colorado Masons Benevolent Fund Association

7955 East Arapaho Court
Suite 1200
Englewood, CO 80112-1362
V: 303-290-8544
No. Awards: varies
Award Amount: varies
Funds Available: $275,000
Features: This association awards scholarships to graduates of high schools in Colorado who will attend college in-state.

Community College Scholarship

Sacramento Bee
P.O. Box 15779
Sacramento, CA 95852
V: 916-321-1000 or 916-321-1791
F: 916-321-1783
E: sblixt@sacbee.com
W: sacbee.com
No. Awards: 5
Award Amount: $1,000-$3,000
Funds Available: up to $15,000
Deadline: mid-March
Features: Applicants must be enrolled in a community college and wish to pursue a career in mass media. Students must live in Sacramento, Calif. circulation area and have a minimum 3.0 cumulative GPA; McClatchy full-time employees and their family members are ineligible. Notifications are made in May.

Duluth Superior Area Community Foundation

Whiteside Scholarship Fund Trust
618 Missabe Bldg.
227 W. 1st Street
Duluth, MN 55802
V: 218-726-0232
No. Awards: varies
Award Amount: $2,400 to $4,200
Features: All applicants must be graduates of Duluth, Minnesota, high schools and rank in the top 10% of the high school class. A 2.75 GPA is initially required; renewal applicants must maintain a 3.0 GPA. Scholarships for local colleges are given in the amount of $2,400. Renewal applicants who choose college locations outside Minnesota receive $4,200.

Ebell Scholarship (and) Charles N. Flint Scholarship Fund

743 S. Lucerne Blvd.
Los Angeles, CA 90005
V: 213-731-1277
No. Awards: varies
Award Amount: varies from $2,000 to $3,000
Features: The Fund awards scholarships to college students who are permanent residents and attend college in Los Angeles County, Calif. The student must also be a registered voter and maintain a GPA of 3.25. Current high school students should not apply.

Rockefeller State Wildlife Scholarship

State of Louisiana
Office of Student Aid Financial Assistance
Scholarship Section
P.O. Box 91202
Baton Rouge, LA 70821
V: 504-388-3103
T: 800-259-5626
F: 504-922-1012
No. Awards: 30
Award Amount: $1,000-$7,000
Deadline: April 1

Features: Applicants must be Louisiana residents attending a public college within the state and studying wildlife, forestry, or marine sciences full-time at a two-year or four-year institution. Must have a minimum GPA of 2.5 and have taken the ACT. Open to non-U.S. citizens. Applicants need to fill out the FAFSA form. This scholarship is renewable for up to five years as an undergraduate and two years as a graduate student. Failure to maintain eligibility will result in permanent cancellation of the scholarship and may result in repayment of all funds received plus interest.

Meliora Grant

University of Rochester, Director of Admissions
Rochester, NY 14627
V: 716-275-3221
F: 716-461-4595
W: http://www.rochester.edu
E: admit@macmail.cc.rochester.edu
No. Award: varies
Award Amount: $5,000
Features: Open to N.Y. residents who are admitted to the University of Rochester.

North Dakota Merit Scholarship Program

North Dakota University System
600 East Boulevard Ave.
Bismarck, ND 58505-0230
V: 701-224-4114 or 701-328-2960
F: 701-328-2961
W: www.nodak.edu
E: wipf@prairie.nodak.edu
No. Awards: varies
Award Amount: varies

Features: The North Dakota Scholarship Program provides tuition scholarships to students who have outstanding academic records. Each high school senior student must rank in the upper 20% of the high school class. Applications and information are available in each high school counseling center.

State of Iowa Merit Scholarship Program

Iowa College Student Aid Commission
200 Tenth Street, 4th Floor
Des Moines, IA 50309-3609
V: 515-242-5067 (or) 800-383-4222
F: 515-242-5996
W: www.state.ia.us/government/icsac/index.htm
E: icsac@max.state.ia.us
No. Awards: varies
Award Amount: varies
Features: This program recognizes high school students who graduate in the top 15 percent of their class. An Iowa State Scholarship application is required along with ACT and/or SAT scores. Applications and information are available in the local high school.

Horace Smith Trust Fund

c/o Fleet Trust Co.
1459 Main St.
Box #3034
Springfield, MA 01101
V: 413-787-8524
No. Awards: varies
Award Amount: varies
Funds Available: over $700,000
Features: This fund was established to award scholarships to residents and students who have graduated from high schools in Hampden County, Massachusetts.

Paul Stock Foundation

P.O. Box 2020
Cody, WY 82414
V: 307-587-5275
No. Awards: 50
Award Amount: varies
Features: Foundation sponsors students with grants in varying amounts to attend college. The student must show demonstrated need and must be a Wyoming resident.

MINORITIES/ HERITAGE/ DISABILITIES

Actuarial Scholarships for Minority Students

Society of Actuaries/Casualty Actuarial Society
475 North Martingale Road, Suite 800
Schaumburg, IL 60173
V: 847-706-3500
F: 847-706-3599
W: http://www.soa.org.
No. Awards: 20-30
Award Amount: $1,000-$1,750
Deadline: May 1
Features: Applicants must be Native American, Eskimo, African-American, or Hispanic and enrolled at a two-year or four-year institution. Students must be planning careers in actuarial science. Applicant must be U.S. citizen. Number and amount of awards vary with merit and financial need.

American Council of the Blind Scholarships

American Council of the Blind
1155 15th Street, NW, Suite 720
Washington, DC 20005
V: 202-467-5081
T: 800-424-8666
No. Awards: 15
Award Amount: $1,500-$4,000
Deadline: March 15
Features: Must submit certification of visual status. To be legally blind, the applicant must have a visual acuity of 20/200 or less in the better corrected eye and/or 0 degrees or less visual field. Applicant must be accepted in an accredited postsecondary school. Undergraduates must send in high school transcripts; graduate students must include undergraduate transcripts. Telephone interviews are made in May.

AMS Minority Scholarship

American Meteorological Society
Attn: Fellowship Scholarship Coordinator
45 Beacon Street
Boston, MA 02108-3693

V: 617-227-2426 x235
E: sarmstrg@ametsoc.org
I: http://www.ametsoc/AMS
No. Awards: varies
Award Amount: $3,000
Features: Must be minority student entering first year of college in Fall 1997; must plan to pursue career in the atmospheric or related oceanic and hydrologic sciences.

Armenian Students' Association of America, Inc.

395 Concord Avenue
Belmont, MA 02178
V: 617-484-9548
W: http://www.asainc.org
No. Awards: 60
Award Amount: $500-$1,500
Deadline: Feb. 15
Features: Applicant must be of Armenian ancestry, be a full-time student who is at least a sophomore attending a four-year accredited college or university in the U.S., demonstrate financial need, have good academic performance, show self sufficiency, and participate in extracurricular activities. Submit an application fee of $5 with completed application.

AT&T ESP Scholarships

Attn: ESP Admin., Room 1E-213
101 Crawfords Corner Road
Holmdel, NJ 07733
V: 908-949-4300
No. Awards: 15
Award Amount: cost of tuition
Deadline: January
Features: Applicant must be a female high school senior and belong to an underrepresented minority group. Engineering major: computer science, mechanical systems, or electrical engineering.

AWIS Educational Awards (See Women)

Albert W. Dent Student Scholarship

Foundation of American College
Healthcare Executives
1 North Franklin Street, Suite 1700
Chicago, IL 60606
V: 312-424-2800
F: 312-424-0023
No. Awards: varies
Award Amount: $3,000
Deadline: March 31
Features: Applicant must be a U.S. or Canadian citizen minority group member, and a Student Associate of the American College of Healthcare Executives. He or she must be a full-time undergraduate in a healthcare management program leading to a graduate program accredited by any regional accrediting association in the U.S. Applicant must not have previously been a recipient.

Dental Assisting Scholarship Program

ADA Endowment and Assistance Fund, Inc.
211 East Chicago Avenue 17th Floor
Chicago, IL 60611
V: 312-440-2567
No. Awards: Up to 25
Award Amount: $1,000
Funds Available: varies
Deadline: Sept. 15
Features: Applicant must be U.S. citizen, full-time student in respective dental program, and have minimum 2.8 GPA. Must be African-American, Hispanic, or Native American. Notification of scholarship awards is made in the fall.

Dental Hygiene Scholarship Program

ADA Endowment and Assistance Fund, Inc.
211 East Chicago Avenue 17th Floor
Chicago, IL 60611
V: 312-440-2567
No. Awards: Up to 25
Award Amount: $1,000
Funds Available: varies
Deadline: Aug. 15
Features: Applicant must be U.S. citizen, full-time student entering second year and attending dental hygiene program accredited by the Commission on Dental Accreditation with a 2.8 minimum GPA. Students must be African-American, Hispanic, or Native American.

Dental Laboratory Technology Scholarship

ADA Endowment and Assistance Fund, Inc.
211 East Chicago Avenue 17th Floor
Chicago, IL 60611
V: 312-440-2567
No. Awards: Up to 25
Award Amount: $1,000 (one year awards)
Deadline: Aug. 15
Features: Applicant must be U.S. citizen entering full-time, first year at a dental laboratory technology school accredited by Commission on Dental Accreditation. GPA 2.8 minimum. Must be African-

American, Hispanic, or Native American. Applicants must demonstrate a minimum financial need of $1,000. Students awarded a full scholarship from another source are ineligible. Notification of scholarship is made in the fall.

Editing Programs (See Communications)

Electronic Industries Foundation Scholarship Program

Electronic Industries Foundation
2500 Wilson Boulevard Suite 210
Arlington, VA 22201
V: 703-907-7400
F: 703-907-7401
No. Awards: 6
Award Amount: $30,000
Deadline: Feb. 1
Features: Financial aid must clearly offset impact of disability on applicant's goals. Candidate must have a disability as defined by the Americans with Disabilities Act of 1990, be accepted at an accredited four-year college or university at time of award and pursuing a degree in electrical engineering, industrial manufacturing, industrial engineering, physics, electromechanical technology, mechanical applied sciences, or similar field directly related to the electronics industry. Please send a self-addressed, stamped envelope.

Foundation of National Student Nurses Association

Ethnic Scholarship
555 West 57th Street, Suite 1327
New York, NY 10019
V: 212-581-2215
F: 212-581-2365
No. Awards: varies
Award Amount: $1,000-$2,500
Deadline: Jan. 31
Features: Applicant must be American Indian, African-American or Asian with financial need, majoring in health services administration. Applicant must enclose a self-addressed stamped envelope with 2 oz. postage for more information and application forms.

GEM PHD Science Fellowship

National Consortium for Graduate Degrees for Minorities in Engineering and Science, Inc.
P.O. Box 537
1118 North Eddy St.

Notre Dame, IN 46556
South Bend, IN 46117
V: 219-631-7771
F: 219-287-1486
W: http://www.nd.edu/~gem
E: gem.1@nd.edu
No. Awards: 20-30
Award Amount: $12,000-$100,000
Deadline: Dec. 1
Features: Applicants must be U.S. citizens who are American Indian, Mexican-American, African-American, Puerto Rican, or Hispanic. Applicants must be graduate students studying life science, mathematics, or physical science and enrolling for doctoral study at a participating GEM institution. Minimum 3.0 GPA is required.

Hallie Q. Brown Scholarship Fund

National Association of Colored Women's Clubs
5808 Sixteenth Street, NW
Washington, DC 20011
V: 202-726-2044
F: 202-726-0023
No. Awards: varies
Award Amount: varies
Deadline: March
Features: Applicant must be minority student, U.S. citizen, and recommended by member of National Association of Colored Women's Clubs. Applicant must be a full-time student in undergraduate studies. Based on financial need. This scholarship is awarded every two years. Applicants must get scholarship packets through members of National Association of Colored Women's Clubs.

Burlington Northern Santa Fe Foundation Scholarship

American Indian Science & Engineering Society
5661 Airport Boulevard
Boulder, CO 80301
V: 303-939-0023
F: 303-939-8150
E: gormanc@stripe.colorado.edu
W: http://www.colorado.edu/AISES
No. Awards: 5 new students awarded each year, totaling 19 students annually.
Award Amount: $2,500 for four years or 8 semesters, whichever occurs first
Funds Available: $47,500
Deadline: March 31
Features: Applicants must reside in AZ, CO,KS, MN, MT, ND, NM, OK, OR, SD, WA,

or CA. Applicant must also be a high school senior and at least one fourth American Indian. Certificate of Indian blood is required. Eligible disciplines: science, business, education, and health administration.

Chicago Association of Black Journalists Scholarship

Chicago Association of Black Journalists
P.O. Box 11425
Chicago, IL 60611
V: 312-409-9392
No. Awards: varies
Award Amount: $1,000
Features: Applicant must be minority, full-time junior, senior, or graduate student enrolled in an accredited college or university in the Chicago metropolitan area; major in print or broadcast journalism.

Duracell Scholarship and Internship Program

National Urban League, Inc.
120 Wall Street
New York, NY 10005
V: 212-558-5450
No. Awards: 5
Award Amount: up to $10,000
Features: Must be minority, junior or sophomore student pursuing full-time studies towards bachelor's degree at accredited U.S. institution of higher learning; interested in engineering, sales or marketing, manufacturing operations, finance or business administration. Must rank within the top 25% of class and maintain ranking throughout participation. Must be interested in summer employment with Duracell between junior and senior years, at a location to be selected by Duracell.

Imasco Scholarship Fund for Disabled Students

Association of Universities and Colleges of Canada
350 Albert Street Suite 600
Ottawa, Ontario K1R 1B1 Canada
V: 613-563-3961
F: 613-563-9745
E: acraig@aucc.ca
I: www.aucc.ca
No. Awards: 10 minimum
Award Amount: $2,000
Funds Available: $20,000 minimum
Deadline: June 1

Features: Must be undergraduate and pursuing a degree at Canadian degree-granting institution, non-degree, Canadian citizen or have lived in Canada for at least two years as a permanent resident, and have a disability.

Agnes Jones Jackson Scholarship

National Association for the Advancement of Colored People
4805 Mt. Hope Drive
Baltimore, MD 21215-3297
V: 410-486-8900 or 9149
F: 410-764-7357
No. Awards: varies
Award Amount: varies
Deadline: April 30
Features: Membership required in NAACP at time of application. Applicant must be a full-time student enrolled at accredited U.S. institution, and recommended (in letter form) by president of NAACP branch, Youth Council or College Chapter, a member of Executive Committee, a member of National Board, a member of SCF Trustees, or an NAACP employee (except those on the Agnes Jones Jackson Scholarship Committee). Graduating high school seniors must have a cumulative GPA of at least 2.5 on a 4.0 scale, undergraduate college students a 2.0, and graduates a 3.0. Only open to U.S. citizens. NAACP employees are ineligible. Recommendation letter should specify sender's title and be on letterhead if possible. Recipients must compete for scholarship renewal. Most recent GPA, NAACP participation, other civil rights activities, and academic awards will be considered. Award may be reduced or denied based on insufficient enrollment (less than full-time) or NAACP participation.

Martin Luther King, Jr. Scholarships

California Teachers Association
Human Rights Department
1705 Murchison Drive
P.O. Box 921
Burlingame, CA 94011-0921
V: 415-697-1400
No. Awards: varies
Award Amount: varies, depends on individuals' demonstrated need.
Deadline: March 15
Features: Based on financial need.

Applicant must be ethnic minority, member or dependent of member of CTA or Student CTA, and pursuing degree or credential for teaching-related career in public education. Scholarships vary annually depending on members' voluntary contributions and applicants' financial need. Applications are available each January.

Kosciuszko Foundation Scholarship

Kosciuszko Foundation, Domestic Grants Office
15 East 65th Street
New York, NY 10021
V: 212-734-2130
F: 212-628-4552
No. Awards: between 65-110
Award Amount: $1,000-$7,000
Deadline: Jan. 16
Features: Applicant must be of Polish heritage to apply for scholarships for study in all areas. Those of non-Polish heritage must be studying Polish subjects. Student must be full-time junior/senior undergraduate or graduate. The majority of scholarships are for graduate students. There is a limited number of scholarships for third and fourth year undergraduates. Financial need is considered. Open to U.S. citizens or permanent residents only. Minimum GPA is 3.0. This scholarship is competitive.

Master's Fellowship

National Consortium for Graduate Degrees for Minorities in Engineering and Science, Inc.
P.O. Box 537
1118 North Eddy St.
Notre Dame, IN 46556
South Bend, IN 46117
V: 219-631-7771
F: 219-287-1486
W: http://www.nd.edu/~gem
E: gem.1@nd.edu
No. Awards: Approximately 300
Award Amount: $25,000-$75,000
Deadline: Dec. 1
Features: Applicants must be U.S. citizens who are American Indian, Mexican-American, African-American, Puerto Rican, or Hispanic. Applicants must be juniors, seniors, or graduate students studying in a life science, mathematics, or physical science program and enrolling in graduate program in same area at a participating GEM institution. Minimum 2.8 GPA is required.

Mattinson Endowment Fund Scholarship for Disabled Students

Association of Universities and Colleges of Canada
350 Albert Street Suite 600
Ottawa, Ontario K1R 1B1 Canada
V: 613-563-1236
No. Awards: varies
Award Amount: $2,000
Funds Available: varies
Deadline: June 1
Features: Applicant must be disabled undergraduate; Canadian citizen or have lived in Canada for at least two years as a permanent resident. Scholarship winners will be notified by August 31. Winners must submit to the Association of Universities and Colleges of Canada confirmation of registration to the educational institution.

Minnie Pearl Scholarship Program

The EAR Foundation
817 Patterson Street
Nashville, TN 37203
V: 615-329-7807
E: earfyi@aol.com
W: www.theearfound.com
No. Awards: 1
Award Amount: $2,000; four year; renewable
Deadline: February 15
Features: Applicants must be high school juniors with a 3.0 GPA. Students must have a significant bilateral hearing loss and must be of mainstreamed hearing-impaired status. All applicants must have been accepted at accredited two- or four-year colleges, universities, or technical schools; plan to attend full time; and be U.S. citizens.

Minority Graduate Research Fellowship

American Society for Microbiology
1325 Massachusetts Avenue, NW
Washington, DC 20005
V: 202-942-9295
E: Fellowships-careerinformation@asmusa.org
No. Awards: varies
Award Amount: $12,000, renewable

Deadline: May 1
Features: Applicant must be minority that is under-represented in the sciences, full-time sophomore or junior with indepen-dent study experience, major in microbiol-ogy or related science. Minimum GPA of 2.0 to renew.

Minority Undergraduate Research Fellowship

American Society for Microbiology
1325 Massachusetts Avenue, NW
Washington, DC 20005
V: 202-942-9295
E: careerinformation@asmusa.org
No. Awards: Not specified
Award Amount: Up to $2,000
Deadline: June 1
Features: Must have completed first college year, be ASM student in the sciences; under-represented minority including African-American, Hispanic, Native American, and Native Pacific Islander.

NABA Scholarship Program

National Association of Black Accountants
7249-A Hanover Parkway
Greenbelt, MD 20770
V: 310-474-NABA ext. 14
No. Awards: over 20
Award Amount: $1,000-$6,000
Features: Applicant must be an under-graduate or graduate accounting student, current member of National Association of Black Accountants. Applicants must also be American Indian, Asian, Hispanic, or African-American. Based on GPA, involve-ment in NABA, financial need, and ability to overcome adversity.

National Achievement Scholarship Program for Outstanding Negro Students

1560 Sherman Avenue, Suite 200
Evanston, Illinois 60201-4897
No. Awards: approximately 600
Award Amount: $2,000 National Achieve-ment Scholarships; corporate-sponsored scholarship amounts vary
Deadline: PSAT/NMSQT test date (in late October)
Features: African-Americans who take the PSAT/NMSQT usually no later than 11th grade and plan to enroll in a bachelor's degree program; U.S. citizens only.

National Italian American Foundation

1860 19th Street, NW
Washington, DC 20009
V: 202-530-3515
No. Awards: 85
Award Amount: $1,000 to $5,000
Funds Available: more than $100,000
Deadline: May 31
Features: Open to Italian-American students of all college majors currently enrolled or entering college who are permanent residents of the U.S. Criteria for selection include academic merit, financial need, and community service.

Nicaraguan and Haitian Scholarship Program

Florida Department of Education
1344 Florida Education Center
Tallahassee, FL 32399
V: 904-487-3260
No. Awards: varies
Award Amount: $4,000-$5,000
Deadline: July 1, postmarked
Features: Applicant must be a Nicaraguan or Haitian citizen or must have been born in Nicaragua or Haiti and currently living in Florida. Student must meet Selective Service registration requirements and have a cumulative high school GPA of at least 3.0 on a 4.0 scale or a 3.0 cumulative GPA for all college work attempted. Candidate must also demonstrate service to the community. Applicant must not owe a repayment of a grant under any state or federal grant or scholarship program. Student must not be in default on any federal Title IV or state student loan program unless satisfactory arrangements to repay have been made. Also, student must be enrolled at a State University System institution for an minimum of 12 credit hours of undergraduate study or 9 credit hours of graduate study. This award is not renewable. However, a person who has received the award may reapply in succeeding years.

NSNA Frances Tompkins Breakthrough to Nursing Scholarship for Ethnic People of Color

The Foundation of the National Student Nurses' Association, Inc.
555 W. 57th Street, Suite 1327
New York, NY 10019
V: 212-581-2215
F: 212-581-2368

W: www.nsna@nsna.org
No. Awards: varies
Award Amount: $1,000-$2,500
Deadline: Jan. 31, postmarked
Features: Applicants must be minority students who are currently enrolled in a state-approved school of nursing or pre-nursing in a program leading to an associate or baccalaureate degree, a diploma, or a generic doctorate or master's degree. Awards are based on academic achievement, financial need, and involvement in nursing student organizations and community activities related to health care. All factors are weighed equally.

Parke-Davis Epilepsy Scholarship Award

c/o IntraMed Educational Group
1633 Broadway, 25th Floor
New York, NY 10019
T: 800-292-7373
No. Awards: 16
Award Amount: $3,000
Deadline: March 1
Features: Must be currently under a physician's care for epilepsy; a high school senior who has applied to a college or university; or a currently enrolled freshman, sophomore, or junior college student; or a college senior who has applied to graduate school. Must have achieved in academics and participated in extracurricular activities. Notification will be made in April.

Sacramento Bee Minority Media Scholarship

Sacramento Bee
P.O. Box 15779
Sacramento, CA 95852
V: 916-321-1000 or 916-321-1791
F: 916-321-1783
E: sblixt@sacbee.com
W: www.sacbee.com
No. Awards: 8 to 12
Award Amount: $1,000-$4,000
Funds Available: $20,000
Deadline: March 15
Features: Applicant must live in Sacramento circulation area, be a first-year college student who has interest in pursuing a career in mass media. Minimum 3.0 cumulative GPA; McClatchy full-time employees and their family members are ineligible. Notifications are in May.

Scholarships and Fellowships

KKG Foundation
P.O. Box 38
Columbus, OH 43216
V: 614-228-6515
No. Awards: Not specified
Award Amount: Average award $1,000; includes educational expenses
Deadline: Feb. 1

Features: Must be a female member of the granting agency; at undergraduate, graduate, or postgraduate level; continue to study at institution where she became a member. Nationality and residency unrestricted. Notification is in the spring.

Supplementary Grant Program

Open Society Institute/CAP
888 Seventh Avenue, 31st Floor
New York, NY 10106
V: 212-887-0175
F: 212-974-0367
No. Awards: approximately 300
Award Amount: average award $6,000
Deadline: May 15
Features: Unrestricted study at all college levels in the U.S.; must be between age 18 and 40 and a Burmese citizen. Grant to address the needs of Burmese students whose college education was disrupted as a result of their active participation in pro-democracy movement of 1988.

Sutton Education Scholarship

National Association for the Advancement of Colored People
4805 Mt. Hope Drive
Baltimore, MD 21215-3297
V: 410-358-8900 or 9149
F: 410-764-7357
No. Awards: Not specified
Award Amount: $1,000 undergraduate students; $2,000 graduate students
Features: Must be full-time college student majoring in education and NAACP member. Graduating seniors may also apply. Minimum cumulative GPA: undergraduates, 2.5; graduates, 3.0. Candidates must be U.S. citizens.

Undergraduate Scholarship Program (UGSP) for Individuals from Disadvantaged Backgrounds (See Health)

Undergraduate Scholarship Program

Amoco Foundation, Inc.
200 East Randolph Drive
Chicago, IL 60601
V: 312-856-6306
Students should check with university department offices or student finaid office for funds donated by Amoco.

Wasie Foundation Scholarship

Wasie Foundation
First Bank Place, Suite 4700
601 Second Avenue South
Minneapolis, MN 55402
V: 612-332-3883
No. Awards: approximately 60
Award Amount: $1,000-$10,000
Funds Available: $250,000
Deadline: April 15
Features: U.S. citizen of Polish ancestry attending specified Minnesota institutions; based on financial need, academic ability, extracurricular activities, and personal qualities.

Roy Wilkins Scholarship

National Association for the Advancement of Colored People
4805 Mt. Hope Drive
Baltimore, MD 21215
V: 410-358-8900 or 9149
F: 410-764-7357
No. Awards: Not specified
Award Amount: $1,000
Features: Must be graduating high school senior and NAACP member. The minimum GPA is 2.5. Applicant must be U.S. citizen and full-time student.

Willems Scholarship

National Association for Advancement of Colored People
4805 Mt. Hope Drive
Baltimore, MD 21215-3297
V: 410-358-8900
F: 410-764-7357
No. Awards: Not specified
Award Amount: $2,000 undergraduate students; $3,000 graduate students
Features: Applicant must be male, NAACP member, and student majoring in engineering, chemistry, physics, or mathematical science. The minimum GPA is 3.0 for

graduate students. Applicants who are graduating seniors or undergraduates must have a minimum GPA of 2.5. Candidates must be U.S. citizens and full-time college students.

Year Abroad Program at the Jagiellonian University at Krakow

Kosciuszko Foundation, Domestic Grants Office
15 East 65th Street
New York, NY 10021
V: 212-734-2130
F: 212-628-4552
No. Awards: 15-17
Award Amount: cost of tuition, dormitory, and partial living expenses
Features: Applicant must study Polish language, history, literature, and culture. Candidate must be enrolled at a U.S. college or university entering third or fourth year of undergraduate study or enrolled in a master's or doctoral program. Open to U.S. citizens or permanent residents only. Minimum GPA is 3.0. This scholarship is competitive.

ORGANIZATIONS/ MEMBERSHIPS

AFCEA ROTC Scholarship Program

Armed Forces Communication and Electronics Association— Educational Foundation
4400 Fail Lakes Court
Fairfax, VA 22033-3899
V: 703-631-6149
T: 800-336-4583 ext. 6149
F: 703-631-4693
E: scholarship@afcea.org
W: www.@afcea.org
No. Awards: 60
Award Amount: $1,500
Funds Available: $90,000
Deadline: April 1
Features: The purpose of this scholarship is to encourage and reward outstanding and deserving students in the ROTC program. Applicants must be U.S. citizens enrolled in an ROTC program who are sophomores or juniors at the time of application. Students must be working toward a degree in electronics, electrical

or communications engineering, mathematics, physics, or computer science or technology. Candidates must also be of good moral character, have proven academic excellence, and demonstrate motivation and potential for completing a college education and serving as an officer of the Armed Forces of the United States. Also based on financial need. This scholarship is distributed equally among the Army, Navy/Marine Corps, and Air Force ROTC programs. Notification of winners will be made in June. Applications are available each year in November.

Air Force Aid Society Education Grant

Air Force Aid Society National
Headquarters
1745 Jefferson Davis Hwy., No. 202
Arlington, VA 22202
V: 703-607-3072
F: 703-607-3022
No. Awards: 4,000 awards for dependent children; 1,000 awards for spouses
Award Amount: $1,500 first year, renewable at $1,000 each year for three years
Funds Available: $5 million
Deadline: forth Friday of March
Features: Applicants must be dependent sons and daughters of Air Force members in one of the following categories: active duty and Title 10 reservists on extended active duty (all other Guard and Reserve are not eligible); retired due to length of active duty service or disability, or retired Guard; Reserve age 60 and receiving retirement pay; widows of Air Force members. Applicants must be enrolled or accepted as full-time undergraduate students in a college, university, or a vocational/trade school whose accreditation is accepted by the Department of Education. Students must maintain a minimum GPA of 2.0. Applicants who are recipients of previous grants must demonstrate satisfactory progress by promotion in school grade level.

AFSA/AMF Scholarship Program

Air Force Sergeants Association
Airmen Memorial Bldg.
5211 Auth Road
Suitland, MD 20746
V: 301-899-3500
F: 301-899-8136
E: afsahq@internetmci.com

No. Awards: approximately 50
Funds Available: $1,500-$2,500
Deadline: January 1 and April 15
Features: Applicants must be single, dependent children, including stepchildren and legally adopted children, of Air Force Sergeants Association members or members of the Association's Auxiliary. Applicants must be high school graduates or in-college students. Based on academic ability, character, leadership, writing ability, and potential for success. Financial need is not a consideration. Pre-freshmen who have not previously attended college and in-college freshmen who will not have completed one full-year of college work by the end of the next spring semester or quarter must submit their SAT results report.Application forms must be requested by sending a self-addressed, postage paid ($.78), # 10 envelope after November 1.

American Federation of State, County, and Municipal Employees, AFL-CIO

AFSCME Family Scholarship
1625 L Street, NW
Washington, DC 20036
V: 202-429-1250
TTY: 202-659-0446
No. Awards: 10
Award Amount: $2,000
Funds Available: $20,000
Deadline: Dec. 31
Features: Applicants must be graduating high school seniors who are children of active AFSCME members. Notification is made by March 31.

American Federation of State, County, and Municipal Employees, AFL-CIO

AFSCME MasterCard Scholarship Award Program
1625 L Street, NW
Washington, DC 20036
V: 202-429-1250
TTY: 202-659-0446
No. Awards: varies
Award Amount: $500-$4,000
Funds Available: $150,000
Features: Applicants must be members, spouses, and children (includes foster, stepchildren, and adopted). Applicants must be accepted into an accredited postsecondary institution including

community colleges, trade, and technical schools. Must submit high school transcript, SAT or ACT scores, and present one reference and 500 word essay. Excludes members' children in graduate school. Members need not be MasterCard holders.

American History Scholarship

National Society, Daughters of the American Revolution
1776 D Street NW
Washington, DC 20006-5392
V: 202-879-3292
No. Awards: varies
Award Amount: $2,000 renewable
Deadline: February 1
Features: Applicants must be U.S. citizens and attend an accredited college or university in the U.S. All applicants must obtain a letter of sponsorship from a local DAR chapter. Applicants must be graduating high school seniors who will be majoring in American History. This application is processed without regard to race, religion, sex, or national origin. Send a SASE for application. Only completed applications submitted in one package will be considered. No records are returned. Annual transcript required for renewal. Only state winners are eligible for judging on the Division level. Division level first and second place winners are judged on the National level. Notification is made in June.

General Henry H. Arnold Education Grant Program

Air Force Aid Society Education Assistance Department
1745 Jefferson Davis Highway, Suite 202
Arlington, VA 22202
V: 703-607-3072
F: 703-607-3022
No. Grants: 5,000
Award Amount: $1,000
Funds Available: $5.5 million
Deadline: March 20
Features: Applicant must be high school graduate accepted as a full-time college undergraduate at a college, university, or vocational/trade school with accreditation issued by the U.S. Department of Education. Minimum GPA: 2.0 (on a 4.0 scale). Applicant must be dependent child of Air Force member in the following categories: active duty and Title 10 reservists on

extended active duty through award disbursement date; Retired Guard/Reserve (age 60 and older), or retired due to length of active duty or disability; Deceased while active or retired, (or) must be spouse of Active duty member or Title 10 Reservists on extended active duty; eligible spouses must live and attend school in the continental U.S., and be legally married to member at time of application and award disbursement. Notification will be made in June.

A.T. Anderson Memorial Scholarship

American Indian Science & Engineering Society
5661 Airport Boulevard
Boulder, CO 80301
V: 303-939-0023
F: 303-939-8150
E: gormanc@stripe.colorado.edu
W: http://www.colorado.edu/AISES
No. Awards: approximately 200
Award Amount: $1,000 for undergraduates, $2,000 for graduates
Funds Available: approximately $219,000
Deadline: June 15
Features: Applicant must be an AISES member ($10 fee); American Indian/ Alaskan Native (minimum 1/4 and or recognized by tribe) full-time student at an accredited institution. Must have knowledge of American Indian cultures (including own). Minimum GPA is 2.0. Certificate of Indian blood is required. Eligible disciplines: business, medicine, natural resources, math and science secondary education, engineering, and sciences. This award is nonrenewable. Students must reapply each year.

Baptist Life Scholarship Benefit

Baptist Life Home Office
8555 Main Street
Buffalo, NY 14221
V: 716-633-4393
F: 716-633-4916
No. Awards: 20
Award Amount: $500 full-time student, $250 part-time student
Funds Available: $10,000
Deadline: May 31
Features: Candidates must be insured on a Baptist Life Association permanent life insurance certificate, term life insurance

certificate, or annuity issued at least one year prior to May 31 of the scholarship application year. Good character and standard entrance level grades required.

California Teachers Association Scholarship

P.O. Box 921
Burlingame, CA 94011
V: 415-697-1400
No. Awards: 17
Award Amount: $2,000
Funds Available: Approximately $34,000
Deadline: Feb. 15
Features: Applicant must be dependent child of active, retired-life, or deceased members and must major in higher education.

Civitan International Foundation

Attn: Scholarship Administrator
P.O. Box 13074
Birmingham, AL 35213-0744
V: 205-591-8910
No. Awards: Approximately 40
Award Amount: $1,000 to $1,500
Deadline: varies
Features: Each candidate must be a Civitan (or a Civitan's immediate family member) and must have been a Civitan for at least two years and/or must be or have been a Junior Civitan for no less than two years. Scholarships are awarded to students pursuing careers which help further the ideals and purposes of Civitan International as embodied in its Creed. Candidates must be enrolled in a degree or certificate program at an accredited community college, vocational school, four-year college or graduate school. If a candidate is not pursuing graduate studies, full-time attendance is required. Send a self-addressed, stamped envelope with postage to cover a 2 oz. U.S. mailing.

Coast Guard Mutual Assistance Education Grants

Coast Guard Mutual Assistance
2100 2nd Street, SW
Washington, DC 20593
V: 202-267-1683 ext. 1682
No. Awards: 80
Award Amount: $500
Features: Must be dependent child of Coast Guard member in one of the following categories: active duty and Title

10 reservists on extended duty; retired due to length of active duty service or disability or retired reserve age 60; deceased while on active duty or retired status. Must be accepted as a full-time undergraduate in 1997-1998 at a college, university or vocational/trade school whose accreditation the Department of Education has accepted. Minimum GPA 2.0. Previous grant recipients must re-apply and demonstrate satisfactory progress; those not qualified to compete for grants may be eligible for CGMA-sponsored loans.

D.A.R. Lillian and Arthur Dunn Scholarship

National Society, Daughters of the American Revolution
1776 D Street NW
Washington, DC 20006-5392
V: 202-879-3292
No. Awards: varies
Award Amount: $1,000, renewable
Deadline: April 15
Features: Applicants must be U.S. citizens and attend an accredited college or university in the U.S. All applicants must obtain a letter of sponsorship from a local DAR chapter. Applicants must be graduating high school seniors whose mothers are current members of NSDAR (no other relationship qualifies). Each application is processed without regard to race, religion, sex, or national origin. Send a self-addressed, stamped envelope for application. Only completed applications submitted in one package will be considered. No records are returned. Annual transcript required for renewal. Notification is made in June.

D.A.R. Enid Hall Griswold Memorial Scholarship

National Society, Daughters of the American Revolution
1776 D Street NW
Washington, DC 20006-5392
V: 202-879-3292
No. Awards: varies
Award Amount: $1,000
Deadline: Feb. 15
Features: Applicants must be U.S. citizens and attend an accredited college or university in the U.S. All applicants must obtain a letter of sponsorship from a local DAR chapter. Applicants must be entering junior or senior year of college and

majoring in either political science, history, governmental, or economics. Each application is processed without regard to race, religion, sex, or national origin. Send a self-addressed, stamped envelope for application. Only completed applications submitted in one package will be considered. No records are returned. Annual transcript required for renewal. Notification is made in June.

D.A.R. Idamae Cox Otis Scholarship

National Society, Daughters of the American Revolution
1776 D Street NW
Washington, DC 20006-5392
V: 202-879-3292
No. Awards: varies
Award Amount: $1,000
Deadline: Feb. 15
Features: Applicants must be U.S. citizens and attend an accredited college or university in the U.S. All applicants must obtain a letter of sponsorship from a local DAR chapter. Applicants must be graduates of Kate Duncan Smith or Tamassee DAR Schools. Applications are handled through the respective school scholarship committees. Each application is processed without regard to race, religion, sex, or national origin. Send a self-addressed, stamped envelope for application. Only completed applications submitted in one package will be considered. No records are returned. Notification is made in June.

D.A.R. Longman-Harris Scholarship

National Society, Daughters of the American Revolution
1776 D Street NW
Washington, DC 20006-5392
V: 202-879-3292
No. Awards: varies
Award Amount: $2,000, renewable
Deadline: April 15
Features: Applicants must be U.S. citizens and attend an accredited college or university in the U.S. All applicants must obtain a letter of sponsorship from a local DAR chapter. Applicants must be graduating seniors of Kate Duncan Smith DAR School. Each application is processed without regard to race, religion, sex, or

national origin. Send a self-addressed, stamped envelope for application. Only completed applications submitted in one package will be considered. No records are returned. Annual transcript required for renewal. Notification is made in June.

Delta Faucet Scholarship Program

National Association of Plumbing-Heating-Cooling Contractors
180 S. Washington Street
P.O. Box 6808
Falls Church, VA 22040-1148
V: 703-237-8100 or 1-800-533-7694
No. Awards: 6 (non-renewable)
Award Amount: $2,500
Funds Available: About $15,000
Deadline: June 1
Features: Student applicant must be recommended by a family member, friend, employee, or NAPHCC member. The student may be a high school senior or first-year college student planning to attend a four-year accredited college. Provide high school or college transcripts, a recommendation letter from a principal, counselor, or dean, a recommendation letter from the NAPHCC sponsor, and a completed application with black and white photo.

Albert W. Dent Student Scholarship (See Minorities)

EPA Tribal Lands Environmental Science Scholarship

American Indian Science & Engineering Society
5661 Airport Boulevard
Boulder, CO 80301
V: 303-939-0023
F: 303-939-8150
E: gormanc@stripe.colorado.edu
W: http://www.colorado.edu/AISES
No. Awards: approximately 68
Award Amount: $4,000
Funds Available: $272,000
Deadline: June 15
Features: Applicant must be a college junior, senior, or graduate student and enrolled full-time at an accredited institution. Certificate of Indian blood is not required. This award is nonrenewable. Students must reapply each year.

E. C. Hallbeck Memorial Scholarship Program

American Postal Workers Union
1300 L Street, NW
Washington, DC 20005
V: 202-842-4268
No. Awards: 5
Award Amount: $1,000 for four years
Deadline: March 1, postmarked
Features: Applicant must be a high school or corresponding secondary school senior during application and plan to attend an accredited college of choice. Student must be a son, daughter, stepchild, or legally adopted child of an active or deceased member of American Postal Workers Union. Winners are judged on the basis of school records, personal qualifications, SAT/ACT scores, and total family income.

International Brotherhood of Teamsters Scholarship Fund

25 Louisiana Avenue, NW
Washington, DC 20001
V: 202-624-8735
No. Awards: 25
Award Amount: (10) $1,500, renewable for four years totaling $6,000; (15) $1,000 non-renewable
Deadline: Jan. 31
Features: Must be child or grandchild of active, retired, disabled, or deceased member of the International Brotherhood of Teamsters who has been or was a member for at least 12 months. Applicants must be ranked in the top 15 percent of their high school class, have or expect to have excellent SAT or ACT scores, and be able to demonstrate financial need. Recipients are selected by an impartial committee of university admissions and financial aid directors on the basis of scholastic achievement, aptitude, personal qualifications, and financial need. Students participating in concurrent enrollment programs, whereby they attend college courses prior to completion of their high school requirements, must apply the year before they begin full-time college course work. Canadian students may apply during junior or senior year, but not both.

Applicants must be sons, daughters, or grandchildren of Teamster's members. Financial dependents (that is, stepchildren and wards) of Teamster's members are eligible if the member contributes in excess of 50% of the applicant's financial support and if the applicant is a financial dependent of the member for federal income tax purposes.

Nancy Lorraine Jensen Memorial Scholarship Fund

The Sons of Norway Foundation
C/O Sons of Norway
1455 West Lake Street
Minneapolis, MN 55408
V: 612-827-3611
T: 800-945-8851
No. Awards: varies
Award Amount: no less than 50% for one term (quarter or semester) and no more than 100% of the tuition for one year
Deadline: March 1, postmarked

Features: Applicant must be a U.S. citizen not younger than 17 and not older than 35 on the date that the scholarship application is submitted. Candidate must be a female member or the daughter or granddaughter of a member of the Sons of Norway, provided that such membership shall have been of at least three years duration on the date the application is submitted. Employment at the NASA Goddard Space Flight Center, Greenbelt, MD, may be substituted in lieu of Sons of Norway. Student must be a full-time undergraduate who has completed at least one term (quarter, semester) of studies majoring in chemistry, physics, or chemical, electrical, or mechanical engineering. The applicant must have attained at least a 1200 SAT score or an ACT score of at least 26. Grants awarded are jointly payable to the student and the institution of learning. Any applicant may receive three awards during undergraduate study.

W.H. "Howie" McClennan Scholarship

International Association of Fire Fighters
1750 New York Avenue, NW
Washington, DC 20006
V: 202-737-8484
No. Awards: Approximately 10
Award Amount: $2,500, renewable
Funds Available: $25,000
Deadline: Feb. 1
Features: Based on financial need, aptitude, promise, and academic achievements. Must be child or legally adopted child of Fire Fighter who died in the line of duty and who was a member in good standing of the International Association of Fire Fighters —AFL-CIO-CLC at the time of death. Applicant must plan to attend an accredited university, college, or school of higher learning in the U.S. or Canada. Transcripts of grades, recommendations from two teachers, and a 200-word statement indicating reasons for continuing education required.

Schuyler M. Meyer, Jr. Scholarship Fund

American Indian Science & Engineering Society
5661 Airport Boulevard
Boulder, CO 80301
V: 303-939-0023
F: 303-939-8150
E: gormanc@stripe.colorado.edu
W: http://www.colorado.edu/AISES
No. Awards: 10
Award Amount: $1,000 for four years or until degree is obtained,
Funds Available: $10,000
Deadline: June 15
Features: Applicant must be a single parent with at least one minor child residing in the household and be enrolled full-time at an accredited institution. Applicant must also be at least 1/4 American Indian or recognized as a member of a tribe. Certificate of Indian blood is required. All disciplines are eligible.

National JACL Scholarship

Japanese-American Citizens League
1765 Sutter Street
San Francisco, CA 94115
V: 415-921-5225
F: 415-931-4671
E: hq@jacl.org

W: www.jacl.org
No. Awards: over 25
Award Amount: $1,000-$5,000
Funds Available: $70,000
Deadline: March 1 for entering freshmen
April 1 for current college students
Features: Applicant must be a U.S. citizen who is a National JACL member.

King Olav V Norwegian-American Heritage Fund

The Sons of Norway Foundation
C/O Sons of Norway
1455 West Lake Street
Minneapolis, MN 55408
V: 612-827-3611
T: 800-945-8851
No. Awards: varies
Award Amount: $250-$3,000
Available Funds: over $200,000
Deadline: March 1, postmarked
Features: Any American, 18 years of age or older, who has demonstrated a keen and sincere interest in the Norwegian heritage and/or any Norwegian who has demonstrated an interest in American heritage, who now desires to pursue further heritage study at a recognized educational institution (arts, crafts, literature, history, music, folklore, and the like) is eligible to apply for a scholarship/grant. Based on GPA, participation in school and community activities, work experiences, education and career goals, and personal and school preferences. No faxed copies will be accepted. **Please note:** The King Olav V Norwegian American Heritage Fund receives a large number of applications and only those that fulfill the above eligibility requirements will go to the scholarship committee for consideration. Applicants may expect to be notified approximately one to two months after the deadline for submission. Checks are made payable jointly to the applicant and his/her school and must be endorsed by both.

General Emmett Paige Scholarship

Armed Forces Communication and Electronics Association
Educational Foundation
4400 Fair Lakes Court
Fairfax, VA 22033-3899
V: 703-631-6149
T: 800-336-4583 ext. 6149

F: 703-631-4693
E: scholarship@afcea.org
W: www.@afcea.org
No. Awards: 10
Award Amount: $1,500
Funds Available: $15,000
Deadline: March 1

Features: The purpose of this scholarship is to promote excellence in scientific and engineering education. Applicants must be U.S. citizens enrolled in an accredited four-year college or university in the U.S. and working toward a bachelor's degree in electrical engineering, electronics, communications engineering, mathematics, computer technology, or physics. Minimum GPA is 3.4. Military affiliation is necessary. Application forms are available from school ROTC units or by contacting the Administrator of Scholarships and Awards at the above address in November. Students competing for other AFCEA scholarships are automatically considered for the General Emmett Paige Scholarship. High school seniors are ineligible, but veterans entering college as freshmen may apply.

Howard Rock Foundation Scholarship Program

Howard Rock Foundation
1577 C Street, Suite 304
Anchorage, AK 99501
V: 907-274-5400
No. Awards: varies
Award Amount: $2,500 for undergraduate students, $5,000 for graduate students
Features: Applicant must be enrolled in a member organization of Alaska Village Initiatives and enrolled in an accredited four-year undergraduate or graduate program. Must be a full-time student for entire scholarship period, majoring in a field of study that promotes economic development and quality of life in rural Alaska. Based on financial need. If a student begins studies later than fall of the year applied for, the scholarship will be awarded in part unless student enrolls full-time during summer term. Must have high school diploma or equivalent and maintain good academic standing. Alaska Village Initiatives Board of Directors and staff, HRF Board of Directors and staff, and immediate families are ineligible.

United Paperworkers International Union Scholarships

United Paperworker International Union
P.O. Box 1475
Nashville, TN 37202
V: 615-834-8590
F: 615-781-0428
No. Awards: 22
Award Amount: $1,000
Funds Available: $22,000
Deadline: March 15
Features: Applicant must be high school seniors who are children of active members in good standing. Winners are limited to two awards per region. Upon receipt of a completed and accepted preliminary application form, a supplemental packet of forms is sent to the applicant.

Vocational Scholarship Program

American Postal Workers Union
1300 L Street, NW
Washington, DC 20005
V: 202-842-4268
No. Awards: 5
Award Amount: $1,000 for three years or until completion of course
Deadline: March 1, postmarked
Features: Applicant must be a high school or corresponding secondary school senior during application and plan to attend an accredited college of choice. Student must be a son, daughter, stepchild, or legally adopted child of an active or deceased member of American Postal Workers Union. SAT/ACT scores must be submitted.

General John A. Wickham Scholarship

Armed Forces Communication and Electronics Association
Educational Foundation
4400 Fair Lakes Court
Fairfax, VA 22033-3899
V: 703-631-6149
T: 800-336-4583 ext. 6149
F: 703-631-4693
E: scholarship@afcea.org
W: www.@afcea.org
No. Awards: 10
Award Amount: $1,500

Funds Available: $15,000
Deadline: March 1
Features: The purpose of this scholarship is promote excellence in scientific and engineering education. Applicants must be U.S. citizens enrolled in an accredited four-year college or university in the U.S. and working toward a bachelor degree in electrical engineering, electronics, communications engineering, mathematics, computer technology, or physics. Minimum GPA is 3.4. Military affiliation is not necessary. Application forms are available from school ROTC units or by contacting the Administrator of Scholarships and Awards at the above address. Students competing for other AFCEA scholarships are automatically considered for the General Emmett Paige Scholarship. High school seniors are ineligible, but veterans entering college as freshmen may apply.

SCIENCES

AMS (American Meteorological Society) Minority Scholarship (See Minorities)

Bausch & Lomb Science Award

Bausch & Lomb Science Award Committee
University of Rochester, Director of Admissions
Rochester, NY 14627
V: 716-275-3221
F: 716-461-4595
W: http://www.rochester.edu
E: admit@macmail.cc.rochester.edu
No. Award: varies
Award Amount: $6,000 minimum, amount varies based on need.
Deadline: Jan. 15
Features: The purpose of this scholarship is to recognize outstanding achievement in the sciences by high school students. Applicants must be selected as Bausch & Lomb medal winners during the junior year of high school. Only students selected by the high school faculties are eligible.

Canadian Society of Exploration Geophysicists (See Teaching/ Education)

GEM PHD Science Fellowship (See Minorities)

Master's Fellowship (See Minorities)

Undergraduate Scholarship Program* (See Minorities/)

Undergraduate Scholarship Program (UGSP) for Individuals from Disadvantaged Backgrounds (See Minorities)

Woods Hole Oceanographic Institution Summer Student Fellowship

Woods Hole Oceanographic Institution
Clark 223, MS 31, Education Office
Woods Hole, MA 02543
V: 508-289-2709
F: 508-457-2188
W: www.whoi.edu
E: education@whoi.edu
No. Awards: 25-30
Award Amount: $3,900 for a 12 week program
Deadline: March 1
Features: Applicants must be in junior or senior year of undergraduate course work studying biology, chemistry, physics, or geology; with an interest in ocean sciences, oceanographic engineering, or marine policy. Application requests may be made in October.

Xerox Award

University of Rochester, Director of Admissions
Rochester, NY 14627
V: 716-275-3221
F: 716-461-4595
W: http://www.rochester.edu
E: admit@macmail.cc.rochester.edu
No. Award: varies
Award Amount: $6,000 minimum, amount varies based on need.
Deadline: Jan. 15
Features: The purpose of this scholarship is to recognize outstanding achievement in the sciences by high school students. Only students selected by their high schools are eligible.

TEACHING/ EDUCATION

Business & Professional Women's Foundation (See Women)

California Teachers Association Scholarship (See Organizations)

Canadian Society of Exploration Geophysicists (See Engineering)

510 5th Street, SW #905
Calgary, Alberta T2P 3S2 Canada

V: 403-262-0015
F: 403-262-7383
W: www.geo.ucalgary.ca/CSEG/
E: cseg@cadvision.com
No. Awards: approximately 25
Award Amount: $1,500 in Canadian funds
Deadline: end of July

Features: Nationality is unrestricted. Applicants must be undergraduate students with above average grades or graduate students at a Canadian college or university pursuing a career in exploration geophysics in industry, teaching, or research.

Golden Apple Scholars of Illinois

Golden Apple Foundation
8 S. Michigan Avenue, Suite 700
Chicago, IL 60603
V: 312-407-0006
F: 312-407-0344
W: www.goldenapple.org
No. Awards: 60
Award Amount: $5,000, renewable for four years
Deadline: July 31
Features: Applicant must be nominated by teacher, counselor, principal, or other non-family adult during student's junior year in high school. Must complete a written application and provide ACT scores and transcripts. Recipients must earn a bachelor's degree at one of 24 Illinois participating universities; must obtain Illinois teacher certification and teach for at least five years in an Illinois school designated in need by Perkins Title One listing and state test scores. Must participate in four summers of Summer Institute and meet conduct standards while in program. 150 finalists are chosen in fall; 60 recipients are selected in December.

Leopold Schepp Foundation

551 Fifth Avenue, Suite 3000
New York, NY 10176
V: 212-986-3078
No. Awards: varies
Award Amount: varies
Deadline: May or December of each year
Features: Applicant must be U.S. citizen or permanent resident, undergraduate (up to the age of 30) or graduate student (up to the age of 40), who wants to pursue

education in the United States or abroad. Based on financial need. Finalists may be asked to go to New York for an interview at their own expense.

Phi Delta Kappa, Inc.

Scholarship Grants for Prospective Teachers
P.O. Box 789
408 North Union Street
Bloomington, IN 47402
V: 814-335-1156
F: 812-339-0018
No. Grants: 43-47
Award Amount: (1) $2,000 award; others $1,000
Deadline: Jan. 31
Features: High school seniors in upper third of class who plan to pursue a teaching career; based on scholastic achievement, school and community activities, recommendations, and essay. Applications are only available at local chapters. Applicants may send self-addressed stamped envelope for listing of closest chapters.

WOMEN

AT&T ESP Scholarships (See Minorities)

Avon Products Foundation Scholarship Program for Women in Business

2012 Massachusetts Avenue, NW
Washington, DC 20036
V: 202-293-1200 ext. 169
No. Awards: approximately 60
Award Amount: $1,000

Features: Applicant must demonstrate critical need for financial assistance ($30,000 or less for a family of four). Must be 25 or older, U.S. citizen, officially accepted in to an accredited program or course of study at a U.S. institution (including institutions in Puerto Rico and the Virgin Islands), expecting graduations 12 to 24 months from date of grant, and planning precisely how to use desired training to upgrade skills for career advancement, career change, or re-entry to the job market. Must study a business-related field, such as management, business administration, marketing, sales, accounting, finance, and entrepreneurial education. Awards may be used for full-time and part-time studies. This scholarship does not cover doctoral studies, correspondence courses, or non-degree programs. Avon officers and their immediate families are ineligible.

AWIS Educational Awards

American Women in Science National Headquarters
1200 New York Avenue, NW, Suite 650
Washington, DC 20005
V: 202-326-8940
F: 202-326-8960
No. Awards: 12-15
Award Amount: $500-$1,000
Features: Must be female student who is enrolled in any life science, physical science, social science, or engineering program leading to a Ph.D. Non-U.S. citizens must be enrolled in a U.S. institution of higher education. Winners traditionally are at the dissertation level of their graduate work. Funds are available for study in the U.S. and abroad. Notification is in May.

Business & Professional Women's Foundation

Career Advancement Scholarship Program
2012 Massachusetts Avenue NW
Washington, DC 20036
V: 202-293-1200 ext. 169
No. Awards: 50
Award Amount: $500 to $1,000
Funds Available: $50,000

Features: Applicant must demonstrate critical need for financial assistance ($30,000 or less for a family of four). Must be 25 or older, U.S. citizen, officially accepted in to an accredited program or course of study at a U.S. institution (including institutions in Puerto Rico and the Virgin Islands), expecting graduation 12 to 24 months from date of grant, and planning precisely how to use desired training to upgrade skills for career advancement, career change, or re-entry to the job market. Must study teacher education certification, computer science, paralegal studies, engineer-

ing or science or for a professional degree (J.D., D.D.S., M.D.). This scholarship does not cover studies at the doctoral level (Ph.D.), correspondence courses or non-degree programs.

BPW Loan Fund for Women in Engineering Studies

Business & Professional Women's Foundation
2012 Massachusetts Avenue NW
Washington, DC 20036
V: 202-293-1200 ext. 169
No. Awards: Not specified
Annual Loan: Up to $5,000
Features: Applicant must demonstrate financial need. Must be U.S. citizen, have academic and/or work experience records that show career motivation and the ability to complete studies. Must have written notice of acceptance for enrollment at a school accredited by the Accreditation Board of Engineering and Technology. Studies may be full- or part-time, but applicant must carry at least six semester hours or equivalent each semester for which the loan is requested. Seven percent interest per annum begins immediately after graduation. Loans are repaid in twenty equal quarterly installments commencing 12 months after graduation.

Business & Professional Women's Foundation

BPW/Sears-Roebuck Foundation Loan Fund
2012 Massachusetts Avenue, NW
Washington, DC 20036
V: 202-293-1200 ext. 169
No. Awards: varies
Award Amount: up to $2,500
Features: Applicant must demonstrate financial need. Must be U.S. citizen, have academic and/or work experience records that show career motivation and the ability to complete studies. Must have written notice of acceptance for enrollment at a school accredited by the American Assembly of Collegiate Schools of Business. Studies may be full or part-time, but the applicant must carry at least six semester hour or the equivalent during each semester for which the loan is requested. BPW Foundation and Sears-Roebuck employees are ineligible.

J.E. Caldwell Centennial Scholarship

Daughters of the American Revolution
1776 D Street NW
Washington, DC 20006
V: 202-879-3292
No. Awards: varies
Award Amount: $2,000
Deadline: April 15
Features: Applicants must be U.S. citizens and attend an accredited college or university in the U.S. All applicants must obtain a letter of sponsorship from a local DAR chapter. Applicants must be outstanding students pursuing a course of graduate study in the subject of historic preservation. This application is processed without regard to race, religion, sex, or national origin. The fund has been made possible through the J.E. Caldwell Company, official jewelers of the NSDAR, in honor of the DAR Centennial. Send SASE for application. Only completed applications submitted in one package will be considered. No records are returned. Notification is in June.

Daughters of the Cincinnati Scholarship Program

Daughters of the Cincinnati
122 East 58th Street
New York, NY 10022
V: 212-319-6915
No. Awards: 10-12 new awards each year, 38-42 annual awards altogether
Award Amount: varies
Funds Available: varies
Deadline: March 15
Features: Applicant must be daughter of a career officer commissioned in the Regular Army, Air Force, Navy, Coast Guard, or Marine Corps (active, retired, or deceased), and a high school senior. Scholarships are awarded based on merit and need for up to four years. The student must plan to attend an accredited institution of higher education.

Daughters of Penelope National Scholarship Award

Daughters of Penelope National Headquarters
1909 Q Street, NW, Suite 500
Washington, DC 20009
No. Awards: varies
Award Amount: approximately $1,500

Funds Available: varies
Deadline: June 20, postmarked
Features: Applicant must be high school graduate, undergraduate, or college graduate female. Applicants must be accepted or enrolled at a college, university or accredited technical school. Student must have a member of the immediate family or legal guardian (court appointed) in the Daughters of Penelope or the Order of Ahepa, in good standing for a minimum of two years, or be a member in good standing for two years of the Daughters of Penelope or the Maids of Athena. (Immediate family means father, mother, or grandparent.) College graduates must be accepted or be currently enrolled in M.S., M.B.A., Ph.D., D.D.S., M.D., or other university post-graduate degree program. College students must also be enrolled for a minimum of 9 units per academic year. Former recipients of the DOP National Scholarship Program are ineligible.

Executive Women International Scholarship Program

Executive Women International
515 South 700 East, Suite 2E
Salt Lake City, UT 84102
V: 801-355-2800
F: 801-355-2852
No. Awards: 130
Award Amount: up to $10,000
Deadline: March 1

Features: Applicants must enter the contest of the local chapter and be available for interview. Applicants must be high school juniors planning to enroll at a four-year institution. Students must be planning careers in any business or professional field of study that requires a four-year college degree. Applicants must reside within the boundaries of a participating chapter. There are 34 chapters in America. U.S. citizenship is not required. Include self-addressed, stamped envelope for application forms.

Gloria Fecht Memorial Scholarship Fund

402 W. Arrow Highway, Suite 10
San Dimas, CA 91773
V: 909-592-1281
F: 909-592-7542
W: www.womensgolf.org
No. Awards: 20-30
Award Amount: $1,000 - $3,000
Funds Available: varies
Deadline: March 1
Features: Applicants must be female residents of Southern California, prove financial need, meet entrance requirements and plan to enroll in an accredited four-year university, and have an active interest in golf. Minimum 3.0 GPA. Preference given to those who play golf regularly, although no skill level is required.

Kappa Kappa Gamma Foundation Scholarship/Fellowship/Grants

Kappa Kappa Gamma Foundation
P.O. Box 38
Columbus, OH 43216-0038
F: 614-228-7809
No. Awards: varies
Award Amount: varies
Deadline: Feb. 1
Features: Must be a member of Kappa Kappa Gamma. Send self-addressed, stamped envelope for more information and an application. Please note chapter membership on your request. Graduate students need to state whether studying full-time or part-time.

LAFRA Scholarship

Ladies Auxiliary of the Fleet Reserve Association
c/o Fleet Reserve Association
125 N. West Street
Alexandria, VA 22314
V: 703-683-1400
F: 703-549-6610
W: www.fra.orgfra
E: news-fra@fra.org
No. Awards: Approximately 5
Award Amount: $500-$2,500
Deadline: April 5
Features: Applicant must be daughter or granddaughter of Naval, Marine Corps, active Fleet Reserve, Fleet Marine Corps Reserve, Coast Guard Reserve, or Coast Guard personnel, retired with pay or deceased. Send self-addressed, stamped envelope. Faxed transcripts are not accepted, but faxed applications are okay.

MANA, a National Latina Organization

1725 K Street NW #501
Washington, DC 20006
V: 202-833-0060 Ext.14 (Ms. Liliana C. Lopez)
F: 202-496-0588
No. Awards: Varies
Award Amount: Varies
Deadline: April 1
Features: Applicants must be female MANA members of Hispanic heritage and enrolled full time in an accredited college or university. Criteria given special consideration are academic achievement, financial need, commitment and contributions to Hispanic issues and Hispanic women's progress. Send self-addressed, stamped envelope for application.

Margaret McNamara Memorial Fund

World Bank
1818 H Street, NW Rm. G-1000
Washington, DC 20433
V: 202-473-8751
No. Awards: 5
Award Amount: $6,000 (estimated)
Funds Available: $30,000 (estimated)

Features: Applicant must be a female at least 25 years old by December 31 and from a selected developing country, but living in the U.S. and studying at an accredited U.S. institution when she applies and during the period the grant covers. Must have a record of service to women and/or children in the applicant's home country and must plan to return to that country roughly two years after date of award. Based on financial need. Students who meet all criteria should write to the above address, listing name, address, country, and institution where they are enrolled. Permanent U.S. residents and relatives or spouses of staff members of any institution in the World Bank group are ineligible.

Nancy Lorraine Jensen Memorial Scholarship Fund (See Organizations)

New York Life Foundation Scholarship for Women in Health Professions

2012 Massachusetts Avenue, NW
Washington, D.C. 20036
V: 202-293-1200, Ext. 169
No. Awards: varies
Award Amount: $500-$1,000
Funds Available: $50,000

Features: Applicants must demonstrate financial need for assistance (defined to be $30,000 or less for a family of four). Applicants must be undergraduates in one of the healthcare fields and must be females over age 24, officially accepted into an accredited course of study at a U.S. institution (including Puerto Rico and the Virgin Islands), and expecting to graduate within 12 to 24 months from date of grant. Scholarships are awarded for full-time or part-time study. The purpose of this award is to assist women seeking the education necessary for entry or re-entry into the work force or advancement within a career in the healthcare field. This scholarship does not cover graduate or doctorate studies, correspondence courses, or non-degree programs. New York Life Insurance Company officers and their immediate family members are ineligible. All awards are granted by BPW Foundation's Financial Aid Committee.

Women's Western Golf Foundation Scholarship

Women's Western Golf Foundation
393 Ramsay Road
Deerfield, IL 60015
V: 847-945-0451
No. Awards: 20
Award Amount: $2,000, renewable for four years
Funds Available: up to $40,000
Deadline: April 5
Features: Academic merit, financial need,

excellence of character, and interest or involvement in the sport of golf. Skill in golf is not required. Must be high school senior female intending to graduate in the year of application and U.S. citizen. Must meet college entrance requirements and plan to enroll in an accredited college or university. Complete preliminary application and the Federal Student Aid Report between January 1 and March 1. Student must have submitted the Free Application for Federal Student Aid (FAFSA). Minimum GPA 3.0. *Deadline to request preliminary applications is March 1.* Final application will be sent later. Must send a self-addressed, stamped envelope for application and information.

Wyeth-Ayerst Scholarship for Women in Graduate Medical Program

2012 Massachusetts Avenue, NW
Washington, DC 20036
V: 202-293-1200 ext. 169
No. Awards: 25
Award Amount: $2,000
Funds Available: $50,000
Features: Applicant must demonstrate financial need for financial assistance (defined to be $30,000 or less for a family of four). Must be female over age 24, officially accepted into an accredited course of study at a U.S. institution (including Puerto Rico and the Virgin Islands), expecting to graduate within 12 to 24 months from date of grant, and have a clear plan for applying training towards career advancement or change, or to enter or re-enter the job market. Must be studying in emerging health field of biomedical research, medical technology, pharmaceutical marketing, public health, or public health policy. Only open to full-time graduate students.

Glossary of Financial Aid Terms

The college money system has become so complex it needs its own glossary. We very much appreciate the kindness of the National Association of Student Financial Aid Administrators in allowing us to use theirs.

Acronyms

ADC	Aid to Dependent Children
AFDC	Aid to Families with Dependent Children
AGI	Adjusted Gross Income
AY	Academic Year
BA	Bachelor's Degree
BIA	Bureau of Indian Affairs
COA	Cost of Attendance
CSS	College Scholarship Service
CPS	Central Processing System
DHHS	Department of Health and Human Services
ED	U.S. Department of Education
EIC	Earned Income Credit
EDE	Electronic Data Exchange
EFA	Estimated Financial Assistance
EFC	Expected Family Contribution (also FC, Family Contribution)
EFN	Exceptional Financial Need Scholarships (health professions)
FADHPS	Financial Assistance for Disadvantaged Health Professions Students
FAFSA	Free Application for Federal Student Aid
FAT	Financial Aid Transcript
FDLP	Federal Direct Loan Programs
FFELP	Federal Family Education Loan Programs
FM	Federal Methodology
FNAS	Federal Need Analysis System
FPLUS	Federal PLUS (Parent) Loan
FSEOG	Federal Supplemental Educational Opportunity Grant
FWS	Federal Work-Study
GPA	Grade Point Average
GSL	Guaranteed Student Loan
HEAL	Health Education Assistance Loan
HHS	Department of Health and Human Services (also abbreviated DHHS)
HPSL	Health Professions Student Loan

INS	Immigration and Naturalization Service
IPA	Income Protection Allowance
IRS	Internal Revenue Service
ISIR	Institutional Student Information Record
LDS	Loans for Disadvantaged Students (health professions)
MDE	Multiple Data Entry
NDSL	National Defense/Direct Student Loan (now known as Federal Perkins Loan)
NHSC	National Health Service Corps
NSLDS	National Student Loan Data System
NEISP	National Early Intervention Scholarship and Partnership Program
NSSP	National Science Scholars Program
NSL	Nursing Student Loan
OSFAP	Office of Student Financial Assistance Programs, U.S. Department of Education
PC	Parental Contribution
PCL	Primary Care Loan Program (health professions)
SAR	Student Aid Report
SAP	Satisfactory Academic Progress
SC	Student Contribution
SDS	Scholarships for Disadvantaged Students
SSIG	State Student Incentive Grant
VA	Veterans Affairs, Department of

Definitions

Academic Credit: The unit of measurement an institution gives to a student when he/she fulfills course or subject requirement(s) as determined by the institution.

Academic Year: This is a measure of the academic work to be accomplished by a student. The school defines its own academic year, but federal regulations set minimum standards for the purpose of determining student financial aid awards. For instance, the academic year at a term school must be a least 30 weeks of instructional time in which a full-time undergraduate student is expected to complete at least 24 semester or trimester hours or 36 quarter hours or 900 clock hours.

Acceptance Form: The written acknowledgment by the student of receipt of an award letter. The form usually provides for acceptance of offered aid, possible declination of all or part of the package, and some means of requesting an appeal, if that is desired, to modify the award. Frequently, acceptance letters and award letters are combined into a single document.

Adjusted Gross Income (AGI): All taxable income as reported on a U.S. income tax return.

Amnesty Applicant: An individual who entered the U.S. without proper documentation, or illegally, who was eligible to apply for temporary (and eventually, permanent) resident status under provisions of the Immigration Reform and Control Act of 1986.

Assets: Cash on hand in checking and savings accounts; trusts, stocks, bonds, other securities; real estate (excluding home), income-producing property, business equipment, and business inventory. Considered in determining expected family contribution (EFC) under the regular need analysis formula.

Assistantship: A type of student employment; usually refers to teaching assistant positions which are available to students.

Award Letter: A means of notifying successful financial aid applicants of the assistance being offered. The award letter usually provides information on the types and amounts of aid offered, as well as specific program information, student responsibilities, and the conditions which govern the award. Generally provides students with the opportunity to accept or decline the aid offered.

Award Year: An award year begins on July 1 of one year and extends to June 30 of the next year. Funding for Federal Pell grants and campus-based programs is provided on the basis of the award year. For example, a student is paid out of funds designated for a particular award year, such as the 1997-1998 award year.

Bachelor's Degree (BA): The degree given for successful completion of the undergraduate curriculum at a four-year college or a university. Also called baccalaureate degree.

Base Year: For need analysis purposes, the base year is the calendar year preceding the award year. For instance, 1996 is the base year used for the 1997-1998 award year. The Free Application for Federal Student Aid (FAFSA) uses family income from the base year because it is more accurate and easier to verify than projected year income.

Budget: The estimated cost of attendance for a student at an institution; usually includes tuition, fees, books, supplies, room, board, personal expenses, and transportation. Other expenses may be included. (See *Cost of Attendance*).

Bureau of Indian Affairs (BIA) Grants: A grant program for enrolled members of a tribe (Indian, Eskimo, or Aleut) pursuing an undergraduate or graduate degree at an accredited postsecondary institution. In order to be eligible for a BIA grant, students must show financial need as determined by the institution they are attending.

Business Assets: Property that is used in the operation of a trade or business, including real estate, inventories, buildings, machinery and other equipment, patents, franchise rights, and copyrights. Considered in determining a family's expected contribution (EFC) under the regular need analysis formula.

Byrd Scholarship: A federally sponsored, merit-based scholarship for academically outstanding high school students.

Campus-based Programs: The term commonly applied to those U.S. Department of Education federal student aid programs administered by institutions of postsecondary education. Includes: Federal Perkins Loan, Federal Supplemental Educational Opportunity Grant (FSEOG), and Federal Work-Study (FWS).

Cancellation of Loan: The condition that exists when a Federal Perkins Loan (or NDSL) borrower has fulfilled requirements to permit cancellation of, or "writing off," a designated portion of the principal and interest.

Central Processing System (CPS): The computer system to which the student's need analysis data is electronically transmitted by the FAFSA processor or MDE. The central processing system performs database matches and calculates the official Expected Family Contribution (EFC) and sends out the Student Aid Report (SAR) to the student and an Institutional Student Information Record (ISIR) to the school.

Citizen/Eligible Non-Citizen: A person who owes allegiance to the United States. Most state and federal financial aid programs are considered domestic assistance programs and are available only to U.S. citizens, U.S. nationals (including natives of American Somoa or Swain's Island), or permanent residents of the U.S., or those who are in this country for other than temporary purposes. Citizens of the Marshall Islands, the Federated States of Micronesia, and the Republic of Palau are eligible for Federal Pell grant, FSEOG, and FWS only.

Collection Agency: A business organization that accepts, from schools and lenders, loan accounts that have become delinquent or are in default, and attempts to collect on those accounts. A fee is charged for the service.

Commercial Lender: A commercial bank, savings and loan association, credit union, stock savings bank, trust company, or mutual savings bank. Can act as a lender for the Federal Family Education Loan Program (FFELP).

Community Service: The National and Community Service Trust Act of 1993 established the Corporation for National Service, which offers educational opportunities through service to American communities. The three programs assist persons who serve communities before, during, or after postsecondary education by rewarding them with educational benefits. Awards may be used to pay for past, present, or future educational expenses, including repayment of portions of their federal education loans.

Commuter Student: A student who does not live on-campus, or in institutionally owned or operated housing; typically, "commuter" refers to a student living at home with his or her parents, but can also mean any student who lives off-campus.

Cost of Attendance: A student's cost of attendance includes tuition and fees, room and board expenses while attending school, and allowances for books and supplies, transportation, loan fees (if applicable), dependent care costs, costs related to a disability, and other miscellaneous expenses. In addition, reasonable costs for a study-abroad program and costs associated with a student's employment as part of a cooperative education program may be included. The cost of attendance is estimated by the school, within guidelines established by federal regulations. The cost of attendance is compared to a student's Expected Family Contribution (EFC) to determine the student's need for aid.

Defaulted (Federal Perkins Loan): A loan for which the borrower failed to make an installment payment when due and such failure persisted (not cured either by payment or other appropriate arrangements). The Secretary of Education considers a loan discharged in bankruptcy not to be in default.

Default (Federal Stafford, Direct Loan, Federal PLUS, or Direct PLUS Loan): The failure of a borrower to make an installment payment when due, or to meet other terms of the promissory note under circumstances where the Secretary of Education or the pertinent guarantee agency finds it reasonable to conclude that the borrower no longer intends to honor the obligation to repay.

Deferment of Loan: A condition during which payments of principal are not required, and, for Federal Perkins and subsidized Federal Stafford and Direct Subsidized Loans, interest does not accrue. The repayment period is extended by the length of the deferment period.

Departmental Scholarship: An award of gift assistance that is specifically designated for a recipient in a particular academic department within the institution.

Dependent Student: A student who does not qualify as an independent student and whose parental income and asset information is used in calculating expected family contribution (see *Independent Student*).

Direct Loan Program (Direct Loans): The collective name for the Direct Subsidized, Direct Unsubsidized, and Direct PLUS Loan programs. Also referred to as William D. Ford Federal Direct Loan Program.

Direct PLUS Loan Program (Parent Loan): Long-term loans made available to parents of dependent students. The government provides the funding. Interest rates are linked to 52-week Treasury bill rates, but may not exceed 9%. May be used to replace EFC.

Direct Subsidized and Direct Unsubsidized Loan Program: Long term, low interest loans administered by the Department of Education and institutions. The government is the source of funding. Variable interest rate not to exceed 8.25 percent. Direct Unsubsidized Loans can be used to replace EFC.

Disbursement: The process by which financial aid funds are made available to students for use in meeting educational and related living expenses. Funds may be disbursed directly to the student or applied to the student's account.

Disclosure Statement: Statement explaining specific terms and conditions of student loans, such as interest rate, loan fees charged, gross amount borrowed, and so on. Disclosure statements must accompany each loan disbursement.

Educational Benefits: Funds, primarily federal, awarded to certain categories of students (veterans, children of deceased veterans or other deceased wage earners, and students with physical disabilities) to help finance their postsecondary education regardless of their ability to demonstrate need in the traditional sense.

Educational Expenses: See *Budget* and *Cost of Attendance*.

Electronic Data Exchange: The Department of Education's service for sending and receiving application information electronically to the CPS.

Eligible Institution: An institution of higher education, or a vocational school, or a postsecondary vocational institution, or a proprietary institution of higher education which meets all criteria for participation in the federal student aid programs.

Eligible Program: A course of study that requires a certain minimum number of hours of instruction and that leads to a degree or certificate at a school participating in one or more of the federal student financial aid programs described in this handbook. Generally, to get student aid, a student must be enrolled in an eligible program.

Employment Allowance: An allowance to meet expenses related to employment when both parents (or a married independent student and spouse) are employed or when one parent (or independent student) qualifies as a surviving spouse or as head of a household. Used in need analysis formula for parents and student, if eligible.

Enrolled: The completion of registration requirements (other than the payment of tuition and fees) at the institution the student is or will be attending; a correspondence school student must be accepted for admission and complete and submit one lesson to be considered enrolled.

Enrollment Status: At those institutions using semesters, trimesters, quarters, or other academic terms and measuring progress by credit hours, enrollment status equals a student's credit hour workload categorized as either full-time, three-quarter-time, half-time, or less-than-half-time.

Entitlement Program: Program which is funded sufficiently to ensure that all eligible applicants are guaranteed to receive maximum authorized awards. As long as the student applicant meets all the eligibility requirements and is enrolled in an eligible program at an eligible institution, he or she will receive the award for which eligibility has been established.

Estimated Financial Assistance: The amount of student financial aid a student may expect from federal, state, school, or other resources, including grants, loans, or need-based work programs.

Exceptional Financial Need Scholarship (EFN): Scholarship program for students studying to earn a doctorate in allopathic or osteopathic medicine or dentistry.

Exceptional Need: An eligibility criterion in the FSEOG and Federal Perkins Loan (NDSL) Programs. Exceptional need for FSEOG is defined in statute as the lowest expected family contributions at an institution. The law does not define the term for the Federal Perkins Loan Program. The definition of exceptional need varies from school to school.

Expected Family Contribution (EFC): The amount a student and his or her family are expected to contribute toward the student's cost of attendance as calculated by a congressionally-mandated formula known as Federal Methodology.

Federal Family Education Loan Programs (FFELP): The collective name for the Federal Stafford (subsidized and unsubsidized) and Federal PLUS Loan programs. Funds are provided by private lenders and guaranteed by the federal government.

Federal Methodology: Formula, defined in statute, and used to determine an expected family contribution (EFC) for Federal Pell grants, campus-based programs, FFEL programs, and direct loan programs.

Federal Pell Grant: A grant program for undergraduate students who have not yet completed a first baccalaureate or bachelor's degree. For many students, Federal Pell grants provide a foundation of financial aid to which other aid may be added.

Federal Perkins Loans: Formerly known as the National Direct Student Loan Program, or NDSL. One of the campus-based programs; a long term, low interest (5%) loan program for both undergraduate and graduate students with exceptional financial need. The school is the lender and the loan is made with government funds.

Federal PLUS Loans: Long-term loans made available to parents with good credit history of dependent students. Interest rates are linked to 52-week Treasury bill rates, but may not exceed 9%. May be used to replace EFC.

Federal Stafford Loan Program (subsidized and unsubsidized): Long term, low interest loans administered by the Department of Education through private lenders and guarantee agencies. Formerly known as Guaranteed Student Loans (GSLs). Variable interest rate, not to exceed 8.25%. Unsubsidized Federal Stafford Loans may be used to replace EFC.

Federal Supplemental Educational Opportunity Grant (FSEOG): One of the campus-based programs; grants to undergraduate students with exceptional financial need who have not completed their first baccalaureate degree and who are financially in need of this grant to enable them to pursue their education. Priority for FSEOG awards must be given to Federal Pell grant recipients with the lowest EFCs.

Federal Work-Study Program (FWS): One of the campus-based programs; a part-time employment program which provides jobs for undergraduate and graduate students who are in need of such earnings to meet a portion of their educational expenses. The program encourages community service work related to the student's course of study.

Fellowship: A grant of money for post-graduate study which may require teaching or research.

Financial Aid Administrator (FAA): An individual who is responsible for preparing and communicating information pertaining to student loans, grants or scholarships, and employment programs, and for advising, awarding, reporting, counseling, and supervising office functions related to student financial aid. He or she is accountable to the various publics which are involved; is a manager or administrator who interprets and implements federal, state, and institutional policies and regulations; and is capable of analyzing student and employee needs and making changes where necessary.

Financial Aid Award: An offer of financial or in-kind assistance to a student attending a postsecondary educational institution. This award may be in the form of one or more of the following types of financial aid: a non-repayable grant, and/or scholarship, and/or student employment, and/or repayable loan.

Financial Aid Package: A financial aid award to a student comprised of a combination of forms of financial aid (loans, grants and/or scholarships, employment).

Financial Aid Transcript: A form used by postsecondary institutions to collect data about any financial aid awards that a student received at other educational institutions.

Financial Assistance for Disadvantaged Health Professions Students (FADHPS): Scholarship program for allopathic and osteopathic medical students and dental students from disadvantaged backgrounds who demonstrate exceptional need for financial assistance.

Financial Need: The difference between the institution's cost of attendance and the family's ability to pay (that is, expected family contribution). May be expressed in the formula: COA - EFC = Need.

Forbearance: Permitting the temporary cessation of repayments of loans, allowing an extension of time for making loan payments, or accepting smaller loan payments than were previously scheduled.

Foreign Student: A student belonging to or owing allegiance to another country. Foreign students are not eligible for the basic federal programs, although there are categories of eligible non-citizens who owe permanent allegiance to the United States and are eligible for student aid.

Free Application for Federal Student Aid (FAFSA): The original input document (aid application) of the Department of Education's need analysis system. The application filled out and filed by a student that collects household and financial information used by the federal government to calculate the Expected Family Contribution (EFC).

FAFSA Express: Electronic method for students to apply directly to the Department of Education for Title IV aid using a PC and a modem.

Full-Time Student: Generally, one who is taking a minimum of 12 semester or quarter hours per academic term in institutions with standard academic terms, or 24 clock hours per week in institutions which measure progress in terms of clock hours.

G.I. Bill Benefits: Special assistance provided by the federal government to eligible veterans for the purpose of financing education or training programs.

Gift Aid: That form of financial aid which does not require repayment or require that work be performed.

Grace Period: The period of time that begins when a loan recipient ceases to be at least half-time and ends when the repayment period starts. Loan principal need not be paid and, generally, interest does not accrue during this period.

Graduate or Professional Student: A student enrolled in an academic program of study above the baccalaureate level at an institution of higher education.

Grant: A type of financial aid that does not have to be repaid; usually awarded on the basis of need, possibly combined with some skills or characteristics the student possesses.

Guaranteed Student Loan (GSL) Programs: Previous collective name used for the Federal Family Education Loan Programs.

Guaranty Agency: A state agency or private, non-profit institution or organization which administers a student loan insurance program.

Health Education Assistance Loan (HEAL) Program: A federal loan program offered through the Department of Health and Human Services, designed to assist students in certain health profession disciplines.

Health Professions Student Loan (HPSL) Program: A long term, low interest loan program designed to assist students in specific health professions disciplines.

Income Protection Allowance: An allowance against income for the basic costs of maintaining family members in the home. The allowance is based upon consumption and other cost estimates of the Bureau of Labor Statistics for a family at the low standard of living.

Independent Student: A student who has attained age 24, or who has not attained age 24 but (a) is an orphan; (b) is a ward of the court; (c) is a veteran; (d) is married or is a graduate or professional student; (e) has legal dependents other than a spouse; or (f) presents documentation of other unusual circumstances demonstrating independence to the student financial aid administrator.

Institutional Student Information Record (ISIR): A federal output record that contains the student's EFC as calculated by the Central Processing System (CPS) and all the financial and other data submitted by the student on the FAFSA. The ISIR can be received electronically by schools that participate in the Electronic Data Exchange (EDE) system. (See *Student Aid Report*.)

Legal Dependent (of Applicant): A natural or adopted child, or a person for whom the applicant has been appointed legal guardian, and for whom the applicant provides more than half support. In addition, a person who lives with and receives at least half support from the applicant and will continue to receive that support during the award year. For purposes of determining dependency status, a spouse is not considered a legal dependent.

Legal Guardian: An individual appointed by a court to be a legal guardian of a person and who is specifically required by the court to use his/her own financial resources to support that person. For 1997-1998, the legal relationship must continue beyond June 30, 1998 for the legal guardian to be considered a parent for the purposes of completing the FAFSA.

Loan: An advance of funds which is evidenced by a promissory note requiring the recipient to repay the specified amount(s) under prescribed conditions.

Loans for Disadvantaged Students (LDS): A federal loan program designed to assist disadvantaged students enrolled in specific health professions disciplines.

Military Scholarships: Reserve Officer Training Corps (ROTC) scholarships available for the Army, Navy, and Air Force at many colleges and universities throughout the United States. These scholarships cover tuition and fees, books and supplies, and include a subsistence allowance.

Multiple Data Entry (MDE): The procedure which allows for the incorporation and transmission of FAFSA data elements so that applicants can apply for Federal Pell Grants and other financial assistance by completing one form. The need analysis service key enters the student's FAFSA data into a computer system and then transmits the data to the Central Processing System. Students receive their eligibility notification directly from the Central Processing System.

Multiple Data Entry (MDE) Servicer: An organization contracted by the Department of Education to provide the means for a student to apply for federal student aid; also known as the FAFSA processor.

National Direct Student Loan (NDSL): Former name of the Federal Perkins Loan Program.

National Health Service Corps (NHSC) Scholarships: Scholarship program for students who pursue full-time courses of study in certain health professions disciplines, and are willing to serve as primary care practitioners in underserved areas after completing their education.

National of the United States: A citizen of the United States or a non-citizen who owes permanent allegiance to the United States.

National Early Intervention Scholarship and Partnership (NEISP) Program: Grants provided to states to encourage states to provide financial assistance and support services to low-income and disadvantaged students interested in pursuing higher education.

National Student Loan Data System (NSLDS): A national database of Title IV loan data and selected Title IV grant data.

National Science Scholars Program (NSSP): Science scholarship available to undergraduate students.

Need Analysis: A system used to estimate a student applicant's need for financial assistance to help meet his/her educational expenses. Need analysis consists of two primary components: (a) determination of an estimate of the applicant's and/or family's ability to contribute to educational expenses; and (b) determination of an accurate estimate of the educational expenses themselves.

Nursing Student Loans (NSL): Loans available to nursing students attending approved nursing schools offering a diploma, associate degree, baccalaureate, or graduate degree in nursing.

Overpayment: Any amount paid to a student which is in excess of the amount he/she was entitled or eligible to receive.

Packaging: The process of combining various types of student aid (grants, loans, scholarship, and employment) to attempt to meet a student's need.

Parent: The student's biological mother or father, legal guardian, or adoptive parent.

Parent Loans: See *Federal PLUS Loans* or *Direct PLUS Loan Program.*

Parents' Contribution: A quantitative estimate of the parents' ability to contribute to postsecondary educational expenses.

Part-Time Student: One who attends an institution on less than a full-time basis as defined by the institution.

Paul Douglas Teacher Scholarship: A scholarship program administered by the states to enable and encourage outstanding high school graduates who demonstrate an interest in teaching to pursue teaching careers at the elementary and secondary levels.

Postsecondary School: Technically, this term refers to any educational institution providing educational services beyond the level of high school. In daily usage, the term is often used to refer to non-higher educational institutions such as propri-

etary schools, trade and technical schools, and a range of non-traditional educational facilities as well as colleges and universities.

Presidential Access Scholarships: Scholarship available to undergraduate students who are eligible for Federal Pell grants and who demonstrate academic achievement.

Primary Care Loan: Loans to assist allopathic medical and osteopathic medical students who intend to engage in primary care residency and practice.

Privacy Acts: Those collective statutes that serve to protect an individual from the release of specified data without the individual's prior written consent.

Professional Student: A student in a professional school, such as a law school student, medical school student. See *Graduate Student.*

Promissory Note: The legal document that binds a borrower to the repayment obligations and other terms and conditions which govern a loan program.

Reauthorization: A Congressional review process intended to refine authorized federal programs to ensure they meet the needs of the populations they are intended to serve.

Refund: The amount due a student who withdraws or fails to pursue his/her course of study when funds have been paid to the institution. When an institution determines that a student is due a refund, if that student has received financial aid funds, a portion of the refund must be allocated to the program(s) from which the student received aid.

Regular Student: A person who is enrolled or accepted for enrollment at an institution of higher education for the purpose of obtaining a degree or certificate.

Renewal FAFSA: The version of the FAFSA that students may use if they applied for federal financial aid the previous award year. If a student is among those allowed to complete a Renewal FAFSA, it will be sent directly to him or her by the FAFSA processor or the school.

Repayment Schedule: A plan, which should be attached to the promissory note at the time a borrower ceases at least half-time study, which sets forth the principal and interest due on each installment and the number of payments required to pay the loan in full. Additionally, it should include the interest rate, the due date of the first payment, and the frequency of payments.

Resident Student: A student who does not live at home (with parents or guardian) during the academic year. An off-campus resident student is one who does not live in the institutionally provided housing. An on-campus resident student is one who lives in housing facilities owned and/or maintained by the institution.

Resources: Resources include, but are not limited to, any: (a) funds the student is entitled to receive from a Federal Pell grant, regardless of whether the student applies for it; (b) Stafford (GSL) Loans; (c) waiver of tuition and fees; (d) grants, including FSEOG and ROTC subsistence allowances; (e) scholarships, including athletic and ROTC scholarships; (f) fellowships or assistantships; (g) insurance programs for the student's education; (h) long term loans, including Federal Perkins and Direct Loans, made by the institution; (i) earnings from need-based employment; (j) veterans benefits; and (k) any portion of other long term loans, including Federal PLUS or Direct Loans, state-sponsored, or private loans, not used as a substitute for the EFC.

Satisfactory Academic Progress: The progress required of a financial aid recipient in acceptable studies or other activities to fulfill a specified educational objective.

Scholarship: A form of financial assistance which does not require repayment or employment and is usually made to students who demonstrate or show potential for distinction, usually in academic performance, at the institution.

Scholarships for Disadvantaged Students (SDS): A federal scholarship program designed to assist disadvantaged students enrolled in certain health profession disciplines.

School Year: See *Academic Year*.

Self-Help Assistance: Funds provided through the work and effort of the student, including savings from past earnings, income from present earnings, or a loan to be repaid from future earnings.

Self-Help Expectation: The assumption that a student has an obligation to help pay for a portion of his/her education. See *Student Contribution*.

Simplified Needs Test: An alternate method of calculating the expected family contribution for families with adjusted gross incomes of less than $50,000, who have filed, or are eligible to file, an IRS Form 1040A, 1040EZ, or 1040TEL, or are not required to file an income tax return. Excludes all assets from consideration.

Statement of Educational Purpose: Statement included on the FAFSA signed by the student financial aid recipient indicating his or her agreement to use all financial aid funds awarded for educational or educationally related purposes only.

State Student Incentive Grant (SSIG): State scholarship/grant assistance for postsecondary students with substantial financial need.

Student Aid Report (SAR): A federal output document sent to a student by the CPS. The SAR contains financial and other information reported by the student on the Free Application for Federal Student Aid (FAFSA). That information is entered into the processing system, and the SAR is produced. The student's eligibility for aid is indicated by the EFC, which is printed on the front of the SAR. (Also see *Institutional Student Information Record*.)

Student Contribution: A quantitative estimate of the student's ability to contribute to postsecondary expenses.

Student Budget: See *Cost of Attendance*.

Student Financial Aid: Funds awarded to a student to help meet postsecondary educational expenses. These funds are generally awarded on the basis of financial need and include scholarships, grants, loans, and employment.

Taxable Income: Income earned from wages, salaries, and tips, as well as interest income, dividend income, business or farm profits, and rental or property income.

Temporarily Totally Disabled: With regard to a student loan borrower, this means an injury or illness which prevents an individual from attending an eligible institution or to be gainfully employed for an extended period of time. With regard to the borrower's spouse or dependent, this means an injury or illness, established by an affidavit of a qualified physician, that requires the borrower to provide care such as continuous nursing (or other similar service) that prevents the borrower from obtaining gainful employment.

Three-Quarter-Time Student: A student who is carrying at least a three-quarter time academic workload as determined by the institution at which the student is enrolled, and which amounts to at least three-quarters of the workload of a full-time student.

Title IV Programs: Those federal student aid programs authorized under Title IV of the Higher Education Act of 1965, as amended. Includes, among others, the Federal Pell grant, Federal Supplemental Educational Opportunity Grant, Federal Work Study, Federal Perkins Loan, Federal Stafford Loan, Federal PLUS, Direct Loan, Direct PLUS, and SSIG.

Totally and Permanently Disabled: Unable to engage in any substantial gainful activity because of a medically determinable impairment that is expected to continue for a long and indefinite period of time or will result in death.

Truth-in-Lending Statement: The document provided to loan recipients that delineates the interest rate and other information relative to the loan the student has received. The use of the statement is required by the Consumer Credit Act.

Undergraduate Student: A student who has not achieved the educational level of a baccalaureate or first professional degree.

Unmet Need: The difference between a student's total cost attendance at a specific institution and the student's total available resources, including financial aid.

Untaxed Income: All income received that is not reported to the Internal Revenue Service or is reported but excluded from taxation. Such income would include but not be limited to any untaxed portion of Social Security benefits, Earned Income Credit, welfare payments, untaxed capital gains, interest on tax-free bonds, dividend exclusion, and military and other subsistence and quarters allowances.

Verification: A procedure in which a school checks the information a student reported on the FAFSA, usually by requesting a copy of signed tax returns filed by the student and, if applicable, the student's parent(s) and spouse. Schools must verify students selected for verification by the federal central processing system, following procedures established by federal regulations. Many schools also select students for verification in addition to those selected by the central processing system.

Veteran: A person who has served on active duty in the Army, Navy, Air Force, Marines. or Coast Guard, or was a cadet or midshipmen at one of the service academies, and who was discharged other than dishonorably. Veterans are considered to be independent. There is no minimum length of service requirement.

Veterans Educational Benefits: Assistance programs for veterans and service persons for education or training.

Vocational Rehabilitation: Programs administered by state departments of vocational rehabilitation services to assist individuals who have a physical or mental disability which is a substantial handicap to employment.

Ward of the Court: A person who is under the care of the court.

*F*ree *A*pplication *for* *F*ederal *S*tudent *A*id
1998–99 School Year

WARNING: If you purposely give false or misleading information on this form, you may be fined $10,000, sent to prison, or both.

"You" and "your" on this form always mean the student who wants aid.

Form Approved
OMB No. 1840-0110
App. Exp.

U.S. Department of Education
Student Financial
Assistance Programs

Use dark ink. Make capital letters and numbers clear and legible.

`E X M 2 4`

Fill in ovals completely. Only one oval per question.

Correct ●

Incorrect marks will be ignored.

Incorrect ⊗ ✓

Section A: You (the student)

1–3. Your name

1. Last name

2. First name

3. M.I.

Your title (optional)   Mr. ○ 1   Miss, Mrs., or Ms. ○ 2

4–7. Your permanent mailing address
(All mail will be sent to this address. See Instructions, page 2 for state/country abbreviations.)

4. Number and street (Include apt. no.)

5. City   **6.** State   **7.** ZIP code

8. Your social security number (SSN) *(Don't leave blank. See Instructions, page 2.)*

9. Your date of birth
Month   Day   Year   `1 9`

10. Your permanent home telephone number
Area code

11. Your state of legal residence
State

12. Month and year you became a legal resident of the state in question 11 *(See Instructions, page 2.)*
Month   Year   `1 9`

13. Your driver's license number. *(If you don't have a license, write in "None.")*
License number

14. State that issued your driver's license.
State

15–16. Are you a U.S. citizen? *(See Instructions, pages 2–3.)*
Yes, I am a U.S. citizen. ○ 1
No, but I am an eligible noncitizen. ○ 2
`A`
No, neither of the above. ○ 3

17. As of today, are you married? *(Fill in only one oval.)*
I am not married. (I am single, widowed, or divorced.) ○ 1
I am married. ○ 2
I am separated from my spouse. ○ 3

18. Date you were married, separated, divorced, or widowed. If divorced, use date of divorce or separation, whichever is earlier.
(If never married, leave blank.)   Month   Year   `1 9`

19. Will you have received a high school diploma or earned a GED before the first date of your enrollment in college?
Yes ○ 1
No ○ 2

20. Will you have your first bachelor's degree before July 1, 1998?
Yes ○ 1
No ○ 2

21. Highest educational level your father completed.
elementary school (K–8) ○ 1
high school (9–12) ○ 2
college or beyond ○ 3
unknown ○ 4

22. Highest educational level your mother completed.
elementary school (K–8) ○ 1
high school (9–12) ○ 2
college or beyond ○ 3
unknown ○ 4

If you (and your family) have **unusual circumstances**, complete this form and then check with your financial aid administrator. Examples:

- tuition expenses at an elementary or secondary school,
- unusual medical or dental expenses not covered by insurance,
- a family member who recently became unemployed, or
- other unusual circumstances such as changes in income or assets that might affect your eligibility for student financial aid.

Section B: Your Plans *Answer these questions about your college plans.*

23–27. Your expected enrollment status for the 1998–99 school year
(See Instructions, page 3.)

School term	Full time	3/4 time	1/2 time	Less than 1/2 time	Not enrolled
23. Summer term '98	○ 1	○ 2	○ 3	○ 4	○ 5
24. Fall semester/qtr. '98	○ 1	○ 2	○ 3	○ 4	○ 5
25. Winter quarter '98-99	○ 1	○ 2	○ 3	○ 4	○ 5
26. Spring semester/qtr. '99	○ 1	○ 2	○ 3	○ 4	○ 5
27. Summer term '99	○ 1	○ 2	○ 3	○ 4	○ 5

28. Your course of study *(See Instructions for code, page 3.)*

Code ☐

29. College degree/certificate you expect to receive
(See Instructions for code, page 3.)

☐

30. Date you expect to receive your degree/certificate

Month | Year
☐☐☐☐☐☐

31. Your grade level during the 1998–99 school year *(Fill in only one.)*

1st yr./never attended college	○ 1	5th year/other undergraduate	○ 6
1st yr./attended college before	○ 2	1st year graduate/professional	○ 7
2nd year/sophomore	○ 3	2nd year graduate/professional	○ 8
3rd year/junior	○ 4	3rd year graduate/professional	○ 9
4th year/senior	○ 5	Beyond 3rd year graduate/professional	○ 10

32–34. In addition to grants, what other types of financial aid are you (and your parents) interested in? *(See Instructions, page 3.)*

32. Student employment Yes ○ 1 No ○ 2

33. Student loans Yes ○ 1 No ○ 2

34. Parent loans for students Yes ○ 1 No ○ 2

35. If you are (or were) in college, do you plan to attend **that same college** in 1998–99?
(If this doesn't apply to you, leave blank.) Yes ○ 1 No ○ 2

36–37. Veterans education benefits you expect to receive from July 1, 1998 through June 30, 1999

36. Amount per month $ ☐☐☐☐ .00

37. Number of months ☐☐

Section C: Student Status

38. Were you born **before** January 1, 1975?	Yes ○ 1	No ○ 2
39. Are you a veteran of the U.S. Armed Forces?	Yes ○ 1	No ○ 2
40. Will you be enrolled in a graduate or professional program (beyond a bachelor's degree) in 1998–99?	Yes ○ 1	No ○ 2
41. Are you married?	Yes ○ 1	No ○ 2
42. Are you an orphan or a ward of the court, or **were** you a ward of the court until age 18?	Yes ○ 1	No ○ 2
43. Do you have legal dependents **(other than a spouse)** that fit the definition in Instructions, page 4?	Yes ○ 1	No ○ 2

If you answered **"Yes"** to any question in Section C, go to Section E and fill out **both the GRAY and the WHITE** areas on the rest of this form.

If you answered **"No"** to every question in Section C, go to Section E and fill out **both the BLUE and the WHITE** areas on the rest of this form.

Section D: Household Information

Remember:
At least one "Yes" answer in Section C means fill out the **GRAY** and WHITE areas.

All "No" answers in Section C means fill out the **BLUE** and WHITE areas.

STUDENT (& SPOUSE)

44. Number in your household in 1998–99
(Include yourself and your spouse. Do not include your children and other people unless they meet the definition in Instructions, page 4.) ☐☐

45. Number of college students in household in 1998–99
(Of the number in 44, how many will be in college at least half-time in at least one term in an eligible program? Include yourself. See Instructions, page 4.) ☐

PARENT(S)

46. Your parent(s)' **current** marital status:

single ○ 1   separated ○ 3   widowed ○ 5

married ○ 2   divorced ○ 4

47. Your parent(s)' state of legal residence

State ☐☐

48. Date your parent(s) became legal resident(s) of the state in question 47 *(See Instructions, page 5.)*

Month | Year
☐☐ 1 9 ☐☐

49. Number in your parent(s)' household in 1998–99
(Include yourself and your parents. Do not include your parents' other children and other people unless they meet the definition in Instructions, page 5.) ☐☐

50. Number of college students in household in 1998–99
(Of the number in 49, how many will be in college at least half-time in at least one term in an eligible program? Include yourself. See Instructions, page 5.) ☐

DRAFT 5/21

Section E: 1997 Income, Earnings, and Benefits

You must see Instructions, pages 5 and 6, for information about tax forms and tax filing status, especially if you are estimating taxes or filing electronically or by telephone. These instructions will tell you what income and benefits should be reported in this section.

	STUDENT (& SPOUSE)	PARENT(S)
	Everyone must fill out this column.	

The following 1997 U.S. income tax figures are from: **51.** *(Fill in one oval.)* **63.** *(Fill in one oval.)*

A—a completed 1997 IRS Form 1040A, 1040EZ, or 1040TEL .... ○ 1   A .... ○ 1

B—a completed 1997 IRS Form 1040 .... ○ 2   B .... ○ 2

C—an estimated 1997 IRS Form 1040A, 1040EZ, or 1040TEL .... ○ 3   C .... ○ 3

D—an estimated 1997 IRS Form 1040 .... ○ 4   D .... ○ 4

E—will not file a 1997 U.S. income tax return .... *(Skip to question 55.)* ○ 5   E *(Skip to 67.)* ○ 5

TAX FILERS ONLY

1997 Total number of exemptions (Form 1040–line 6d, or 1040A–line 6d; 1040EZ filers— *see Instructions, page 6.*) **52.** ☐ **64.** ☐

1997 Adjusted Gross Income (AGI: Form 1040–line 31, 1040A–line 16, or 1040EZ–line 4—*see Instructions, page 6.*) **53.** $ _____ .00 **65.** $ _____ .00

1997 U.S. income tax **paid** (Form 1040–line 44, 1040A–line 25, or 1040EZ–line 10 **54.** $ _____ .00 **66.** $ _____ .00

1997 Income earned from work (Student) **55.** $ _____ .00 (Father) **67.** $ _____ .00

1997 Income earned from work (Spouse) **56.** $ _____ .00 (Mother) **68.** $ _____ .00

1997 Untaxed income and benefits (yearly totals only):

Earned Income Credit (Form 1040–line 54, Form 1040A–line 29c, or Form 1040EZ–line 8) **57.** $ _____ .00 **69.** $ _____ .00

Untaxed Social Security Benefits **58.** $ _____ .00 **70.** $ _____ .00

Aid to Families with Dependent Children (AFDC/ADC) **59.** $ _____ .00 **71.** $ _____ .00

Child support received for all children **60.** $ _____ .00 **72.** $ _____ .00

Other untaxed income and benefits from Worksheet #2, page 11 **61.** $ _____ .00 **73.** $ _____ .00

1997 Amount from Line 5, Worksheet #3, page 12 *(See Instructions.)* **62.** $ _____ .00 **74.** $ _____ .00

Section F: Asset Information   **ATTENTION!**

Fill out Worksheet A or Worksheet B in Instructions, page 7. *If you meet the tax filing and income conditions on Worksheets A and B, you do not have to complete Section F to apply for Federal student aid. Some states and colleges, however, require Section F information for their own aid programs. Check with your financial aid administrator and/or State Agency.*

Age of your older parent **82.** ☐

	STUDENT (& SPOUSE)	PARENT(S)

Cash, savings, and checking accounts **75.** $ _____ .00 **83.** $ _____ .00

Other real estate and investments value *(Don't include the home.)* **76.** $ _____ .00 **84.** $ _____ .00

Other real estate and investments debt *(Don't include the home.)* **77.** $ _____ .00 **85.** $ _____ .00

Business value **78.** $ _____ .00 **86.** $ _____ .00

Business debt **79.** $ _____ .00 **87.** $ _____ .00

Investment farm value *(See Instructions, page 8.)* *(Don't include a family farm.)* **80.** $ _____ .00 **88.** $ _____ .00

Investment farm debt *(See Instructions, page 8.)* *(Don't include a family farm.)* **81.** $ _____ .00 **89.** $ _____ .00

DRAFT 5/21

Section G: Releases and Signatures

90–101. What college(s) do you plan to attend in 1998–99?
(Note: The colleges you list below will have access to your application information. See Instructions, page 8.)

Housing codes	1—on-campus	3—with parent(s)
	2—off-campus	

	Title IV School Code	College Name	College Street Address and City	State	Housing Code
XX.	0 5 4 3 2 1	EXAMPLE UNIVERSITY	14930 NORTH SOMEWHERE BLVD. ANYWHERE CITY	S T	XX. 2
90.					91.
92.					93.
94.					95.
96.					97.
98.					99.
100.					101.

102. The U.S. Department of Education will send information from this form to your state financial aid agency and the state agencies of the colleges listed above so they can consider you for state aid. Answer "No" if you **don't** want information released to the state. *(See Instructions, page 9 and "Deadlines for State Student Aid," page 10.)* ....**102.** No ○ 2

103. Males not yet registered for Selective Service (SS): Do you want SS to register you? *(See Instructions, page 9.)* ....**103.** Yes ○ 1

104–105. Read, Sign, and Date Below

By signing below, you certify that all the information on this form is true and complete to the best of your knowledge. If asked, you agree to give proof of the information, which may include a copy of your U.S. or state income tax form. If you purposely give false or misleading information, you may be fined $10,000, sent to prison, or both. You also certify that:

- you will use any federal student aid funds received during the award year covered by this application solely for educational expenses related to attendance during that year at the institution of higher education that determined eligibility for those funds;
- you are not in default on a title IV educational loan, or you have repaid or made satisfactory arrangements to repay your loan if you are in default;
- you do not owe an overpayment on a title IV educational grant, or you have made satisfactory arrangements to repay that overpayment; and
- you will notify your school if you do owe an overpayment or are in default.

Everyone whose information is given on this form should sign below. The student (and at least one parent, if parental information is given) must sign below or this form will be returned unprocessed.

104. Signatures *(Sign in the boxes below.)*

1 Student

2 Student's Spouse

3 Father/Stepfather

4 Mother/Stepmother

105. Date completed | Month | Day | Year
1998 ○
1999 ○

Section H: Preparer's Use Only

For preparers other than student, spouse, and parent(s). Student, spouse, and parent(s), sign in question 104.

Preparer's name (last, first, MI)

Firm name

Firm or preparer's address (street, city, state, ZIP)

106. Employer identification number (EIN)

OR

107. Preparer's social security number

Certification: All of the information on this form is true and complete to the best of my knowledge.

108. Preparer's signature   Date

School Use Only

D/O ○   Title IV Code

FAA Signature

MDE Use Only
Do not write in this box   Special handle

MAKE SURE THAT YOU HAVE COMPLETED, DATED, AND SIGNED THIS APPLICATION.
Mail the original application (NOT A PHOTOCOPY) to: Federal Student Aid Programs, P.O. Box 4008, Mt. Vernon, IL 62864-8608

 **1997-98**

10000289
444-44-4444
STEVE X JOHNSON
X   Application 0

Complete all sections of this PROFILE Application except Questions 1, 2, 24, and 25. Be certain that everyone giving information on the application signs it.

Section A - Student's Information

1. How many family members will the student (and spouse) support in 1997-98? <u>Always include the student and spouse.</u> List their names and give information about them in Section M. See instructions.

2. Of the number in 1, how many will be in college at least half-time for at least one term in 1997-98? Include yourself.

3. What is the student's state of legal residence?

4. What is the student's citizenship status?

a. 1 ○ U.S. citizen (Skip to Question 5.)

  2 ○ Permanent resident (Skip to Question 5.)

  3 ○ Neither of the above (Answer 'b' and 'c' below.)

b. Country of citizenship?

c. Visa classification?
  1○ F1 2○ F2 3○ J1 4○ J2 5○ G 6○ Other

Section B - Student's 1996 Income & Benefits

If married, include spouse's information in Sections B, C, D, and E.

5. The following 1996 U.S. Income tax return figures are (Fill in only one oval.)

  1 ○ estimated. Will file IRS Form 1040EZ, 1040A, or 1040TEL. Go to 6.

  2 ○ estimated. Will file IRS Form 1040. Go to 6.

  3 ○ from a completed IRS Form 1040EZ, 1040A, or 1040TEL. Go to 6.

  4 ○ from a completed IRS Form 1040. Go to 6.

  5 ○ a tax return will not be filed. Skip to 10.

Tax Filers Only

6. 1996 total number of exemptions (IRS Form 1040, line 6d or 1040A, line 6d or 1040EZ - see instructions.)

7. 1996 Adjusted Gross Income from IRS Form 1040, line 31 or 1040A, line 16 or 1040EZ, line 4 (Use the worksheet in the instructions.) $ _____ .00

8. 1996 U.S. income tax paid (IRS Form 1040, line 44 or 1040A, line 25 or 1040EZ, line 10) $ _____ .00

9. 1996 Itemized deductions (IRS Form 1040, Schedule A, line 28. Write in "0" if deductions were not itemized.) $ _____ .00

10. 1996 income earned from work by student (See instructions.) $ _____ .00

11. 1996 income earned from work by student's spouse $ _____ .00

12. 1996 dividend and interest income $ _____ .00

13. 1996 untaxed income and benefits (Give total amount for year.)

  a. Social security benefits (See instructions.) $ _____ .00

  b. Aid to Families with Dependent Children $ _____ .00

  c. Child support received for all children $ _____ .00

  d. Earned Income Credit (IRS Form 1040, line 54 or 1040A, line 29c or 1040EZ, line 8) $ _____ .00

  e. Other - write total from worksheet, page 4. $ _____ .00

14. 1996 earnings from Federal Work-Study or other need-based work programs plus any grant and scholarship aid required to be reported on your U.S. income tax return $ _____ .00

Section C - Student's Assets

Include trust accounts only in Section D.

15. Cash, savings, and checking accounts $ _____ .00

16. Total value of IRA, Keogh, 401k, 403b, etc. accounts as of December 31, 1996. $ _____ .00

	What is it worth today?	What is owed on it?
17. Investments (Including Uniform Gifts to Minors. See instructions.)	$ _____ .00	$ _____ .00
18. Home (Renters write in "0".)	$ _____ .00	$ _____ .00
19. Other real estate	$ _____ .00	$ _____ .00
20. Business and farm	$ _____ .00	$ _____ .00

21. If a farm is included in 20, is the student living on the farm?   Yes ○ 1   No ○ 2

22. If student owns home, give

  a. year purchased   1 9 __ __   **b.** purchase price $ _____ .00

Section D - Student's Trust Information

23. a. Total value of all trust(s) $ _____ .00

  b. Is any income or part of the principal currently available?   Yes ○ 1   No ○ 2

  c. Who established the trust(s)?   1 ○ Student's parents   2 ○ Other

Section E - Student's 1996 Expenses

24. 1996 child support paid by student $ _____ .00

25. 1996 medical and dental expenses not covered by insurance (See instructions.) $ _____ .00

Page 1 of 4

CSSAP1

Section F - Student's Expected Summer/School-Year Resources for 1997-1998

		Amount per month	Number of months
26.	Student's veterans benefits (July 1, 1997 - June 30, 1998.)	$ .00	

		Summer 1997 (3 months)	School Year 1997-98 (9 months)
27.	Student's (and spouse's) resources (Don't enter monthly amounts.)		
	a. Student's wages, salaries, tips, etc.	$ .00	$ .00
	b. Spouse's wages, salaries, tips, etc.	$ .00	$ .00
	c. Other taxable income	$ .00	$ .00
	d. Untaxed income and benefits	$ .00	$ .00
	e. Grants, scholarships, fellowships, etc. from other than the colleges or universities to which the student is applying (List sources in Section P.)		$ .00
	f. Tuition benefits from the parents' and/or the student's or spouse's employer		$ .00
	g. Contributions from the student's parent(s) for 1997-98 college or university expenses		$ .00
	h. Contributions from other relatives, spouse's parents, and all other sources (List sources in Section P.)		$ .00

Section G - Parents' Household Information - See page 5 of the instruction booklet.

28. How many family members will your parents support in 1997-98? Always include the student and parents. List their names and give information about them in Section M.

31. What is the current marital status of your parents? (Fill in only one oval.)
   1 ○ single   3 ○ separated   5 ○ widowed
   2 ○ married   4 ○ divorced

29. Of the number in 28, how many will be in college at least half-time for at least one term in 1997-98? Include the student.

30. How many parents will be in college at least half-time in 1997-1998? (Fill in only one oval.)
   1 ○ Neither parent   2 ○ One parent   3 ○ Both parents

32. What is your parents' state of legal residence?

Section H - Parents' Expenses

		1996	Expected 1997
33.	Child support paid by the parent(s) completing this form	33. $ .00	$ .00
34.	Repayment of parents' educational loans (See instructions.)	34. $ .00	$ .00
35.	Medical and dental expenses not covered by insurance (See instructions.)	35. $ .00	$ .00
36.	Total elementary, junior high school, and high school tuition paid for dependent children		
	a. Amount paid (Don't include tuition paid for the student.)	36. $ .00	$ .00
	b. For how many dependent children? (Don't include the student.)		

Section I - Parents' Assets - If parents own all or part of a business or farm, write in its name and the percent of ownership in Section P.

		What is it worth today?	What is owed on it?
37.	Cash, savings, and checking accounts	$ .00	
41.	Business	$ .00	$ .00
38.	Monthly home mortgage or rental payment (If none, explain in Section P.)	$ .00	
42. a.	Farm	$ .00	$ .00

39. Investments — What is it worth today? $ .00   What is owed on it? $ .00

42. b. Does family live on the farm? Yes ○1   No ○2

40. a. Home (Renters write in "0".) — $ .00 $ .00

   b. year purchased 1 9 | | c. purchase price $ .00

43. a. Other real estate — $ .00 $ .00

   b. year purchased 1 9 | | c. purchase price $ .00

Section J - Parents' 1995 Income & Benefits

44. 1995 **Adjusted Gross Income** (IRS Form 1040, line 31 or 1040A, line 16 or 1040EZ, line 4)　　　$ _____ .00

45. 1995 **U.S. income tax paid** (IRS Form 1040, line 46, 1040A, line 25 or 1040EZ, line 10)　　　$ _____ .00

46. 1995 **itemized deductions** (IRS Form 1040, Schedule A, line 28. Write "0" if deductions were not itemized.)　　$ _____ .00

47. 1995 **untaxed income and benefits** (Include the same types of income & benefits that are listed in 55 a-k.)　$ _____ .00

Section K - Parents' 1996 Income & Benefits

48. The following 1996 U.S. income tax return figures are (Fill in only one oval.)

　1 ○ estimated. Will file IRS Form 1040EZ, 1040A, or 1040TEL. Go to 49.
　2 ○ estimated. Will file IRS Form 1040. Go to 49.
　3 ○ from a completed IRS Form 1040EZ, 1040A, or 1040TEL. Go to 49.
　4 ○ from a completed IRS Form 1040. Go to 49.
　5 ○ a tax return will not be filed. Skip to 53.

Tax Filers Only

49. 1996 **total number of exemptions** (IRS Form 1040, line 6d or 1040A, line 6d or 1040EZ - see instructions)　　**49.** ⌷⌷

50. 1996 **Adjusted Gross Income** (IRS Form 1040, line 31 or 1040A, line 16 or 1040EZ, line 4)　　**50.** $ _____ .00

Breakdown of income in 50

　a. **Wages, salaries, tips** (IRS Form 1040, line 7 or 1040A, line 7 or 1040EZ, line 1)　　**50.** a. $ _____ .00

　b. **Interest income** (IRS Form 1040, line 8a or 1040A, line 8a or 1040EZ, line 2)　　b. $ _____ .00

　c. **Dividend income** (IRS Form 1040, line 9 or 1040A, line 9)　　c. $ _____ .00

　d. **Net income (or loss) from business, farm, rents, royalties, partnerships, estates, trusts, etc.** (IRS Form 1040, lines 12, 17, and 18). If a loss, enter the amount in (parentheses).　　d. $ _____ .00

　e. **Other taxable income such as alimony received, capital gains (or losses), pensions, annuities, etc.** (IRS Form 1040, lines 10, 11, 13, 14, 15b, 16b, 19, 20b and 21 or 1040A, lines 10b, 11b, 12, and 13b or 1040EZ, line 3)　　e. $ _____ .00

　f. **Adjustments to income** (IRS Form 1040, line 30 or 1040A, line 15c)　　f. $ _____ .00

51. 1996 **U.S. income tax paid** (IRS Form 1040, line 44, 1040A, line 25 or 1040EZ, line 10)　　**51.** $ _____ .00

52. 1996 **itemized deductions** (IRS Form 1040, Schedule A, line 28. Write in "0" if deductions were not itemized.)　　**52.** $ _____ .00

53. 1996 **income earned from work by father**　　**53.** $ _____ .00

54. 1996 **income earned from work by mother**　　**54.** $ _____ .00

55. 1996 **untaxed income and benefits** (Give total amount for the year. Do not give monthly amounts.)

　a. **Social security benefits**　　**55.** a. $ _____ .00

　b. **Aid to Families with Dependent Children**　　b. $ _____ .00

　c. **Child support received for all children**　　c. $ _____ .00

　d. **Deductible IRA and/or Keogh payments** (See instructions.)　　d. $ _____ .00

　e. **Payments to tax-deferred pension and savings plans** (See instructions.)　　e. $ _____ .00

　f. **Amounts withheld from wages for dependent care and medical spending accounts**　　f. $ _____ .00

　g. **Earned Income Credit** (IRS Form 1040, line 54 or 1040A, line 29c or 1040EZ, line 8)　　g. $ _____ .00

　h. **Housing, food and other living allowances** (See instructions.)　　h. $ _____ .00

　i. **Tax-exempt interest income** (IRS Form 1040, line 8b or 1040A, line 8b)　　i. $ _____ .00

　j. **Foreign income exclusion** (IRS Form 2555, line 43 or Form 2555EZ, line 18)　　j. $ _____ .00

　k. **Other - write in the total from the worksheet in the instructions, page 7.**　　k. $ _____ .00

WRITE ONLY IN THE ANSWER SPACES. DO NOT WRITE ANYWHERE ELSE.

Section L - Parents' 1997 Expected Income & Benefits

If the expected total income and benefits will differ from the 1996 total income by $3,000 or more, explain in Section P.

56. 1997 **income earned from work by father**　$ _____ .00　　　**58.** 1997 **other taxable income**　$ _____ .00

57. 1997 **income earned from work by mother**　$ _____ .00　　　**59.** 1997 **untaxed income and benefits** (See 55a-k.)　$ _____ .00

10000289 CSSA 20 1-00011001-05 5 1 5/5 00011001　　　　　　　　　　CSSAP3

Section M - Family Member Listing - Give information for all family members entered in question 1 or 28, but don't give information about yourself.
List up to seven other family members here. If there are more than seven, list first those who will be in school or college at least half-time. List the others in Section P

60.

	Full name of family member	Use codes from below.	Age	Claimed by parents as tax exemption in 1996? Yes? No?	1996-1997 school year Name of school or college	Year in school	Scholarships and grants	Parents' contribution	1997-1998 school year Attend college at least one term full-time / half-time	School or college Type	Name
1	**You - the student applicant**										
2				○ ○					1○ 2○		
3				○ ○					1○ 2○		
4				○ ○					1○ 2○		
5				○ ○					1○ 2○		
6				○ ○					1○ 2○		
7				○ ○					1○ 2○		
8				○ ○					1○ 2○		

Write in the correct code from the right. ↑ 1 – Student's parent, 2 – Student's stepparent, 3 – Student's brother or sister, 4 – Student's husband or wife, 5 – Student's son or daughter, 6 – Student's grandparent, 7 – Other

Write in the correct code from the instructions on page 8.

Section N - Parents' Information

61. Fill in one: ○ Father ○ Stepfather ○ Legal guardian ○ Other (Explain in P.)

a. Name _____ Age |__|__|

b. Fill in if: ○ Self-employed ○ Unemployed - Date: _____

c. Occupation _____

d. Employer _____ No. years _____

e. Work telephone |__|__|__|–|__|__|__|–|__|__|__|__|

f. Retirement plans: ○ Social security ○ Union/employer ○ Civil service/state ○ IRA/Keogh/tax-deferred ○ Military ○ Other

62. Fill in one: ○ Mother ○ Stepmother ○ Legal guardian ○ Other (Explain in P.)

a. Name _____ Age |__|__|

b. Fill in if: ○ Self-employed ○ Unemployed - Date: _____

c. Occupation _____

d. Employer _____ No. years _____

e. Work telephone |__|__|__|–|__|__|__|–|__|__|__|__|

f. Retirement plans: ○ Social security ○ Union/employer ○ Civil service/state ○ IRA/Keogh/tax-deferred ○ Military ○ Other

Section O - Divorced, Separated, or Remarried Parents
(to be answered by the parent who completes this form if the student's natural or adoptive parents are divorced, separated, or remarried)

63. a. Year of separation |__|__| Year of divorce |__|__|

b. Other parent's name: _____
   Home address _____
   _____
   Occupation/Employer _____

c. According to court order, when will support for the student end? |__|__| |__|__|
   Month   Year

d. Who last claimed the student as a tax exemption? _____
   _____ Year? |__|__|

e. How much does the other parent plan to contribute to the student's education for the 1997-1998 school year? $ _____ .00

f. Is there an agreement specifying this contribution for the student's education? Yes ○ No ○

Section P - Explanations/Special Circumstances
Use this space to explain any unusual expenses such as high medical or dental expenses, educational and other debts, child care, elder care, or special circumstances. Also, give information for any outside scholarships you have been awarded. If more space is needed, use sheets of paper and send them directly to your schools and programs.

Certification:

All the information on this form is true and complete to the best of my knowledge. If asked, I agree to give proof of the information that I have given on this form. I realize that this proof may include a copy of my U.S., state, or local income tax returns. I certify that all information is correct at this time, and that I will send timely notice to my schools/programs of any significant change in family income or assets, financial situation, college plans of other children, or the receipt of other scholarships or grants.

1 _____
Student's signature

2 _____
Student's spouse's signature

3 _____
Father's (stepfather's) signature

4 _____
Mother's (stepmother's) signature

Date completed: |__|__| |__|__| Month Day

1 ○ 1996
2 ○ 1997
3 ○ 1998

CSS Use Only |__|__|

Page 4 of 4

10000299

CSSAP4

COLLEGE SCHOLARSHIP SERVICE
The College Board

Date:

Your Name:

Your CSS Number:

Your Social Security Number:

SECTION A - STUDENT'S INFORMATION

Question Name and Number		You Reported
Last Name	1*	
First Name	1*	
Middle Initial	1*	
Mailing Address	2*	
City	2*	
State	2*	
Zip Code	2*	
Home Telephone Number	3*	
Title	4*	
Date of Birth	5*	
Social Security Number	6*	
Year in School	7*	
Marital Status	8*	
US Veteran?	9*	
Orphan/Ward of Court?	10*	
Legal Dependents?	11*	
Natural Parents Sep./Div.?	12*	
Parents Own Business/Farm?	13*	
97-98 Financial Aid Status	14*	
Number Family Members	1.	
Number in College	2.	
State of Legal Residence	3.	
Citizenship Status	4a	
Country of Citizenship	4b	
Visa Classification	4c	

SECTION B - STUDENT'S 1996 INCOME & BENEFITS

Question Name and Number		You Reported
U.S. Tax Figures	5.	
Number of Exemptions	6.	
Adjusted Gross Income-AGI	7.	
U.S. Taxes Paid	8.	
Itemized Deductions	9.	
Student's Work Income	10.	
Spouse's Work Income	11.	
Dividend & Interest Income	12.	
Social Security Benefits	13a.	
Aid to Families with Children	13b.	
Child Support Received	13c.	
Earned Income Credit	13d.	
Other Untaxed Income	13e.	
Work Study, etc. Earnings	14.	

SECTION C - STUDENT'S ASSETS

Question Name and Number		You reported
Cash, Savings, Checking	15.	
IRA/Keogh Plans	16.	
Investments Worth	17.	
Investments Debt	17.	
Home Worth	18.	
Home Debt	18.	
Other Real Estate Worth	19.	
Other Real Estate Debt	19.	
Business & Farm Worth	20.	
Business & Farm Debt	20.	
Living on Farm?	21.	
Home Purchase Year	22a.	
Home Purchase Price	22b.	

SECTION D - STUDENT'S TRUST INFORMATION

Question Name and Number		You Reported
Value of Trusts	23a.	
Principal Available Now?	23b.	
Trust Established By?	23c.	

SECTION E - STUDENT'S 1996 EXPENSES

Question Name and Number		You Reported
Child Support Paid	24.	
Medical/Dental Expenses	25.	

SECTION F - STUDENT'S 1997-1998 RESOURCES

Question Name and Number		You Reported
VA Benefits Amount	26.	
VA Benefits No. of Months	26.	
Summer Wages, etc.	27a.	
School Year Wages, etc.	27a.	
Spouse's Summer Wages	27b.	
Spouse's Sch. Yr. Wages	27b.	
Other Taxable Inc. (Sum.)	27c.	
Other Taxable Inc. (Sch. Yr.)	27c.	
Untaxed Inc./Ben. (Sum.)	27d.	
Untaxed Inc./Ben. (Sch. Yr.)	27d.	
Grants, Scholarships, etc.	27e.	
Tuition Benefits	27f.	
Contribution from Parents	27g.	
Contribution from Relatives	27h.	

FINANCIAL AID TRANSCRIPT

Instructions: If you ever attended another postsecondary institution, you *must* complete Part I of this form and submit it to the Financial Aid Office of that institution. Federal regulations require that a Financial Aid Transcript request be sent to *every* institution you previously attended, regardless of whether you received aid to attend that institution.

Name_____ Social Security # _____

Last   First   M.I.   Maiden

Name used at previous institution (if different from above) _____

Student's Address:_____

I request that the Financial Aid Office at

_____

which I attended from _____ to _____ provide the information requested in Part II to the institution shown to the left.

I ☐ did ☐ did not receive aid while a student at this institution.

Student's Signature (optional):

(Fold here for window envelope)

_____

Complete either: • Sections A, B and F; OR
                 • Sections A, and C through F.

SECTION A Other Institutions Attended (Everyone must complete this section).

The institution has information indicating the student attended institutions other than this institution.

☐ No, our records show no previous institution attended.
☐ Yes, our records indicate that the student has attended the following institutions: _____

_____

SECTION B To be completed if the institution is not completing Sections C, D, and E.

The information requested in Sections C, D, and E is not provided because:

☐ The student neither received nor benefited from any Title IV aid while at this institution.
☐ The transcript pertains solely to years for which the institution no longer has and is no longer required to keep records under the Title IV recordkeeping requirements.

If you have completed Section A and checked one of the reasons in Section B, and are not required to provide any other information, skip Sections C, D, and E, and complete Section F. Otherwise, proceed with Section C.

SECTION C Complete the first statement and check all others that apply.

1. The student first received Title IV aid at this institution for award year: _____ through: _____

   mo/yr   mo/yr

2. Check all that apply:
   ☐ The student received increased Federal Perkins Loan/NDSL at this institution due to Expanded Lending Option or study abroad.
   ☐ The student received increased FSEOG at this institution due to study abroad.
   ☐ The student had an outstanding balance on an NDSL at this institution on July 1, 1987, *which is still outstanding as of today's date.*
   ☐ The student had an outstanding balance on a Federal Perkins Loan/NDSL at this institution on October 1, 1992, *which is still outstanding as of today's date.*
   ☐ The student owes a refund due to overpayment on a Federal Pell Grant, FSEOG or Federal Perkins Loan/NDSL at this institution.
   ☐ The student is in default on a Federal Perkins Loan/NDSL/Income Contingent Loan (ICL) at this institution.
   ☐ The institution is aware that the defaulted Federal Perkins Loan/NDSL/ICL has been discharged in bankruptcy.
   ☐ The institution knows the student owes a refund due to overpayment on SSIG received for attending this institution.
   ☐ The institution knows that the student is in default on a Federal Family Education Loan (FFEL) or a Federal Direct Student Loan (FDSL) received for attendance at this institution (including consolidation loans).
   ☐ The institution is aware that the defaulted FFEL or FDSL has been discharged in bankruptcy.

Revised 4/11/94

For ALL federal aid programs: When indicating totals, deduct any refunds, repayments, or Federal Pell Grant recoveries which have been returned due to an overpayment or student withdrawal. Do NOT deduct Federal Perkins Loan/NDSL and ICL prepayments or payments made according to a repayment schedule.

Sources of Assistance		Current Year Amounts 19___-___	Cumulative Total (include current year)
Federal Pell Grant:	Total Disbursement		xxxxxxxx
	Scheduled Award (full time, full year)		xxxxxxxx
Does the school expect to make additional disbursements to the student after this transcript is signed? If so, indicate when:_____		xxxxxxxx	xxxxxxxx
FSEOG			xxxxxxxx
Income Contingent Loans (Report ICL separately even if merged with Federal Perkins/NDSL funds. ICL does not count toward Federal Perkins/NDSL aggregates.)		xxxxxxxx	
Federal Perkins/NDSL Loans			
Federal SLS Loan or PLUS Loan (ALAS) (borrowed by the student)			
Federal PLUS/Federal Direct PLUS Loan (borrowed by parents for the student)			xxxxxxxx
SSIG/State Grant/Other aid* (optional – identify each)			

* If this school participates in health professions aid programs through the Department of Health & Human Services, include them here.

List the loan period and amount for each of the following Title IV loans received for attendance at this institution. Include current loans.

Subsidized and Unsubsidized Federal Stafford/Federal Direct Stafford Loan			Additional Unsubsidized Federal Stafford/Federal Direct Stafford Loan (Include only amounts which exceed Federal Stafford/Federal Direct Stafford Loan eligibility for independent or graduate students, or dependent students whose parents cannot borrow PLUS)		
Loan Period	Grade Level	Amount	Loan Period	Grade Level	Amount

Authorized Signature _____ Date _____

Typed Name _____ Title _____

Name of Institution _____

Address _____

_____

Telephone _____

COMMENTS _____

_____

Form developed by the National Association of Student Financial Aid Administrators.

Revised 4/11/94

Index

WHY APPLY!?

Apply! is a unique CD-ROM that eases the arduous college search and application process by enabling students to use their personal computers to find, apply to, and pay for college. As typewriters become obsolete and harder to find, *Apply!* provides a stress-free solution. Students simply fill in applications onscreen, print out completed forms, and submit them to colleges.

Apply! helps ease the tension of the application and admissions processes by giving students the tools they need to easily and effectively find the right colleges for them and then complete the applications. Features of the software include:

- A college search database with information on more than 1,500 colleges.
- Exact duplicates of the applications to more than 500 colleges with the ability to fill in basic information just once!
- Information on more than 180,000 scholarships, loans, and grants.
- A financial aid area with an estimated financial need calculator and a student loan application.
- 30 days of FREE Internet access and a free copy of Internet Explorer.

Best of all, this truly innovative software is available **FREE of CHARGE** thanks to the generosity of national sponsors a the participating colleges. Do not miss the opportunity to order your free copy today!

EDUCATION TRUST
A SallieMae LENDER

The **APPLY! Education Trust** is the answer to the question, *"Now that I've been accepted, how am I going to pay for college?"* A partnership with Sallie Mae allows Apply Technology to provide the most comprehensive borrower benefits available with the most flexible, lowest cost, education loans you can find anywhere. For more information or a loan application, please call 888-888-3469.

**Visit *Apply!* on the web
www.weapply.com
or call 203.740.3504 to order.**

Please clip and mail to:
Apply! '98, P.O. Box 8406, New Milford, CT 06776-9848

YES... I want to order the free *Apply!* CD-ROM!

Name

Address

City

State _____ Zip

School _____ Grad Year

☐ **Windows**   ☐ **Macintosh**

Orders begin shipping in September, 1997.
Orders received after 3/1/98 will be considered pre-orders for *Apply!* '99.